W9-BLY-487

Why Do You Need This New Edition?

If you're wondering why you should buy this fourth edition of *Writing in Political Science*, here are five good reasons!

1. **Guide your research.** With updated URLs, an expanded list of Internet research sources, and updated sections on Internet research and Internet source evaluation, you'll be able to locate and verify information quickly, while new examples highlight the changes in researching legislative analysis, policy evaluation, and policy recommendation. A section on literature reviews helps you to research and manage past and present literature in the political science field.

2. **Guide your writing.** Avoid making common mistakes with an updated plagiarism section that reflects current trends and problems you might experience during the research and writing process. New reference pages on Internet citations give you comparative formats for MLA, *The Chicago Manual of Style*, APA, and APSA styles so you can document your resources correctly.

3. **Guide your studies.** With the increased quality and accessibility of raw data, new examples show you how to read and create tables and graphs from previously unpublished data now available on government and private organizational Web sites. Chapter 5 has been expanded to include a section on classificational analysis, constructing conceptual models, and typologies to reflect the current trends in data presentation.

4. **Guide your communication.** New sections on media applications and PowerPoint presentations reflect current trends in student-to-student communication, and an additional section on 508 compliance (ADA) for accessibility in presentations prepares you for communicating in a public sector position.

5. **Guide your future.** New sections on policy memos, grant writing, and project report writing show you how to apply your political science writing skills in the public, nonprofit, and private sectors, and updated advice on composing job and graduate school application materials prepares you for your post-college endeavors.

PEARSON

WRITING IN
POLITICAL SCIENCE

A PRACTICAL GUIDE

Fourth Edition

Diane E. Schmidt
California State University, Chico

Longman

Boston   Columbus   Indianapolis   New York   San Francisco   Upper Saddle River
Amsterdam   Cape Town   Dubai   London   Madrid   Milan   Munich   Paris   Montreal   Toronto
Delhi   Mexico City   Sao Paulo   Sydney   Hong Kong   Seoul   Singapore   Taipei   Tokyo

Editor in Chief: Eric Stano
Marketing Manager: Lindsey Prudhomme
Senior Media Producer: Regina Vertiz
Production Manager: Savoula Amanatidis
Project Coordination, Text Design, and Electronic Page Makeup: GGS Higher Education
    Resources, A Division of PreMedia Global Inc.
Senior Cover Design Manager/Cover Designer: Nancy Danahy
Cover images: Copyright © Digital Vision/Getty Images, Inc.
Senior Manufacturing Buyer: Dennis J. Para
Printer and Binder: R. R. Donnelley and Sons Company—Crawfordsville
Cover Printer: R. R. Donnelley and Sons Company—Crawfordsville

Library of Congress Cataloging-in-Publication Data

Schmidt, Diane E.
Writing in political science: a practical guide / Diane E. Schmidt.—4th ed.
    p. cm.
    Includes bibliographical references and indexes.
    ISBN-13: 978-0-205-61736-4 (alk. paper)
    ISBN-10: 0-205-61736-0 (alk. paper)
    1. Political science—Authorship—Style manuals.   2. Political science—Research—
Handbooks, manuals, etc.   3. Academic writing—Handbooks, manuals, etc.   I. Title.

JA86.S36 2010
808'.06632—dc22

2009024303

Copyright © 2010, 2005, and 2000 by Pearson Education, Inc.

All rights reserved. No part of this publication may be reproduced, stored in a retrieval system,
or transmitted, in any form or by any means, electronic, mechanical, photocopying, recording, or
otherwise, without the prior written permission of the publisher. Printed in the United States.

Longman
is an imprint of

www.pearsonhighered.com

1 2 3 4 5 6 7 8 9 10—DOC—12 11 10 09

ISBN-13: 978-0-205-61736-4
ISBN-10: 0-205-61736-0

To

Alan, Casey, Jonathan, and Margie

and

in memory of Margaret and Ausby

CONTENTS

PREFACE

As political scientists, we are rarely directly involved in politics; instead, we write about it the same way sports commentators report on baseball games. We theorize and conjecture, but rarely play the game. Some of us keep statistics about our players, some of us just provide the color commentary while the players are in the arena, and some of us analyze the actions of the players to see how the winners won and the losers lost. Mostly, we study and learn by observing and providing a reasoned perspective about political activities.

What political scientists do best is write. Part of what this book is about is writing in political science. It is not a formal book of style, nor is it a tome on what it means to think critically about politics or to be a political scientist. It is a practical, sometimes irreverent, and usually serious guide to becoming a color commentator, armchair quarterback, or an expert on politics. It is about becoming a professional in political science and communicating with a community of students and scholars of government and policy. In other words, this book is a guide to communicating about political events, about political ideas, about political passions, and about political agendas. It is not just about writing; it is about *thinking* about politics, *reading* about politics, and *arguing* about politics.

There are many reasons why I wrote this book. I noticed early in my teaching career that students in my courses, regardless of their major or class standing or grade point average, exhibited a general confusion about what and how to communicate in political science assignments. My first response was to condemn the public high school system and the English department for not training students to write coherently. But that was too easy. Upon investigation, I found that there was a different approach to writing among political science, English composition, and the hard sciences. At approximately the same time I discovered the Writing Across the Curriculum approach, and I received the best, most instructive assessment of the problem from a retiring English composition professor. She said, "I'm not surprised that your students are having problems. We teach them to write for us. If you want them to write well in political science, teach them to write for political science." That, in a nutshell, is what Writing Across the Curriculum promotes. That, in a nutshell, is what this book is intended to accomplish.

I wrote this book for political science majors and for students who are passing through the discipline as an elected activity. But this guide is more than an abridged writer's guide with explicit references to political science writing assignments. In addition to outlining a standard form for student assignments, the guide provides practical information and advice about criteria used to evaluate student assignments. It provides and uses the vocabulary of the political science discourse community while keeping the directions and formats simple enough to understand and execute without guidance from an instructor. Anyone who can follow a recipe in a cookbook, read an auto repair manual, or use an automatic teller machine at a bank, can follow the instructions in this book and turn out a professional-level, high-quality manuscript concerning politics.

Unfortunately, this book is not a jump-start for writing and the directions must be followed closely. The advice in this book cannot compensate for poor effort or preparation. Although many parts of this guide mirror sections of general stylebooks and English composition textbooks, it is not a substitute for a comprehensive style guide or a course in composition. This guide stresses the application of general principles of expository writing to common projects and assignments given to students in political science classes. The style and composition sections are designed to enhance and refresh skills already acquired through introductory composition coursework. These sections build on standard writing forms while applying them to the kind of study and investigation conducted in the discipline of political science.

In many ways, this guide is an extended information sheet, not unlike those given to students by their professors. In addition to stating criteria for assignments, it includes gentle reminders about critical thinking, research habits, and general formatting of manuscripts. The guide provides instruction and examples of political science writing assignments that help students begin and end in the right direction for meeting the instructor's expectations.

More importantly, the guide provides examples—yes, examples—of actual student manuscripts written for the sole purpose of getting a grade. None of the student papers was written expressly for the book. Some were written before I ever conceived the idea of writing the book. A few of these examples are from the first edition of the book and are somewhat timeless. Many examples are from current student work reflecting issues, research approaches, and/or data availability contemporary to the state of the art for political science research. With a few exceptions, the papers were written by students in my courses and reflect some of the best examples of papers produced by following the format and structure directions for the particular type of writing assignment required in those courses.

In fact, the examples in this guide are some of its most distinguishing and beneficial aspects. Unlike standard guides for writing research papers or even guides to writing in political science, this guide provides, in exhaustive detail, an explanation about the difference between writing an analysis of legislation or an analysis of a public policy *and* how to write them both. Because it is important for students to see, and not to be just told, that different courses and different subfields in political science have different forms and expectations for written research, there is an example for every exercise and every assignment listed in the book.

Because the book includes both the directions concerning form and examples that exhibit an application of such forms, students will, with or without an instructor's help, be able to choose and narrow a topic, formulate a research agenda, execute a study, write about the findings, and learn something about politics at the same time. The examples in this guide, though very good, are not necessarily the most spectacular work performed concerning the topic or assignment requirements. Those standards are difficult and almost impossible for most people to achieve. No, the examples reflect the efforts of good, hard-working, conscientious students who followed directions, researched their topics earnestly, and produced fine manuscripts that encompass a reasoned perspective on their topics. With the instructor's help, students can use the advice and examples as templates for classroom work. Without the instructor, students may reasonably assume that some approximation of an example related to the course focus will be a good approach.

There is one aspect of this book that may not seem obvious at first that I should explain. The examples in this guide are particularly skewed toward American government, public policy, public law, and public administration. There are several reasons for this. Although I am cross-trained in all subdisciplines in political science, I currently teach American government, public administration, and public policy. The examples come from my students because I know their potential. I set the goals, structured the incentives for achieving them, and measured how closely they were achieved. The examples are testimony to the utility of providing the students a clear statement of goals, expectations, and standards for assignments. I know these techniques work because they have worked for me at every course level from introductory to graduate classes.

Because the techniques used in this guide are based on a Writing Across the Curriculum perspective, they have also worked for colleagues and students in several subfields, several disciplines, and several institutions who adopted this book in draft form. In fact, my book was used to help train Lithuanian students in a Master's in Public Administration program in Lithuania! From freshman to graduate level, from history to anthropology, this guide has been helpful for instructors and students alike. Just like a recipe for cheesecake or barbecue, the application of these techniques varies among users. Instructors put in their own personal touches, accents, and emphasis. In contrast, my students sent copies to friends and siblings and have taken the guide along to law or graduate school because of its versatility and straightforward, understandable advice.

Nonetheless, the principles and advice in the guide can be applied to political theory, comparative government, and international relations. Wherever possible and appropriate, I have provided instruction and advice about using the materials in these fields. The topic section has examples of choosing subfield-specific topics for all subfields. The sections on enhancing comprehension and synthesis, as well as the section on handling and processing class materials, are standard. The section on conventional papers includes a short discussion of how such papers are used in other subfields. Finally, the advice concerning assignments requiring special analytical techniques and assignments in applied political science can be utilized for any institutional level regardless of the country on which or in which it was performed.

Thus, what this guide lacks in discipline breadth, it makes up for in depth and comprehensiveness related to instructing on the discourse, the professional standards, and the method of discovery in political science as a profession. The examples were taken from a cross-section of student writing styles and issues of interest to many students. While each paper exhibits a unique perspective, the thread that ties them together is the salient and controversial nature of each topic. As with any work, some gross errors were made by students and thus corrected. Some typographical errors are my fault. I have never been a good copyeditor for my own work. For the most part, the papers clearly reflect the students' efforts. Small mistakes in logic, as well as some usage errors, were preserved to maintain the personality and spirit of the writers. As teaching tools, they are instructive. As statements on political events, they are interesting and well reasoned. As examples, they set standards that are attainable. This combination makes these student papers assets to the guide and makes the goals of the guide attainable.

New to the Second, Third, and Fourth Editions

I added material and expanded sections on Internet research, Internet source evaluation, reading tables and graphs, creating tables and graphs, editorials, case studies, referencing, plagiarism, PowerPoint presentations, literature reviews, policy memos, report writing, and grant writing. For Chapter 1, I moved and expanded the section on plagiarism to reflect the current trends and problems experienced by students. In Chapters 2 and 3, I clarified explanations. In Chapter 3, I revised the topic selection to reflect the current political climate.

In Chapter 4, for the third edition, I added a section on Internet searching. The section on Internet research was co-authored by a political science librarian according to the American Library Association's standards for research literacy. Unlike other Internet guides that are written by technicians or scholars in the field, this section provides practical techniques *actually used by students* for student research. So much of the available advice is written for users who actually enjoy "surfing" the net. I have found that my students prefer direct practical advice for locating information fast. This section provides the minimum information on Internet terminology while focusing the student's attention on efficient Internet use. I updated all the URLs for the fourth edition and expanded the research sources.

In the third edition, for Chapter 5, I also added an expanded section on research methods and statistical research. Because the Internet provides a dearth of data, and because spreadsheet technology is so user-friendly, I added a section about locating and using data. I included a section on primary research for conducting interviews, creating surveys, and analyzing surveys. Included in this section is advice on reading and constructing tables, graphs, and figures. I also included a section on finding secondary sources and data on the Internet. Finally, I provided Web site addresses and advice for using Web-based information. I further expanded this chapter in the fourth edition to include a section on classificational analysis, constructing conceptual models, and typologies to reflect the current trends in data presentation.

In both the third and fourth editions, for Chapters 6 and 7, I mainly clarified and tightened the presentation of the information. In addition, for the fourth edition, I included an expanded section on approaches.

For Chapter 8 in the fourth edition, I made important and needed changes to include expanded examples. I expanded and added examples of executive summaries, abstracts, tables of contents, and lists of tables and figures. While the third edition includes an expanded and improved referencing section, in the fourth edition I added many more formats for Internet citations, both in the text as well as in the reference page. I also provided comparative formats for MLA, Chicago Manual of Style, APA, and APSA styles. For each type of source, I provided an example from each of the four styles in separate sections rather than as a comparison among styles for each item.

In addition, for Chapter 9 in the third edition, I added editorials and case studies; for the fourth edition I added a section on media applications. Editorial writing is a skill that helps students participate in the process after leaving their educational institutions. Furthermore, unlike concept or position papers, the case study approach to the study of politics provides opportunities for students to apply what they learned in class to a specific agency or entity. I included two types of case studies. The first type is an academic case study approach where students learn to evaluate analysis problems in organizations. The second type is a problem-solving case study where the student chooses a particular problem, researches it, and provides a recommendation for resolving the problem. Finally, as media has become increasingly important in presenting and communicating political ideas, I added a section reflecting on class concepts using media applications.

For Chapter 10, in the third edition, I added new examples of annotated bibliographies to reflect current research approaches and sources. For the fourth edition, I added a new section on PowerPoint presentations to reflect current trends in student-to-student communication. This section emphasizes 508 compliance (ADA) for accessibility in presentations for which students in public sector positions will be responsible. Also for the fourth edition, I deleted the section on Briefing Cases for a variety of reasons; beyond space limitations for the text, students now have access to on-line briefs making the guidance for composing briefs a bit dated.

For Chapter 11, I added a new section on literature reviews. This is in response to popular requests from colleagues and students. The section focuses on instructing students on researching and managing the literature by applying classificational approaches to organizing and classifying information as a review of the past and present literature in the field.

In Chapter 12, in both the third and fourth editions, I added new examples of legislative analysis, policy evaluation, and policy recommendations. These new examples highlight changes in researching in these fields, particularly given the wealth of information available through government and private organizational Web sites. More than any other type of research, the quality of data available for policy research has expanded exponentially with improvements in access to previously unpublished data, as well as documents previously available only by request. These new examples reflect the depth and breadth of qualitative and quantitative data now available through the Internet. I also added new sections on policy memos, grant writing, and project report writing for the fourth edition. Policy memos involve applied research and writing skills that are particularly useful in public, nonprofit, and private-sector positions. As students increasingly become involved in internships, civic engagement projects, and other types of experiential learning, having the skills to create a policy memo will greatly enhance their experiences within the organizations for which they work. In addition, students involved in experiential learning activities are increasingly being asked to participate in grant writing and project reports for organizations they work with or for in their studies. I included simple instructions and examples to help students approach these tasks within their assignments. Finally, I moved the Participant/Observation/Internship Report section into Chapter 12 for greater coherence in linking this specialized writing to project report writing.

Finally, Chapters 13, 14, and 15 have been eliminated for the fourth edition not only to keep the cost of the book down, but also because changes in technology and common practice have made these chapters somewhat obsolete. These chapters included advice for clipping files, storage of notes, and resume writing that, at the time, were state of the art paper-based projects. Now such assignments can be more easily conducted through electronic, paperless processes. I would like to hear from readers about ideas for including help for these kind of projects for the fifth edition. Please email me at dschmidt@csuchico.edu.

In sum, this is not just another writing guide. It is a complete guide for being or becoming a professional in political science. It can be used from freshman- to graduate-level coursework, from entering a student career to graduating and pursuing a professional career after graduation. It is a style guide, a class handout, and a writing manual. It is everything students need to begin their research, their writing, and their careers. Enjoy!

Acknowledgments

I wish to express my appreciation to the many people who encouraged me and helped me in the preparation of the first, second, third, or fourth editions of this book, including (but in no special order) Bruce Appleby, Bob Lorinskas, Terry Plain, Sari Ramsey, Jerry Hostetler, Amy Andrews, Leila Niehuser, Cecilia Lause, Mark Toews, Beth McMillin, David Phihour, Jon Ebeling, Kathi Fountain, Rich Meade, Chris Trowbridge, Steffan Winkler, Eric Stano, Saraswathi Muralidhar, Rick Ruddel, Gilbert Duenas, Jennifer White, Alicia Gifford, Josh Ford, Kari Carter, Alyssum Root, and Leni Reus. I am also indebted to my students and colleagues who have been complimentary and supportive of my efforts in each edition to help students develop professionally.

Finally, I am indebted to friends and family for their unconditional support of this project including (but in no special order) Kay Heidbreder, Marji Morgan, Suzy Parker, Teresa Murphy, Sherlie McMillan, Cindy McKinney, Cindy McGee, Jim Mallien, Bonnie Hallman, Nicole Thompson, Don McBride, Donna Kemp, Frank Alvarez, Cortney Nelson, and Jennifer Oman. They have been friends when I needed them. I also want to thank my family, especially my mother Margie Brown, my sisters Sharon Rankin and Karon Houck, and sister-in-law Joan Brown for their support and pride in my accomplishments. Last, but not least, I wish to thank my sons, Casey and Jonathan, for being patient during my never-ending string of projects, and my husband, Alan, for his contributions to the text and his support and understanding when I was too involved in this project to worry about less pressing matters. These are the people I cherish most and who have been my greatest inspiration. Thank you.

Diane E. Schmidt, Professor
California State University, Chico

CHAPTER 1

POLITICAL INQUIRY

Introduction

This writing guide is designed to help students sharpen, reinforce, and develop good writing and research habits in political science. Writing is a process through which we learn to communicate with others. No one expects students to be perfect writers. We all learn and help each other learn. Through organization, writing and rewriting drafts, and logical presentation of our ideas, we engage in an intellectual process which helps us grow and be a part of the discourse community of political science.

What the Guide Is Supposed to Do:

1. Sharpen writing skills particular to political science.
2. Provide information about standards and expectations concerning political science writing.
3. Help differentiate between writing for political science and other disciplines.

What the Guide Cannot Do:
1. This material does not teach primary writing skills.
2. This material is not intended to be a substitute for a formal class in writing.
3. This material will not teach grammar, spelling, or punctuation.
4. This material cannot substitute for poor preparation.

The Art of Political Inquiry Defined

Many students are unaware that writing assignments for political science classes require different skills from those required for English composition, creative writing, and journalism courses. Although the basic skills are the same, political scientists, as members of a discipline:

1. Ask different questions and seek different answers to questions than those of the humanities and physical sciences.
2. Are interested in more than a description of what happened, where something happened, or when something happened.
3. Are interested in the political process or the causal connections between political events.

An event or a phenomenon must be politically relevant for it to be of interest to political science scholars. Of course, the standard definition of what is politically relevant is often in the eye of the beholder! A general rule for writing in political science classes is for students to always ask, before they write anything: What are the politics or power relationships existing in a political event?

Professional Research

Professional research in political science is based on the acquisition of scientific knowledge. Locating scientific knowledge requires developing or applying theories either through induction (based on observations) or deduction (based on prior expectations). According to Jones and Olson (1996 and 2005), such theories include:

1. *Systems Theory:* This theory explains political activities as part of a process or system. Researchers using this theory explain political phenomena by examining elements in the political environment (citizen activism, parties, interest groups, etc.).
2. *Power Theory:* This theory explains political activities by examining the power relationship between individuals or groups.
3. *Goals Theory:* This theory explains political activities by examining the purpose or goals of political phenomena.
4. *Rational Choice Theory:* This theory explains political activities as a result of individuals' preferences and self-interest.

Professional Methods of Investigation

There are a variety of approaches to examining political phenomena and there are a number of student paper examples that approximate these professional approaches.

1. *Philosophical Method:* Those using this approach examine the scope, purpose, and values of government activity. Often, those using this method ask how government

should act. This approach is inherently deductive (see "Example of a Political Argument" in Chapter 2 and "Example of an Analytical Essay" and "Example of an Editorial" in Chapter 9).

2. *Historical Method:* Those using this approach examine what conditions contributed to the occurrence of government activity. The focus of this research is on the structure of a historical event and how this structure may condition the outcome of future events (see "Example of an Analytical Case Study" in Chapter 12).

3. *Comparative Method:* Those using this approach compare and contrast experiences of governments, states, and other political entities (see "Example of a Comparative Paper" in Chapter 11).

4. *Juridical Method:* Those using this approach examine the legal or procedural basis for government activities. This approach is sometimes also referred to as institutional research (see "Example of a Legislative Analysis" in Chapter 12).

5. *Behavioral Method:* Those using this approach study the behavior of political actors by examining data collected on actual political occurrences. Often referred to as positivism or empiricism, this value-free approach approximates the scientific method to examine causal relationships and test theories on actual events (see "Example of an Analysis" in Chapter 11 and "Example of a Policy Evaluation" in Chapter 12).

6. *Post-behavioral Method:* Those using this approach examine, sometimes with mathematical models, not only observed behavior but values associated with the behavior. Often referred to as post-positivist, this method supports the argument that examining values and ethics, as well as observed events, is important (see "Example of a Position Paper" in Chapter 11 and "Example of a Policy Recommendation" in Chapter 12).

For more information on political inquiry in political science, policy, and public administration, see Jones and Edwards (2005), Schrems (2004), and Rabin (2003).

Types of Student Writing

Although professional-level research is rarely expected of students, political science assignments often emulate professional research. The following is a list of common types of writing assignments required in political science classes.

Analysis: These assignments usually ask students to examine the relationships between the parts of a political document or some political events or political outcome. Typically, these assignments require the student to provide a perspective or reasoned opinion about the significance of an event or a document (such as a policy). For example, students may be required to assert and defend an opinion about the most important features in the Bill of Rights (see examples in Chapter 12).

Argument: These assignments often require the student to prove or debate a point. Typically, these assignments ask for normative assertions supported by evidence and examples. For instance, instructors may ask students to provide an argument supporting (or not) automatic voter registration, random drug testing, or a constitutional amendment protecting the flag (see "Example of a Political Argument" in Chapter 2 and "Example of an Analytical Essay" in Chapter 9).

Cause and Effect: These assignments typically require the student to speculate about the reasons why some political event has occurred. For example, students may be asked why people vote, why members of Congress worry about their images, what caused the Civil War, or why some people are disillusioned with government (see "Example of an Analysis" in Chapter 11).

Classify: These assignments usually ask the student to identify a pattern or system of classifying objects, such as types of voters, types of political systems, or types of committees in Congress (see "Example of a Literature Review" in Chapter 11).

Compare or Contrast: These assignments usually ask the student to identify the differences and similarities between political roles, political systems, or political events (see "Example of a Comparative Paper" in Chapter 11).

Definition: These assignments usually ask the student to define a political concept, term, or phrase such as democracy, socialism, or capitalism. Students must provide examples of distinguishing features and differentiate the topic from others in its functional class (see "Sample Answer: Essay Test Question" in Chapter 9).

Process: These assignments usually ask the student to describe how some political phenomena relate functionally to other political phenomena. For example, students may be asked to describe how media influence voting behavior or how decisions are made in committees (see "Example of a Position Paper" in Chapter 11).

The Process of Political Inquiry

Professional political scientists, as part of a discourse community, engage in a process of political inquiry that involves using research techniques, critical thinking skills, and theory building. In general, political inquiry involves posing a question (a hypothesis), collecting data, analyzing the data, and drawing conclusions about whether the data support the hypothesis.

Understanding the nature of evidence and uses of data to support an assertion or hypothesis is critical to the inquiry process. The process functionally relates questions to evidence to conclusions to knowledge:

Hypothesis
⬇
Evidence
⬇
Conclusions
⬇
Knowledge

A **hypothesis** is a generalization that can be tested. Hypotheses state **expected** relationships between the *dependant variable* (the event being explained) and the *independent variables* (occurrences that caused or are associated with causing the event). Most importantly, hypotheses assert precisely how a change in the independent variable(s) changes the dependent variable.

Data are **evidence.** There are two kinds of data:

> **Quantitative evidence:** objective or numerical data usually from surveys, polls, tests, or experiments.

> **Qualitative evidence:** subjective or authoritative data usually from interviews, firsthand observations, inference, or expert opinions.

Conclusions are assertions made by the author concerning the relationship between the hypothesis and the evidence.

Knowledge is what we have learned from political inquiry. The goal of all political inquiry is to contribute to a universal body of knowledge. As scholars, we are obliged to learn and contribute to this body of knowledge.

The Author's Argument: The Nature of Assertions

Sometimes, in conversation with friends and colleagues, we take for granted that assertions or statements are true or are reasonably close to being correct. Sometimes we even switch from opinions to beliefs to facts as though they were of the same class of statements. These terms, however, have specific meanings and, as critical thinkers, we need to distinguish clearly between statements of fact, of opinion, of belief, and of prejudice.

Beliefs are convictions based on personal faith, values, perceptions of morality, and cultural experiences. They are not based on fact or evidence. Like facts, they cannot be disproved and are not subject to argument.

Facts are verifiable information. They do not make good assertions because the truth of a fact is not debatable.

Opinions are judgments based on facts. A thesis sentence of an argument is an opinion. Opinions are testable and arguable because they are viewpoints arrived at through the examination of facts and evidence. Opinions are not arguments—arguments with supporting evidence are used to support opinions.

Prejudices are opinions that have been formed on insufficient or unexamined evidence. They are often thoughtless oversimplifications and typically reflect a narrow-minded view of the world. They are testable and easily refutable by the presentation of facts and evidence.

The Author's Evidence: Supporting an Argument with Data

The strength of an argument rises and falls based on the evidence or data presented by the writer to support an assertion. Specificity and breadth are the main characteristics of good supporting evidence. To convince readers of the correctness of an assertion, writers must provide readers with evidence that is accurate and relevant (relating directly to the point).

Data and evidence are essentially the same thing. We typically use the word *data* to refer to numerical evidence. This, however, need not be the case. Whatever we use to support our arguments can be seen as data. We use our own observations or those of others to back up our assertions. Evidence varies in strength based on its individual properties and the contexts of its use. Whether these data are facts, expert opinions, examples, or statistics, we use them, in combination, to support our arguments.

Examples are specific references or instances of the point being made and are typically referred to as anecdotal evidence. The strength of anecdotal evidence is found in its generalizability and representativeness.

Expert opinions are judgments made by authorities based on their experiences with evidence and assessment of the facts. When facts are unavailable, expert opinions are the next strongest evidence a writer can supply to support an argument. Expert opinions are some of the strongest kinds of evidence a writer can use.

Facts are statements that can be verified. They are the strongest proof or evidence a writer can supply to support an assertion. They are also the most difficult kind of evidence to obtain.

Statistics are often called probabilistic evidence because they are based on probabilities of correctness and depend on strict adherence to representative sampling techniques. Statistics are not facts: they are the next best things to facts when facts are unavailable. Unfortunately, statistics alone provide weak support for an argument. Together with expert opinion and examples, however, statistics can provide powerful support for arguments.

Professionalism, Ethical Considerations, and Plagiarism

Professional research in political science also involves the ethical use of evidence to support claims and assertions developed as part of political inquiry. Ethically, all information used to support an argument must be referenced. Although most students realize that direct quotations from a source or a fact taken from a table must be referenced, they often do not realize that a paraphrase of someone else's work or their own work must be referenced as well. Each writer makes a stylistic contribution to the communication of ideas and information. Paraphrasing without acknowledging the author of the idea or information, and/or without acknowledging the author's unique contribution, is considered plagiarism. In general, cautious students should include at least two references per paragraph in the body of their papers and make sure all terminology, phrasing, or ideas are referenced frequently and directly. Introductions and conclusions generally do not need references unless the phrasing of the information is particular to someone else. (The information for some of the following discussion has been adapted or based on Babbie 1998; OWL 1995–2004; University of California, Davis 2001; Standler 2000; Indiana University, Bloomington 2004.)

Controversies About Plagiarism

Plagiarism is using other people's ideas and data without acknowledgment. Although researchers are expected to build on other people's work, they are not supposed to take credit for other people's work. When researchers take credit for words, ideas, or facts created by others, they commit an act of plagiarism.

What Is Plagiarism?

Plagiarism is the intentional or unintentional use of someone else's ideas, phrasing, terminology, or words without providing an acknowledgment in the form of a footnote, endnote, parenthetical reference, or direct comment in the text. Although copyright laws allow the *fair use* of a limited amount of other authors' materials, such laws do not grant permission or license to use such materials without attributing credit to the original author. To use another person's materials, students must provide full documentation of the source in the text of their papers as well as in the reference page (see Chapter 8 on documentation and referencing criteria and formats). Failing to document and attribute the source of any belief, fact, opinion, or statistic that is not original or that is not common knowledge is considered plagiarism. There are different types of plagiarism.

Text Plagiarism. Copying text word for word where either the words are identical to the original text, the tone or style is nearly identical to the original text, or the structure of the words used together is nearly identical to the original text is plagiarism if students do not acknowledge the relationship between the words they used in their papers and the original source of those words.

- **Direct quotes without using quotation marks.** Plagiarism is using someone else's exact words without quotation marks and a reference. This includes paragraphs, sentences, and unique phrasing of words. For example, Robert Salisbury published an article in 1968 where he wrote on page 151 the words *Public policy consists in authoritative or sanctioned decisions by governmental actors.* To use these words, a student must put quotation marks in front of the word *Public* and after the period in the sentence. The student must then report in the form of a footnote, endnote, parenthetical reference, or direct comment in the text the author's name, the publication year, and the page number where the words can be found.

- **Paraphrasing by using synonyms.** Plagiarism is using someone else's words from a text and rewriting them by substituting synonyms (words that mean the same thing) without a reference and without stating that the words have been changed. For example, a student who changes Robert Salisbury's words *Public policy consists in authoritative or sanctioned decisions by governmental actors* to *Public policy is made up of official decisions by people in government* is plagiarizing unless the statement is prefaced by "To paraphrase Salisbury (1968, 151), public policy is made up of official decisions by people in government."

- **Paraphrasing by shifting order of words.** Plagiarism is using someone else's words from a text and rewriting them by shifting the order of the words without referencing the author and without stating that the order of the words from the original text has been changed. For example, a student who shortens and/or rearranges Robert Salisbury's words *Public policy consists in authoritative or sanctioned decisions by governmental actors* by writing *Government actors create public policy through authoritative or sanctioned decisions* is plagiarizing unless the statement is prefaced by "To paraphrase Salisbury (1968, 151), *government actors create public policy through authoritative or sanctioned decisions.*"

Idea Plagiarism: Summarizing Without Attribution. Adopting or adapting ideas, models, theories, hypotheses, arguments, assertions, perspectives, and/or opinions without acknowledging that they are someone else's original thoughts is plagiarism if the student does not reference the source from which the information was taken. Plagiarism is using someone else's ideas and so on without referencing the author of these ideas. This includes any and all ideas expressed in writing or orally. For example, a student who wishes to use Robert Salisbury's ideas communicated in the sentence *Public policy consists in authoritative or sanctioned decisions by governmental actors* (1968, 151) by writing a paraphrase such as *Public policy is defined by actions* *taken by government officials* is plagiarizing Salisbury's idea unless the statement is accompanied by a reference at the end of the sentence that includes the name of the author, the year of publication, and the page number where the idea can be found.

Fact Plagiarism: Quoting Without Attribution. Using facts, data, statistics, figures, charts, graphs, tables, pictures, findings, or research results that were gathered and reported by someone else without referencing the source of these "facts" is plagiarism.

- Any number or numerical information taken from a source must be referenced with the author's name, the year of publication, and the page number where the number can be found. The reference should be placed at the end of the sentence where the fact is reported.

- If students use a graph, chart, etc. from someone else's original work, they are plagiarizing unless the graph, chart, etc. is copied exactly as reported by the original author and fully referenced (usually at the bottom of the illustration) with the author's name, the title of the publication, the place of publication (for books) or the source (for articles and electronic media), the year of publication, and the page number where the source can be located (or in the case of electronic sources, the full URL and accessed date).

- If students use data created by someone else to create an illustration (chart, graph, etc.), they are plagiarizing unless the data used to create these illustrations are recorded exactly as they are reported by the author. A complete reference must be provided at the bottom of the illustration, including the author's name, the title of the publication, the place of publication (for books) or the source (for articles and electronic media), the year of publication, and the page number where the source can be located (or in the case of electronic sources, the full URL and accessed date).

Why Is Plagiarism Wrong?

Plagiarism is wrong because it infringes on property rights and perpetuates academic dishonesty. Just as stealing a car is wrong, using someone else's intellectual property without permission or outside of fair use provisions is against the law. Along with cheating on tests, plagiarism is an act of academic dishonesty at best, and fraud at worst.

Property Rights Violations: Plagiarism violates the intellectual property rights of individuals. Protecting intellectual property is one of the first protections of private property created by the framers of the U.S. Constitution. Article I, Section 8, Clause 8 of the Constitution grants exclusive rights to authors. To further define and support these rights, the Copyright Act of 1790 (and many amendments, revisions, and court interpretations to this law as well) implemented and set constraints on the use of other people's work (Association of Research Libraries 2002). Under fair use policies, researchers are allowed to reference and use the intellectual properties of others as long as the owners of the property are acknowledged and/or compensated according to the conditions set by these regulations.

Dishonesty: Plagiarism impedes intellectual growth because those who plagiarize take credit for ideas and information that are not a product of their intellectual investment. Essentially, plagiarism is lying by misrepresenting one's intellectual investment.

In this sense, plagiarism is a form of cheating and of academic dishonesty. Plagiarism further perpetuates intellectual property crimes because those who do so are stealing the property of others. In serious cases, especially where an entire source has been copied (an article, a purchased term paper, etc.), the act of plagiarism can be prosecuted as a crime.

Why Plagiarism Happens

There are a variety of reasons why people plagiarize the work of others. The most disturbing is the deliberate intention to steal other people's work. The most generous perspective on plagiarism is that it is accidental or based on poor training.

Deliberate Misrepresentation: Some people cheat; the reasons are generally personal, but sometimes plagiarism is a choice people make when they are ignorant, poorly organized, or lazy. Sometimes students are unsure about how to perform a task required by an instructor so they simply copy somebody else's work to comply with the requirements of the course. Sometimes students misjudge how long or difficult an assignment is and run out of time to finish the work. To finish an assignment, they resort to cutting and pasting the work of others without synthesizing (merging ideas together) and putting the ideas into their own words. Finally, some students are just lazy. For them, it is easier to purchase or copy material and represent it as their own work. Using work performed by others without acknowledgment, even if it is purchased, is deliberate misrepresentation and fraud.

Mistakes: Some students are disorganized or poorly trained for research. Sometimes students accidentally plagiarize material created by others because they did not organize their research efforts. Without good organization and note-taking skills, students often forget where they found information. This often happens when they have used cut-and-paste software tools for taking notes from electronic resources. In addition, poorly trained students may not know how or understand when they must acknowledge the source of their information. Although students often know they must provide a source for their materials, they may not understand the difference between quoting, paraphrasing, and summarizing information.

Confusion: Some students are confused about how to write a paper that is creative and based on their own work when their work is based on the intellectual property of others. Students sometimes fail to differentiate *writing creatively* with *writing something that is unique* or original. Creative writing and research using secondary research sources (other people's work) are based on *how the intellectual properties of others are used as evidence* to support the students' ideas and perspectives on the topic. It is the synthesis, organization, variety, depth, and breadth of the secondary sources students use for writing about the topic that generate a research paper that becomes their intellectual property.

What Sources Must Be Referenced or Acknowledged?

Students must reference all information that is taken directly from secondary sources or rephrased from someone's or something's intellectual property. Compliance with this requirement is important because experts on the topic (such as professors) not only recognize the origins of such secondary source information but are also familiar with the unique phrasings and style of the sources' authors. Shifts in style and language in a student's paper are strong indicators of plagiarism, especially when such shifts in language and presentation are not accompanied by references or acknowledgments. Students also should be aware that many educational institutions are acquiring software programs designed to flag or identify plagiarism. Thus, all electronic sources of information of any type, as well as all secondary sources of information in more traditional formats, must be referenced directly and accurately.

Secondary Sources of Information

A secondary source is a set of information created by someone or something other than the researcher or writer of the research paper. When using some other person's, organization's, or entity's creative work from any communication source, students must reference the source. This includes:

- Writings and findings from all books, journals, pamphlets, electronic media, billboards, broadcast media, entertainment media, conversations, graphs, tables, etc. that the student has not personally created.
- Anything written, observed, visually presented, spoken, and/or heard in any form or format not created by the student for the research paper or project.

Unique or Distinctive Words or Sets of Words

When using some other person's, organization's, or entity's unique or distinctive words, wording, phrasing, or conceptualization (model), students must reference the source. This includes direct (word-for-word) quotes, paraphrasing (modified wording), or summarizing (condensing).

Electronic Sources of All Types

Plagiarism software generally uses one or more databases to search for text that is copied verbatim or paraphrased. Students should be careful when taking notes, especially when those notes have been cut and pasted from electronic sources, to attribute that information to the source if used in research papers, because plagiarism software programs identify suspect words or phrases (usually underlined or highlighted) and the original source is usually linked to these words or phrases. If a student has cut and pasted a document from an electronic source, the software will identify material as possible plagiarism. A well-documented research paper should have no difficulties when scanned by plagiarism software.

Student Researcher's Manuscripts

Students must reference themselves when using research findings and/or text from manuscripts that they created for other research projects, regardless of whether or not these manuscripts have been published. It is common for researchers to build on their previous studies, but once they produce a manuscript, use of any part of the manuscript should be referenced. For students, this means that if they write a paper for one class, they should not use any part of that paper for any other class without referencing the original and/or asking permission of the professor they wrote the paper for and of the professor for whom they are writing the new paper.

What Sources Do Not Have to Be Referenced or Acknowledged?

There is no information or communication that does not have to be acknowledged in some way. Yet, the burden of reference is lighter for personal experiences, common knowledge, and conclusionary statements. The decision to reference or not to reference in these instances must be made on a case-by-case basis.

Personal Experiences

Personal experiences do not have to be referenced, although students must identify the context (where, when, how, and why) of such experiences. As such, even personal experiences have references.

Original Research

Findings from primary data research do not have to be referenced, although students must identify and reprint the methodological process for creating original or primary data. As such, results from primary or original research are referenced by the methodological process through which the student collected the data or findings.

Common Knowledge

Common knowledge need not be referenced, although what is considered common knowledge is contextually determined by culture, profession, and time. Common knowledge differs by generations, political or social cultures, and fields or subfields within a professional area of study. Unless the information is *obviously* part of the traditions and socialization of the audience (e.g., that Thomas Jefferson wrote the Declaration of Independence is common knowledge in America), even common knowledge should be referenced.

Personal Conclusions

Generally, the conclusion sections of papers do not need to include references; however, the conclusions must be a product of the student's own analysis and efforts. If students use unique or distinctive words, wording, phrasing, or anything else that is *not* based on their own thoughts or insights and/or if the conclusions are *not* clearly based on the analysis in the body of the paper, then this information should be referenced.

How to Avoid Plagiarizing Due to Mistakes and Confusion

Students can minimize and/or prevent plagiarism problems or being accused of plagiarizing by being organized and informed about the use of intellectual property. By organizing their research methodically around attributing information as it is collected in the research process, students may avoid plagiarism that results from mistakes and confusion. By improving their skills and strategies for referencing in the writing process, students may avoid problems, especially ones that arise from manuscripts being processed through plagiarism software, that are a result of mistakes and confusion about how to reference secondary sources.

Avoiding Plagiarism in the Research Process

Set up a Binder: Keep references for every source of communication (books, articles, etc.) in a binder.

- Before reading anything, write the complete bibliographic information of the source on paper; one sheet of paper per source.

- If the source is electronic, copy the URL (and as much other bibliographic information available from the source) using cut-and-paste tools while still in the file. Paste these items into a word processing file and save them for creating the reference page. Print out the source reference and put it into the binder.
- Record, on paper, the author, date, and place where the information was heard, seen, experienced, or observed.
- Keep the references in the binder in alphabetical order.

Organize Notes: When taking notes on a source, place the name of the author (person, organization, entity) and year of publication at the top of the first note page and every page of notes made from that reference. When there is no author, use an abbreviated title (just as for a citation in the paper) that clearly links to the bibliographic page created in the binder.

Annotate Quotes: When copying the author's information to notes word for word, write the word *QUOTE* first, then the page number(s), and finally, put quotation marks around the words.

- Quotes can be any text in the source.
- Quotes are quantitative or concrete information such as numbers or facts unique to the source.
- Quotes can be abstract or qualitative information such as opinions or concepts.

Annotate Paraphrases: When paraphrasing in the notes, underline the words that are modified or similar to the author's exact words. Write the word *PARAPHRASE* and the page number(s).

- Using a thesaurus to change the author's words is paraphrasing.
- Using different forms of the words, such as using the past or present tense of verbs or different pronouns to modify the nouns, is paraphrasing.

Annotate Summaries: When summarizing an author's work, page numbers may or may not have to be used in the reference; remember, however, that using a thesaurus to change the author's words is not summarizing. Summarized information *should not be* similar in form, style, cadence, phrasing, personality, or wording to the original author's wording. The summary should reflect the student's writing style and personality.

- When summarizing a distinct set of ideas or information from an author's work, write the word *SUMMARY* and the page numbers for the information and then put the information in other words.
- When summarizing the entire contents of an author's work, as is often done for annotated bibliographies, write the words *SUMMARY-PURPOSE* and then summarize the purpose of the work in a few short sentences. Then write the words *SUMMARY-SIGNIFICANCE*, and summarize the conclusions of the author and state the importance of the findings to the field and/or the research topic in a few short sentences.

Avoiding Plagiarism in the Writing Process

Quoting, paraphrasing, and summarizing have different formats, techniques, and requirements for attribution.

Quotes: Acknowledge exact or modified quotes (information taken word for word from an author's text) by attributing the words to the author directly before or after the quote. All quotes must be introduced directly by using words and phrases such as *said, says, according to, argued, stated*, etc. The quotation marks are placed before the words from the author's text begin and after the words from the author's text ends. If the student is only quoting a portion of a statement, often the attribution is latent (at the end). Students must identify any modifications to the author's exact phrasing using brackets, for information changed, or ellipsis (three periods), for information excluded. In either case, students must be careful not to change the meaning or context of the original author's text when using a direct quote. Quotes that are over four lines long are placed in a separate paragraph and indented and do not have quotation marks (see Chapter 8 on formatting).

Quoting Techniques

For example, to acknowledge Robert Salisbury's work on public policy, students may quote and reference using any of the following techniques. (These examples are in *The Chicago Manual of Style* parenthetical citation format.)

Technique 1: Unmodified text, direct attribution Salisbury (1968, 151) says, "Public policy consists in authoritative or sanctioned decisions by governmental actors. It refers to the *substance* of what government does and is to be distinguished from the processes by which decisions are made."

Technique 2: Unmodified text, latent attribution According to Salisbury, "Public policy consists in authoritative or sanctioned decisions by governmental actors. It refers to the *substance* of what government does and is to be distinguished from the processes by which decisions are made" (1968, 151).

Technique 3: Modified text by omitting part, direct attribution Many scholars have argued about the definition of public policy, yet Salisbury states clearly that "[p]ublic policy . . . refers to the *substance* of what government does and is to be distinguished from the processes by which decisions are made" (1968, 151).

Technique 4: Modified text by omitting part, latent attribution For this research paper, public policy is defined as "the *substance* of what government does" (Salisbury 1968, 151).

Technique 5: Modified text by omitting several parts, latent attribution Public policy is not defined by the "processes by which decisions are made"; it is "the *substance* of what government does" (Salisbury 1968, 151).

Paraphrase: Acknowledge modified or similar wording by attributing the information to the author by using phrases such as *according to, suggested, argued, found, discussed, reasoned, intimated*, etc.

Paraphrasing Techniques

For example, in a discussion of Robert Salisbury's work on public policy, students may attribute **paraphrased** ideas by using the following techniques. (These examples are in *The Chicago Manual of Style* parenthetical citation format.)

Technique 1: According to Salisbury (1968, 151) public policy is defined by government actions and not the decision processes.

Technique 2: Policy, as suggested by Salisbury (1968, 151), is not about decision-making processes; it is about the essence of what governments do in society.

Technique 3: Yet, Salisbury (1968, 151) indicated that public policy is not defined by government processes, but by government actions.

Technique 4: Salisbury (1968, 151), in his article defining the meaning of public policy, explained that it is what governments *do* that defines policy.

Technique 5: Salisbury (1968, 151) elaborates as well as disagrees with other scholars' definition of public policy; he argues that policy is what governments do.

Summaries: Acknowledge summarized information by attributing the information to the author using a reference to the author at the end of the sentence or set of sentences used to summarize the author's contribution to knowledge. If the information is summarized from a unique portion of the author's work, then use page numbers in the citation. If the information is a summary of the purpose and/or the contributions and findings of the author's work, then the reference need not have page numbers included in the citation.

Summarizing Techniques

For example, in a discussion of Robert Salisbury's contribution to the field of public policy analysis, students may attribute a **summary** of his work by the following techniques. (These examples are in *The Chicago Manual of Style* parenthetical citation format.)

Technique 1: Public policy analysis, as a field, has been the subject of intense academic debate. Policy scholars disagree on whether policy is best understood by case studies of policy outcomes or by examining the ways in which decisions are made and implemented within a society (Salisbury 1968, 151–153).

Technique 2: Public policy is more than a process; it is defined by the characteristics of policy outcomes. How those outcomes are distributed, particularly when there are implications of zero-sum results, is important to defining and understanding constraints on political behavior (Salisbury 1968).

CHAPTER 2

CRITICAL THINKING ABOUT POLITICS

Critical Thinking: The Cornerstone of Political Inquiry

If we as political scholars are obliged to contribute to a body of knowledge, then we must learn to ask questions that are politically interesting. Critical thinking skills separate students who are information sponges from those who are information filters.

- **Sponges** indiscriminately, unquestioningly absorb information.
- **Filters** sort information and ask questions not only about the information provided but also about the validity of the evidence and assumptions used to produce the information. Filters sort the politically relevant from the irrelevant. Not all information is worth analyzing.

Critical Thinkers

- Define problems, examine evidence, and analyze the assumptions leading to a conclusion.
- Question arguments, causal theories, evidence, broad generalizations, and simple correlation.

- Are open to both sides of an argument.
- Are prepared to examine and "poke holes" in all arguments, even their own.

Critical Thinking Defined

When listening to a speaker or reading a document, essay, article, or book, students must first identify the structure of the author's argument. A good argument usually identifies an issue, provides reasons, and concludes something. Second, the student must examine the structure of the author's conclusion. Within each structure, we can ask questions about the validity of the evidence and assumptions. Critical thinkers generally do the following (adapted from Richard Paul and Linda Elder. 2006. *The thinker's guide to the art of Socratic questioning*. Dillon Beach, CA: Foundation for Critical Thinking):

- Classify and clarify information.
- Examine assumptions.
- Analyze reasons and evidence.
- Identify viewpoints and perspectives.
- Scrutinize implications and consequences.
- Discover application and significance.

How to Think Critically

The first step in obtaining critical thinking skills is identifying what to look for in a written work (Schmidt et al. 1989; Fowler and Aaron 1989, 128–158).

First: Identify the author's argument or hypothesis.
- Ask what is the author's point?
- Look for the thesis statement.
- Know what an argument is and is not.
  - An argument is not a fact, a definition, an example, or descriptive information.
  - An argument or a hypothesis poses a testable question.

Second: Identify what the author uses as evidence.
- Find out how the author supports the point made in the work.
- Look for data.
- Identify what kind of data or types of evidence are used.
  - Is it qualitative or quantitative?
  - If it is statistical data, examine the method used to collect it.
  - If it is qualitative data, examine the context in which it is being used.
- Know what evidence is and what it is not.
  - Evidence is facts, survey results, authoritative opinion, and examples.
  - Evidence is not hearsay, the author's personal opinion, speculation, or values espoused by the author.

Third: Identify the author's conclusion.

- What does the author say about the relationship between the hypothesis and the evidence?
- Know what a conclusion is and is not.
  - A conclusion is not a fact, a definition, an example, or descriptive information.
  - A conclusion asserts that the question posed is either supported or not by the evidence.
- Look for identifying or indicator words to locate the conclusion: Words such as, *thus, therefore, in fact, it follows that, as a result, the point is,* and *it has been shown* indicate a concluding statement.

Critical Thinking and Reasoning

Learning to think and write critically means commanding a sense of what properties a well-reasoned argument should possess. Reasoning is essential to the writing process. In fact, sound reasoning is more important in political science writing than creativity and eloquence. Political science writing depends heavily on arguments about the structure of political or power relationships. Because of this, communicating a point about an issue is dependent on a clear, well-reasoned exposition of the evidence.

Much of the work of political scientists is based on a scientific method of inquiry. The scientific method is based on inductive and deductive reasoning as well as inference and generalization. Here are some brief definitions of these terms (Fowler and Aaron 1989, 132–137).

Inductive Reasoning: Generalizing from observations or attributing a cause to a set of observed circumstances.

Deductive Reasoning: Applying generalizations or conclusions that are accepted as true to slightly different but similar situations or issues.

Inference: A conclusion based on evidence. This is based on inductive reasoning.

Generalization: A characterization based on the assumption that what applies in one set of circumstances also applies in similar circumstances.

Political Inquiry and Inductive Reasoning

Inductive reasoning involves a process of collecting enough data or evidence to make a confident assertion about political or power relationships. We can infer a conclusion after examining and collecting information about what an author thinks about an issue.

- Inference and inductive reasoning are important steps in the process used by political scientists to identify the causal relationships between political phenomena.
- Inference and inductive reasoning provide the mechanism by which political scientists use data to increase the body of political knowledge.
- Inference and inductive reasoning promote sound conclusions based on sound evidence.

Most of what we know or think we know about politics and political behavior is based on inductive reasoning. Conclusions in voting studies, for example, are primarily based on inductive reasoning from empirical evidence. If we want to know what factors influence the voting turnout of the elderly, we would need to observe some behavior:

Observation: After conducting a survey based on a representative random sample of the elderly, we observe that most of the elderly say that they vote only when Social Security is in jeopardy.

Observation: We find that exit polls show that when Social Security is an issue, a large number of the elderly vote.

Conclusion: Based on these two pieces of evidence, we can reasonably conclude, through inductive reasoning, that most of the elderly are motivated to vote when their interests are threatened.

Political Inquiry and Deductive Reasoning

Political scientists also use deductive reasoning, but it is less obvious than the use of inductive reasoning. Deductive reasoning underlies many of the arguments used in political science writing. Through deductive reasoning, we can use the generalizations we asserted through inference to make an argument about specific cases.

Deductive reasoning is composed of at least two factual statements (premises) and a conclusion. This constitutes a syllogism. A syllogism is simply two premises stating facts or judgments that together lead to a conclusion. The conclusion must derive from the premises.

Example of Deductive Reasoning

Premise: Most elderly citizens vote when their interests are threatened.

Premise: Many of the elderly are worried about the stability of the Social Security system.

Conclusion: Many of the elderly will vote in the next election.

Unfortunately, not all deductive arguments are presented clearly. Some deductive arguments will rely on either unstated (implied) premises or will overstate a premise.

Example of Implied Premise

Many of the elderly are worried about the stability of the Social Security system, so they will vote in the next election.

The premise, that the elderly vote when their interests are threatened, is left unstated.

Example of Overstated Premise

The elderly always vote when their interests are threatened. Many of the elderly are worried about the stability of the Social Security system, so they will vote in the next election.

The first premise overstates the generalization because it would be hard to apply it to all circumstances. Absolute words such as *all, no one, never,* or *always* force the generalization to apply strictly to every case and circumstance. Premises that cannot be applied to every case use limiting words such as *some, many,* and *often.*

Common Problems in Critical Thinking

Once an argument is offered, the author is obligated to address the argument directly with evidence and then reach a reasonable conclusion. There are, however, common problems in logical exposition of an argument that influence the reasonableness and validity of an author's point (Fowler and Aaron 1989, 137–143).

Examine the following lists of common problems in critical thinking. After the definition of each problem is an example. These examples were taken from student answers to an essay question concerning the desirability of requiring poor women with small children to work in order to receive public aid. (For further help and a comprehensive list of logical fallacies with examples, see Stephen Downes, http://onegoodmove.org/fallacy.toc.htm.)

BEGGING THE QUESTION An argument begs the question when the author treats a debatable opinion as a proven fact.

> **Example:** "Welfare mothers should have to work for their money because they only have children to collect free money."
>
> **Problem:** This author assumes that receiving money without working for it causes women to have babies, which is a highly questionable generalization at best.

IGNORING THE QUESTION An argument ignores the question when the author appeals to the reader with reasons that have nothing to do with the issues raised. The most common occurrence of these errors is found in political campaign slogans and commercial advertising. Authors ignore or evade the question when they engage in one or more of the following:

Emotional appeals—appeals to the reader's sense of decency, fear, or pity.

> **Example:** "Any self-respecting woman would not take money she did not earn, even from the government."
>
> **Problem:** The author suggests that poor women are not good, decent people but provides no proof of that assertion. The author is appealing to the reader's sense of decency.

Snob appeal—appealing to the reader's desire to be like someone they admire.

> **Example:** "Pioneer women were able to raise families without government aid while their husbands were off on cattle drives or fighting wars."
>
> **Problem:** The author is appealing to a glorified image of rugged women settlers. The author is suggesting that women who are able to take care of their families alone are like pioneer women and those who cannot take care of their families are not living up to their potential. While the assertion itself is debatable, the example of pioneer women is inappropriate because it is based on a stereotypical image, not reality.

Bandwagon approach—appealing to the reader's desire to be like everyone else.

> **Example:** "Every hard-working American resents giving money to people who do not work for it."
>
> **Problem:** The author creates an impossible situation for the reader. Because many people like to think of themselves as hard workers, to be part of this group the reader must adopt the same attitude toward cash assistance for poor women. The assertion is debatable and presents an inappropriate reason for being against cash assistance.

Flattery—projecting qualities on the reader.

Example: "As an intelligent and hardworking person, you should resent giving people money for doing nothing."

Problem: The author is projecting the qualities of being intelligent and hardworking onto the reader. The statement implies that disagreeing with the author is tantamount to admitting that the reader does not exhibit these qualities.

Ad hominem—personalizing the issue by concentrating on the real or imagined negative characteristics of those who hold different or opposing views.

Example: "Because most people work hard for their money, the only people who continue to support free money to lazy women are old, drugged-out hippies and know-it-all liberal scholars."

Problem: The author projects the currently and socially unacceptable negative images of old hippies and overbearing liberals onto the supporters of cash assistance to poor women. The author is counting on the reader to reject cash assistance for poor women based on its association with those unpopular stereotypical images.

FAULTY REASONING   Fallacies, or errors in reasoning, are problems because they weaken the author's argument.

Hasty generalizations—a generalization that is based on very little evidence or which overstates the facts.

Example: "Welfare mothers are just lazy. I know of two welfare mothers who do nothing but watch television all day."

Problem: The author is generalizing about all poor women receiving public assistance on the basis of two such women he or she has observed. A selection of two observations is much too small a sample to make a generalization about an entire class of people.

Oversimplification—stating that one event caused another when there is either no relationship or when other causes exist.

Example: "Providing free money to mothers may actually cause more harm than good for their children. Children of welfare mothers rarely excel in school."

Problem: The author suggests that cash assistance to mothers discourages their children from achieving in school. There is no reason to believe that cash assistance causes poor scholastic achievement. There are a host of other causes, however, which contribute to low achievement among children in general. Cash-poor schools, overcrowding, malnutrition, and poor health care are but just a few alternative causal variables in poor scholastic achievement, regardless of the source of the child's family income.

Post hoc fallacy—jumping to the conclusion that event A caused event B just because event A occurred earlier.

Example: "The availability of free money to poor families causes these families to break up. Fathers leave so that their families can collect welfare."

Problem: The author suggests that the only reason fathers leave their families is the availability of cash assistance. Application for public aid is a response to families in trouble; it does not necessarily follow that public aid causes families to break up. Fathers leaving their families is not a necessary or sufficient condition for receiving public aid.

False dilemma—stating that a complex question has only two answers that are both good, both bad, or one good and one bad.

Example: "By continuing to provide free money to poor mothers, we can expect only a continuation of poverty or an erosion of the American work ethic."

Problem: The author suggests that continuing public aid to poor mothers can only result in two undesirable conditions. The author neglects to identify other possible resulting conditions that are desirable, such as a reduction in the number of children who are malnourished, from continuing public aid.

Non sequitur—when two ideas are presented with no logical connection.

Example: "Providing free money has done nothing to improve the quality of life among the poor. Wealthy and middle-class citizens continue to take tax deductions for charitable contributions."

Problem: The author is suggesting that because people still make contributions to charity, no change in the situation of the poor has resulted from public assistance to poor mothers. There is no logical connection between public assistance and tax deductions for charity. The contribution need not be for the poor to be deductible.

False analogy—assuming that things that are alike in one respect are alike in other respects.

Example: "In general, welfare mothers are characterized by poor work skills and little work experience. Few will take the initiative to acquire new skills or work at low-skilled jobs without a coercive incentive, such as working for their welfare checks."

Problem: Although the author's assertion about the skills and experience of welfare mothers may be valid, there is no logical reason to accept that all welfare mothers will resist acquiring training unless coerced. If given the opportunity to acquire job skills and experience, some may do so and some may not. We cannot predict, based on receiving public aid, whether or not a person will seek to improve his or her marketability.

Tips for Critical Thinking

The following is a summary checklist with a detailed set of questions that students should ask themselves as they read a book, an article, or an essay. There are two classes of questions. One set examines the author's argument and evidence. The other set of questions examines the author's conclusions. (The summary and the detailed questions are based on material from Fowler and Aaron 1989; and Schmidt et al. 1989.)

Summary Checklist for Reading or Writing Critically

Here is a checklist for students to use in checking their arguments as well as those of other authors.

1. Has the author stated the central point or assertion of the essay, article, or book in a thesis sentence?
2. Does the body of the work demonstrate the validity of the thesis sentence by breaking it down into other statements or assertions?
3. Has the author reasoned inductively or deductively?

4. Is the evidence provided varied, representative, relevant, and inclusive of facts, examples, and expert opinion?

5. Are there areas where the argument exhibits problems of faulty reasoning or where the author did not face the question posed?

Detailed Set of Questions to Ask About the Author's Argument and Evidence

(Adapted from Ruggiero 1991, 54–64, 149–157.)

Issues

A. Look for an explicit reference to the issue. Often authors will use subjective language to introduce the issue and their point of view. For example, here is a statement: "Should flag desecration be a crime?"

1. Students should ask what the author's definition of flag desecration is and which forms of flag desecration the author is concerned about.

2. Students should ask under what conditions misuse of the flag would be considered punishable or not punishable, according to the author.

B. Look for implicit references to the issue.

1. This may involve examining the closing or concluding remarks of the author.

2. Authors will often use words that sum up or suggest relationships in the conclusion that imply what issue has been examined in the work.

Reasons

A. Authors are obligated to give readers reasons why their points are true or valid.

B. Students should look for clues in the literature to identify the evidence.

1. Look for identifying words such as *because, since, for one thing, also.*

2. Look for ordered paragraphs starting with *first, second, third, finally.*

3. Look for statistics, graphs, or tables.

Ambiguity

A. Look for words or phrases that may seem obvious but have multiple meanings.

B. Look for ambiguous or abstract words.

1. Words such as *liberal, conservative, freedom, equality,* and *justice* are abstract and lack specificity.

2. Students should make sure they know how such words are being used. Look for qualifying references and definitions.

C. Understand all the terms, concepts, and phrases used, including professional jargon.

D. Beware of tautologies or truisms.

1. Tautologies or truisms are statements that are always true and cannot be disproved by any evidence or data.

2. One example of a truism is that either people will vote or they will not. Whether people vote or do not vote does not matter because either way the statement remains true.

Value Assumptions

A. Look for the author's stated ideas or beliefs about what influences behavior or choices.

    1. Does the author base points and arguments upon values concerning the desirability of competition, justice, freedom of speech?

    2. Does the author make assumptions about behavior or choices that are generally true?

B. Look for the author's unstated beliefs about what influences behavior or choices. Read between the lines.

C. Students should realize what their personal values and biases are and be prepared to accept defeat in light of a well-reasoned, factually based argument made by someone else.

    1. Students should identify the stated and unstated value assumptions that are consistent with their own.

    2. Students should identify the stated and unstated value assumptions that conflict with their own.

Evidence

A. If empirical (quantitative) data are used as evidence, then examine the data fully.

    1. Are the data representative (in size, breadth, and randomness) of the target population being studied?

    2. Look for misleading use of percentages: comparisons of percentages and reporting, especially large percentages, are often suspect.

    3. Know the sample size on which the percentages were based. Small sample sizes often produce misleading results.

    4. Remember that correlation is not the same thing as causation. When two things are correlated (occurring at the same time), they may not necessarily be causally related (one thing causing the occurrence of the other thing).

B. If the evidence is qualitative, then examine the context of the evidence.

    1. Be sure that the evidence is from an objective and respected authority.

    2. For example, a recommendation by the American Medical Association for action concerning a disease would be an appropriate piece of evidence. Alternatively, a recommendation by the American Medical Association concerning national health insurance is suspect because that organization has a personal stake in the outcome and cannot be considered an objective authority.

    3. Be cautious of one compelling example used as evidence. Remember, as data, the example would be a nonrepresentative sample composed of one data point.

Logical Errors

A. Be sure that the evidence fits the conclusions.

    1. Form conclusions from the data and check them against the author's conclusion.

    2. If the author's conclusion differs, go back and check the author's reasoning, value assumptions, and qualifying terms and definitions.

B. Reject evidence when it exhibits the following flaws:

1. Attacks an individual's character rather than the issue.

2. Creates a false dilemma by oversimplifying the choices or alternatives.

3. Diverts the reader's attention by changing subjects within the argument.

4. Begs the question by using a reason that repeats the conclusion in different words.

Omissions

A. Has more than one viewpoint been presented?

1. Have credible contrary views been acknowledged?

2. Have the contrary views been explained and reasons given why they are not acceptable?

B. Is the evidence supporting the argument or thesis overwhelming? Has anything been left out?

C. Has the author examined the underlying reasons concerning an issue?

D. Has the author gone beyond his or her argument and added a normative idea?

1. A positive argument deals with an issue, provides reasons, and concludes based on those reasons.

2. A normative argument goes beyond the reasons presented and prescribes a solution about what should be done. This prescription is based on value assumptions and biases that require a separate analysis.

Reading Critically to Write Critically

So far, we have examined specific examples of arguments and evidence used to support an opinion. Rarely are arguments so contrived to fit the evidence or is the evidence clearly presented. In the following pages is an example of an editorial concerning the controversy over funding art that is politically unacceptable to a political majority of citizens. Read the essay and mark the text to find the critical point made by the author using the suggestions presented on this and the previous pages. Then look at the annotated examination of the essay immediately following the essay. Reading the annotations should provide a better understanding of the elements of expository writing in political science.

In particular, reading critically simply means asking questions while reading and noting where the arguments, evidence, and conclusions are weakest or strongest. Not all information must be remembered verbatim or memorized. Use shorthand symbols to mark in the margins of personal copies of books, articles, and essays for easy retrieval of information. Students should be able to identify at least the important points, the hypothesis, the evidence, and the conclusion in a piece of literature.

Here are some suggestions for identifying critical points in a piece of literature:

1. Use a "T" to identify the theory, hypothesis, or thesis sentence.

2. Use a star (°) to identify an important point. The more important the point, the more stars in the margin.

3. Use an "E" to identify quantitative evidence and information that is proven or known to be true.

4. Use an "S" to identify suggestive or qualitative evidence.

5. Use a "V" to indicate where the author has used a value assumption to make a point.

6. Use a question mark (?) to indicate where the author's reasoning is unclear or use of evidence is suspect.

7. Use an "X" to indicate where the author's evidence or point is not valid.

8. Use a "C" to identify a conclusion based on an assertion about the relationship between the author's hypothesis and the evidence presented.

An Example of a Political Argument

(Reprinted by Permission)

FEDERAL FUNDING FOR NEA
AND
THE ROLE OF THE ARTS IN A DEMOCRACY
By Alan G. Schmidt

The controversy over federal funding for the arts has moved to center stage again, as Congress—faced in an election year with the possibility of having to raise taxes—considers the budget for the National Endowment for the Arts (NEA). Emotions run high on both sides of the issue, and there are valid arguments to support both sides. On the one hand, it can be argued that culture is something that rises naturally out of the common values of a community and not something that can be dictated from a centralized bureaucratic source. It follows from that argument that America would not suddenly be without culture if a budget cut forced a trim in the NEA's funds. On the other hand, when artists are subsidized, they should not be subjected to political censorship and denied their First Amendment rights as a condition for public funding. Although public funding of the arts is not a cultural necessity, denial of funding for artists who express politically unpopular views erodes the value of important constitutional guarantees of equal protection, free speech, and minority rights.

One of the important issues in the debate over funding politically offensive art is whether public funds should support undesirable activities. This issue, however, obscures a hidden problem of equal protection. Public funds have been and are used to support undesirable activities. For example, tobacco farmers are given public subsidies to produce a crop that will kill half a million people every year. These tobacco farmers are given subsidies in spite of acknowledged government and public support for banning smoking as an undesirable, socially unacceptable activity.

Another important issue in the debate over public funding targets is not socially undesirable activities, but politically oriented activities that may or may not be politically unacceptable. The crux of this argument stems from a desire to prevent tax dollars from being spent by individuals engaging in political debate. Unfortunately, this argument is flawed and inconsistent with standard tax subsidies provided to non-profit organizations. For example, according to this argument, the tax-exempt status for churches should be abolished. The Catholic Church spends over a million dollars a year on political lobbying against abortion and yet it pays no taxes. A tax exemption has the same effect as a tax subsidy—money from taxes which could be used for other public purposes is given (not collected) to churches for private use. No one seems to be asking Cardinal O'Connor or Jerry Falwell or Pat Robertson to stop engaging in politics as a condition of their organizations' tax-exempt status. Political expression, even that which is espoused by leaders of tax-exempt churches, is protected by the First Amendment.

At the very least, it seems that some consistency in what is considered protected rights and obligations is in order for examining public funding for the arts. There is one argument against funding the NEA, however, that could prove dangerous for all Americans, no matter what their feelings about the current controversy. Jonathan Yardley of *The Washington Post* has argued that public funds should not be granted to artists who engage in political expression. Although it was not clear who would judge an artist's work as political or apolitical and because assessing the content of a work is a subjective process, what Yardley apparently meant was that funding should be withheld for artists whose political agendas do not agree with his political agenda.

Again, constitutional provisions establishing equal protection and minority rights which inhibit arbitrary and subjective government activities help diffuse, but not disarm, this argument. Yardley's idea is disturbing because he expects artists who live in an open, democratic society to produce work totally devoid of democratic ideas. Much, if not all American art—from the poetry of Walt Whitman to the films of Frank Capra to the music of Elvis Presley—is inherently political. If American arts do not reflect the ideals and the conflicts in society, what purpose would they serve in society? Tolerance of statements about government and society, as promulgated by political philosopher J. S. Mill, is necessary for the maintenance of a democratic society and is at the very heart of the American experiment with democracy.

The basic artistic values and ideals of American culture were inherited from the ancient Greeks, for whom art (along with politics and good citizenship) was considered an essential act of public service. To refuse to fund works by artists for budgetary reasons is vastly different from refusing to fund works because they reflect political values. An artist has just as much right to express political ideas as anyone else. How can Americans promote their experiment to the world as an exemplary model of democratic government if they refuse to allow political discourse in the publicly funded arts?

The debate over tax-supported arts is one that may be on the public agenda for a long time. It is difficult to predict how it will resolve. Judging from Yardley's arguments, the debate will be centered on confusing rhetoric and a manipulation of emotions. Nonetheless, artists have just as much right to use their skills to influence political outcomes as anyone else. Public funding for NEA has helped to secure the right to political expression for artists whose activities are not often valued monetarily. Some federally funded art may indeed be offensive and objectionable to the majority of Americans, but to deny funding to the arts because of their political nature should be offensive and objectionable to all Americans.

Analysis of *Federal Funding for NEA and the Role of the Arts in a Democracy*

The following material is an annotation of the political argument immediately preceding. The essay has been critically reviewed based on the validity of the arguments and evidence presented below. Although a diagram of the reasoning would help to evaluate questionable parts of the argument, the annotations concentrate on only those problems or errors that correspond to the material discussed in Chapters 1 and 2. The author of the essay uses many kinds of evidence discussed in Chapter 1 and types of arguments examined in this chapter. The essay is broken down into logical development of the argument, uses of evidence, and conclusions based on induction or deduction.

Introduction to the Problem

"The controversy over federal funding for the arts has moved to center stage again, as Congress—faced in an election year with the possibility of having to raise taxes—considers the budget for the National Endowment for the Arts (NEA)."

- The introduction quickly identifies the issue of federal funding for the arts as controversial.
- A critical thinker should be wondering what the controversy is about and why it is important.

Context of the Problem

"Emotions run high on both sides of the issue, and there are valid arguments to support both sides. On the one hand, it can be argued that culture is something that rises naturally out of the common values of a community and not something that can be dictated from a centralized bureaucratic source. It follows from that argument that America would not suddenly be without culture if a budget cut forced a trim in the NEA's funds. On the other hand, when artists are subsidized, they should not be subjected to political censorship and denied their First Amendment rights as a condition for public funding."

- The author explains what the controversy concerns. He does this in two ways. He begins with deductive reasoning; he establishes the first part of the argument in the following way. Conclusion B is one part of the controversy, yet Premise 1 is overstated. The word "all" makes this statement apply to all cases. It is an unstated value assumption that all art is culture. Because Premise 1 is weak, this weakens conclusions A and B.

Premise 1:	(*implied*) All art is culture.
Premise 2:	Culture arises from common values of the community.
Conclusion A:	(*implied*) All art arises from common values of the community.
Premise 3:	Common values cannot be dictated from government.
Premise 4:	Culture exists without public funding.
Conclusion B:	(*implied*) All art will exist without public funding.

- The author also sets up the second part of the argument. Unlike the first part of the controversy, the second part is mostly implied. The author now has established the second view, that denial of public funding is unlawful.

(*all implied*)

Premise 1:	Art that conforms to politically correct values receives funding.
Premise 2:	Art that does not conform to politically correct values does not receive funding.
Premise 3:	Denying funds for political reasons is censorship.
Premise 4:	Censorship is a violation of First Amendment rights.
Premise 5:	Violating First Amendment rights is unlawful.
Conclusion:	Denying funds to artists for political reasons is unlawful.

Thesis

"Although public funding of the arts is not a cultural necessity, denial of funding for artists who express politically unpopular views erodes the value of important constitutional guarantees of equal protection, free speech, and minority rights."

- The author establishes his perspective on the issues.
- He is implying that although the first view has some validity, it misses the point. The real problem is that denial of funding for political reasons violates the constitution.

Assertion 1: An Expressed Opinion

"One of the important issues in the debate over funding politically offensive art is whether public funds should support undesirable activities. This issue, however, obscures a hidden problem of equal protection. Public funds have been and are used to support undesirable activities."

- In this first assertion, the author begins his defense of his thesis and a further examination of the important issues in the controversy.
- He presents one issue and proceeds to show, through inductive reasoning, that the objection to public funding is inconsistent with other kinds of public funding.

Evidence Supporting Assertion 1: A Statistic

"For example, tobacco farmers are given public subsidies to produce a crop that will kill half a million people every year."

- The author is supplying a statistic to support the implied assertion that tobacco consumption is an undesirable activity.
- A critical thinker should be asking, where did this figure come from? Is it a fact that tobacco kills people? Could this be a case of begging the question by treating a debatable theory as a fact? Could this be a case of a false analogy between politically offensive art and tobacco consumption?

Evidence Supporting Assertion 1: An Example

"These tobacco farmers are given subsidies in spite of acknowledged government and public support for banning smoking as an undesirable, socially unacceptable activity."

- The author argues that the public objects to tobacco consumption. But is this valid?
- He implies that all of the public objects to smoking. Is this true? Is this a case of a hasty generalization? Who acknowledges this support?

Assertion 2: An Expressed Opinion

"Another important issue in the debate over public funding targets is not socially undesirable activities, but politically oriented activities that may or may not be politically unacceptable."

- In this assertion, the author expresses an opinion about what issues he believes contribute to the controversy.
- He is suggesting that the issue is not social, but political, activities that are defined as problems.

Assertion 3: Assertion 2 Interpreted

"The crux of this argument stems from a desire to prevent tax dollars from being spent by individuals engaging in political debate. Unfortunately, this argument is flawed and inconsistent with standard tax subsidies provided to non-profit organizations."

- Without actually explaining the difference between social activities and political activities, the author redefines the issue to focus on political activities. Is there a difference? Does differentiating between social and political debate create a false dilemma?
- He concludes that the issue is the use of public money to fund political activities. But who are the people who do not desire this? The author's reference to "desire" is vague.
- Nonetheless, the author proceeds to show that such a desire is inconsistent with other policies.

Evidence Supporting Assertion 3: A Factual Example

"For example, according to this argument, the tax-exempt status for churches should be abolished. The Catholic Church spends over a million dollars a year on political lobbying against abortion and yet it pays no taxes. A tax exemption has the same effect as a tax subsidy—money from taxes which could be used for other public purposes is given (not collected) to churches for private use."

- Using a conclusion resulting from deductive reasoning, the author argues that subsidizing church organizations that engage in political activities makes the separation between subsidizing only social activities and not subsidizing political activities invalid.

Evidence Supporting Assertion 3: An Example

"No one seems to be asking Cardinal O'Connor or Jerry Falwell or Pat Robertson to stop engaging in politics as a condition of their organizations' tax-exempt status."

- The author is using an appeal to emotions here.
- For an appeal to be effective, the reader must know that the individuals referenced here are highly controversial, politically outspoken religious leaders.

Evidence Supporting Assertion 3: A Fact and an Example

"Political expression, even that which is espoused by leaders of tax-exempt churches, is protected by the First Amendment."

- The author uses a fact to establish the credibility of his assertion that protection of political expression is applied to politically questionable people who receive public subsidies.
- If readers accept the previous evidence, then they accept assertion 3.
- By accepting assertion 3, readers concede acceptance of assertion 2.

Assertion 4: An Expressed Opinion

"At the very least, it seems that some consistency in what is considered protected rights and obligations is in order for examining public funding for the arts. There is one argument against funding the NEA, however, that could prove dangerous for all Americans, no matter what their feelings about the current controversy."

- Having set up his argument so that he has invalidated objections to public funding in principle and in particular instances where political expression is concerned, the author then questions the credibility of the key opponents, asserting that one of them has ideas that are dangerous to the public.
- He then begins to present an example.

Evidence Supporting Assertion 4: An Example

"Jonathan Yardley of *The Washington Post* has argued that public funds should not be granted to artists who engage in political expression. Although it was not clear who would judge an artist's work as political or apolitical and because assessing the content of a work is a subjective process, what Yardley apparently meant was that funding should be withheld for artists whose political agendas do not agree with his political agenda."

- The author restates the opposition's case and identifies a problem with the opponent's position.
- The author implies that the danger is using subjective measures of political activity.
- He implies that this subjectivity could be abusive and self-interested.
- But who is Yardley anyway? Is his opinion worth noting? Can he act in any effective way on his opinion?
- As critical thinkers, students first need to be certain that Yardley's view is representative of the opposition to public funding.
- Second, students need to decide whether they trust the author to interpret the opposition's intentions correctly.
- In this matter, the author personalizes the issue—ad hominem—by concentrating on imagined negative characteristics.

Assertion 5: An Expressed Opinion

"Again, constitutional provisions establishing equal protection and minority rights which inhibit arbitrary and subjective government activities help diffuse, but not disarm, this argument. Yardley's idea is disturbing because he expects artists who live in an open, democratic society to produce work totally devoid of democratic ideas."

- The author builds on the reader's acceptance of assertion 4 to continue interpreting the opposition's view as being unacceptable.

- He implies that Yardley's commitment to or understanding of democratic society is questionable.
- The author is attempting to cast doubt on the credibility of the opponent's view by suggesting that the opponent is not knowledgeable about the issue.
- Again, the author is appealing to the negative characteristics—ad hominem—of his opponent.
- To accept this as valid evidence, students must trust that the author is fairly representing the opponent's credentials.

Evidence to Support Assertion 5: An Example

"Much, if not all American art—from the poetry of Walt Whitman to the films of Frank Capra to the music of Elvis Presley—is inherently political. If American arts do not reflect the ideals and the conflicts in society, what purpose would they serve in society?"

- The author is using a set of examples to show that the distinction between social and political activities is not valid when applied generally to art.
- He is implying that to reflect societal values is by definition a reflection of political values in society.
- The author supports this, however, by using what appears to be the beginning of a non-sequitur form of reasoning.
- He presents two ideas that have no obvious connection. The first idea questions what thing art reflects. The second idea is what purpose art serves in society.
- He is hoping to induce the reader to accept that art serves a role in society, which is to reflect its ideals and conflicts. Yet, he did not say how reflecting an ideal relates to serving society.

Evidence to Support Assertion 5: An Expert Opinion

"Tolerance of statements about government and society, as promulgated by political philosopher J. S. Mill, is necessary for the maintenance of a democratic society and is at the very heart of the American experiment with democracy."

- Now the author makes the connection for the reader by paraphrasing a famous political philosopher and commentator.
- Historical accounts of the early days of the framing of our constitution tell us that the framers were highly influenced by the teachings of Mill.
- The author is using an appeal to authority to convince the reader that tolerance of political statements serves to preserve democratic society.

Evidence Supporting Assertion 5: A Fact

"The basic artistic values and ideals of American culture were inherited from the ancient Greeks, for whom art (along with politics and good citizenship) was considered an essential act of public service."

- This piece of evidence is being used as additional support for the connection between art, societal ideals, and preservation of democracy. It is also setting up the next assertion by appealing to the emotions—to the romanticism about and reverence for those ancient cultures that were among the first to experiment with democratic government. It implies that to be against political art is to deny America's ancient and sacred cultural heritage.

Assertion 6: An Opinion

"To refuse to fund works by artists for budgetary reasons is a vastly different matter than refusing to fund works because they reflect political values. An artist has just as much right to express political ideas as anyone else."

- The author is now granting that for nonpolitical, civic, or objective reasons, refusing to fund the arts could be acceptable. It is the act of refusing funding for political reasons that is a denial of rights.
- The author is using a bandwagon approach akin to "everybody does it, so why can't they?"
- He implies that political expression should not come with a political cost. Does everyone have the right to freely express himself or herself and be guaranteed protection from political costs?

Evidence Supporting Assertion 6: An Example

"How can Americans promote their experiment to the world as an exemplary model of democratic government if they refuse to allow political discourse in the publicly funded arts?"

- The author expresses a belief here and uses it as evidence supporting the notion that the American democratic experiment holds special historical significance in the preservation of democratic ideals.
- Again, the author appeals to the emotions, especially to patriotism, to induce support from the reader.
- There is no question, by now, about the author's understanding of democracy. Is this true? He has firmly established his appreciation of and commitment to democratic values. Or has he?

Conclusion 1

"The debate over tax-supported arts is one that may be on the public agenda for a long time. It is difficult to predict how it will resolve. Judging from Yardley's arguments, the debate will be centered on confusing rhetoric and a manipulation of emotions."

- The author now restates the problem and identifies the causes more clearly.
- By referring to Yardley, his first conclusion implies that emotional, not rational, reasons are used by opponents as evidence against public funding as a way of censoring views held by artists who are in the political minority.

Conclusion 2

"Nonetheless, artists have just as much right to use their skills to influence political outcomes as anyone else."

- The author reasserts his contention that the problem with denying public funding to the arts is a matter of equal protection.

Conclusion 3

"Public funding for NEA has helped secure the right to political expression for artists whose activities are not often valued monetarily."

- The author reasserts his position that public funding helps ensure minority rights and free speech.

- This is implied by the reference to artists who do not profit from their activities related to political expression and may not be able to pay the costs of expressing unpopular views.

Knowledge

"Some federally funded art may indeed be offensive and objectionable to the majority of Americans, but to deny funding to the arts because of their political nature should be offensive and objectionable to all Americans."

- What have we learned from this argument?
- In essence, the author has shown us that to be against funding art, especially if it is political in nature, is (at best) to be ignorant of American values or is (at worst) un-American!
- Are you convinced that this is true?
- If readers accept all the assertions made and evidence presented as valid, then they must accept this conclusion.

CHAPTER 3

TOPIC SELECTION

Choosing a Topic

Open-ended writing assignments are opportunities to develop long-term professional interests. Each subdiscipline in political science offers a set of rich and varied subjects for students to explore. Students may wish to combine one or more types of topics to limit the scope of their research. They can also limit the scope of their research by examining a characteristic of an object associated with a concept. The combinations are limited only by the nature of the course and constraints set by the instructor.

Objects: Things That Can Be Seen Physically

Players: These are people who are politically important. Presidents, members of Congress, interest group leaders, bureaucrats, and judges are examples of political players.

Institutions: These are any body that engages in routinized patterns of interaction. Affiliations, associations, alliances, and political organizations such as Congress, bureaucracies, political parties, interest groups, and even families are institutions.

Events: These are occurrences or situations that led to political outcomes or consequences or are political outcomes. The Kent State Massacre, political assassinations, campaigns, the Great Depression, and the Nixon resignation are examples of events.

Policies: These are or can be any decision made by any public official in any branch of government that has the force of law. Policies also include customs as well as nondecisions on problems. Congressional legislation, bureaucratic regulations, presidential orders, judicial decisions, and common law are policies.

Concepts: Things That Are Believed, Acknowledged

Dilemmas: These are undesirable situations or problems that seem to be difficult to resolve. They are often associated with unwanted and unsatisfactory conditions. They can also be related to a difficulty in achieving some preferred outcome. Political apathy, political intolerance, providing for social welfare during a recession, providing for cleaner air without devastating the coal industry, and reconciling individual liberties with the public good are examples of dilemmas.

Processes: These are observable patterns of political behavior in people and groups. They are associated with procedures and mechanisms for using, acquiring, and distributing political power. The methods and structure of congressional, judicial, and bureaucratic decision making are examples of processes. Democracy, federalism, confederation, oligarchy, monarchy, feudalism, socialism, and communism are all different processes for organizing government.

Values: These are outlooks, perspectives, and subjective or biased opinions. Values are often associated with irrational, moral, or ethical judgments. A value is a sentiment that may or may not be socially acceptable. For example, support for a political party or for racial supremacy is a value that sustains vastly different levels of public support. Patriotism, individualism, collectivism, racism, and loyalty are examples of values.

Beliefs: These are a state of mind related to a conviction or unconscious trust in a statement that is not fact-based or based on objective evidence. Beliefs are often associated with faith or custom. Natural rights, liberty, justice, freedom, and self-sufficiency are examples of beliefs.

Principles: These are doctrines or codes of conduct that are usually held in high esteem. Self-determination, limited government, constitutionalism, the rule of law, and legitimacy are examples of principles.

Ideologies: These are integrated bodies of ideas, values, beliefs, and aspirations that constitute a sociopolitical program. They are associated with a desire, a need, a moral obligation, or a utopian vision. The ideas, beliefs, or values need not be socially acceptable; all that is needed is that the ideas, beliefs, and values are linked coherently. Liberalism, conservatism, anarchism, authoritarianism, pacifism, imperialism, Marxism, fascism, Nazism, libertarianism, and nationalism are examples of ideologies.

Theories: These are sets of plausible statements or general principles offered to explain phenomena or events. Theories offer testable hypotheses or speculations about the causes of political outcomes. Theories are often modified or constrained by ideological perspectives. Democratic theory, corporatism, the Downesian model of party competition, egalitarianism, the American voter model, the domino theory, feminism, elitism, and pluralism are all theories.

Tips for Choosing a Topic

When choosing a topic, students must keep in mind that whatever they have chosen to write about must relate to the course material, be interesting to study, and adhere explicitly to the instructions and limitations set by the instructor. Failing to keep these three criteria in mind when choosing a topic will, in most instances, result in an undesirable grade. There are a number of ways that students can assure that their topic contains these characteristics.

Look at the table of contents in the course textbooks.

1. Make a list of the people, institutions, or other objects that seem interesting.
2. Make a list of any theories, ideologies, or other concepts that seem interesting.
   - Do not waste time worrying about whether a concept fits into a particular category.
   - If the thing is something that cannot be touched, then it is a concept.
3. Combine the list of objects and concepts in different ways.
4. Choose the combination that most piques curiosity.
5. Use verbs and qualifiers to transform the combination of objects into a question.

Check the handout, syllabus, or whatever the instructor provided that states the requirements for the assignment.

1. Note any special information or questions that must be addressed in the written assignments.
2. Use these in combination with the abstract and concrete topics from the textbooks to pose the topic question.
3. Focus the topic so that it clearly addresses the requirements of the instructor.
4. Follow up on an interesting comment or idea presented in a class, seminar, or workshop.

Limit the time frame so that the topic can be addressed within the page limits set by the instructor.

1. A five-page paper can support only a very narrow topic. Combine an abstraction and a concrete topic and specify a short time frame to narrow the topic.
2. A ten-page paper can support a focused, but very specific, topic. Combine two concepts or combine a concept and an object, but limit the period to no more than a decade.
3. A fifteen-page paper can support a complex topic. Combine two or more objects with a concept, but be careful that the period or scope does not become all encompassing or historical.
4. A twenty-page paper or longer can support a complex topic and some description of historical context. Combine several objects with one or more concepts and keep the period manageable.

Example of Combining Objects and Concepts

AMERICAN GOVERNMENT

OBJECTS		CONCEPTS	
PLAYERS:	Hillary Clinton	**DILEMMAS:**	Reconciling government aid with balanced budget
INSTITUTIONS:	Presidency		
EVENTS:	Scandal		
POLICIES:	Health Care		
		PROCESSES:	Congressional voting
		VALUES:	Individualism
		BELIEFS:	Social justice
		PRINCIPLES:	Limited government
		IDEOLOGIES:	Libertarianism
		THEORIES:	Egalitarianism

POSSIBLE COMBINATIONS

Combination One: Hillary Clinton and Health Care Reform

Combination Two: Reconciling Government Aid with a Balanced Budget and Congressional Voting

Combination Three: Health Care and Limited Government

Combination Four: Scandal and the Presidency

Combination Five: The Presidency, Libertarianism, and Justice

Combination Six: Hillary Clinton and the Presidency

Combination Seven: Libertarianism, Social Justice, and Limited Government

Combination Eight: Scandal and Congressional Voting

Combination Nine: Health Care and Reconciling Government Aid with a Balanced Budget

Combination Ten: Hillary Clinton, Egalitarianism, and Individualism

Example of Combining Objects and Concepts

INTERNATIONAL RELATIONS

OBJECTS		CONCEPTS	
PLAYERS:	Iraq	**DILEMMAS:**	Presidential authority to deploy troops
INSTITUTIONS:	United Nations		
EVENTS:	9/11 Attack		
POLICIES:	Pre-emptive Strike	**PROCESSES:**	Religious terrorism
		VALUES:	Patriotism
		BELIEFS:	Radical Islam
		PRINCIPLES:	Rule of law
		IDEOLOGIES:	Nationalism
		THEORIES:	Global patriarchy

POSSIBLE COMBINATIONS

Combination One: 9/11 Attack, the United Nations, and Presidential Authority to Deploy Troops

Combination Two: Radical Islam and Patriotism

Combination Three: The United Nations and Nationalism

Combination Four: The Preemptive Strike Doctrine and Rule of Law

Combination Five: Iraq and the United Nations

Combination Six: Patriotism and Global Patriarchy

Combination Seven: Radical Islam and Religious Terrorism

Combination Eight: Patriotism and Religious Terrorism

Combination Nine: Presidential Authority to Deploy Troops and the United Nations

Combination Ten: Nationalism and Patriotism

COMPARATIVE POLITICS

OBJECTS		CONCEPTS	
PLAYERS:	Tony Blair	**DILEMMAS:**	Political
INSTITUTIONS:	Parliament		intolerance
EVENTS:	London Bombing	**PROCESSES:**	Parliamentary
POLICIES:	Public		decision making
	Surveillance	**VALUES:**	Patriotism
		BELIEFS:	Privacy rights
		PRINCIPLES:	Legitimacy
		IDEOLOGIES:	Totalitarianism
		THEORIES:	Elitism

POSSIBLE COMBINATIONS

Combination One: Tony Blair and the Growth of Political Intolerance

Combination Two: Parliament, the London Bombing, and Privacy Rights

Combination Three: Tony Blair, Parliamentary Decision Making, and Elitism

Combination Four: Parliamentary Decision Making, Tony Blair, and Legitimacy

Combination Five: The London Bombing and Patriotism

Combination Six: Political Intolerance, Privacy Rights, and Public Surveillance

Combination Seven: Totalitarianism, Elitism, and Tony Blair

Combination Eight: Public Surveillance, Legitimacy, and Parliament

Combination Nine: Parliament and Parliamentary Decision Making

Combination Ten: Public Surveillance and Political Intolerance

Example of Combining Objects and Concepts

CRIMINAL JUSTICE

OBJECTS		CONCEPTS	
PLAYERS:	John Ashcroft	**DILEMMAS:**	Protecting civil liberties and antiterrorism restrictions
INSTITUTIONS:	FBI		
EVENTS:	Terrorist attack		
POLICIES:	Patriot Act 2001		
		PROCESSES:	Democracy
		VALUES:	Patriotism
		BELIEFS:	Justice
		PRINCIPLES:	Rule of law
		IDEOLOGIES:	Authoritarianism
		THEORIES:	Rehabilitation

POSSIBLE COMBINATIONS

Combination One: John Ashcroft and the Patriot Act

Combination Two: John Ashcroft, the FBI, and Patriotism

Combination Three: Terrorist Attacks and the Rule of Law

Combination Four: FBI, the Patriot Act, and Authoritarianism

Combination Five: John Ashcroft, Terrorist Attacks, and Democracy

Combination Six: The FBI, Civil Liberties, and Antiterrorism Regulations

Combination Seven: Rehabilitation, Democracy, and Justice

Combination Eight: The Patriot Act, Individual Liberty, and the Rule of Law

Combination Nine: John Ashcroft, Authoritarianism, and the Rule of Law

Combination Ten: The Rule of Law, Justice, and the Patriot Act

Example of Combining Objects and Concepts

PUBLIC ADMINISTRATION

OBJECTS		CONCEPTS	
PLAYERS:	Michael Brown	**DILEMMAS:**	Reconciling
INSTITUTIONS:	Congress		bureaucratic
EVENTS:	FEMA scandal		discretion with
POLICIES:	Revenue sharing		accountability
		PROCESSES:	Bureaucratic
			decision making
		VALUES:	Loyalty
		BELIEFS:	Liberty
		PRINCIPLES:	Legitimacy
		IDEOLOGIES:	Liberalism
		THEORIES:	Elitism

POSSIBLE COMBINATIONS

Combination One:	Congress and Reconciling Bureaucratic Discretion with Accountability
Combination Two:	Michael Brown, Congress, and the FEMA Scandal
Combination Three:	Revenue Sharing and Reconciling Bureaucratic Discretion with Accountability
Combination Four:	Congress, Revenue Sharing, and Bureaucratic Decision Making
Combination Five:	Michael Brown, Loyalty, and Legitimacy
Combination Six:	Congress, Loyalty, and Bureaucratic Decision Making
Combination Seven:	Michael Brown, the FEMA Scandal, and Bureaucratic Decision Making
Combination Eight:	Revenue Sharing, Liberty, and Liberalism
Combination Nine:	Congress, Loyalty, and the FEMA Scandal
Combination Ten:	Congress, Elitism, and Bureaucratic Decision Making

Example of Combining Objects and Concepts

PUBLIC LAW

OBJECTS		CONCEPTS	
PLAYERS:	Earl Warren	**DILEMMAS:**	Political intolerance
INSTITUTIONS:	The family		
EVENTS:	Civil rights marches	**PROCESSES:**	Judicial decision making
POLICIES:	Abortion	**VALUES:**	Racism
		BELIEFS:	Liberty
		PRINCIPLES:	Limited government
		IDEOLOGIES:	Conservatism
		THEORIES:	Egalitarianism

POSSIBLE COMBINATIONS

Combination One: Justice Warren and Egalitarianism

Combination Two: Justice Warren, Racism, and Limited Government

Combination Three: Civil Rights Marches, Political Intolerance, and Liberty

Combination Four: Abortion, the Family, and Limited Government

Combination Five: Judicial Decision Making, the Family, and Abortion

Combination Six: Political Intolerance, Abortion, and Conservatism

Combination Seven: Civil Rights Marches, Racism, and Justice Warren

Combination Eight: Racism, Limited Government, and Civil Rights Marches

Combination Nine: Abortion, Conservatism, and Liberty

Combination Ten: Judicial Decision Making and Racism

Example of Combining Objects and Concepts

POLITICAL THEORY

OBJECTS		CONCEPTS	
PLAYERS:	Thomas Jefferson	**DILEMMAS:**	Reconciling liberties with the public good
INSTITUTIONS:	Congress		
EVENTS:	American Revolution	**PROCESSES:**	Democracy
POLICIES:	The Bill of Rights	**VALUES:**	Individualism
		BELIEFS:	Freedom
		PRINCIPLES:	Self-determination
		IDEOLOGIES:	Nationalism
		THEORIES:	Corporatism

POSSIBLE COMBINATIONS

Combination One: Thomas Jefferson and Democracy

Combination Two: Congress and Reconciling Individual Liberties with the Public Good

Combination Three: The Bill of Rights and Reconciling Individual Liberties with the Public Good

Combination Four: Thomas Jefferson, the Bill of Rights, and Self-Determination

Combination Five: Bill of Rights/Corporatism

Combination Six: The American Revolution: Thomas Jefferson and Self-Determination

Combination Seven: Corporatism and Freedom

Combination Eight: Congress, the Bill of Rights, and Democracy

Combination Nine: Democracy, Reconciling Individual Liberties with the Public Good, and Congress

Combination Ten: Congress, Reconciling Individual Liberties with the Public Good, and Freedom

Locating Research Materials Using Indexes, Databases, and the Internet

Coauthored by Kathleen Carlisle Fountain
Reference/Political Science and Social Work Librarian
California State University, Chico

Introduction

Thorough, well-documented research is the basis for all good writing. This chapter provides students with the basic tools for engaging in professional-level, high-quality research. Regardless of the scope of a research assignment, students need to master the search and retrieval skills for locating high-quality information to learn about a topic as well as to support arguments or perspectives about the topic. The suggestions in this chapter are written in compliance with standards developed by the Association of College and Research Libraries in *Information Literacy Competency Standards for Higher Education* (Association of College and Research Libraries 2000). Using the information in this chapter should provide students with the opportunity to demonstrate information literacy in writing projects.

Characteristics of Sources Used in Research Papers

A well-written paper is only part of what determines whether a manuscript is a good scholarly effort. Scholarly research requires professionalism in the choice of resources used for locating information about the relationship between concepts and objects involved in the research topic. Professionalism is determined by the care and thoughtfulness invested in the collection of resources from different resource formats that fit the scope of the research effort. A well-documented research paper is characterized by sources that are clearly relevant and of high quality and that exhibit depth, breadth, and variety.

Relevance

Students should remember that identifying and sorting information is an important part of the research process. To support their hypotheses and arguments in the paper, students will have to locate supporting arguments, perspectives, qualitative data and/or quantitative data as evidence. To provide balance, students must also locate similar information that does not support their views and explain how such information changes (or not) the types of assertions that students can make about their topics.

Quality

Remember that the quality of the report depends on the quality of the materials used in the research. Different types of research projects require a different mix of evidence. There are a variety of types of information available to students to provide background information, discussions of the issues involved in their topics, and evidence to support their assertions. Sources that have been produced by scholars, reputable professionals in the field, research organizations, and/or government agencies provide the foundations and evidence for a high-quality, well-researched paper.

Depth and Breadth

A well-researched paper has, at minimum, a blend of existing information from different resources that are organized by the student's original thoughts about the topic. Students must learn to synthesize (blend) historical and current information to provide a new perspective on a topic or issue when writing a research paper. Both recent and older information sources serve the valuable purposes of informing and supporting student research.

Current Sources: As in all disciplines, it is important in political science research to find and cite the most current research available on the topic. Not only is it necessary to read recent scholarship to understand the latest arguments being made about a topic but many topics require references to the latest related laws, regulations, or data. When searching for information, students should pay close attention to *when* (the time period) the author or publisher produced the information. Students must make a special attempt to ensure that the information used is the most current and relevant for the research topic.

Historical Sources: The need to use current scholarship does not imply that historical scholarship, that is, older articles or books or data, is useless or invalid for student research. In fact, graduate students of political science spend a great deal of time learning the foundational literature of the discipline, some of which is considered classic in the field. Academic research is essentially a conversation among scholars, and authors of new articles will reference past contributions to the conversation on their topic. Conducting a research project allows students to contribute their own insights to this long-standing scholarly conversation. To do so, it may be necessary to make references to the same landmark literature as other scholars do.

Variety

Students should use a variety of information from different types of resources to support the research question. It is *never* appropriate to base the entire research paper on a single resource such as one book, one article, Web sites, or mass media such as newspapers. *A well-researched political science paper should include, at minimum, references to books, scholarly journal articles, and government documents* as the foundation for most of the research. Additional references may include Web sites, mass media, personal interviews, or secondary analyses of text or data.

Distinguishing Between Types of Information

It is important not only to know that information is available in a variety of resource formats such as books, journal articles, videos, audio tapes, CDs, or DVDs but to understand the purpose and content of those sources as they relate to the unit of analysis and scope of the research investigation. There are two kinds of information, qualitative (descriptive) and quantitative (numerical) information, that are available in primary or secondary sources.

Primary Sources

Primary sources contain evidence gathered in the form of archival documents (qualitative information) or raw data (quantitative information) that has been analyzed by the student researcher. Projects that attempt to determine causal relationships will likely require some primary sources. Including primary sources within the scope of the research project takes more time and often requires information searches that extend beyond the services offered through university or college libraries. (See Chapter 5 for a description of the types of archival and raw data and for strategies and techniques used to create evidence from such primary sources.)

Secondary Sources

A secondary source contains arguments and information gathered by other researchers and *does not include data created by student researchers*. In particular, secondary sources are *published* reports, discussions, or data based on primary research. The quality and currency of the information contained in secondary sources depend on whether the material is intended for a mass-market (popular) or academic (scholarly) audience. Both popular and scholarly source literature are available through university or college library services. Popular materials tend to be better sources of current-event reporting for the average person, whereas scholarly sources tend to be better sources for informed or expert opinion and professional analysis by researchers in the field. The *content* of secondary sources can be analyzed to create primary raw data; the *information* provided in secondary sources is primarily used to locate facts for research projects. For example, a student researcher may analyze the content of newspapers to create *primary raw data* about the tone and amount of news coverage of a political candidate or may use newspaper articles to gather *secondary data,* such as facts about positions or polling numbers associated with a candidate.

Popular or Mass Media

Popular or mass-media materials are intended for the average adult. These materials appeal to mass audiences and typically cover current news events. Examples include any newsstand magazine like *Newsweek* and *Time,* newspapers such as the *New York Times* and *Washington Post,* television programs on CNN or other networks, or webzines like *Slate.* (The novel *Primary Colors,* which spoofed President Clinton's campaign, could also be considered popular literature.) These types of materials are available through libraries, Web sites, or commercial publishers and distributors. Many newspapers and magazines are available through microfilm, microform, and/or online services. The purpose of these sources is to provide general information about current events. Popular literature provides information, but it generally does not include the detailed analysis and historical context offered by scholarly literature. The characteristics of popular literature include:

Authors: The information is written by staff writers employed by the magazine, newspaper, or television show. Although the authors are generally given credit, in some formats they are not identified. The authors are rarely scholars or experts in the field or on the topic of the work. Decisions to publish the information are made by media owners and editors.

Cited Sources: Popular literature rarely includes direct citations. Although the author may mention sources within the text of the work, the documents will not include footnotes with complete citation information.

Language: The language used to provide the information is generally simple and easy to understand.

Graphics: Generally, substantial advertising and extensive photographs accompany mass-media information.

Quality Professional Publications and Law Reviews

These types of materials are intended for professionals and knowledgeable individuals in the field. Quality professional publications generally cover current events, controversies, and phenomena. Examples include the *Congressional Quarterly Weekly Reports, National Journal, The Congressional Digest, Monthly Labor Review,* and *Clement's International Report.* Law reviews contain articles about various aspects of local, state, and federal law that often are written by practitioners or legal experts but edited by law students. The purpose of these sources is to provide information about, and thoughtful analysis of, current political and legal activities and events for professionals in the field.

These sources may also provide historical context. The characteristics of quality publications and law reviews include:

Authors: The information is written by and for skilled professionals in the field. Although the authors may not be scholars, they are respected as specialists.

Cited Sources: Direct citation of sources may occur in quality professional publications but is sporadic throughout the text. Law review articles, however, include frequent citations to relevant laws, cases, and other literature. When citations are made, the text will include footnotes or endnotes with complete citation information.

Language: The language used to provide the information is generally professional and geared toward a specialized and educated audience.

Graphics: There is generally very little advertising and the graphics are professionally presented and discussed in the text.

Government Documents

For the most part, government documents are *official records* of the public activities of individuals working in either a legislative or executive office. At the federal level, government documents are published by the Government Printing Office or placed on the Internet by individual agencies. Government documents include agency reports, congressional hearings, the *Congressional Record*, congressional reports, and reports of the president.

Authors: The information is written by skilled professionals working for the institutions. The authors may be highly trained, may or may not be named directly, and may or may not work at the institution full-time. Some documents may also be direct transcripts of the statements made to and by government officials.

Cited Sources: The authors may make references to sources. If references are used, they are typically infrequent and the text will include footnotes or endnotes with complete citation information.

Language: The language used to provide the information is generally professional and geared toward a professional or educated audience.

Graphics: There is no advertising, and the graphics are professionally presented and discussed in the text.

Legal Documents

Legal documents are laws, regulations, and court opinions that govern the activities of individuals and groups. These publications are *official documents* of the legislature, regulatory agencies, and courts. Examples include the *United States Supreme Court Reports*, *Federal Reporter*, *United States Code*, and *Code of Federal Regulations*.

Authors: The information is carefully written by skilled legal professionals, including legislators, federal bureaucrats, and judges.

Cited Sources: The authors often use references to support their assertions. When references exist, the text will include footnotes or endnotes with complete citation information.

Language: The language used is specialized for a legal audience.

Graphics: There is no advertising or graphics.

Scholarly Materials

Most scholarly literature appears in the form of journal articles and books. Some professors may refer to this type of literature as "academic," "peer reviewed," or "refereed." Regardless of what it is called, scholarly literature exists to inform an educated audience of fellow researchers in a particular discipline. It analyzes specific academic topics, provides historical context, and makes conclusions based on in-depth research.

Authors: The literature is written by scholars, usually professors working for universities, and the article or book should mention the author's credentials. The decision to publish the material is generally based on recommendations by experts in the field (peers) through a blind review process.

Cited Sources: The information sources are cited in footnotes, endnotes, or parenthetical references, and the document will include complete citation information. A list of references or a bibliography should appear at the end of the piece unless these are provided in footnotes or endnotes.

Language: The authors will use professional language, jargon, or terms understood by scholars in the field. For example, scholars may mention Latin legal terms, political theories, or work by other scholars without significant explanation because it is expected that the readers will know these commonly used discipline-specific concepts.

Graphics: Scholarly literature most commonly includes charts or graphs directly related to the content of the writing. Photographs are rarely included. Some advertising may appear, but the products marketed are more likely to be books or other academic products rather than commercial consumer products.

Secondary Raw Data

Secondary raw data are generally original data that were gathered by other researchers, used in their research, and then made available to other researchers for reanalysis. These "raw" data may be available to students free of charge, through subscription services, and/or for a fee. The advantage of using data collected by others is that students save time and, in some cases, money. The disadvantage of using existing data sources is a loss of control over content and method of collection. (See Chapter 5 for a discussion of these data sources.)

Retrieval Systems for Locating Sources

Printed indexes, databases, and the Internet are the three main retrieval systems for locating both primary and secondary sources. In the past, students depended on printed materials such as indexes and card catalogs to locate information in their libraries. The advent of personal computers created opportunities for providing alternative systems for locating materials, including computerized library catalogs, databases on CDs, and online databases. Some libraries continue to rely on printed indexes, but most libraries provide databases that are accessed directly or indirectly via the Internet. The research identified by the indexes, databases, and the Internet bears no relationship to the holdings of individual libraries. Instead, these resources allow students and other researchers to become aware of published scholarship and information available from all over the world.

In general, these systems differ by organization, subject coverage (single or multiple), and search-term language. Single-subject systems focus on information from specific disciplines or sources. Multidisciplinary systems compile references to information on many subjects.

The methods used to search print indexes, databases, and the Internet also vary because of the way those systems are constructed. Printed indexes use *controlled vocabulary*; whereas databases and the Internet primarily use *keyword searching*. Controlled vocabulary searching involves using specially selected words from an established list of terms to find information. Keyword searching, however, involves using any relevant word or set of words that matches the author, title, subject, or text of a document to locate information.

Printed Indexes

Printed indexes organize published literature (books and articles) into annual volumes. Like online databases, these indexes include references (including author, title, journal, date, etc.) to scholarship related to a particular topic. In fact, many online databases simply provide electronic access to the information contained in a printed index. For example, *PAIS* initially existed as a printed index to public policy literature, but the publisher migrated the content into an electronic version called the *PAIS Database* and sold it to libraries across the country.

Printed indexes continue to serve a valuable purpose in library research. Because they predate databases, scholars may often need to use them to identify scholarship published before the development of the database counterpart. Also, some libraries are unable to afford the cost of a database and thus choose to continue subscribing to the print version of an index.

Organization

Before using a printed index, students need to determine how it is organized. Fortunately, each index includes a description of its organization at the beginning of the volume (e.g., by subject headings, category, or author). Nonetheless, reference librarians are an important source of aid/help in interpreting how to use these indexes. In general, the indexes are organized by author and/or by subject in annual volumes. Each volume contains a list of bibliographic citations by author or subject for approximately one year of scholarship. To find all of the relevant material for research topics over time, the same topic or author must be looked up in multiple volumes. Some print indexes have a cumulative index that provides references to literature covering several volumes, which makes it easier to search across many years at a time.

With most indexes, a subject or author listing in the cumulative index will usually refer to a description of an article on a particular page or section of the index. The description should include the author, article title, journal title, volume, issue, number, date of publication, and abstract. After finding a reference to an article, students must determine if the journal is available in the library or online.

Subject Coverage

Subject coverage in print indexes can be by single subject or by multiple disciplines. Specialized indexes exist for political science, law, criminal justice, and public administration. In addition, some printed indexes cover a wide variety of sources either by type of information or by topic. For example, a printed index may cover the stories published in a particular newspaper (e.g., the *New York Times*), or it may reference only social science literature from journals. Some of the more common single-subject print indexes include *ABC Political Science*, *International Political Science Abstracts*, and *Index to Legal Periodicals & Books*. Some of the more common multidisciplinary print indexes include *Social Science Citation Index*, *Social Science Index*, *Book Review Digest*, and *Readers' Guide to Periodical Literature*.

Search Term Language

Students may locate information in print indexes either by using controlled vocabulary or by the author's name. Controlled vocabulary means that all topics covered by the index are grouped into *subject headings* and those subjects then describe all related articles. This allows similar articles to be grouped into one section of the index, although students must determine which term the index uses to describe their topic.

The language, or controlled vocabulary, used to describe particular topics will vary from publisher to publisher. For example, for items in library catalogs, the Library of Congress produces a list of terms in its *Library of Congress Subject Headings* that dictates how libraries can describe the books they own. This controlled vocabulary, then, sets the protocol for selecting search terms. Because every index has its own controlled vocabulary and lists a limited number of subjects, it is important to search for the subject in the way the index describes it. For example, in the *Library of Congress Subject Headings*, World War II is described as "World War, 1939–1945," so a student looking for World War II books should look them up using "World War, 1939–1945." Further, single-subject indexes may use professional language and jargon to organize subjects, whereas multidisciplinary indexes generally use simpler, more common terms for their subject headings. Reference librarians can advise students on what kind of search language terms to use with each index. Students may also consult a thesaurus for the index if the publisher issues one.

Example: Controlled Vocabulary in Indexes

For the topic "regulation of garbage services," search for:
  "Waste Management" in *ABC Political Science*
  "Solid Waste Management" in *Index to Legal Periodicals & Books*
  "Refuse and Refuse Disposal" in *Readers' Guide to Periodical Literature*

Databases

Databases are often the *online* versions of printed indexes. They may contain only descriptions of articles or they may provide direct, full-text access to the document. The quality of information retrieved from databases is more reliable than information from the Internet because databases are purposefully constructed collections of material. Although they are accessed through the Internet via the World Wide Web, databases are not part of what most people consider the Internet, nor are they organized or searched the same way as the Internet. Importantly, use of databases is not free and open to the public; database access is *purchased* by libraries for use by patrons and accessed through library facilities.

Organization

Unlike searches using printed indexes, databases allow searching and retrieving references to and/or copies of published documents for more than one year at a time. One search attempt may retrieve references to related research from the most recent journals and to articles published as many as 15 years earlier. The time period limit for searching is determined by the publisher of the database and the journal publishers with whom the publisher does business. A good rule of thumb is to expect databases to provide references to literature written beginning in the late 1980s. Databases typically provide a list of publications included in the collection and the dates of coverage.

At a minimum, databases offer a *search box* that allows the user to type in a keyword or words related to their research topic. Many offer more advanced searches whereby the user may limit the search to a particular time period, publication, full-text availability, and scholarly (refereed) documents. Many databases also allow the user to expand the search beyond the title, author, or abstract to include searches of the text of the document or words related to the keyword typed in by the user. Depending on the type of database, the search results generally include complete bibliographic information (author, article title, journal title, volume, issue, number, date, pages, etc.) for published materials. Databases most often direct researchers to journal and magazine articles, but some also include books, government documents, and newspapers.

With the exception of searches for books, most databases provide opportunities to download, e-mail, or print copies of most types of documents free of charge either as PDF full-text or HTML full-text versions. PDF full-text documents are essentially *pictures* of the pages of the document as it was originally published; HTML versions are documents that have been reformatted by the database publisher. This is an important distinction for two reasons.

The information provided in the two documents may not be the same: PDF versions are identical to the published version of the document. HTML versions may or may not include the charts, tables, graphs, or photos from the original article and rarely identify page breaks in the article. If given a choice, always print or save the PDF version.

Referencing a PDF article in a research paper is easier than citing an HTML version: Because the PDF is identical to the original publication, the original page numbers are preserved, which allows citation of specific page numbers. HTML versions, however, tend to eliminate any mention of the original pagination. For that reason, references to HTML versions *must* include the name of the database and/or subscription service where the article was obtained online. Citations may need to include a section heading instead of a page number to indicate the source of a particular quote in the article. For example, as shown below, in referencing an article from the *ABA Journal* retrieved in PDF format from the *Academic Search* database (sometimes referred to as EBSCOhost or epnet.com), the page numbers of the original article in the citation may be used. In general, if the same article is retrieved in HTML format, the citation should include page numbers, if possible, and must reference the name of the database and the date the document was retrieved from the database. Although most reference styles regard the date of access as optional, we recommend that students provide the date. (For examples of other citation styles, see Chapter 8.)

CITING DATABASE ARTICLES IN *CHICAGO MANUAL OF STYLE* FORMAT

PDF reference format:
Chanen, Jill Schachner. 2000. Daddy's home. *ABA Journal.* 86 (11): 90–91.

HTML reference format:
Chanen, Jill Schachner. 2000. Daddy's home. *ABA Journal* 86 (11): 90.
    http://www.epnet.com (accessed August 27, 2003).

Subject Coverage

Individual databases exist for political science, law, criminal justice, and public adminis-tration. Because databases are often online versions of print indexes, they may cover a single subject or may be multidisciplinary. Currently, the two most important online databases for general political science research are *Worldwide Political Science Abstracts* and *International Political Science Abstracts.*

Search Term Language

The subscription services also use controlled vocabulary to organize their subjects, but the flexibility of searching online allows researchers to use a broader range of language. Always refer to the "help" option in each database for specific searching recommenda-tions. Single-subject databases may use professional language and jargon; multidiscipli-nary databases often use simpler terms as their subject headings. Besides searching using controlled vocabulary, databases also allow for *keyword searching* of subject headings, abstracts, or even full-text articles, and most allow for three different types of keyword searching :

Field Searching: This function allows the user to search a particular field. A "field" is a segment of the item description and commonly includes author, article title, journal title, subject headings, and abstract. Specialized databases may also include special-ized fields, which will be described in the database itself. Author field searching can be particularly useful to find literature written by known experts on a subject.

Phrase Searching: This function allows the user to search for a particular title or a particular phrase. Most databases automatically search multiple word strings as phrases. For example, a search using the phrase *chewing tobacco* as search terms pro-duces articles only with both words in that exact order. Phrase searching may be com-bined with *field searching* and *Boolean searching* (see below) to further limit the number of results.

Boolean Searching: Unlike print indexes, databases have sophisticated searching capabilities, called Boolean operators, that allow researchers to limit their search results to the most useful items. Boolean operators are terms (*AND, OR, NOT,* etc.) placed between keywords. These terms control the relationships between the key-words and determine the results retrieved. In general, database searches will yield fewer yet more relevant results when the keyword search includes more combina-tions and narrow concepts and/or objects. Broad database keyword searches will yield a larger number of results, but these results tend to be more irrelevant because they are searched with broad, less precise terminology.

Commonly Used Database Search Operators

AND   Reduces the number of results by requiring both words in the same article. The more words included, the fewer results. Example: *smoking AND regulation AND advertisements.*

OR   Expands the number of results by allowing one or the other word to appear. Example: *smoking OR tobacco.*

NOT   Reduces the number of results by eliminating unwanted references. This is best used after a first search found too many articles or documents about an unrelated topic. Example: *tobacco NOT chewing.*

*   Use at the end of the word to find a root word and all its variations. Particularly useful for finding singular and plural forms of the same word. Users must check to see if the database employs the exclamation point (!) or the question mark (?) instead of an asterisk (*). Example: *advertis** finds *advertisements, advertising, AND advertise.*

( )   Parentheses group search terms together to create more complex searches. Example: *(smok* OR tobacco) AND (regulation* OR rule*)*

The Internet   (Written with the assistance of Leila Niehuser)

The Internet has become a useful tool to use when searching for information sources. When used correctly, the Internet can reduce research time. When used incorrectly, the Internet can be at best a waste of time and at worst can provide false or misleading information. Because the Internet is unregulated, information provided through an Internet source (Web site) can be as reliable as information found in government documents or as unreliable as information provided in terrorist propaganda—and just as dangerous. To use the Internet efficiently, students must first understand how it is organized. Second, students must become proficient in Internet search techniques. Third, students must learn how to evaluate Internet sources for quality and reliability.

Organization

The Internet (also called the World Wide Web or Web) is not like any other known entity that provides or processes information. It links users to freely available content from companies, universities, governments, and organizations, and as a worldwide system of computer networks linked together, it provides a forum for sharing information and resources. But the Internet is not free: there are real costs and implicit costs. The real costs are the costs of setting up an Internet account and any fee the information provider wishes to charge. The implicit costs involve how the information is collected and the time it takes to retrieve information.

When material is retrieved from a Web site, the entire Web address for the document as well as the author, title, subtitles, date of creation or last update (day-month-year), and date of access must be referenced in the bibliographic citation. It is not acceptable to use the date of access in place of the date of creation (or last update). It is the student's responsibility to locate this information. Quality Web sites generally provide this information; for all others, students may have to search the document or seek the information from any links or menus available at the Web site. (For examples of citation styles, see Chapter 8 or go to http://www.bedfordstmartins.com/online/citex.html.)

INTERNET REFERENCES IN *CHICAGO MANUAL OF STYLE* FORMAT

With an Author:
Galinsky, Ellen, Stacy Kim, and James Bond. 2001. *Feeling overworked: When work becomes too much.* Families & Work Institute. http://www.familiesandwork.org/announce/workforce.html (accessed May 21, 2007).

Without an Author:
Center for Work and Family. 2000. *Workplace flexibility: A powerful strategy for today's dynamic marketplace.* http://www.bc.edu/centers/cwf/research/highlights/ (accessed May 21, 2007).

Because no one authority controls Internet information, each network is free to set its own standards and rules. Although the Web path or address is fairly standardized, other important information about the Web site, such as author, title, and date of publication, is not standardized across domains. Some will be authored by individuals and others will be authored by the sponsoring organization. Some Web sites will include a clearly stated month-date-year for the creation or date the site was updated, but such information will not be easy to find in other sites. Although no one controls the Internet content, there are some common requirements.

COMMON REQUIREMENTS FOR THE INTERNET

Web Access: All Internet connections require software providing protocols, an Internet service provider, and a modem to provide the connection to the computer. Access to the World Wide Web is gained through a browser such as Microsoft's *Internet Explorer.*

Resource Characteristics: Information on Web sites is stored in files often referred to as Web pages or home pages. These Web pages are structured by HTML, or Hypertext Markup Language.

URL: In addition, each information source has a unique electronic mail address called a Uniform Resource Locator (URL). The URL is sensitive to errors and must be typed in precisely as given, including any capitalization, punctuation marks, underlining, and characters. A simple URL format is generally as follows:

protocol://domain.name/directory/subdirectory/filename.ext

Protocol: Each URL contains a protocol (type of link) or service. Each service requires a different piece of software. The most commonly used protocols include:

World Wide Web service is *http://*

E-mail service is *mailto://*

Telnet service is *telnet://*

FTP for file transfer service is *ftp://*

Network News Transfer Protocol *usenet://*

Domain.name: Each URL contains a domain name that identifies the owner of the Web site. The domain name has at least two parts separated by a "dot." The word before the dot is called the second-level domain and the word after the dot is called the top-level domain. Some URLs will contain third and fourth level domains as well. The most important is the top-level domain, which tells the user the type of organization that owns the domain. These include but are not limited to:

> **.edu** for colleges and universities
>
> **.gov** for government institutions
>
> **.org** for nonprofit organizations
>
> **.com** for commercial organizations
>
> **.net** for networking services
>
> **.mil** for military sites
>
> **.us** for United States (or any other two-letter Internet country code)

Directory: Some URLs contain a path (directory and subdirectories) to the information on the Web site. The directories are simple organizing mechanisms for the stored information. These directories are separated in the URL by a "/" or slash. Some paths also may include a "~" (tilde) that often indicates who in the organization is assigned that particular directory.

Filename.ext: The filename and extension, which are separated by a dot, are the most specific reference to information in a file. The filename can be brief or lengthy. The extension is generally, for most Web pages, *.htm* or *.html* for text material. Some material will have a .pdf extension, which is read by *Adobe Acrobat Reader.* Some material is still readable as ASCII text, as indicated by the .txt extension.

Subject Coverage

Subject coverage on the Internet may include single-subject or multidisciplinary directories. Web sites can usually be found by using a search engine or a meta-search engine to surf (explore, search) for information if the URL for a Web site is unknown. Although the difference between directories and search engines has become increasingly blurred over time, there are some quality differences in the way that information about Web sites is classified and retrieved.

> *Subject Directories:* Subject directories (also called subject guides or Web directories) provide links to Internet sources by subject. The links in the subject directories are specially selected and organized hierarchically from most general to most specific keywords in "layers" or levels of information. In general, most subject directories are searchable by keywords as well. There are two basic types of directories. *Commercial* directories, such as *Yahoo!*, are created to serve the general public and are not appropriate for scholarly research. *Professional* directories, such as *INFOMINE*, are generally created by subject experts to serve as research tools. Students should use professional subject directories when they have a broad topic and/or wish to locate high-quality information. The links in these directories are generally chosen for their relevance and quality for academics and professionals in the field. Some professional

subject directories provide a broad range of searchable materials; others are narrowly tailored to political science. Some of the more common professional subject directories include:

Professional General Subject Directories	Political Science Subject Directories
INFOMINE [http://infomine.ucr.edu]	National Politics Index [http://www.politicalindex.com]
AcademicInfo [http://www.academicinfo.net]	Political Science Resources on the Web [http://www.lib.umich.edu/govdocs/polisci.html]
WWW Virtual Library [http://vlib.org]	International Affairs Resources on the World Wide Web [http://www.etown.edu/vl/]
BUBL LINK [http://bubl.ac.uk]	Library of Congress Resources [http://www.loc.gov]
Librarian's Index to the Internet [http://lii.org]	Political Resources on the Net [http://www.politicalresources.net/]

Search Engines: A search engine is a database of Internet sources. Search engines use "spiders" or "robots" to retrieve individual Web pages or documents from Web sites listed either because the author of the engine prefers to list the Web site or because the Web site owner has asked to be listed. Search engines tend to "index" (record by word) all of the terms in a given Web document. Alternatively, they may index all of the terms within the first few sentences, the Web site title, or the document metatags.

The two types of search engines are individual search engines and meta-search engines. *Individual search engines* retrieve information for their indexes using their own spiders. Older or first-generation search engines retrieve information that contains some or all of the search terms requested. Second-generation search engines rank the results based on the quality of the Web page links. *Meta-search engines* combine several search engines simultaneously. Often referred to as parallel search tools, these meta-search engines do not build their own databases; they use the search engines and directories created by others.

The best way to find information fast is to conduct a meta-search. The meta-search tools identify the most relevant sites across numerous individual search indexes for the information requested. Most of these search engines retrieve documents that have been set up to be accessed from Web pages. Some of the more sophisticated search engines may also search the databases and nontext files (graphics, etc.) in the "deep Web" (sometimes referred to as the invisible Web). *Google*, *AltaVista*, and *Lycos* will search the deep Web. For an excellent list and discussion of the deep Web, visit the following Web site, http://toolguide.searchhelpcenter.com/search_tool_guide_for_effective_internet_search_tool_abilities.html. Here is a list of some of the search engines currently being used on the Internet for scholarly research that are considered award-winning, top-choice, or popular by *SearchEngineWatch.com*:

Individual Search Engines	Meta-Search Engines
Google [http://www.google.com]	Vivisimo [http://www.vivisimo.com]
All the Web	Fazzle [http://www.fazzle.com]
[http://www.alltheweb.com]	Ixquick [http://www.ixquick.com]
AltaVista	Mamma Meta-search [http://www.mamma.com]
[http://www.altavista.com]	Dogpile [http://www.dogpile.com]
MSN Search	Excite [http://www.excite.com]
[http://search.msn.com]	MetaCrawler [http://www.metacrawler.com]
InfoPlease [www.infoplease.com]	Turbo10 [http://turbo10.com]
HotBot [http://www.hotbot.com]	Ithaki [http://www.ithaki.net]
Lycos [http://www.lycos.com]	

Search Term Language

Unlike indexes and databases, Internet search engines rely on natural language searches to retrieve results. In plain English, this means that databases return results based on the words searched that match the words on the Web page. Subject directories and search engines generally operate in the same way as database searching using Boolean logic. Refer to the "help" menu for specific details on the type of search operators or terms the search subject directory and search engine use. Some will use the Boolean "AND" and "OR" operators (see the examples in the Commonly Used Database Search Operators box) and some will use implied Boolean symbols for these, such as "+" or "−".

INTERNET SEARCH OPERATORS

" " Requires that more than one word be found as a phrase. *Example*: *"tobacco manufacturer."*

+ The plus sign next to or placed directly in front of the keyword will assure that the search will result in documents that include that keyword. By placing additional plus signs in between a list of keywords, students may further limit the search to documents that contain only the terms listed. This works like the Boolean term "and." *Example*: *+child +sex +abuse.*

− The minus sign next to or placed directly in front of the keyword will assure that the search will result in documents that do not include the keyword. Using the minus sign in conjunction with the plus sign will remove unwanted documents from the hit list. This works like the Boolean term "not." *Example*: *+child −sex −abuse.*

Saving Materials from the Web

It is important to save and/or print any materials to be used in the research project and *record the date that the material was accessed on the Internet*. Internet materials, unlike any other sources available, are subject to frequent revisions (minute by minute, daily, weekly, monthly, annually)—George Orwell's *1984* was an easier world for research than ours! In Orwellian fashion, not only are Web sites updated, they can be rewritten with new information that is different, even contrary, to that posted earlier. "Here today, gone tomorrow" is common for Web sites. Unlike books and articles that are available through interlibrary loan if not available at the school library, Web sites removed temporarily or permanently cannot be reconstructed on demand. *Because Internet information is so unstable, material should be printed or saved to a disk to preserve it and the date noted on which the Web site was accessed in addition to the URL for that Web page.* For the purposes of research, students must be able to produce the materials they used when instructors ask for them. Many instructors randomly check student sources or subscribe to software services that search for evidence of plagiarism. For books and articles, instructors can check the library. For Web materials, it is not always possible to find the materials when the source has been discontinued or changed. It is the student's responsibility to provide evidence of the validity and reliability of the Web materials.

To save the entire Web page

- Insert a floppy disk (rewritable CD or USB drive) into the computer.
- Select *File,* then select *Save As,* then select the drive the floppy is in.
- Give the file a name.
- Select *Plain Text* (.txt) or *Web Page* (.htm or .html).
- Select *OK.*
- Copy and paste the URL (address), and record the time the document was found online.

To Save Part of a Web Page

- Click and hold the left mouse button at the beginning of the text.
- Drag the cursor over the range of text to be saved. Release the button.
- From the menu bar, select *Edit* then select *Copy.*
- Open a word processing application.
- From the menu bar of the word processing application, select *Edit* then select *Paste.*
- Put quotes around any part of the document copied directly from the Web.
- Type the name of the Web page—include all titles and subtitles.
- Copy and paste the URL (address), and record the time the document was found online.
- Save the file with a filename.

To save a Web Address with a Title

- Click and hold the left mouse button at the beginning of the address in the box marked Netsite.
- Drag the cursor over the range of text to be saved. Release the button.
- From the menu bar, select *Edit* then select *Copy.*

- Open a word processing application.
- From the menu bar of the word processing application, select *Edit* then select *Paste.*
- Repeat the process for the title of the Web page.
- Edit and change the font of the text, if necessary.
- Annotate (write about) the site with any other descriptive information or notes about the site.
- Do not forget to record the date of creation or date the Web site was last updated.
- Save the file with a filename.
- Copy and paste the URL (address), and record the time the document was found online.

Selecting the Right Search Tools for Locating Research Materials

For nearly every topic researched by students of political science, one can find information in a range of resources. News articles, journal articles, laws, or books may provide arguments and facts to help prepare a research paper. Because students often research current events and issues, they need to understand how the information industry affects the availability of research sources over time. After determining what might be available, students should then choose the appropriate tool for retrieving that information.

The Information Time Line

As current events and issues unfold in the public eye, writers and scholars begin to generate research sources. Depending on the format of the source, however, information *may not* be available shortly after a significant political event. The availability and type of sources for research are highly determined by the time period. For example, if a student chooses to research the attacks against the World Trade Center in New York City and the Pentagon in Washington, DC on September 11, 2001, the information available the day after the event would be limited to newspaper articles, video from broadcast or cable sources, and news on Web sites. It would be difficult to find the variety of sources necessary to write a thoroughly researched ten-page paper using only information from September 12, 2001. Scholars and government officials may have begun research about the event, but September 12 would have been too early to have any of their research published. In sum, locating information requires a clear understanding of what purpose the source serves and how each type of source fits into the research process. Each provides information in different formats and time periods. The following chart describes the availability of resources available over time. Use this chart to determine what source will provide the type of information needed.

The Information Time Line

Time Period	Source(s)	Type of Information	Authors	Audience
Day of the Event	Nonprint news reports: radio, television, & Internet news services	General: who, what, and where (not necessarily why)	Journalists	General public
1–3 Days	Print & nonprint news: newspapers, radio, television, Internet news services	Varies: some articles include analysis, statistics, photographs, editorial opinions	Journalists	General public
Week	Popular & mass-market magazines (e.g., *Time* & *Newsweek*)	Still in reporting stage (who, what, where, & why); general; editorial & opinions; statistics; photographs; usually no bibliography available	Journalists (usually not specialists in the field)	General public to educated layperson
Months	Scholarly journal articles	Research results, detailed & theoretical discussion; bibliography available	Specialists & scholars in the field	Scholars, specialists, & students
Two years	Books & conference proceedings	In-depth coverage of a topic; edited compilations of scholarly articles related to a topic; bibliography available	Specialists & scholars in the field	General public to scholars
Ten years	Reference sources (e.g., specialized encyclopedias)	General overview giving factual information; bibliography available	Specialists & scholars in the field	Scholars, students, laypersons

Source: Chart based on UCLA College Library's "Flow of Information" tutorial located at: http://wwwtest.library.ucla.edu/libraries/college/help/flow/index.htm (Johnson and Blakselee 2004).

Search Tools by Format

There is a set of efficient search tools for each type of source format (i.e., books and articles). The availability of tools such as indexes and databases varies for each library, so students should determine what sources their libraries offer by checking the library's Web site.

Books

Every library offers a library catalog (a database) that lists books owned by the library. The catalog should also include all other items in the library—journals, videos, CDs, maps, and government documents. Searching in multilibrary catalogs (databases that include the holdings of many libraries) identifies items owned by libraries around the world and these can be requested via the library's Interlibrary Loan services.

Important Book Search Tools			
Source	Indexes	Databases	Web Sites
Single Library	Card catalog (if available)	Local library's online catalog	Internet Public Library [http://www.ipl.org/div/books/]
		Library of Congress [http://catalog.loc.gov/]	Online Books Page [http://onlinebooks.library.upenn.edu/lists.html]
Multi library		Melvyl [http://melvyl.cdlib.org]	Project Gutenberg [http://promo.net/pg]
		WorldCat	WorldCat [http://www.worldcat.org]
Commercial	Books in Print	Located on any publisher's Web site	Library of Congress [http://www.catalog.loc.gov/]
		Books in Print	Amazon.com [http://www.amazon.com]

Scholarly Journal Literature

Scholarly, peer-reviewed, and law review articles are found in journal databases or printed indexes. If searched by subject, the database or index provides information about published journal articles matching the subject. Online databases may even include the complete text of the article, so it can be e-mailed or printed directly. Printed indexes, however, offer only a citation and require the user to find out if the journal mentioned is available in the local library. Databases and indexes may be multidisciplinary, covering a wide variety of academic subjects, or single-subject, representing the literature of a single discipline like law or political science. Web sites are generally poor sources for locating scholarly journal publications, but there are e-journals that publish scholarly, peer-reviewed articles. The e-journals are often not included in searchable databases, so locating them is sometimes difficult. Also, e-journals may charge a fee for access to materials on their Web sites.

Important Journal Search Tools

Discipline	Indexes	Databases	Web Sites
Social Science	Reader's Guide to Periodical Literature	Academic Search	Directory of Open Access Journals [http://www.doaj.org/]
	Social Science Citation Index	Expanded Academic	The Alliance [http://www.coalliance.org/]
	Social Sciences Abstracts	JSTOR	All Academic [http://www.allacademic.com/index.html]
	Social Sciences Index	Social Sciences Abstracts	Social Science Online Periodicals [http://www.unesco.org/shs/shsdc/journals/shsjournals.html]
		InfoTrac	INFOMINE [http://infomine.ucr.edu]
		SocINDEX with Full Text	Google Scholar [http://scholar.google.com]
		ASSIA: Applied Social Sciences Index and Abstracts	
		Social Science Index	
		International Bibliography of Social Sciences	
Political Science	ABC Political Science	International Political Science Abstracts	Social Science Online Periodicals [http://www.unesco.org/shs/shsdc/journals/shsjournals.html]
	CSA Political Science & Government	Political Science Abstracts	Directory Political Science Journals [http://dir.yahoo.com/Social_Science/Political_Science/Journals/]
	International Political Science Abstracts	Worldwide Political Science Abstracts	Worldwide Political Science Abstracts [http://www.cdlib.org/inside/resources/choosecampus/polisciabs.html]
Criminal Justice	Criminal Justice Periodicals Index	Criminal Justice Periodicals Index	National Criminal Justice Reference Service [http://www.ncjrs.gov]
		Criminal Justice Abstracts	
		SocINDEX with Full Text	
		Sociological Abstracts	
International Relations	International Periodical Index	Columbia International Affairs Online	Directory Political Science Journals [http://dir.yahoo.com/Social_Science/Political_Science/International_Relations/Journals/]
Public Administration	Public Administration Abstracts	ABI/Inform	U.S. Government Accountability Office [http://www.gao.gov/]
	PAIS	PAIS	Directory of Open Access Journals [http//:www.doaj.org/]
		Business Source	Electronic Hallway [http://www.hallway.org/index.php]
		Academic Search	ERIC (Education Resources Information Center) [http://www.eric.ed.gov/]
Public Policy	PAIS	PAIS	Directory Political Science Journals [http://dir.yahoo.com/Social_Science/Political_Science/Public_Policy/Journals/]
		ABI/Inform	ERIC (Education Resources Information Center) [http://www.eric.ed.gov/]
		Academic Search	

Quality Professional Publications (for Law Reviews, see *Law* below)

Industry experts often consider professional publications "trade publications" because they are articles written by experts for experts. Many libraries subscribe to such trade magazines and journals, and they can often be searched through journal databases (see "Scholarly Journal Literature" above). Government-issued magazines, like *FBI Law Enforcement Bulletin* or the *Monthly Labor Review*, can be searched in sources that focus on U.S. government reports.

Important Quality Publication Search Tools		
Indexes	Databases	Web Sites
PAIS	CQ Weekly	The Alliance [http://www.coalliance.org/]
CSA Political Science and Government	CQ Public Affairs Collection	E-journals [http://nnlm.gov/rsdd/ejournals/]
Social Sciences Abstracts	Library of Congress Government Web Resources	Library of Congress Government Web Resources [http://www.loc.gov/rr/news/extgovd.html]
	PAIS	Poly-Cy: Internet Resources for Political Science [http://www.polsci.wvu.edu/PolyCy/]
	ABI/Inform	e-journals.org [http://www.e-journals.org/]

Law

Academic libraries, especially those that support pre-law programs or law schools, buy legal documents, including state and federal codes, opinions, and regulations. Increasingly, this same information can be found online for free, though access may be limited to recent information. Databases purchased by libraries for their students generally include a broad range of historical and current legal documents.

Important Court Decisions, Laws, and Regulations Search Tools

Indexes	Databases	Web Sites
U.S. Supreme Court Digest	LexisNexis Academic	Findlaw [http://www.findlaw.com]
West's Federal Practice Digest	Westlaw Campus Research	Legal Information Institute [http://www.law.cornell.edu]
		LexisOne [http://www.lexisone.com]
		American Legal Publishing Online Library [http://www.amlegal.com/library/]

Important Law Review Articles Search Tools

Indexes	Databases	Web Sites
Index to Legal Periodicals and Books	LexisNexis Academic	Legal Periodicals and E-Journals [http://www.ncf.edu/novak/vl/legaljournals.html]
	Westlaw Campus Research	Findlaw [http://www.findlaw.com]

Government Reports

The federal government issues an array of official information in the form of statistical data, reports, or laws. This information is not protected by copyright and is, thus, often packaged in for-profit databases by enterprising businesses; it can be found for free online from the government directly. Many libraries also hold collections of government documents, which can be found by searching the library catalog. In addition, state and local governments also issue an array of official information in the form of statistical data, reports, or laws. Much of this information can be found for free online at government sites. Many libraries also hold collections of state documents, which can be found by searching the library catalog. Some libraries have special collections housing local documents.

Important U.S. Government Search Tools

Indexes	Databases	Web Sites
American Statistics Index	LexisNexis Congressional	USAsearch [http://www.usasearch.gov]
Monthly Catalog of Government Publications	Government Periodicals Index	Google Uncle Sam [http://www.google.com/ig/usgov]
	PAIS	GPO Access [http://www.gpoaccess.gov]
	LexisNexis Statistical	Catalog of U.S. Government Publications [http://catalog.gpo.gov]

Important State and Local Government Search Tools

Indexes	Databases	Web Sites
Statistical Reference Index	LexisNexis Statistical	USAsearch [http://www.usasearch.gov]
Monthly Checklist of State Publications	PAIS	State & Local Government on the Net [http://www.statelocalgov.net/]
		American Legal Publishing Online Library [http://www.amlegal.com/library/]

International Reports

The United Nations and its auxiliary organizations produce a substantial number of important documents related to individual countries and international issues. A select number of large universities serve as depositories for UN documents, and much like other libraries, are U.S. depositories. Access to their publications can also be found through databases and the UN Web site.

Important International Report Search Tools

Indexes	Databases	Web Sites
Index to International Statistics	AccessUN	United Nations [http://www.un.org]
Index to United Nations Documents and Publications	LexisNexis Statistical	NationMaster [http://nationmaster.com]

Popular or Mass Media (News)

Newspaper and magazine articles may be searched in a variety of locations, including databases, on the Internet, or on microfilm. Databases allow the searching of the full text of articles from around the world over a long period of time. The Internet provides recent articles and audio and video clips, though online news sources may charge fees to view some articles and video. Microfilm preserves very old issues of newspapers and magazines, which helps when researching historical topics.

Important Popular or Mass Media Search Tools

Indexes	Databases	Web Sites
New York Times Index	Factiva	Newslink [http://newslink.org/]
Readers' Guide to Periodical Literature	LexisNexis Academic	Metagrid [http://www.metagrid.com/]
	Newstand	NewsTrawler [http://www.newstrawler.com/]

Private Reports

Businesses, interest groups, educational institutions, and think tanks may issue private reports. As mentioned earlier, this information is typically difficult to find. The reference sections of most libraries carry a variety of organizational directories that can provide published addresses for these private organizations and sometimes provide Web site addresses as well. A growing number of databases and Internet sites, however, provide access to information disseminated to the public. Effective searching through Internet search engines may identify useful reports.

Important Private Report Search Tools		
Organizational Directories	Databases	Web Sites
Encyclopedia of Business Information Sources	PolicyFile	Public Agenda Online [http://www.publicagenda.org]
Gale's Encyclopedia of Associations		Political Advocacy Group [http://www.csuchico.edu/∼kfountain/]

Research Strategies for Locating Sources: A Simulation

Be aware that there is a hard way and an easy way to locate source material for a research paper.

The Hard Way: Read everything that can be found that is connected to the topic in two weeks or less. This means that interlibrary loan materials, books, journal articles, and government reports will probably not be available in time for finishing the research paper.

The Easy Way: Let the experts be the guides. This section illustrates the process by which a student could investigate and locate resources for a paper examining tobacco regulation in a policy evaluation course.

Step One: Review Expectations of the Assignment and Choose a Topic

Students should have a clear idea of what the professor expects for the assignment. If students are unsure, they should check with the instructor for clarification on the requirements and the appropriateness of the chosen topic. (See Chapter 3 for more information on choosing a topic.) For this example, the topic "Regulation of Tobacco and the Protection of Minors" combines two objects and a concept (policy, players, and values).

Set Up a Research Folder with Expectations and Topic Options Prominently Displayed

Begin the process of setting up a project folder. Essentially, students should keep notes, copies of information, bibliographies, etc. in a folder or binder that is specific to the project. Students should also keep a copy or list the specific research requirements and expectations that the instructor provided as part of the class assignment in this folder.

Keep Careful Records

Students should plan to save all relevant citation information of sources as they engage in the research process. This is essential for anything students plan to cite in the paper.

Journal Article (printed or PDF copy): author, article title, journal title, date of publication, volume, issue or number, pages.

Journal Article (HTML copy): author, article title, journal title, date of publication, volume, issue or number, pages, database name, date of retrieval.

Government Report: author (a person or an agency name), title of the report, place and date of publication, and publisher. If retrieved online, include Web address and date of retrieval.

Book: author, title, place and year of publication, and publisher.

Law: title of the law, title of the book, volume number, section number, and date.

Case: party names, case citation including volume, book title abbreviation, pages, and year.

Web Page: author, title, date of last update, Web address, date of retrieval.

Step Two: Find Background Information

Gathering background information will provide knowledge that will help *identify* leading authors in a research area, *focus* the research on a manageable topic, and *evaluate* the information collected from secondary sources. To research a project involving tobacco regulation, students should be looking for information about the history of government regulation of tobacco and the smoking rates of young people to determine the nature of the problem. To find this information, students should:

Look in the Assigned Textbook for the Course

Read essays, sections, or chapters that relate to the topic. Not only will this provide course-specific information but it will be presented in a context that is relevant to the class. Take special note of any authors, issues, examples, or relevant facts mentioned.

Look in Reference Books Related to the Topic

The most useful books will be encyclopedias with brief essays (about three to five pages). These typically summarize the recent research and identify some of the most influential scholars and current areas of debate. Specialized dictionaries may also help by defining theories or concepts central to the research topic. To find reference books:

- Ask a reference librarian for relevant recommendations.
- Browse the "J" (for Political Science) or "K" (for Law) call number area of the reference collection in the library.
- Browse the school library's Web site to see if there are any links to useful sources. Many libraries organize research tools by subject. Look for recommendations for political science, law, public administration, and related fields.

For example, for the topic "Regulation of Tobacco and the Protection of Minors," reference books, including *Statistical Abstract of the United States, Encyclopedia of American Public Policy*, and *CQ Researcher* contain the following important facts:

- In 1985, 29.4% of youths aged 12–17 considered themselves current users of cigarettes. By 1999, that percentage dropped to 15.9%.
- Congress passed several laws regulating the marketing and distribution of cigarettes. Among them are the Cigarette Labeling and Advertising Act (1965) and the Public Health Cigarette Smoking Act of 1969.
- Cigarette companies recently faced public criticism for targeting their advertisements to young people to create loyal, lifelong smokers.

Browse Government Web Sites or Government Documents

With few exceptions, most topics involving government and/or politics are addressed in some way in government documents. Policy evaluations, for example, should always begin with locating the public law and the legislative history of the policy. For example, using the database *Lexis/Nexis Congressional*, a search of U.S. Codes using the keywords *Public Health Cigarette Smoking Act AND (child OR children OR minors)* locates a document that identifies and/or links to current amendments, the legislative history, the controlling bureaucratic agency, court decisions, and the parts of the legislation that relate to regulation of smoking by minors.

Step Three: Write a Preliminary Research Hypothesis or Question

After doing some preliminary investigation of a topic, the variety of available primary and secondary sources of research will emerge. The brief articles in reference sources will highlight issues of legitimate inquiry. Use this information to develop an initial research hypothesis or question. For example, preliminary research into tobacco regulation and children suggests that the target of the policy is tobacco advertising. As a result, the research question could be "How has the regulation of tobacco advertising affected teen smoking?" or the hypothesis could be "Regulation of tobacco advertising has reduced teen smoking." Either way, the focus and purpose of the research is to evaluate the effectiveness of regulating advertising as a means of reducing teenage smoking.

Step Four: Identify Types of Sources Needed for the Project

Different tools, such as databases or catalogs, find different sets of material. For a thoroughly researched political science paper, depending on the scope of the assignment, students generally need:

Sources required for all political science papers:

- Research or scholarly articles that examine objects and/or concepts related to the topic
- Books that examine objects and/or concepts related to the topic

Sources that may be available or required involving the objects and/or concepts related to the topic:

- Government documents (reports, hearings, and/or debates)
- Federal, state, or local laws
- Federal, state, or local court cases

- Quality publications (especially law review articles and professional publications)
- Relevant mass media (especially editorials or investigative reports/analysis)
- Expert analysis (especially provided by think tanks, scholarly institutes, reputable organizations)
- Quantitative data (primary or secondary)

For example, to research the topic "Regulation of Tobacco and the Protection of Minors," the student must find scholarly articles, government sources, books, and some quality publications. In particular, the student will benefit from locating books or an edited book with a summary article on the history of tobacco regulation.

Step Five: Build a Set of Search Terms

The preliminary research on the topic should provide a set of words or terms and synonyms for those terms that can be used as keywords for locating additional sources. Once additional sources are located, additional terms can found to locate even more sources. As knowledge and familiarity with the topic increase, the quality, relevance, and usefulness of search results increase as well. To do this:

Create Keywords from the Hypothesis or Research Question

For example, the keywords for the research question "How has the regulation of tobacco advertising affected teen smoking?" are *tobacco, advertising, regulations, teen,* and *smoking.*

Develop Synonyms Based on These Keywords

List synonyms for the keywords identified in the research question or hypothesis. A thesaurus can identify synonyms, and many word processing programs have a built-in thesaurus. Importantly, the information from the preliminary research should be used to note different terms or ways of expressing/describing the same things. For example, to research tobacco regulations and use by minors, the following terms and their synonyms would be keywords:

- Tobacco, cigarettes, nicotine, smoking
- Advertising, commercials, billboards, advertisements, infomercials, ads
- Regulations, rules, restrictions, control, limitations, limits, policies
- Teen, adolescent, young adult, underage, kid, teenager, children
- Smoking—same as "tobacco"
- Philip Morris, manufacturer, company (to describe the major tobacco industry players)
- Public Health Cigarette Smoking Act (to find information about a particular law)
- Department of Health, Education, and Welfare, Food and Drug Administration, Alcohol Tobacco and Firearms, and agencies (to find information on federal agencies and their role in tobacco regulation)

Step Six: Searching in Relevant Indexes, Databases, and Internet Sites

Remember that indexes, databases, and search engines use different searching technology and that searches should be structured to reflect these differences.

There *should not* be a "perfect" article that covers the entire topic exactly as stated in the research question.

Students should be telling their own stories and supporting their own arguments based on the unique combination of secondary and/or primary sources they have collected in the research process. No single article, book, or report will be or should be identical to the focus, purpose, justification, hypothesis, method of inquiry, or the results of the student's efforts.

Begin a Search for Secondary Sources Using All Available Resources

Indexes: Look up different terms from the keywords list in an index. One of them will lead to relevant literature. For example, "tobacco" can be looked up in:

- The school library's *Online Catalog* to see if there are books on any aspect of the topic
- *ABC Political Science* to find the cross-reference "see smoking." The heading for "smoking," then, will list a number of interesting articles.

Databases: Search some of the keywords in combination with Boolean operators. Choose no more than one term for each concept or object, and combine them to find articles that address the topic. *Importantly, in most databases, unless a search of the full text of the article or document is specifically requested, the database search will be limited to titles and abstracts/summaries of the article. For a thorough search for secondary sources of research on the topic, indicate (often by marking the box "search within text") that the entire document should be searched for the keywords.* Doing this will find more documents that address the objects and concepts related to the topic that, although they directly address the topic, did not contain the specific keywords used in the keyword search. As an added bonus, most database programs will identify the keyword in bold each time it appears in the text. For example, documents related to tobacco regulation and minors may be found using:

- *LexisNexis Congressional* for information about Congress's role in regulating tobacco
- *LexisNexis Academic-Law Reviews* for law review articles related to regulating tobacco
- *PAIS* to find articles and government reports about public policies
- *Academic Search* to find scholarly articles from many different fields (such as political science and medical journals)
- *CQ Weekly* to find quality articles written by professionals covering Congress

To locate documents with these databases, use the following keywords related to tobacco regulation and minors:

- *Tobacco AND regulation AND advertising*
- *Smoking AND policies AND teens*
- *Tobacco AND regulat° AND advertis°*
- *Smok° AND polic° AND teen°*

Search Engines: Visit Web sites recommended for each type of resource format (reports, laws, etc.). Search within these sites, particularly if they have directories or a search option before moving on to more general search engines like *Google* or

MetaCrawler. In particular, because *USA.gov* searches only government Web pages, it automatically filters results so that the documents retrieved will generally be useful and relevant. For example, documents related to tobacco regulation and minors may be found using:

- *USA.gov Web site* for reports and statistics from the federal government
- Web sites for the American Lung Association and the American Cancer Association for high-quality nongovernmental reports and data regarding tobacco consumption and regulation

To locate documents with these search engines, use the following keywords related to tobacco regulation and minors:

- *Tobacco regulation "Food and Drug Administration"*
- *Cigarette +advertisements +teens +smoking*

Modify Keywords and Search Terms Based on Search Results

Because computers try to match the words typed to the words in a database or on a Web page, different terms may be needed to find more information. Are there words appearing in results that can be added to the original keyword list? Do the indexes and databases offer subject headings that could be searched? If so, modify the list of keywords with these new terms.

For example, after searching using the keyword list derived from the research question, the student may discover that a legal settlement reached between the states and the tobacco industry companies affected the way in which tobacco products could be marketed. Because of this new information, the student begins searching for more information about the settlement. The new keywords are:

- *settlement, lawsuit, case, litigation, class action*
- *prevention, public health, health policy*

These new keywords can be combined with the original keywords. For example:

- *Tobacco AND settlement AND advertisements*
- *Smoking AND prevention AND settlement°*
- *Smoking AND teen° and prevent° AND lawsuit°*
- *Lawsuit AND market° AND cigarette°*

Try Searching in Many Indexes, Databases, and Search Engines

This ensures that students will find the most current, relevant, and important information on the topic. In addition, the diverse sources provide a range of perspectives. For example, searching *PAIS* for articles on tobacco regulation may turn up a particularly relevant court case. To search the court case, the student moves the search from the *PAIS* database to *LexisNexis Academic* to conduct research on legal information regarding the case and its impact on tobacco regulation.

Step Seven: Examine the Bibliographies of Materials Retrieved

Once reference texts, books, and articles are located, the bibliographies, references, footnotes, endnotes, and/or works cited pages of those sources should be reviewed. The references listed by the authors of these documents provide a rich supply of additional research sources that may have been untapped by searches in indexes, databases, and/or the Internet.

Remember: All Document Retrieval Systems Have Source and Time Limits

Students should remember that indexes, databases, and Internet search engines are limited to the document sources that *their sponsors choose to include* in the search criteria. All of these document retrieval systems have time limits as well. Research documents that existed before the index was published, the database was compiled, or are not accessible to the Internet are unacknowledged. There is no universal source for all research. Yet, there is a wealth of creditable research that is left out of searches using these retrieval systems that are known to scholars in the field. Identifying these scholars and their publications provides students with access to more documents.

Locate References to the Same Authors in Several of the Documents

Authors who are knowledgeable, credible, respected, and renowned for their expertise tend, with a few exceptions, to be considered experts in the field. Although not all scholars in the field may agree with these authors' viewpoints or perspectives, their published research in scholarly books and articles has been peer reviewed (evaluated by other scholars) and deemed a significant contribution to the field. Students need to acknowledge the work of these authors and locate relevant research published by such experts. Often the work of these authors is referenced in many publications. To find their work, do the following:

Identify Authors Referenced in Textbooks and/or Reference Books. When an author or a particular document by an author is listed or referenced in a textbook and/or reference books, it is usually because the author is considered to have made an important contribution to the field related to the student's topic.

Identify Authors Referenced in Several Documents. If an author is listed in the references of several books and/or articles, it is very likely that this author is considered a highly recognized scholar or authority in the field related to the student's research topic. Make a list of authors of books and articles that are related to the research topic and list the titles of the referenced documents under each author's name.

Search for More Articles by These Expert Authors

Return to appropriate indexes, databases, and Web sites for the topic. Search for the expert authors identified in textbooks, reference books, and listed in many sources. Most databases are particularly useful for locating these publications because searches can be limited to author's name, the title of the book or monograph, the title of the article and/or the title of the publication. To find publications by these authors, do the following:

Do Full-Text Searches by Author's Name. The full-text search will find documents written by the author as well as documents by other authors who referenced that author in their research. This activity will provide additional sources as well as an indication of how important this author is to the field.

Do Full-Text Searches by Document Title. Also do a full-text search in databases using the exact title of the author's publication in quotations or marking the *"phrase search"* box (whichever applies to the database) so that every available document that references the article or book is retrieved in the search. Again, this provides additional sources as well as an indication of how important the document is in the field.

Do an Internet Search by Author's Name. Often, leading scholars in the field will publish research results on academic and nonacademic institutional Web sites. Indexes and databases do not search these sources, but Internet search engines often do. This is especially true of the search engines that search the "invisible Web."

Evaluating the Quality and Reliability of Sources

All materials retrieved for a research project must be evaluated before they can be used. Regardless of whether they are books, articles, or Web materials, each item should be evaluated based on the author's credentials, accuracy of the information, objectivity, timeliness, focus, audience, and origins of the evidence. Students may want to access Widener University's "Evaluate Web Pages" tutorial at http://www3.widener.edu/ Academics/Libraries/Wolfgram_Memorial_Library/Evaluate_Web_Pages/659/. For an evaluation of a site, read *Web Wisdom: How to Evaluate and Create Information Quality on the Web* by Jan Alexander and Marsha Ann Tate (Lawrence Erlbaum Assoc., 1999) or use the guidelines below.

Examine the Author's or Source's Credentials

Students should be wary of any source that does not have an identifiable author. Sometimes the author is listed as an organization, sometimes as a series of individuals, and sometimes as a single individual. Some of the questions students should ask about the author of the materials include:

General Guidelines

- If the author is an individual, what are the author's credentials and educational background? Academic scholars—those authors who are listed as faculty at a university—typically produce more scientifically based research.
- Are there multiple sources written by the same author? If so, the author may be a leader in the field.
- Who published the sources—a government agency, a nonprofit institution, a university, etc.? For example, sources on Web sites with a domain name ending in .gov, .us, or .edu have higher credibility than unknown individuals or some obscure organization. Books published by university presses have a higher reputation than those published by commercial (mass-market) publishers and nonacademic associations.

Web Guidelines

- Read Web sources carefully. Some Web sites will try to confuse the researcher by using domain names that sound like governmental or university organizations but are really owned and maintained by individuals. Look for a statement that the content has been approved by the organization or that the organization holds the copyright. If it is not clear that the organization is responsible for the contents of the page, the Web site may not be credible.
- If there is any doubt about the origin of the Web site, find out who operates it by going to http://www.internic.net/. Click on the "Whois" search database of registered domain names and type in the domain name of the Web site. Another way to

locate this same information is through another Web site supported by Network Solutions. Network Solutions maintains the central database for domain registration on the domain name central server. See http://www.networksolutions.com/en_US/whois/index.jhtml.

- A tilde (~) in the Web site address generally means that it is an individual's home page. Be very careful of these types of home pages. Even some .gov and .edu Web sites will include these pages. Remember that an individual home page regardless of the domain still represents just the individual's viewpoint.

- Web sites with long, complicated addresses are also suspect. Such Web sites are generally so imbedded and distant from the Web site owners that the researcher cannot easily find out who the owner of the site is. For such sites, start by deleting parts of the address from right to left until the domain name and home page appear. This is like peeling an onion; the purpose is to get to the owner of the Web site.

Assess the Accuracy of the Information

Just because it is published does not make information true or accurate. All information needs verification.

General Guidelines

- Look for references to other sources for any factual information. One way to assess the accuracy of the information is to find it in two different sources. If it can be found in two places—preferably at least one government, academic, or university source—the information is probably accurate.

- Another way to assess a resource is to look for relative balance in the information presented. Does the author present alternative views? Is the author associated with an organization with an interest in the outcome?

Web Guidelines

- Web sites with hyperlinks (links to sites) that only link the user to the same author or server are also suspect. Hyperlinks in Web sites should direct the user to additional information and corroborating sources not authored or provided by the same server.

- Just because a credible Web site lists additional sites does not mean those sites are equally credible.

- Web sites that refer users to resources in print form (books and journals, for example) have a higher credibility than those that refer users to nothing else or to their own servers.

- Web sites with frequent grammatical and spelling errors are also suspect. Credible servers/authors professionally maintain their Web pages.

Does the Source Demonstrate Objectivity?

Assessing objectivity is difficult if the researcher is unfamiliar with general information about the topic. Until the researcher is better informed, using verbal clues and cues will help determine the value of the information. Value-laden, manipulative, belief-driven, baseless information is of very little value in academic research. Other than being used as an example of a type of opinion or perspective, the information contained in such sources is often tainted by the author's biases. Assess the information using the following questions:

- Is the language used in the document neutral or persuasive?
- Are the terms used value-neutral or value-laden?
- Are the author's assertions based on beliefs or quantifiable, reliable data?
- Does the author express opinions with or without factual evidence?

Identify the Timeliness of the Source or Data Used in the Source

Timeliness is an important characteristic if the research project requires current information or data. All data and facts in the source should contain the date when they were collected and/or some indicator of the context in which they were collected.

General Guidelines

- Check statistics and any numerical facts for a date collected or compiled. If there is no indication of when the data were collected, do not use the data.
- Check statistics and any numerical facts for the context of the time period. Any numbers that are used as indicators should have a reference or footnote stating time period or year to which they are indexed or referenced.

Web Guidelines

- Make sure to record the date the material was accessed on the Web. Web sites are frequently changed, updated, corrected for errors, removed, etc.
- Examine when the Web site was last updated. Assertions about current trends based on Web information that has not been updated for years will not be valid.

Identify the Focus of the Source

The focus of the information is important. Searches identify any source that has a word matching the keyword requested. Such searches result in sources that have the research topic as the focus as well as sources that may mention the keyword in a footnote or as an aside. The better sources are those that have the research topic as the focus of the information.

- Does the source have the keyword in the title?
- Does the source include material unrelated to the keyword?
- Does the source discuss the topic in depth?

What Is the Purpose of the Content?

The best sources are those that are compiled for educational, scholarly, academic, and informational purposes. Expectations for such sources are high. If the purpose of the content is popular, entertaining, recreational, or promotional, the value of this source diminishes and it is not appropriate for student research.

- Does the content include data professionally presented in charts and graphs or with glitzy icons, music, flashing characters, etc.? Scholarly information rarely incorporates glitzy presentations.

- Does the content provide references in the form of parenthetical citations, footnotes, or endnotes? Scholarly material, as a rule, provides full disclosure of where and how evidence used was collected.
- Does the content include a request for money, product offerings, advertising, membership invitations, or other inducements? Scholarly material rarely includes any such inducements or advertisements.

What Are the Origins of the Data?

The source's content may include primary or secondary data or evidence. If the source uses primary (original) data or resources, examine how, when, where, and why the data or resources were collected. For primary data or resources, the researcher must investigate the methods of collecting the information; for secondary data or resources, the researcher must investigate how the material has been used or manipulated in view of its intended purpose.

- Does the author discuss the methods of data or resource collection? Are the methods reasonable, understandable, and in agreement with generally accepted practices?
- Does the author reference work by other researchers without discussing the context of the work? If so, look at the original work before referencing or using any assertions by the author about that work.

CREATING EVIDENCE WITH PRIMARY AND SECONDARY DATA

Introduction

Students should identify the information (data) they need for their research early in the research process. If it is not available in secondary form, students must then determine if it is feasible within the research project's time frame to use primary data to produce the information they need for the project. Primary data are produced either by locating raw data or creating the data. To produce primary data as evidence, students must collect it either from original documents, a questionnaire, or personal interviews. If such research is being done on human beings and in conjunction with coursework or campus activities, students generally must obtain permission to do the research from their school's Human Subjects Committee. Once collected, primary data must be processed through one or more methods of data reduction.

This chapter begins with an overview of secondary data sources and then progresses to a discussion of primary data collection. To assist students in deciding how to use such data as evidence, this chapter also provides a primer on data reduction methods.

Secondary Sources of Quantitative Data

A secondary data source is a set of data that is not collected by the student. Students who do not have the time or the need for primary data collection may analyze existing sources of data to provide evidence for their research papers. Such data is often collected by public agencies, private organizations, and scholars for particular purposes. The data collected by others and used to create their analyses may be available free of charge, through subscription services, and/or for a fee.

Secondary data can be used in a variety of ways. It can be used in its raw form, through data reduction methods, or merged with primary data. The advantage of using data collected by others is that students save time and, in some cases, money. The disadvantage of using existing data sources is that students do not control content and method of collection.

Public Data

Unless data are classified, public institutions are required by law to make data that they use as the basis of their government reports available to the public. Many federal and state datasets are available by request, and some datasets are available on government Web sites. For information not available locally or on a Web site, students may have to file a Freedom of Information Act (FOIA) request to obtain the data needed for a project (be aware that FOIA requests may take as long as 3 months from request to delivery). Using data acquired through FOIA requires significant preplanning and knowledge of precisely what the data are and where they are held or collected. Some of the most common data sources used in political research include the following.

Federal Data

Census Bureau Data: The Department of Commerce, Bureau of the Census, compiles data on many topics in addition to demographic data about the population. The census is taken every 10 years (since 1790); however, various kinds of data are collected every 5 years. The *Census of Governments* and *USA Counties* provides information on local governments. In addition, the *Current Population Survey* includes demographics and employment data collected once a month. The *County and City Data Book* provides demographic characteristics and lists services by county and city. A simplified version of these data can often be found in the *Statistical Abstract of the United States.*

Other Bureaucratic Agency Data: The U.S. Departments of Commerce, Education, Health and Human Services, Justice, Labor, and State, as well as independent agencies (e.g., the Environmental Protection Agency) and independent commissions or boards (e.g., the SEC, NLRB, EEOC, OSHA) routinely collect data on services, spending, enforcement activities (e.g., OSHA citations, number of small business loans granted, cases processed), and current conditions of clientele and jurisdictions (statistics on labor, economy, business, land use, etc.). Many of these types of statistics are compiled into yearbooks such as the *Statistical Abstract of the United States, Sourcebook of Criminal Justice Statistics, United States Health, Digest of Education Statistics, Handbook of Labor Statistics,* and *Vital Statistics on American Politics.*

Federal Records

National Archives: This archive includes a collection of historical data collected by the U.S. government.

State and Local Data

The Book of the States: This data book provides information about state governments in the United States, including state services, laws, and finances.

Federal Agencies: Federal agencies collect and disseminate extensive data on state and local regions. Check census and other federal data sources for information about cities, counties, and states.

International and Comparative Nations Data

United Nations: The UN publishes a variety of data sources, including the *Statistical Yearbook*, *Demographic Yearbook*, and the *Yearbook of the United Nations*, that provide data on production, population, employment, health, death rates, birth rates, etc.

Europa Publications: This publisher offers specialty handbooks on international issues and data, including the *Europa World Year Book* and the *International Yearbook*.

Private Data

Unless the material is related to publicly regulated activities, private and nonprofit organizations are under no obligation to make their data available to the public. Organizational Web sites provide data authorized for public dissemination. For information not available on Web sites or in public documents, students may have to request information directly from the organization's staff. Most medium- to large-size private and nonprofit organizations employ public relations staffs who handle requests for information from the public.

Professional and Special Interest Organizations

The American Lung Association, American Cancer Society, Sierra Club, National Rifle Association, National Organization of Women, AFL-CIO, and American Bar Association are examples of organizations that conduct studies and collect data. Some of these data are made available through their publications and some are available by request.

Think Tanks

Organizations such as The Brookings Institution, The Urban Institute, Hubert H. Humphrey Institute of Public Affairs, RAND, and the Organization for Economic Co-operation and Development (OECD) collect data and provide some public access to their collections.

Corporations

R.J. Reynolds Tobacco Company, General Motors, and many other large corporations collect industry data and provide some data through press releases. Other data are available to the public by request.

Commercial Data

Numerous organizations disseminate information for a fee. Some of these data are available in raw form through subscription services and some are available for purchase. Subscription services are generally offered to organizations and institutions, but not to students as individuals. Here are some examples of data sources:

ICPSR

The Inter-University Consortium for Political and Social Research (ICPSR) provides access to the world's largest compilation of computerized data on human behavior. ICPSR provides user support to assist in identifying relevant data. The holdings include collections of a wide variety of data on populations, wars, education, public opinion, elections, and more, compiled at the local, state, national, and international levels.

Gallup Poll

The Gallup Organization routinely compiles polling data, including demographic, opinion, and behavioral data, usually by contract, to client organizations. It has expanded to collect comparative data overseas as well. The data are collected by professionals, provided to the client, and later made available to the public either in publications or for a fee.

Field Poll

Field Research Corporation is a national consumer marketing and public opinion survey research firm that collects data for business, industry, and government. It is the most prestigious state-level poll in the United States. Generally administered four times a year during nonpresidential election years and six times during presidential election years, it is also administered for special occasions, such as the California recall of the governor.

NORC

The National Opinion Research Center conducts an annual General Social Survey (GSS) for the National Science Foundation. This survey is done annually to collect data opinions, beliefs, and behavior related to contemporary social and political issues in the United States. It is considered one of the finest U.S. data-collection sites.

Roper

The Roper Center for Public Opinion Research collects opinion data on political and social issues in the United States and numerous other nations.

Creating Primary Data

Primary (raw) data are *created by the student researcher* using qualitative research techniques such as survey research questionnaires or direct collection from a source. Creating evidence using primary sources involves a two-step process. First, qualitative data are created by researching specific information found in sources, such as original text documents, observations, and/or by conducting interviews. Once the qualitative data are collected, the student must then engage in data reduction by conducting a content analysis, creating a quantitative data set from the qualitative data, or writing a descriptive analysis of the results.

Creating Qualitative Data from Original Text Documents

Original text documents (often referred to as archival or historical documents) can be used to gather descriptive or evaluative information. Original text documents may provide the foundation for descriptive evidence about events and attitudes over time. Students may want to analyze newspaper coverage over a period of years or evaluate a set of historical documents (such as presidential letters or congressional hearing reports) to describe changes in attitudes or treatment of events. To research in original text documents, students must formulate a research question and hypothesis that identifies the nature and variety of information needed from the documents. This requires prior research, not only on the topic of the student's research, but also on the availability of the materials for the research time frame. While newspapers and magazines may be available on microform or online for a long time period, some documents, such as local government meeting minutes, may be available only for a short time period.

In general, there are several types of archival materials available for analysis. Students may use ***public documents***, such as government proceedings, hearings, reports produced by any institution of government to document events, political positions, or any other political phenomena for historical research. Students may also use ***private documents***, such as annual reports, news releases, letters, writings, and public relations materials, for documenting events or changes in the organizations' or an individual's political, economic, or social position. Finally, students may analyze ***media***, such as the content of books, newspapers, broadcast or cable news media (CNN, ABC, PBS, NPR, etc.), magazines, videos, DVDs, or CDs to discover conceptual patterns in the attitudes and substance of the materials. Many newspapers and magazines are available through microfilm, microform, and/or online services. The following steps outline the procedure for creating data from original text documents:

1. **Determine the information needed.** Students must formulate a research question and hypothesis that identifies the nature and variety of information needed from a set of documents. This requires prior research on the topic of the student's research. Students need to know what kind of information (descriptive, evaluative, or both) they need as evidence in their research project. Students also need to know if they need to use a complete set of documents for the time frame of the research project or if a random sample of documents is sufficient to support their research.

2. **Locate the copies of the original text documents for the entire scope of the study.** Prior to committing to a study that includes information gathered from historical or archival documents, students should make sure that copies of these documents are available. Although securing personal copies of such materials is best, it is not always possible because of restrictions on the document's use or because it may be costly to produce copies. Students should obtain permission to use and conduct research in advance for original text documents that are not public documents or readily available to the public.

3. **Construct a set of research questions.** Students should have a set of research questions they intend to answer using original text documents. Ordinarily, student researchers choose to formulate their research questions based on testing theories related to issues involving their topics. Using these theories, they construct a set of variables that they expect to find information about in the text documents.

4. **Engage in data reduction.** Read and evaluate each text document individually. Using the research questions and the identified set of variables, engage in classifying and analyzing the text document. Use either descriptive analysis or content analysis techniques for the data reduction. (See the following discussion for a description of data reduction techniques.)

5. **Write about the results.** Once the information has been collected and analyzed, either descriptively or through content analysis, use the data as evidence in the research paper. Students must report the documents used to collect the data (with full citations for each document), the method of selecting the documents (complete set or random sample), any problems involving the validity or accuracy of the documents, and how they reduced the data for analysis (descriptive or content analysis).

Creating Qualitative Data from Direct Observation/Field Research

Observational or field research involves student researchers directly in the subject of their research. Data created through this technique are based on information that researchers collect while participating in and/or observing activities or events. Student researchers can be either directly involved by participating in events, they can be direct observers, or they can be some combination of participant and observer. Collecting information as a ***participant observer*** requires that the student participate in the activities they are observing. For example, a student may want to volunteer as a campaign worker to collect information on how a candidate's campaign headquarters is organized. (See Chapter 12 for an example of this type of research combined with an internship.) Alternatively, collecting information as a ***nonparticipating observer*** requires that students remain detached from the activities they are observing. For example, a student may attend court hearings once a week for two months to observe and identify patterns in the types of people and issues brought before the court over that time period. (See Chapter 12 for an example of keeping a log or journal that might save formatting issues.)

This type of data collection is perhaps the most flexible and experiential for students studying any topic. Field research can be highly focused and theory-based, whereby students formulate a hypothesis and, through observation of and/or participation in events, find evidence that supports a theory or hypothesis. Alternatively, students may also simply participate in events or observe behavior and formulate their own impressions. Because the student researcher is physically "in the field," field research is also one of the least objective and generalizable techniques of gathering qualitative data. Although other forms of data collection can be replicated, field research cannot be reproduced because it is conducted on a unique population and at a specific point in time. Furthermore, even though field research is rarely completely unbiased, it is especially useful for validating theories or assertions about human behavior. Students must make a special effort to prevent or minimize their personal biases in how they record and analyze the data they collected from their experiences. Students should also understand that by being involved, either actively through participation or passively through observation, they may influence the nature and quality of the information they are collecting. This is especially true if the population involved in the event knows the student is collecting information and therefore the subjects alter their behavior.

Although there are no particular rules for conducting field research, there are a number of expectations that students must address when conducting research projects:

1. **Determine the information needed.** Develop a set of clear-cut objectives for the field research. Although students need not have a thesis or hypothesis, they should have a reason for conducting field research. Students may want to conduct field research to learn about how people interact within a particular context and use that information to focus and inform their library research. Alternatively, students may have a well-developed set of theories or hypotheses that they wish to validate or test by observing people or events. In addition, if students are engaged in collecting information at a nonpublic event that involves particular people, they should obtain permission to do the research from their campus Human Subjects Committee.

2. **Choose the context and time frame.** Prior to committing to the research, students should be informed about the events and the population they are observing. Based on this information, students must choose the events and the time frame of the field research. Depending on what students want to observe, they may either choose to engage in continuous monitoring or randomly select the set of events to observe. For example, observing court proceedings by one judge every Tuesday for a month does not provide as much diversity and validity as observing on a randomly selected day in different courtrooms for two months, or observing such court proceedings every day for two months. Students should not, however, switch back and forth from continuous monitoring to random selection.

3. **Choose a role to play.** Students must decide before beginning their research how they are observing and who knows about their research. Students may not change their roles after they have begun their research. Students must decide whether they are fully participating or strictly observing; students may not switch their level of participation during the data collection activity. Students must also decide whether or not to fully inform the population that they are the subjects of a research project. If the subjects who are not informed about being observed discover, during the observation period, that the student is collecting information, the research project must be stopped at that point.

4. **Choose a level of depth and breadth of the field notes.** Students must be willing to regularly record (usually through journals or logs) both objective information, as well as their subjective impressions. Students should describe what they see, hear, and feel. They should identify in their notes which information is objective (just describing) and which information is the student's reaction or impressions of the events observed. Students should never tape record, take pictures, or video tape any activities without getting permission from the subjects of the observations. Students should carefully describe what they observed and note their reactions to the following:

   - *Context:* Log the context of the place in which the event is being held.
   - *Demographics:* Log the characteristics of the population involved in the activities.
   - *Activities:* Log how people interact, how they behave, how they react, and what they do. If a participant, and not just an observer, describe personal interactions and what was contributed. Ask questions where possible and appropriate.

- *Distinguish between expected and unexpected events:* Log the routine activities and be sure to note which activities were unexpected.
- *Collect documentation:* Secure copies of free public information. Students should not take private or public documents without permission.

5. **Analyze the results through data reduction.** Transcribe field notes as soon as possible. Then engage in classifying and analyzing the notes using descriptive data reduction techniques.

6. **Write about the experience.** All observation information related to individuals must be kept confidential, unless the student has the individual's permission to use identifying characteristics in the analysis. Report complete information about when and where observations were conducted in the text, footnotes/endnotes, or reference section of the analysis.

Creating Primary Qualitative Data from Personal Interviews

Data created through personal interviews are based on information from face-to-face, unstructured interviews with specific people. Personal interviews are valuable for providing background information, individual perspective, and insider information about political events. To conduct a personal interview:

1. **Determine the information needed.** Students must formulate a research question and hypothesis that identify the nature and variety of information needed from a particular person (respondent). This requires prior research, not only on the topic of the research but on the respondent as well. Students should contact their Human Subjects Committee for prior approval. The information sought may include facts that cannot be otherwise found in public documents, and it may also include the respondent's opinions about trends, events, or remedies for problems related to the subject of the student's research. Finally, this information could also provide context or background information known only to insiders in the organization the respondent represents.

2. **Contact the person.** Always call or write for permission to do the interview. Tell the respondent about the purpose and focus of the interview, and arrange a date and time for the interview.

3. **Construct a set of interview questions.** Students should prepare written questions and arrange them in order from vague to specific. The vague or more general questions should be asked first, and then progress to the most specific questions. Students should be prepared to ask follow-up or explanatory questions based on the respondent's answers. More detail is better than less detail! All responses should be recorded either by a tape recorder or through note-taking. Students must get permission from the respondent to tape-record the interview.

Example of Interview Questions

Question 1:   Please describe the process through which you were hired for the director's position in the National Labor Relations Board Regional Office in St. Louis, Missouri.

Follow-up: What credentials were most helpful in securing this position?

Question 2:   Since taking the position, describe the kinds of organizational problems you have addressed most frequently.

Follow-up: How would you describe the relationship between the national office and your regional office staff?

Follow-up: Do you sense antagonism between the national office and your staff?

Follow-up: Do you sense antagonism between your legal and nonlegal staff?

4. **Attend the interview.** Arrive at the interview shortly before the prearranged time, dress professionally, and be prepared to begin on time.

5. **Thank the persons interviewed.** Write a thank-you note to each of the respondents.

6. **Clean and analyze the results through data reduction.** Transcribe notes or recordings as soon as possible. Then classify and analyze the responses through data reduction.

7. **Write about the results.** All interview information is to be kept confidential unless the student has the respondent's permission to report the source. Include information about when the interviews were conducted in the research paper and list the questions in an appendix. If the respondent permits identifying the source, then the respondent's name, position, and date of interview should be listed in the reference page and the source cited in the text.

Creating Primary Qualitative Data from Focus Groups

Data created through focus groups are based on information that researchers collect while facilitating discussions between and among prearranged small groups of individuals. Focus groups are valuable for providing background information, individual perspectives, and group perspectives about political events. The purpose of a focus group is to explore the feelings, attitudes, and perceptions of a set of individuals. Often, focus groups are used in exploratory research to identify a range of opinions or issues involving a particular topic. Although focus groups are used to generate an understanding of the issues, the results cannot be generalized or applied to the general population. To conduct a focus group:

1. **Determine the information needed.** Develop a set of clear objectives for the focus group. Prepare a set of questions based on the research topic and a hypothesis that identify the nature and variety of information needed from the group. This requires prior research and identification of what information is available without a focus group and what kind of information is available only through a focus group. Students should secure Human Subjects Committee approval of their project and questions before beginning their focus group research.

2. **Determine the population sample.** Identify and recruit a set of individuals who represent a range of opinions about the research topic while also exhibiting diversity of demographic characteristics (e.g., education, occupation). Focus groups are generally as small as six or as large as twelve individuals. Professionals often provide incentives for participating in the focus group. Depending on the topic and range of opinions needed for the study, participants may be identified through membership lists, referrals, or random sampling. Regardless of how the participants are identified, each participant must be contacted (usually by telephone) to request participation and provide details about the purpose of the study, their role in the study, and the location as well as the duration of the study.

3. **Plan the meeting and recruit assistants.** To conduct the focus group, students will need a staff, a location, refreshments, and equipment. The staff includes a moderator, an assistant moderator, and note-takers. The location should be a room with comfortable chairs. The refreshments and amenities should be available to all participants. The equipment should include tape recorders, flip charts with markers, and notepads.

4. **Prepare a set of focus group questions.** Prepare ten to twelve questions to stimulate group discussion. The moderator should be prepared with follow-up questions for each question asked. To do so, the moderator must be knowledgeable about the topic. If demographic characteristics (age, gender, occupation, income, etc.) are important to the study, be sure to collect this information separately from the focus group meeting.

5. **Convene the participants.** Once the group is convened, the moderator should first set up the ground rules for the discussion (one person talking at a time, raising hands, etc.) and assure participants of the confidentiality of the recording. After a brief introduction, the moderator asks the first question followed by comments that encourage responses from each participant. Based on the responses, if all comments are about the positive aspects of the issue, then the moderator should follow up with the questions about the negative aspects of the issue. This continues until the questions and/or time allotted for the discussion have been exhausted.

6. **Thank the participants.** Thank each participant and follow up with a thank-you note the next day after the meeting. Any inducements to participate should be delivered as promised.

7. **Clean and analyze the results.** Classify and analyze the responses through data reduction.

8. **Write about the results.** All responses are to be kept confidential unless the student has written permission to report their source. In their research paper, students should include information about when the focus group was conducted, recruitment methods, the demographic characteristics of the focus groups, and a list of the questions in an appendix.

Creating Primary Data from Questionnaires or Surveys

Data created through questionnaires and surveys are based on information collected from a structured interview or survey of a subset of the public, that is, they are a sampling of public opinion. Questionnaires or surveys create quantitative data from qualitative or opinion assessments. Students should remember that unless sampling a target population specifically designed to include respondents who are knowledgeable about the topic, survey opinion is not necessarily informed opinion. To conduct such a survey:

1. **Determine the information needed.** Formulate a research question and hypothesis that identify the nature and variety of information needed to study political problems, political actors, and/or public policies. Decide what kind of factual and/or attitudinal data must be obtained.

   - *Factual information* generally consists of demographic data about the respondent (occupation, age, sex, education, income, etc.).
   - *Attitudinal information* includes how people think or feel about public policies or societal problems.

2. **Determine the population sample.** Identify the target population for the survey. A target population is the portion (sample) of the public whose attitudes are important to the study. The individuals in the sample being asked the questions are called respondents. There are various ways to gather a sample.

   - *Representative sample* is a random selection from the target population, whereby the types of respondents included in the sample are reasonably close to their proportions in the general population. For example, if women comprise 52 percent of the target population, the sample should contain approximately 52 percent women. The result is a relatively objective survey of respondents who represent the target population. Under these conditions, the sample results can be used to describe attitudes in the target population.
   - *Nonrandom sample* is a sample of respondents who are not selected randomly and/or does not include respondents in the same proportion as they occur in the general population. One example of this is a sample of the first 100 people encountered in a shopping center. The result is a biased survey. Such a survey may be used to describe only the sample population and cannot be used to describe the attitudes in the target population.

3. **Determine the method of contact.** Decide on how the respondents are to be contacted. Surveys may be mailed or conducted door-to-door (face-to-face), by telephone, or through e-mail or on the Internet. The costs and the response rates (percentage of survey responses completed of all respondents contacted) are lower for mailed surveys than they are for the door-to-door or telephone formats. The expected response rate for mailed surveys is less than 50 percent; for telephone surveys, the expected response rate is less than 75 percent; for face-to-face surveys, it is less than 90 percent. E-mail and Internet survey response rates vary according to the currency of the respondent lists but are generally expected to be lower than those of mailed surveys.

4. **Decide whether to use existing survey questions or create new ones.** Students may use questions written by professional survey research designers (from published studies, for example) or write their own questions. A pretest of the questionnaire before distributing to the target population can help identify problems in the construction of the questionnaire. Good surveys are short, clear, and direct.

   - *Short.* The total questionnaire should be fewer than six pages. The questions should use about twenty words or less per question.

- *Clear.* Questions should address one issue at a time. Questions requiring a reference to a time period should be clearly stated with the time frame in the question; for example, "Did you vote in the 2000 presidential election?" The responses should be mutually exclusive (fit in only one category) and exhaustive (all possible responses are provided as choices). Professionals often include an "other, please specify" category in case the respondent has an answer that was unanticipated by the researcher.

- *Direct.* The questions and responses use value-neutral and simple language. This means using words that are as objective as possible; avoid using words with strong emotional or value connotations. Also avoid using jargon or technical terms with sample populations drawn from the general public. Broad, less controversial questions should be placed at the beginning of the questionnaire, and personal questions should be placed at the end.

5. **Decide on question format.** Decide whether the survey will provide an opportunity for the respondents to answer the questions as they wish (open-ended questions) or constrain the respondents to a choice of predetermined answers (close-ended questions). Open-ended questions are best used in surveys that also include close-ended questions.

- *Open-ended.* Open-ended questions (with space for the respondent's own words) require content analysis and a coding scheme for data reduction and analysis. Because an open-ended question does not provide a list of choices, respondents are free to answer with any information they wish to provide, regardless of its relevance to the question. Questions such as "What do you think your local government should do about homeless people in your community?" provide the respondent with an opportunity to offer an opinion without being constrained to a fixed set of choices. Open-ended questions provide the researcher with an opportunity to discover unanticipated ideas and perspectives.

- *Close-ended.* Close-ended questions generally are formatted as multiple-choice questions with fixed answers.

6. **Decide answer format for close-ended questions.** Consider whether the close-ended questions must elicit nominal, ratio, ordinal, or interval data from the answers. Regardless of the answer format, the answer choices should include an option for "don't know," "no opinion," or "refused." This allows the researcher to identify those respondents who do not know how they feel about the subject or do not want to answer the question.

- *Nominal.* Questions designed to elicit nominal information from the answers provide two or more choices, which may be, for example, "*yes*" or "*no*," 1 = *Democrat*, 2 = *Republican*, 3 = *Other (specify)*. This type of data is often referred to as categorical data because the choices provided are in categories. The numbers attached to the choices have no numerical value other than identifying the choice. For example, *Republican* is not valued twice as much as *Democrat*.

- *Ratio.* Questions designed to elicit ratio information provide answer choices that are ordered, measurable, and of equal distance. These questions often ask, for example, about income, number of children, etc. It is also possible for the answer to be zero, because it is possible that someone can have zero income or zero children.

- *Interval.* The answers to interval questions have exact and constant values. The responses are ordered and continuous but have no absolute zero point. IQ scores are an example of interval data.
- *Ordinal.* The answers to questions that are intended to elicit ordinal information can be scaled or rank-ordered to measure the direction and intensity of the opinion. The choices generally progress from highest to lowest or from lowest to highest values.

7. **For ordinal answer formats, choose a scale such as Likert or Guttman scales.** Ordinal answer formats are frequently used to measure the intensity of opinions across a set of questions.

- *Likert scale:* This format provides a choice of options from *Strongly Agree* to *Strongly Disagree* or from *Very Poor* to *Excellent* with usually no more than seven responses for a series of questions.

Example of a Likert Scale

> **Would you strongly support, somewhat support, neither oppose nor support, somewhat oppose, or strongly oppose rules that would restrict smoking on campus?**
>
> | 1 | 2 | 3 | 4 | 5 | DK |
> |---|---|---|---|---|---|
> | Strongly Oppose | Somewhat Oppose | Neither Oppose nor Support | Somewhat Support | Strongly Support | Don't Know |

- *Guttman scale:* This format provides options, such as *"Agree or Disagree, Yes or No, Check all that you agree with,"* for a series of statements arranged from the most general to the most specific. Each question item is assigned a value based on the intensity of the item content. The respondent is then asked to check statements they agree with in the list. Agreement with the last item in the list implies agreement with the statements preceding it. The respondent's answers are then summed across these questions to create a score.

Example of a Guttman Scale

> **People have different opinions about smoking tobacco products in public. Read each statement below. Circle either the answer *Yes* or the answer *No*.**
>
> People should refrain from smoking tobacco products in public places. (Yes No)
> People should not smoke tobacco products in public places. (Yes No)
> People should not be permitted to smoke tobacco products in public places. (Yes No)
> People should be fined for smoking in public places. (Yes No)
> People should be arrested for smoking in public places. (Yes No)

8. **Clean and analyze the results through data reduction.** Once the survey is conducted and the questionnaires completed, describe and analyze the data. All the open-ended questions and the "other, please specify" categories in close-ended questions must be examined by means of a content analysis and coded into categories of responses. Once the data are coded, the frequency of answers chosen

per question should be examined. Students may want to compare responses based on demographic characteristics, such as gender, age, income, party affiliation, or occupation. These summary results (often referred to as descriptive statistics) can then be presented graphically or in table form. For more sophisticated analysis of the answers chosen by different types of respondents (cross-tabulation), students should use a statistical processing program to calculate the mean, standard deviation, adjusted error, and significance tests. Many computer spreadsheets are capable of calculating these statistics, creating tables, and graphing data.

9. **Write about the results.** When writing about the data results, students should report the total number of respondents in the sample, the response rate, and when, where, and how the sample was administered. Students should also report the mean, standard deviation, error, and significance tests if these were calculated.

A Primer on Qualitative Data Reduction Methods

Once data are collected, researchers engage in data reduction by which they summarize textual information through descriptive analysis or create quantitative data through content analysis.

Descriptive Analysis

Descriptive analysis is a method of describing patterns and tendencies in the information collected via documents. This is a particularly important type of analysis for communicating information created through interviews and observation. To perform descriptive analysis:

1. **Summarize the fundamental nature of the information.** Generalize—across all discussions, observations, and/or coded information—about what the data suggest concerning the hypothesized relationships.

2. **Look for trends and patterns.** Report any trends and patterns that appear to emerge from the examination of the data. Group similar responses or events by demographic characteristics (supportive comments by gender, etc).

3. **Record frequency.** Identify and discuss the value of information that is frequently found in the document.

4. **Report observed behavior.** For interviews (both face-to-face and focus groups) and observation notes, report and indicate the significance of body language observed during data collection.

5. **Identify meaningful statements.** Identify and report verbatim quotes from source documents or interviews to illustrate the validity of generalized assertions about the findings. Students should use people's names only if granted permission to do so prior to writing the report. Otherwise, all references to individuals should be designated by a nondescriptive characteristic (Defendant 1; Legislator 2, etc.).

6. **Keep information confidential.** All information is to be kept confidential unless the student has permission to report the source. In research papers, students should include information about when and where the data were collected.

Content Analysis

Content analysis is a system for defining categories of information and coding the basic units of each category. Content analysis can be used to summarize information taken from original documents, journal entries, notes recorded during observations, or comments recorded in focus groups. To do so:

1. **Select a sample.** For original text documents, students must select a sample of the documents. Students must formulate a research question and hypothesis prior to the examination of the documents. The collection of documents should be manageable for the period of the student's coursework.

2. **Identify information.** For all types of documents, students must identify the kind of information that they are looking for in the text.
   - *Subject matter* that relates to the student's hypothesis about the relationship between the objects and concepts in the research project.
   - *Frequency of occurrence* of the subject matter.

3. **Define categories.** Based on the kind of information needed, define categories of the subject matter and expected characteristics of each category as indicators of hypothesized relationships. The list of categories and characteristics comprise the *coding scheme* for the study. The coding scheme must include categories, and the characteristics must be exhaustive and mutually exclusive.
   - *Exhaustive:* The characteristics include all known characteristics.
   - *Mutually exclusive:* The characteristics in each category must not overlap.

   For example, for party membership, the categories and characteristics may be *Democrat–registered, Democrat–not registered, Republican–registered, Republican–not registered, Other–registered (specify), Other–not registered (specify).*

4. **Pretest.** Students should pretest the list of categories and characteristics on a small sample of the documents to make sure the categories exhibit validity, reliability, and objectivity.
   - *Validity* is determined by whether the category measures what it is supposed to measure.
   - *Reliability* is determined by the ability to reproduce the results.
   - *Objectivity* is determined by whether the results are unbiased.

   One way to do this is to have two or more people examine a small sample of the documents (ten each) using the list of categories and characteristics. If each reviewer finds the same information, or very nearly the same information, then the categories and characteristics will exhibit validity, reliability, and objectivity. Professionals calculate and report an *intercoder reliability* score. To calculate the score for two coders, count the number of times the coders agree, multiply that number by 2 (the number of coders), and then divide that number by the total number of codings by each. For example, if each person coded ten documents, and they agreed on eight out of ten codings, then the calculation would be

   Intercoder reliability score: $(8 \times 2) / (10 + 10) = 16/20$, or 80%

The result should be 80 percent or greater; any score less than 80 percent means the coding scheme needs clarification and revision.

5. **Code all documents.** Once the coding scheme is pretested, read and code all the documents using data sheets organized by the coding scheme. Generally, coding involves recording an identifying characteristic (e.g., date and page number of the newspaper, observation date and journal page, respondent number and note-page) and then recording the characteristic. For instance, suppose a student wants to study support for recreational use of public lands in California. To learn more on decisions about public land use, the student may examine the meeting minutes of the California Bureau of Labor Management Resource Advisory Council regarding off-highway vehicle (OHV) use of public lands. The following example shows how the first three lines of data from a content analysis coding sheet might look for such a study:

Example: Abridged Content Analysis Coding Sheet

MEETING DATE	RAC MEMBER COMMENTS 1 = *Pro use* 2 = *Against use*	TOPIC 1 = *OHV use on public lands* 2 = *OHV designated areas* 9 = *Other (specify)*
3/30/2000	1	1
3/31/2000	1	9 (grants to build more trails)
7/13/2000	2	2

6. **Count frequency per characteristic.** Count the frequency of the occurrences of each characteristic in each category (e.g., the number of times each characteristic of each category was found in the text). For example, the following table could be the result from a content analysis on the Resource Advisory Council meeting minutes:

Example: Content Analysis of California RAC Meeting Minutes 2000

RAC Member Comments Support OHV Use	Frequency	RAC Member Comments Limit/Oppose OHV Use	Frequency
OHV use on public lands	12	OHV designated areas	6
More demand of OHV use	6	Limit OHV access	6
More demand for recreational opportunities	3	Stop inappropriate OHV use	1
Outdated land use plans related to OHV access	2	Management/Guidelines for OHV trails	11
Need for more OHV trails	4	Limit OHV trails	10
Need more OHV grant funds/more OHV trails	2	Conserve natural resources, protect plants, animals	13

Data source: http://www.ca.blm.gov/news/rac.html RAC Meeting Dates: March 30, March 31, June 28, June 29, July 13, July 14, and August 29, 2000. Adapted from *Policy Implementation and the Collaborative Management Process* by Gilbert Peña Dueñas (Chico, CA: California State University, Chico, 2003), Table 1, 39.

7. **Summarize and interpret.** Finally, interpret the findings as they relate to the hypothesis. Use tables, graphs, or models to illustrate the findings. The data may be reduced further by collapsing the main categories into one or several main themes, as the following example demonstrates:

Example: Interpretation of California RAC Meeting Minutes 2000

RAC Member Comments Support OHV Use	Frequency	RAC Member Comments Limit/Oppose OHV Use	Frequency
Need more OHV trails/access	8	Limit/Stop proliferation of OHV trails/access	30
Promote OHV use as recreation	21	Discourage OHV because of environmental problems	13
Total Support for OHV	*29*	*Total Opposition for OHV*	*43*

Data source: http://www.ca.blm.gov/news/rac.html RAC Meeting Dates: March 30, March 31, June 28, June 29, July 13, July 14, and August 29, 2000. Adapted from Gilbert Peña Dueñas, *Policy Implementation and the Collaborative Management Process* (Chico, CA: California State University, Chico, 2003), Table 2, 40.

8. **Discuss the results.** Discuss each illustration fully and describe how it supports or does not support the assertions or assertions made by others. Also include with the illustrations as well as in the reference pages information about the source of the text analyzed by the content analysis. Finally, include a copy of the coding sheet in an appendix.

Classification Analysis

Classification analysis, the results of which are often reported as a concept map or typology, is a simple, descriptive method for sorting and categorizing information about events, objects, or people based on inductive reasoning (reasoning from specific cases to a generalized concept). Classification analysis is especially useful for sorting theories for literature reviews, identifying policy alternatives, and conducting comparative studies. Although classification analysis is also used as a data reduction method to sort and classify quantitative data (especially using cluster or factor analysis), it is commonly used for collecting and processing categorical data (nominal or ordinal variables), observational data, and best-practice investigations. This method involves systematically collecting information about a topic and sorting it into two or more groups, classes, subclasses, or categories based on similarities and differences in characteristics or attributes (see Bailey 1994; Dunn 2008, 99–102).

Generic Classification

The purpose of classification is to create meaningful categories from a set of qualitative information to show conceptual patterns or relationships within that information. To do this, students must first research the various indicators (items or cases) of the topic, then compare cases looking for similarities, and from this analysis, create categories and subcategories based on similarities between these items or cases. When analyzing the information, it is important to sort the items logically and based on valid criteria, including (Dunn 2008, 99–100; Bailey 1994, 3):

- **Substantive relevance:** The groups, categories, or classes must conform closely to reality. While creatively combining information is part of the research process, how the information is sorted into groups should be based on a theoretical concept or a realistic definition of the problem. For example, classifying governments into democracies and autocracies would be based on a credible definition of the problem based on conceptual definitions of the characteristics of democracies and autocracies.

- **Exhaustiveness:** All the items collected must fit into a category, group, or class. This means that every case or item in the dataset of information must be placed into a class or group. If there is an item or case that does not fit into a group, category, or class, then another category may have to be created or the criteria for placement may have to be reevaluated. Either way, the test of a valid classification is the ability to place all items in a suitable class or group.

- **Disjointedness (mutual exclusiveness):** All categories, classes, or groups must be unique with no overlapping characteristics. This means that the categories and subcategories must be mutually exclusive. To be mutually exclusive, the categories, classes, or groups must be defined by clear indicators of the class or group characteristic or attribute, which requires a clear set of criteria for determining when an item belongs into category 1 or category 2. In other words, there must be an explainable reason for placing each item into a class or group and this must be done consistently across all categories and items. If the item has characteristics that overlap into more than one category, make a decision about where to place the item based on logical reasoning. For example, voting researchers created red states (Republican-dominated) and blue (Democrat-dominated) states. Yet, where would the purple states (both parties are competitive) be placed in this classification?

- **Hierarchical distinctiveness:** The categories and subcategories must be distinguished between and among each other. There must be a hierarchy from broadest category to narrowest subset of the characteristics that distinguish the category. One category may have two subcategories and another category may have three subcategories. Subcategories should have distinguishing attributes within the category. Subcategories between categories should not overlap either. For example, political surveys often ask for a respondent's political identification as Democrat, Republican, or Independent. The subcategories for Independent are often Independent Leaning Democrat, Independent, and Independent Leaning Republican. The main categories are distinctive, and the subcategories of the Independent category are distinctive within that category.

Once the information (data) is collected and sorted, the results can be represented simply by creating a table that identifies the categories and subcategories. The attributes or characteristics are then listed below the category. In the body of the paper, the student must then discuss, explain, and evaluate how each attribute fits into each category or subcategory. For example, in the following classification table regarding events occurring prior to flight that create unsafe conditions for flying, the researcher illustrates that there are two categories of events and that there are two subcategories within each event category:

Example: Generic Classification Table

PRECONDITIONS FOR UNSAFE ACTS BY AIRCREWS	
Substandard Conditions of Operators	Substandard Practice of Operators
Adverse Mental States	*Crew Resource Mismanagement*
Distracted	Failed to communicate/coordinate
Mental fatigue	Failed to conduct adequate brief
Life stress	Failure of leadership
Adverse Physiological States	*Personal Readiness*
Medical illness	Excessive physical training
Physical fatigue	Self-medicating
Impaired physiological state	Violation of crew rest requirement

Data adapted from Shappell and Wiegmann 2000, 7, Table 2.

Under each category, the researcher provided a list of behaviors or acts by aircrews that are characteristics or attributes of the subcategory. In the text, for example, the researcher explained the *personal readiness* category as follows:

> *Personal Readiness.* In aviation, or for that matter in any occupational setting, individuals are expected to show up for work ready to perform at optimal levels. Nevertheless, in aviation, as in other professions, personal readiness failures occur when individuals fail to prepare physically or mentally for duty. For instance, violations of crew rest requirements, bottle-to-brief rules, and self-medicating all will affect performance on the job and are particularly detrimental in the aircraft. It is not hard to imagine that, when individuals violate crew rest requirements, they run the risk of mental fatigue and other adverse mental states, which ultimately lead to errors and accidents. Note, however, that violations that affect personal readiness are not considered "unsafe act, violation" since they typically do not happen in the cockpit, nor are they necessarily active failures with direct and immediate consequences (Shappell and Wiegmann 2000, 9).

Concept Model/Map Based Classification Data

A concept model or map is a graphical technique for representing relationships between concepts. The concepts, in this case, symbolize objects or events, designated by a representative label. The relationship between the concepts is linked by lines and/or arrows. The arrows can be one way or two ways depending on the relationship between the

are zero should be displayed, and data that are near zero should be displayed in decimal form (.003).

Interpreting a Table

1. **Take a little bit at a time!** Identify the items that are interesting and relevant to the paper.
2. **Identify the outliers (extreme values):** Look for values that are much higher or lower than the most common values. Are they reasonable and do they fit with reality? If not, there might be an error in the dataset.
3. **Examine the context:** Identify information that challenges theories or contradicts what is generally known and assumed.
4. **Be conservative:** Do not overstate the importance of the data results.

Example of a Table Using Primary Data

In the following example, the authors use a table to exhibit the association between party dominance in each chamber of Congress and confirmation of presidential appointees. At first glance, the table appears as just a set of numbers. Now, notice the outliers. The large values in President Kennedy's and President Clinton's **number of withdrawn nominees** are different from those of the rest of the presidents. Why? Kennedy and Clinton both faced a Democratic Congress, so why did they withdraw so many more of their nominees than other presidents? Does this contradict or confirm what is known or assumed? How important are these results? Why did Presidents Carter, Bush, and Clinton have so many nominees left unconfirmed? What does this say about their presidencies or their abilities to work with Congress?

PRESIDENTIAL NOMINATIONS AND SENATE ACTION BY POLITICAL DIVISION SINCE 1960[a]

Congress	President	Democrats in the Senate	Republicans in the Senate	Number of Confirmed Nominees	Number of Withdrawn Nominees	Number of Rejected Nominees	Number of Unconfirmed Nominees
87th	Kennedy	64	36	100741	1279	0	829
88th	Johnson	67	33	120201	0	6	1953
89th	Johnson	68	32	120865	0	173	1981
90th	Johnson	64	36	118231	0	4	1966
91st	Nixon	58	42#	133797	2	487	178
92nd	Nixon	54	44#	114909	11	0	2133
93rd	Nixon	56	42#	131254	15	0	3069
94th	Ford	61	37	131378	6	0	3801
95th	Carter	61	38	124730	66	0	12713
96th	Carter	58	41	154665	18	0	1458
97th	Reagan	46	53°	184844	55	7	1346
98th	Reagan	46	54°	97262	4	0	610
99th	Reagan	47	53°	95811	16	0	3787
100th	Reagan	55	45#	88721	23	1	5933
101st	Bush	55	45#	88078	48	1	7951
102nd	Bush	56	44#	75349	24	0	756
103rd	Clinton	57	43#	76122	1080	0	2741
104th	Clinton	48	52°	73711	22	0	8472

[a]Data taken from U.S. Congress n.d.; Kurian 1994; Mackenzie 1996; Stanley and Niemi 1998. Table created by Diane Schmidt and Shelly Tall (1999). [b] ° indicates Republican dominance. [c] # indicates close Republican margin.

Graphical Displays

Graphical displays, often referred to as graphs, figures, diagrams, and charts, are dramatic visual illustrations of data. Like tables, graphical displays may be used with raw or statistically transformed data.

Types of Graphical Displays

- **Bar Graph.** Bar graphs display ordinal or nominal data either horizontally or vertically by category. The height or length of the bar represents the frequency of occurrences for each category.
- **Histogram.** Histogram displays interval data using bars. The height and width of the bars relate to the size of the interval. The area of the bar represents the frequency of the occurrences.
- **Pie Charts.** Pie charts display the proportion of each part of a nominal or ordinal category. The circle represents the entire category (e.g., voters) and the divisions show the different parts to the category (e.g., the proportion of Democrats, Republicans, and Independents).
- **Pictograms.** Pictograms are another way of presenting pie charts. The only difference is that an icon or picture is used to represent the proportion of each category.
- **Line Diagram.** Line diagrams display interval data by connecting all the cases with a continuous line. These graphs show how the data change over time.

Format of Graphic Displays

- **Title.** The title should tell the reader what the data refer to, where the data were collected, when the data were collected, what kind of data are listed, source of the data, and categories in the graphical display. The information can be listed in the title or in a footnote at the bottom of the illustration.
- **Amount of Data.** The data listed in illustrations should be presented simply and should exhaust the category—that is, include all parts of the category.
- **Labels.** Each part of the illustration must be labeled. For line graphs, whatever is being explained is usually listed on the left-hand side and whatever is being used to explain it is listed across the bottom of the graph. For figures, charts, and pictures, each division must be labeled clearly. Distinctions are generally made by color coding, creating a legend, or using shading.
- **Cells Complete.** Each space (cell) in the illustration should include information. The illustration should make complex data and ideas simpler to understand.

Interpreting Graphic Displays

A good graphical display should communicate concepts and ideas with precision and efficiency. The illustration should show the reader visually the nature of the relationship between two or more events.

1. **Size Matters.** Notice the size of the bars, proportions, or "peaks and valleys" in the illustration. Identify the events that are interesting and relevant to the research topic.
2. **Identify Dramatic Shifts in Values.** Look for values that are much higher or lower than the other values. What does this say about the relationship between the events?
3. **Examine the Relative Proportions.** Identify relative relationships that challenge theories or contradict what is generally known and assumed.

Example: Two Types of Graphs

Look at the two following illustrations. Both use data from the table of presidential nominations shown earlier; however, the data presented in the graphs are from only one category and one part of the data. Which one is easier to read? Which one best illustrates the relationship between presidential administration and number of nominees left unconfirmed?

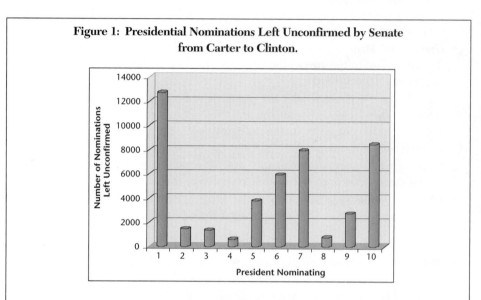

Figure 1: Presidential Nominations Left Unconfirmed by Senate from Carter to Clinton.

Figure 2: Presidential Nominations Left Unconfirmed by Senate from Carter to Clinton.

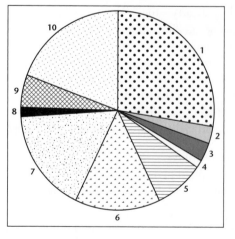

Legend: 1=Carter (95th), 2=Carter (96th), 3=Reagan (97th), 4=Reagan (98th), 5=Reagan (99th), 6=Reagan (100th), 7=Bush (101st), 8=Bush (102nd), 9=Clinton (103rd), 10=Clinton (104th)

Source: Data taken from U.S. Congress n.d; Kurian 1994; Mackenzie 1996; Stanley and Niemi 1998.

A Primer on Data Analysis

In more advanced political science courses, instructors may give students the opportunity to include quantitative evidence that has been produced or summarized through data analysis. Whether students have collected the data themselves (primary data collected through a content analysis, survey, or directly from the source) or used a data set produced by someone else (secondary data), it is likely that the data are in "raw" form. This means that the data are in the form of lists of numbers. To make these data meaningful, it is often necessary to summarize the data.

Data Reduction with Simple Descriptive Statistics

Analysts use simple descriptive statistics in mass media, advertisements, political speeches, and informal conversation to summarize or reduce data into manageable, understandable forms. Data used in descriptive analysis include frequencies, means, modes, percentages, and ratios. Analysts use these measures to describe the current state or level of things. Frequencies indicate the absolute value of variables, whereas means, modes, percentages, and ratios specify the relative value of variables. In particular, means, modes, and percentages describe the central tendency (typical values) of a variable in different ways and, because of this, can lead the researcher to different conclusions depending on which statistic is used. As such, each type of descriptive statistic has a different use, purpose, and meaning for summarizing or describing data. Many computerized statistical programs can calculate these statistics.

Frequency: A frequency is how many different items are in a group or category. Find this by counting the number of each item in a category. For example, there are three categories for a variable measuring political party affiliation. Of the 125 people who were asked their party affiliation, 60 said they were Democrats, 45 said they were Republicans, and 20 said they were Independent.

The frequency of Democrats is 60, of Republicans is 45, and of Independents is 20.

Mean: A mean is an average. In other words, a mean indicates the typical value found in the data. This is only true if the data do not have some unusual extreme values (often referred to as outliers). When the data include a limited number of very high or very low values compared to the other values in the data, a mean will misrepresent the typical value. Where the data include comparatively few very high values, the mean will be higher than it should be. Where the data include comparatively few very low values relative to the other values, the mean will be lower than the typical value. To address this, sometimes researchers will exclude an outlier from the mean and simply note the exclusion and a reason why they excluded the value. To find a mean, add all the numerical values in one category together to find the sum (total). Next, divide the sum by the number of items in the category. If students prefer a whole number as a result, they should round the number to the nearest preferred value. For example, the test grade for student A is 99, student B is 85, student C is 71, student D is 60, and student F is 52. To find the mean:

Add: 99 + 85 + 71 + 60 + 52 = 367
Divide: 367/5 = 73.4
Round to 73. This is the average grade.

Median: The median is often used in place of a mean when the data contain outliers that cannot or should not be dropped from the dataset. The median is the middle value when the data values are listed from smallest to largest. (If there is an even number of data values, then the two middle values in the list should be added together, then divided by 2. The result is the median for a list of data values when there is an even number of values.) For example, the test grade for student A is 99, student B is 85, student C is 71, student D is 60, and student F is 52. To find the median:

Add: $99 + 85 + 71 + 60 + 52 = 367$
Locate the value in the middle of the list of these five numbers.
The median is 71.

Percentages: Percentages are proportions of the total of the variable. To find a percentage, divide the number of a specific type of thing by the total number of all items in a category and multiply by 100. For example, in a survey of 125 people, 60 people identified themselves as Democrats. To find the percentage of people in the study who identified themselves as Democrats:

Percentage voting: $60/125 = .48 \times 100 = 48\%$

Percentage Change: A percentage change measures the change in the frequency of an event over time. It is calculated by examining the amount of change in two frequencies of the same variable from one period to the next. To calculate this, subtract the frequency of the earlier event from the frequency of the later event and divide by the frequency of the earlier event. Then, transform the result into a percentage by multiplying by 100. The formula is [(Event in time 2) − (Event in time 1)/(Event in time 1)] × 100. For example, a county had 2800 people in 1988 and 3500 people in 1998. To find the percentage change in population:

Calculate: $(3500 - 2800)/2800 = .25$
Change the figure into a percentage: $.25 \times 100 = 25\%$ *increase in population*

Mode: A mode is the category with the greatest number of cases. Find this by looking for repeated values. For example, the grade for student A is 75, student B is 75, student C is 64, and student D is 56.

Two students received 75 and one student each received 64 and 56: The mode is 75.

Ratios: Ratios show a relative proportion. It is used to compare the proportion of one number to another for relative value. Find this by creating a fraction out of the two numbers. Reduce the fraction until it cannot be reduced any further. The ratio is the larger number compared to the smaller number in the fraction. In a group of 4500 female and male public administrators, there are 3000 men and 1500 women. To find the ratio of men to women:

Create a fraction: $3000/1500$
Reduce it: $30/15 = 2/1$
The ratio of men to women is 2 to 1.

Rates: Rates compare the number of occurrences of an event in a jurisdiction to the total population of that jurisdiction. This is done by dividing the frequency of the occurrence by the total population in the jurisdiction. Because the denominator (total population) is so much larger than the numerator (the frequency of occurrence), it is necessary to multiply them by a base number (such as 100 or 1000 or 10,000) to convert the small decimal number into a whole number. The formula is (Events/Population) × (Base number).

For example, a county of 15,600 people had 32 accidents last year. To find the accident rate per 1000 people:

> *Do the following: 32/15,600 = .00202*
> *Multiply .00202 by a base of 1000: (.00202) × 1000 = 2.02*
> *The rate is 2.02 per 1000 of population.*

Data Reduction Using Statistical Methods

Data reduction using statistical methods provides the researcher with opportunities to examine relationships between variables in a structured and systematic way. Some of the statistical techniques are simple and others are quite complicated. The best way to approach data analysis is through a social science statistics course. Students who have already taken a statistics course may wish to refresh their memories by obtaining a copy of *Essential Statistics for Public Managers and Policy Analysis* by Evan M. Berman (Washington, DC: Congressional Quarterly Press, 2002), a copy of *Interpreting Basic Statistics: A Guide and Workbook Based on Excerpts from Journal Articles*, 3rd ed., by Zealure C. Holcomb (Los Angeles, CA: Pyrczak Publishing, 2002), and/or a copy of *The Research Methods Knowledge Base*, 2nd ed., by William Trochim (Cincinnati, OH: Atomicdog Publishing, 2001, or online at http://www.atomicdog.com). These books have just about everything a student needs to know about data analysis. They are written without jargon in a readable and simple format. Without burdening the reader with details, the authors describe and provide examples of simple elementary statistical analysis, as well as more sophisticated techniques . Together, they are handy reference guides for looking up statistical terms and explanations of significance tests that are frequently used in scholarly political science materials as evidence of a theory's validity.

Another way to learn about statistical techniques for data analysis is to view a Public Broadcasting Service (PBS) series entitled *Against All Odds: Inside Statistics*. This is available on VHS videocassettes. There are twenty-six individual half-hour programs that demystify statistical methods by providing living examples of using mathematical formulas to measure social phenomena. The series appeared on PBS television stations in the fall of 1989 and was produced for a mass audience. Check the college or university tape and film library to see if it contains a copy of this series. If not, obtain a copy through an interlibrary loan. The programs examine everything from a definition of statistics, to time series analysis, to conducting a case study.

Finally, another way to learn about statistical methods for social science is to browse through or study the many books produced by Sage Publications, Inc. The *Quantitative Applications in the Social Sciences Series* and the *Applied Social Research Methods Series* together contain over seventy books on methodology in social science. Students can view a list of books in these series at http://www.sagepub.com.

Even if students are not conducting a statistical analysis for their research projects, they should be aware of how other researchers use statistical evidence to support their assertions or conclusions. Researchers use a set of terms and measures to support their assertions about political relationships. Following is a list of common terms used in data analysis to describe research methods.

Hypothesis: This is a term that describes researchers' theories about how events or conditions relate to each other. Researchers pose a hypothesis about the structure of these relationships. They also pose a null hypothesis that the relationships do not exist or are a result of coincidence or chance. Using evidence to test the strength and structure of these relationships, researchers either reject or accept the null hypothesis. In other words, researchers test whether the evidence supports their theories about how things relate or not.

Variables: These are things such as attitudes, characteristics, policies, etc., usually measured by numbers that vary (change) in the frequency (how often) or level in which they occur. Employment rates or the percentage of people voting in an election will differ from one time to the next. They are variables because neither occurs at a constant rate. There are different kinds of variables:

Dependent Variable: A dependent variable is a measure of what researchers are interested in explaining. For example, if students want to learn about public support for smoking regulation, their dependent variable could be data gathered on public opinion about smoking regulation. If they want to study college student support for smoking regulations at their school, their dependent variable could be data gathered regarding college student opinions about regulating campus smoking.

Independent Variable: Independent variables are measures of things researchers believe cause or influence the dependent variable. For example, if students are interested in investigating what kind of individual characteristics are associated with support for smoking regulations, they may collect data on individuals' age, gender, smoking habits, family smoking habits, peer smoking habits, etc. Each of these characteristics exist for each individual regardless of whether he or she supports regulation or not. A person who is 60 years old, male, smokes a pack a day, has family and friends who smoke, lives in Kentucky, and works for tobacco growers is not likely to support tobacco regulation. A person who is 25 years old, female, never smoked, has no family or friends who smoke, lives in California, and works for a hospital is likely to support tobacco regulation.

Dummy Variable: A dummy, or control, variable is a special kind of measure that is created as a way to indicate (or control for) whether a condition or an event has or has not occurred. The data for dummy variables are usually coded into 0s and 1s, where 0 is the absence of the condition or event and 1 indicates the presence of the condition or event. For example, a student may create a dummy variable to indicate whether an individual lives in a tobacco-producing state. In this case, the researcher would create a dummy variable called *Tobacco-State* and enter a one (1) for each of the respondents who live in a tobacco producing state and a zero (0) for each of the respondents who do not live in such a state. By comparing this variable and a person's support for regulation, a student could examine whether those who live in states that do not produce tobacco show more support for smoking regulations than those who live in tobacco-producing states.

Constant: This is a term that describes a characteristic that is common to all the data. For example, if a researcher is studying roll-call voting in the Senate, then Senate membership is a constant because all subjects of the study are members of the Senate.

Causal Relationship: This term describes the relationship between variables; where one or more variables (independent) cause another variable (dependent) to move either *positively* (as the independent variable increases, the dependent variable increases), *negatively* (as the independent variable decreases, the dependent variable decreases), or *inversely* (as the independent variable increases, the dependent variable decreases; or as the independent variable decreases, the dependent variable increases). For a causal relationship to exist, the change in one variable must be plausibly related to the change in another variable. For example, there may be a positive causal relationship between smoking a pack a day and a person's lack of support for tobacco regulation. This is plausible (believable) because it would be illogical for smokers to want constraints on their ability to smoke.

Cross-tabulation: Cross-tabulation allows the researcher to examine the relationship between two (bivariate) categorical variables or sometimes three (multivariate) categorical variables. A cross-tabulation is a process whereby the frequency of one categorical variable is measured against the frequency of another categorical variable. This is best conducted by using a statistical program. For example, if a dataset on college smoking habits included a variable that measured the amount of smoking (none, less than a pack a day, at least a pack a day) and a variable recording the respondent's gender, the student researcher could cross-tabulate the amount of smoking variable with the gender variable. The result would show how many male respondents do not smoke, how many male respondents smoke less than a pack a day, and how many male respondents smoke more than a pack a day. The same kind of results would be available for female respondents.

Contingency Tables: Contingency tables record the frequency for each combination between two variables. Where there is a causal relationship hypothesized, the dependent variable is listed horizontally (in rows) and the independent is listed vertically (in columns); otherwise, it does not matter which variable is placed on the row or column. The table usually has row and column totals. For example, to examine the relationship between college smoking habits and gender, the labels for the row variable would be the different categories for the variable measuring smoking habits. The labels for the column variable would be the different categories of the gender variable. The table would then contain the numerical frequency of each combination of characteristics.

Correlation: This term describes how characteristics or variables vary together. They can be correlated in the same direction (positive) or in opposite directions (negative). Correlation suggests that variables only change in these directions, not that one variable causes another's movement. For example, personal smoking habits may correlate positively with family smoking habits (i.e., increases in amount of smoking are correlated with increases in number of family members who smoke), yet personal smoking habits cannot be said to cause family smoking habits, or vice versa. Something else could be causing both variables to increase. If something else is causing both variables to vary together, then that is considered a *spurious* (coincidental or accidental) correlation.

Standard Deviation: This is one of the most often used measures of volatility in the variation or change in a variable. The standard deviation measures the degree to which a value of a variable differs from the mean (average) of the entire set of data on that variable. Most computer applications will calculate this measure. For variables such as age, the values could be widely dispersed (18, 39, 72) or narrowly dispersed (18, 22, 23). The standard deviation indicates how widely or narrowly the data are dispersed in the dataset. Discussions of trends in data are generally more meaningful where most of the data are more narrowly dispersed around the mean of the data.

Significance: This is a term used to indicate whether the results from data analysis used to measure relationships between variables are reasonable or valid. Often, researchers will refer to a measure as significant at a probability level of .05 or .01. These are probabilities (the odds) that the researchers are wrong about the nature of the relationship between variables or items. In other words, a significance level of .05 (reported as $P = .05$) indicates that there is a 5 percent chance that the researchers' hypothesis about the relationship between the dependent variable and independent variables is false, when they claim it is true. This means the data results can be used as evidence that the hypothesized relationships are probably valid. Most computer applications can produce a variety of statistics for testing significance (especially chi-square, t-tests, R-square), and researchers specify which types of tests they want conducted on their data analysis results. Most computerized statistical programs will calculate both a test statistic and the significance level for each type of test requested.

Chi-square (χ^2) *test:* This is a statistical test used to measure the existence and strength of the relationship between two categorical variables. The test is a mathematical formula that basically compares the expected value (usually the mean) to the actual values (observed frequency) for the two variables while controlling for the size (often referred to as N) of the dataset. When the actual values deviate from the expected value in a pattern, then the results suggest that the relationship in that pattern is not coincidental.

Student's t-distribution (t-test): This is a statistical test used to measure the existence and strength of the relationship between a continuous and a group variable. Using a mathematical formula, a statistical computer program can calculate whether the means for each group differ in a discernible pattern. For example, a t-test can be used to test whether smoking habits differ by gender.

R-square (R²): This is a statistical measure of the amount of variance in the dependent variable that is explained by the variance of independent variables. It is more often used in multivariate analysis. The mathematical formula for this measure also controls for the size of the dataset and the number of independent variables associated with the dependent variable. For example, an R^2 can be used to suggest how the combination of variables such as smoking habits, gender, and age will determine attitudes toward smoking regulation. To measure the strength of the relationships, the formula creates a statistical result between 1 and 0; the closer the number is to 1, the "tighter" or stronger the relationship is between the dependent variable and the independent variables.

PROPERTIES OF ESSAYS AND RESEARCH PAPERS

Properties of a Good Essay or Research Paper

A well-written, well-documented essay or research paper has three basic parts: an introduction, a body, and a conclusion. The **introduction** must include a thesis sentence that structures and focuses the paper on an assertion or a hypothesis about the relationship between concrete and/or abstract political objects. The **body** of the paper must include arguments, assertions, or points that provide reasons why the thesis sentence is true and counterarguments against the thesis. The body also includes evidence to back up each reason or assertion. There is no absolute number of reasons required for supporting a thesis. The following diagram shows the thesis supported by three arguments with evidence for illustrative purposes only. The **conclusion** generally summarizes the main supporting points and clarifies the functional or logical relationships between the evidence and the inferences made by the author.

Properties of an Essay or Paper

PROPERTIES OF AN ESSAY OR PAPER

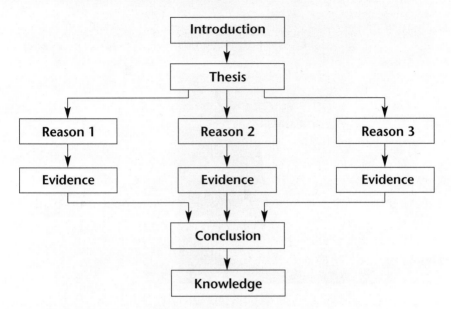

Recognizing and Writing a Good Thesis Sentence

Functions of a Thesis Sentence
- A thesis sentence sums up the main ideas that the writer wants to make.
- A thesis sentence asserts something about the topic.
- A thesis sentence conveys the writer's purpose.
- A thesis sentence acts as a working guide to organize the writer's points.
- A thesis sentence provides a concise preview of the major subtopics addressed in the written work.

Requirements of a Thesis Sentence
- Does it make an assertion about the topic?
- Does it convey a purpose?
- Is it limited to an assertion of only one main point?
- Is the assertion specific?
- Does it suggest a plan for the paper or essay?

Writing a Thesis Sentence for an Essay or Essay Test

Essay exams are designed to demonstrate the student's specific knowledge of a subject. Students are responsible for choosing the right facts and organizing them coherently to demonstrate what they know.

Definition of Terms

An essential element in constructing a thesis sentence is to understand the question being asked. Students must first read the question thoroughly and identify the key words that determine the meaning of the question. Very often, the verb determines the meaning of the question and the nature of the answer. Here is a list of important terms and definitions that are commonly used in political science essays (Corder and Ruszkiewicz 1998, 631).

Analyze: give main divisions or elements

Classify: arrange into main divisions

Compare: point out the likenesses

Contrast: point out the differences

Criticize: provide a perspective on good and bad features

Describe: name the features of or identify the steps

Discuss: examine in detail

Evaluate: provide a perspective on the value or validity

Explain: make clear, give reasons for

Illustrate: give one or more examples of

Interpret: give an explanation or clarify the meaning of

Justify: defend, show to be right

Review: examine on a broad scale

Significance: show why something is meaningful

Summarize: briefly go over the essentials

Common Problems in Answering Essay Questions

Here are some common problems that students have experienced in writing opinion essays or essays for exams. An instructor may use an acronym to signify these problems. An example of each problem follows each explanation based on the following essay question:

Essay Question: Describe the important changes that would occur in the structure of power relationships in Congress if the outcomes of the House and Senate elections resulted in a change in party dominance.

Good Answer: *"If the Republicans were to recapture control of either chamber, the changes would not be nearly as radical in the Senate as they would be in the House because the Democrats have dominated the House leadership positions for a very long time."*

Reason: This sentence answers the question directly by describing the changes as radical in the House and less radical in the Senate. In particular, it provides reasons why this would be true.

Begs the Question (BQ)

These types of thesis sentences do not answer the question asked. They typically make assertions about some small aspect of the question without really answering the question at all.

BQ Answer: *"There would be a dramatic change in the structure of power relationships in Congress if the outcome of the Senate elections resulted in a change in party dominance."*

Reason: This sentence begs the question by answering only a small part of the question. It does not address the comparison between the House changes and the Senate changes.

Ambiguous or Vague (AV)

These types of thesis sentences typically need clarification and/or limiting. They usually lack specific detail about the topic. Such thesis sentences result in the reader asking such questions as, "So what? So why should we worry about that?"

AV Answer: *"If the outcome of the elections resulted in a switch from one party to another, some say it would have little impact."*

Reason: This sentence is vague. It does not tell the reader why such a change would not have much of an impact. In addition, it does not say who says that a change in party dominance would not have much of an impact.

Descriptive or Historical (DH)

These types of answers are typically factually correct but do not provide a critical or analytical response to the question. Very often, these thesis sentences prepare the reader for a chronology of events without addressing the controversy associated with the events or relationships.

DH Answer: *"Party dominance has changed from one party to another in both chambers and has changed the structure of power relationships in them many times, yet Congress continues to function."*

Reason: This sentence, although it may appear to answer the question, actually prepares the reader for a chronology of elections where the party dominance has changed in one or both chambers. It does not address the comparative intent of the question.

Writing a Thesis Sentence for a Research Paper

Research paper assignments help students demonstrate an ability to organize their thoughts about a topic or subject. Such assignments help students clarify their understanding of political phenomena. More than any other assignment, a research paper requires synthesizing and integrating information and opinions.

- Research papers require students to organize material coherently to support an argument or statement.
- Research papers are most often assigned without any particular question to answer.
- Research papers require students to think critically and formulate an opinion or a perspective about their topics that is both interesting and supportable within the scope of the assignment.

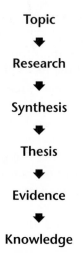

Topic

⬇

Research

⬇

Synthesis

⬇

Thesis

⬇

Evidence

⬇

Knowledge

Understanding the Function of the Thesis Sentence in a Research Paper

Students often have trouble understanding the reason for having a clearly stated thesis sentence in their papers. The thesis sentence is usually found in the first paragraph. This thesis lays out the plan for the paper by incorporating the major subtopics or points within the statement. The function of the thesis sentence is to provide a preview of the main supporting ideas and the order in which the writer will address these ideas. One way to think of the function of a thesis sentence for a research paper is to:

1. **Visualize the thesis as a defendant in a murder case.**
2. **Students should visualize themselves as Clarence Darrow presenting a classic legal defense.**
3. **In the opening statement to the jury, after presenting some background information, declare a thesis sentence. For example, the client is not guilty for the following reasons:**
   - He has exhibited a lifetime commitment to nonviolence.
   - He had no motive.
   - He was with someone else at the time of the murder.
4. **The thesis sentence is on trial for being a false statement. It is up to the student to defend it through:**
   - Sound reasoning.
   - Presenting material and evidence supporting one's position.
   - Defending one's position against contrary evidence.
5. **The jury can reasonably expect the summary:**
   - To summarize every valid point asserted in the thesis.
   - To summarize every point refuted but asserted in the thesis.

Formulating a Thesis Sentence for a Research Paper

1. **Once students have picked out their topics, they must do some preliminary research to narrow and limit the focus of their papers.**
   - Only after students do this preliminary research can they begin to develop a preliminary thesis sentence or hypothesis.
   - This hypothesis is a statement that can be tested and confirmed (or disconfirmed) through the presentation of empirical evidence.
   - Here is one *example* of a hypothesis that is testable through the presentation of information and data: *"Women's issues have a greater chance of getting on to the congressional agenda when Democrats control the White House and the Congress."*

2. **Once students have formulated their preliminary thesis, subsequent research should either lend support or disprove their assertion.**
   - Students should expect to refine and revise their thesis sentences many times throughout the course of their research.
   - As the thesis is narrowed and focused, it takes on a more controversial tone.
   - An increasing knowledge base allows students to ask more sophisticated and critical questions about the topic.
   - The more knowledgeable students become about their topics, the more focused they should become with their assertions about the topic.

3. **For most student papers, a thesis statement with one main idea supported by three subtopics is usually sufficient and preferable to more complex and complicated thesis sentences.**
   - The rule of thumb is to keep the thesis sentence simple, narrow, and specific.
   - The best way to do this is to capsulize and state succinctly the causal relationships between the main point and the subtopics.
   - *A word of caution*: The length of the manuscript and the nature of the topic will influence the structure and desirability of having more or less than three subtopics in the thesis statement.

Example of Narrowing and Refining a Thesis

To give students a better idea of how a thesis can be revised over time, the following are examples of revisions, from start to finish, of one thesis sentence. As you read each revision, notice how each statement further refines and focuses the main idea. Each subsequent statement also reflects a greater and greater sophistication and mastery of the material.

1. **"Labor union leaders, during the past decade, have been less effective than business leaders in mobilizing worker or political support."**
   - This thesis sentence, though narrow enough, is vague.
   - What does effectiveness mean? Political support from whom? Why have they been less effective?
2. **"Lane Kirkland was not the leader Walter Reuther was in safeguarding his union against economic blackmail upheld by the NLRB, market fluctuations, and a union-busting president."**
   - This thesis sentence is focused too narrowly on one person and one union and is vague about the causal relationship between the variables.
   - The thesis does not specify what economic blackmail is, nor does it refer to any specific time period.
3. **"Labor unions, as political-economic groups, have fallen onto hard times in the past decade due to a hostile presidential administration, the recession, and new techniques in union busting."**
   - This thesis sentence is more specific about the causal relationship between the variables.
   - The thesis does not identify the important political actors or the intervening relationships that helped produce this political problem.
4. **"Next to management's advanced, state-of-the-art techniques for busting unions with the support of the Reagan administration appointees to the NLRB, efforts by union leaders such as Lane Kirkland were dwarfed in comparison when conducting organizing campaigns during the worst U.S. recession since the Great Depression."**
   - This thesis sentence, while quite complex, fully describes the context, the players, and the variables associated with problems in union organizing.
   - This thesis is testable.

Tips for Writing a Thesis Sentence for Papers with Specific Requirements

Sometimes students are given a paper assignment for which the instructor has provided the reading materials, a question to be answered, and/or that requires certain types of questions to be answered within the text of the paper. This should not alter the student's ability to construct an effective thesis statement. It does, however, limit the range of ideas and points that can be made in the paper.

1. **To construct a thesis sentence for an assignment for which the instructor has specified the reading materials and a specific question to answer:**
   - Use the essay test thesis sentence format.
   - Answer the question directly and reference the reading material to support the main points of the thesis.

2. **To construct a thesis sentence for a research paper that must answer specific questions within the text:**
   - Reflect the paper's main idea in the thesis sentence and subdivide the paper so that it reflects the answers to the questions.
   - Structure the paper's main arguments to comply with the requirements of the assignment.

Common Problems in Constructing a Thesis

Here are some common problems that students have experienced in writing a thesis sentence for a research paper. An instructor may use an acronym to signify these problems.

Ambiguous or Vague (AV)

These types of thesis sentences are usually worded very generally and typically need clarification and/or limiting. They often lack specific detail about the topic.

Example 1: *"Labor union members have different voting patterns than non-union workers."*
- Such thesis sentences result in the reader asking questions like "How are they different and why is this information important to know?"

Example 2: *"Many men and women do not fully participate in the political system."*
- These types of statements result in the reader asking questions such as "So what? So, why should we worry about that? How many? What is considered full participation? Which political system?"

Not Unified (NU)

These types of thesis sentences typically attempt to link two different ideas without suggesting how they are related.

Example: *"Workplace participation can help reinforce democratic values even if people do not vote."*
- Such thesis sentences result in the reader asking questions like "What does this mean? Does one part cause the other?"

Too Factual or Obvious (TF)

These types of thesis sentences typically declare or assert some opinion or perspective that is not controversial.

Example: *"Automatic voting registration would require the government to spend money."*
- Such thesis sentences result in the reader asking questions like "What will the rest of the paper be about? So, tell me something I do not know!"

Recognizing and Writing a Good Paragraph

Paragraph construction in expository or argumentative writing is both similar to and different from other kinds of writing, such as technical or creative writing. All types of writing use the same grammatical rules for sentence and paragraph structure. Nevertheless, the paragraphs and the sentences within the paragraphs constructed for expository writing must logically and functionally relate to one another. This is not always the case in creative or even technical writing.

Functions of a Paragraph

All paragraphs do not function in the same way nor do they have the same properties.

There are three types of paragraphs:

- Introductory paragraphs
- Supporting or explanatory paragraphs in the body
- Concluding or summary paragraphs

Each of these types of paragraphs has a special job to do in communicating the writer's goals and ideas to the reader. There is no absolute number of paragraphs required for supporting an introductory paragraph. The following diagram shows the introductory thesis paragraph supported by three explanatory paragraphs for illustrative purposes only.

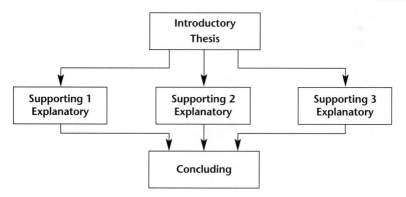

Properties of an Introductory or Opening Paragraph

An opening paragraph should capture the reader's attention and interest in the topic, specify what the writer will be discussing, and set the tone, direction, scope, and content of the essay or paper. An opening paragraph should contain at least three sentences, including:

- A general statement (a topic or thesis sentence)
- A clarifying sentence
- An explanatory sentence

The best opening paragraph begins with a general statement, followed by a clarifying statement or two, and ends with the thesis sentence.

Advice for Constructing Introductory Paragraphs

Try one of these ways of constructing the first paragraph:

- State the subject.
- Use a meaningful or thought-provoking quotation.
- Ask a question.
- Make a historical comparison or contrast.
- State an important fact.

DO NOT use these methods in an introductory paragraph:

- Vague generalities
- "The purpose of . . ." in the first line
- The title of the paper in the first line
- "According to . . ." in the first line
- Truisms and statements of the obvious

Example: Introductory Paragraph (Sullivan 1988)

The political dynasty, in the American context, is an organization usually centered on a family that transcends traditional norms in campaign and voter perception. By transcending these norms, the dynasty develops the image of American "royalty." The Kennedy and Rockefeller families have evolved as the most dominant examples of political dynasties in the twentieth century. The phenomena, as evidenced in these examples, appear to center around one individual and build from there. Once established, this mutation of American politics becomes its own organization, nearly independent of their respective parties in power and strategy. Even though the later elements of the dynasty benefit from their link to the overall public perception, they are, at times, mistakenly associated and credited with the dynasty's accomplishments as well.

Properties of a Concluding Paragraph

A concluding paragraph is not just the last paragraph; it concludes or summarizes the author's main points, completes the writer's thoughts about the topic, and ties the ending to the beginning of the paper or essay. The concluding paragraph must contain at least three sentences:

- A general statement
- A clarifying sentence
- An explanatory sentence

The best concluding paragraph restates the thesis and summarizes the evidence.

Advice for Constructing Concluding or Closing Paragraphs

Use these methods to construct a closing paragraph:

- Summarize the paper's main assertions or points.
- Clarify, qualify, and restate the main issues.
- Answer the question asked in the introduction.
- Suggest a course of action based on the evidence.

DO NOT use these methods to construct a closing paragraph:

- New arguments or information
- Restating the introduction.
- Concluding more than is reasonable from the material and arguments presented in the paper
- Apologizing for materials or views presented

Example: Concluding Paragraph (Sullivan 1988)

The success of the Kennedy and the Rockefeller families, as two prime examples of American dynasties, exemplifies the primary political dynamics that are essential to being part of American political life. These dynamics are instant name recognition for family members, instant empathy from the electorate for the family member's position on issues, nonrational voting based on residual biases associated with the family, and ability to exhibit independence from party politics. The practical effect of establishing a political dynasty is political survival. The societal effect is much less noticeable; political dynasties package political change as familial continuity and thus provide for the survival of their family's influence as well as goals for society. Because of this, political dynasties built in the past shape present political life and have uncommon influence over the America's destiny.

Properties of a Paragraph in the Body of the Paper

The paragraphs in the body of the written work function to support the thesis sentence and explain the writer's perspective on the topic in detail.

- The paragraphs in the body of the work help to break down the thesis sentence into subtopics and ideas.
- The paragraphs in the body of the work break down the central point or thesis into manageable parts, discuss each part, and relate each part to the others.
- Because the writer makes a commitment to the reader in the thesis sentence, paragraphs that follow must inform readers by filling in details, supporting claims, and giving examples.

Each Paragraph Must Contain Three Types of Sentences

- A general statement or topic sentence
- A specific or clarifying and limiting sentence
- A sentence that provides details or examples

Example: Paragraph for the Body of the Paper (Sullivan 1988)

Each political dynasty, however, is different; each dynasty has its own dynamics that separates it from the rest of the political community. The Kennedys, for example, are a nationally recognized political family even though the family center or core is in Massachusetts. The Rockefellers, while equally nationally known, have spread their political dominance over the governor mansions in New York, Arkansas, and West Virginia (Salmore 1989, 125). While both families exhibited a drive for dominance, the political bases of their influence span the spectrum from highly centralized to decentralized (Clinch 1973, x).

Properties of a Topic Sentence

Every paragraph, except the paragraph that holds the thesis sentence, needs a topic sentence. Like a thesis sentence, a topic sentence states the central idea and the writer's perspective about it. Topic sentences, however, elaborate on parts of the thesis sentence in the body of the paper. In particular, the topic sentence states the main idea of the paragraph, and every sentence following it supports that one idea.

Where to Place the Topic Sentence

Most of the time the topic sentence is placed at the beginning of the paragraph. Sometimes, writers put the topic sentence at the end of the paragraph. The structure of the rest of the paragraph depends on where the topic sentence is placed.

Try thinking of a paragraph as a car, a stick-shift vehicle used to get an idea or point to the reader. If the topic sentence is placed at the beginning, then downshift. If it is placed at the end, then shift up. Upshifting cars with stick shifts without enough speed results in the car losing power. Downshifting too fast results in grinding the gears and may damage the transmission.

A Visual of the Two Patterns of Paragraph Construction

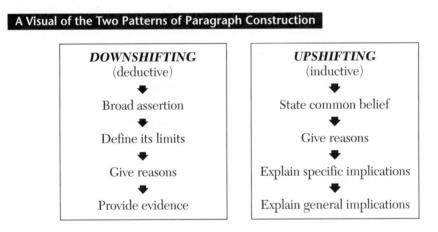

DOWNSHIFTING (deductive)	**UPSHIFTING** (inductive)
⬇	⬇
Broad assertion	State common belief
⬇	⬇
Define its limits	Give reasons
⬇	⬇
Give reasons	Explain specific implications
⬇	⬇
Provide evidence	Explain general implications

Writing a good explanatory paragraph takes as much skill and attention as shifting a car. Just as a car's transmission can be damaged by improper shifting, the "transmission" of an argument to the reader can be equally damaged by improper shifting from idea to evidence to conclusion. Clearly state the idea in a topic sentence, support the topic sentence with explanatory and supporting sentences (at least one), and resolve the paragraph with a sentence.

Be careful! Shifting from an idea or belief to a resolution without explaining the point clearly will weaken the assertion and the general argument will lose power. Shifting from a broad assertion to a resolution without limiting the assertion and backing it up with evidence may bring the argument to a grinding halt. Political scientists are in the business of communicating and evaluating information. Writers must be careful that ideas or points are not lost in the transmission due to poor explanatory paragraph development.

Tips for Reasoning Once the Topic Sentence Has Been Placed in a Paragraph

When Placed at the Beginning of a Paragraph:

- The topic sentence is the first sentence when it introduces a general point or idea.
- It is the second sentence when the author has made a transition from one point to the next. The first sentence in this case is a transition sentence.
- Writers must use deductive reasoning for constructing the rest of the paragraph.
- This means that the topic sentence will make a broad statement that is then supported, enriched, and expanded by other sentences.

Example: Topic Sentence at the Beginning of the Paragraph (Sullivan 1988)

Although political dynasties may benefit similarly from the same sources of power, the political bases of their influence span the spectrum from highly centralized to decentralized (Clinch 1989, x). Each political dynasty is different. Each dynasty has its own dynamics that separates it from the rest of the political community. The Kennedys, for example, are a nationally recognized political family even though the family center or core is in Massachusetts. The Rockefellers, while equally nationally known, have spread their political dominance over the governor mansions in New York, Arkansas, and West Virginia (Salmore 1989, 125).

When Placed at the End of a Paragraph:

- The topic sentence is the last sentence when it makes a general statement about the implications of an idea or point.
- Writers must use inductive reasoning for constructing the rest of the paragraph.
- This means that the topic sentence will make an assertion about how some specific idea applies generally.
- This method requires a climactic order, from least important to most important, from most familiar to least familiar, or from simple to complex supporting reasons or examples.

Example: Topic Sentence at the End of a Paragraph (Sullivan 1988)

Each political dynasty, however, is different. Each dynasty has its own dynamics that separates it from the rest of the political community. The Kennedys, for example, are a nationally recognized political family even though the family center or core is in Massachusetts. The Rockefellers, while equally nationally known, have spread their political dominance over the governor mansions in New York, Arkansas, and West Virginia (Salmore 1989, 125). While both families exhibited a drive for dominance, the political bases of their influence, however, span the spectrum from highly centralized to decentralized (Clinch 1989, x).

Advice for Constructing Paragraphs in the Body of the Paper

Use a commitment and response pattern for paragraphs.

1. Make a commitment in the topic sentence to a controlling idea or claim
2. Then, make sure each sentence in the paragraph contributes to explaining and supporting that idea.
3. DOWNSHIFT! When all else fails, start general and get specific.

ALWAYS ALWAYS ALWAYS Use a Topic Sentence

1. Make a point in one sentence with a single descriptive, judgemental, or argumentative idea in a declarative statement.
2. In the draft copy of the paper, highlight the topic sentence in every paragraph.
3. Then, make sure each sentence in the paragraph says something about the point made in the topic sentence.

Use Transitions

Use transition sentences and transitional words or phrases to keep the paragraph unified and coherent. These link ideas together between sentences or between paragraphs. (See the section "List of Transitional Expressions.")

1. **Vary sentence structures and styles by using transitional words and phrases to keep the ideas in the paragraph coherently linked together.**
   - Repeat important words; use synonyms.
   - Use connecting words such as *however, for example.*
   - Use pointer words such as *first, second*, and *finally* to keep track of supporting ideas.
2. **Provide a bridge between the current paragraph and the previous paragraph with transitional sentences.**
   - Transitional sentences help the writer make a change in direction without losing the reader.
   - Transitional sentences point back to the previous idea and forward to the new one at the same time.
   - A major change in direction may require more than one transitional sentence.
   - The topic sentence then comes after the transitional sentence.
   - All supporting information comes after the transitional sentences.

List of Transitional Expressions

The following terms should be used to link sentences together within a paragraph. Most are used at the beginning of a sentence. Some terms, such as *however*, should be used only within a sentence; for example: "This policy, however, failed to remedy the problem of malnutrition." (Adapted from Fowler and Aaron 1989, 95–96.)

To add or show sequence: again, also, and, and then, besides, equally important, finally, first, further, furthermore, in addition, in the first place, last, moreover, next, second, still, too

To compare: also, in the same way, likewise, similarly

To contrast: although, and yet, but, but at the same time, despite, even so, even though, for all that, however, in contrast, in spite of, nevertheless, notwithstanding, on the contrary, on the other hand, regardless, still, though, yet

To give examples or intensify: after all, an illustration of, even, for example, for instance, indeed, in fact, it is true, of course, specifically, that is, to illustrate, truly

To indicate place: above, adjacent to, below, elsewhere, farther on, here, near, nearby, on the other side, there, opposite to, to the east, to the left

To indicate time: after a while, afterward, as long as, as soon as, at last, at length, at that time, before, earlier, formerly, immediately, in the meantime, in the past, lately, later, meanwhile, now, presently, shortly, simultaneously, since, so far, soon, subsequently, then, thereafter, until, until now, when

To repeat, summarize, or conclude: all in all, altogether, as has been said, in brief, in conclusion, in other words, in particular, in short, in simpler terms, in summary, on the whole, that is, therefore, to put it differently, to summarize

To show cause or effect: accordingly, as a result, because, consequently, for this purpose, hence, otherwise, then, therefore, thereupon, thus, to this end, with this object

Do Not Use These Methods To Begin a Topic Sentence

- A proper name (such as Bill Clinton was . . .)
- A date (September 11, 2001 is . . .)
- Because or Since
- A prediction
- A question
- Statistics or an undisputed fact
- Truisms (obvious truth) or definitions
- An irrelevant detail

Common Problems in Constructing Paragraphs

Here are some common problems that students have experienced with paragraphs. An instructor may use an acronym to signify these problems.

Not Unified (NU)

Paragraphs exhibiting this problem usually include an idea or point that is unrelated to the topic sentence.

- These paragraphs are not focused on a central point.
- The reader will typically ask the question, "How does this contribute to the central point (topic sentence)?"

NU Example: *"The structure of our federalist government has influenced the ways people act in society today. It helps to set the standards that influence people's lifestyles. It is not only one person who enforces these rules but a set of institutions. In our society, the people elect representatives to these institutions that shape and enforce the rules of the government."*

Problem: It includes points and ideas that are unrelated to the topic sentence.

Solution: Take out all sentences and information that do not directly contribute to the central point made in the topic sentence. In this case, that is everything after the second sentence.

Incoherent (IC)

Paragraphs exhibiting this problem usually have sentences that do not establish a clear relationship between ideas or points.

- These paragraphs are generally confusing because the writer has not linked the sentences together logically or functionally.
- The reader will typically ask the question, "How do the sentences relate to the main topic or to one another?"

IC Example: *"The goal of regulating national powers became mandatory for the framers. The national government, like the state and local government, has three law-making bodies: the executive, the legislative, and judicial branches of government. The president makes up the executive branch. Congress makes up the legislative branch, and the Supreme Court makes up the judicial branch."*

Problem: The sentences do not establish a clear relationship between the ideas or points.

Solution: Use transitional expressions to link important ideas and sentences together. In this case, we could say, "one way the framers sought to achieve this goal was to divide. . . . For example. . . ."

Too Long (LG)

Paragraphs exhibiting this problem usually encompass more than one idea.

- The writer has failed to communicate the main point of the paragraph clearly and confuses the reader.
- The reader will generally ask the question, "Which point does the information support?"

LG Example: *"The U.S. constitution and tradition provide the office of the presidency with many powers and responsibilities. His role represents a fusion of the stature of a king and the power of a prime minister. While his role as the symbolic leader of the nation provides him societal support, the president's veto power also gives him much influence over the congressional agenda. The persuasive ability of the individual holding the office of the presidency also contributes to the president's power. The ability of the president to harness and focus competing groups inside and outside of the government, especially in Congress, greatly influences his effectiveness in promoting his agenda. To be effective, the president must be able to persuade others to follow his lead."*

Problem: The paragraph tries to cover more than one main idea.

Solution: Break up the paragraph where the sentences change in time, place, direction, focus, or emphasis. In this case, break the paragraph before the sentence concerning the president's persuasive abilities.

Too Short (ST)

Paragraphs exhibiting this problem fragment an idea between two or more paragraphs. Often these paragraphs are only one or two lines long.

- The writer fails to establish the main point of the paragraph and/or does not support the point with sufficient evidence or limiting information.
- The reader will generally ask the question, "What is the point of giving me this information?"

ST Example: *"Media, interest groups, and political parties become important political influences on mass attitudes. Even if at times they are criticized, our political system would not work as well without them."*

Problem: The paragraph is too short. It does not make a point, nor does it follow through with evidence and supporting information.

Solution: Expand on the central idea expressed in the topic sentence by including additional limiting information, evidence, or examples. In this case, expand on the desirable and undesirable ways that media, interest groups, and political parties similarly influence mass attitudes.

First Aid for Bad Paragraphs

Break up long paragraphs wherever the sentences in the paragraph shift in time, place, direction, focus, or emphasis.

1. **Remember: use only one main point or idea per paragraph.**
2. **A unified, coherent paragraph is usually no longer than half of a typed, double-spaced page with 1-inch margins.**
3. **A quick way to tell visually if paragraphs are too long:**
   - Measure—if a paragraph is longer than 5 inches, then it is too long. Keep an 8"-by-5" index card handy to use as a template to measure during revision.
   - There should be at least two paragraphs on a typed, double-spaced page.

Develop the ideas in a short paragraph or combine the paragraph with adjacent paragraphs.

1. **If the paragraph makes a point that is different from those of previous and following paragraphs, then:**
   - Develop the idea sufficiently by narrowing the assertion.
   - Provide evidence to support the topic sentence.
2. **If the paragraph does not make a point that is different from those of previous and following paragraphs, then:**
   - Identify the topic sentence in each of the previous and following paragraphs.
   - Identify which topic sentence would be best supported by the information provided in the short paragraph.
   - Merge the short paragraph with that paragraph.
3. **A quick way to tell visually if paragraphs are too short:**
   - If a paragraph is smaller than the width of two fingers placed side by side, then it is too short.
   - There should be no more than three paragraphs on a typed, double-spaced page.
   - If a paragraph is only three lines long, then it is too short.
   - If a paragraph does not contain at least three sentences (a topic, a specific, and an explanatory sentence), then it is too short.

CHAPTER 7

COMMON WRITING PROBLEMS

Common Stylistic Problems

Although some stylistic problems are particular to the individual writer, many are common to even some of the best writers. Good writing requires diligence and persistence in learning to recognize functional errors. Although stylistic problems are not the primary cause of poor communication of ideas, they interfere in the relationship between the writer and the reader. Stylistic problems create confusion at best, and at their worst, they reflect negatively on the writer's credibility. (See *The Elements of Style* by William Strunk Jr. and E. B. White for an excellent discussion of how to identify and correct stylistic problems.)

Misinterpreting the Audience

Students must define their audience before putting even one word on a page. Letters written to a friend, a senator, a parent, and a judge differ in tone, content, and mutual expectations. This is true of academic writing as well.

Avoid the following in written assignments:
- Students should not assume that the audience is composed of friends or relatives. This encourages familiar, informal, and pedestrian writing.
- Students should not write for themselves. This encourages incomplete thought and shallow explanations.

Target the following audiences when writing a paper for a class:
- Students should write for scholars in the field. This encourages approaching the assignment in a professional way.
- Students should write for the professor and keep in mind what his or her expectations and objectives are for the assignment.
- Students should write for the class as well as for the professor. This will keep the student's approach at a less pompous level than it might be if written for the professor alone.
- Students should write for the intelligent nonspecialist. This will keep the student's writing approachable, clear but not simplistic.

Using the Wrong Voice

Students should approach their assignments in a serious, thoughtful, respectful, and professional way. The voice for an assignment should be formal, unless the professor directs otherwise.

Choose the appropriate approach for the scope and nature of the assignment: Some assignments may involve multiple approaches.
- **Descriptive:** Use this approach when writing about the present or past but the focus is on providing factual information or explaining information or events. These are simple descriptions of the context or characteristics of events such as *"Labor leaders expressed concern about the decline in worker benefits over the past two years."*
- **Predictive:** Use this approach when arguing the likelihood of an event occurring in the future. Most of these assertions include phrases or words indicating causally related actions (including "will" or "leads to"), such as *"Without additional program funding, the problem will continue to worsen."*
- **Evaluative:** Use this approach when providing a statement based on values, not facts, about whether an event is good or bad. Most of these assertions include a value judgment expressed by an emotive modifier before or after a verb or noun, such as *"Infants are dying needlessly from poor nutrition"* or *"Working mothers are in an appalling position."* The words *needlessly* and *appalling* are value expressions that transform the sentence from being descriptive to evaluative.
- **Prescriptive:** Use this approach when providing a statement prescribing or encouraging an action. Most of these statements include words such as *must* or *should*, for example *"Government officials must address the education funding for disadvantaged students."*

Avoid the following in written assignments:
- Students should not use colloquial language, such as *"The senator gave the majority leader the slip on that piece of legislation."*

- Students should not preface opinions or assertions with a first-person reference. Statements such as *"It is my opinion that . . .,"* or *"I believe that . . .,"* or *"I can only conclude that . . ."* are inappropriate and weaken the arguments.

- Students should not use contractions in written work. Such words as *don't, won't, didn't, she'd,* and *can't,* although technically correct, reduce writing to an informal or pedestrian level.

- Students must never use vulgar, profane, or obscene language or references in written work. Statements such as *"The senator really kicked butt on the floor"* have no place in professional writing. This type of language weakens the credibility of the author as well as the argument.

Linguistic Bias

Racial, class, and sexual stereotyping have no place in academic writing. These kinds of linguistic biases demean individuals and weaken the writer's arguments. Unfortunately, it is difficult to break old habits. Although linguistic biases may not be intentional, students should carefully edit to avoid the most obvious linguistic biases (see Ward 1990, 1–5, 29–32, Appendix 4).

Avoid problems of linguistic bias by:

1. Referring to race in a socially acceptable manner.

- Attach the word *American* when referring to an individual's heritage. For example, use *African American* to refer to U.S. citizens of African heritage.
- *Black* is still acceptable in referring to people of African heritage.
- *Minorities* and *people of color* are acceptable in referring to people who are not of Caucasian heritage residing in the United States.

2. Refer to the problems of the poor or disadvantaged as a problem of society, not as a character flaw in individuals belonging to that class.

- Avoid overgeneralizing about preferences and characteristics of individuals classified based on social or economic criteria.
- Avoid attributing problems experienced by one set of people as a class problem.

3. Change the structure of sentences and terminology to reflect gender-neutral language.

- Substitute a plural for a gender pronoun or alternate between female and male pronouns.
- Substitute the words *someone, anyone, person,* or *people* for references to men and women in general (such as "people who become police officers . . .").
- Refer to people by occupation or role only (such as "parents are concerned about child care . . .").
- Use more specific terms rather than the suffix "man" to refer to people's occupations (such as "members of Congress" rather than "congressmen").
- Avoid using *man* as a catch-all term to refer to a group (such as "all men were created equal").
- Avoid descriptions that imply stereotypical behavior (such as "rugged men" and "delicate women").

Punctuation

Issues of punctuation plague us all. The best way to properly punctuate is to keep sentences simple. Long, complex sentences are difficult to read and comprehend. Sometimes it is necessary, though, to create complex sentences. Punctuation, then, provides the mechanism for helping the reader absorb the complexities of the thought the sentence represents.

Capitalization: Capitalize proper nouns (names of people, places, and things, e.g., *Alabama*) and proper adjectives (adjectives created from proper nouns (e.g., *American* flag). In general, capitalize titles, any geographic location, names of organizations, names of types of people (race, ethnicity).

Colon: Use a colon when introducing a list or description of items. Whenever possible, the list or description should be a complete sentence.

Semicolon: Use a semicolon in a sentence to connect two complete thoughts directly. Both parts of the sentence must be complete sentences as well.

Commas: Use a comma to punctuate complex sentences that include either descriptive clauses or a series of information.

Apostrophes: An apostrophe is used for two reasons: Either to show possession for a noun (e.g., *dog's bone*) or to indicate a contraction (e.g., *won't*). Pronouns (such as *she* or *it*) never use apostrophes to show possession. The only time a pronoun appears with an apostrophe is to indicate a contraction (*she's* for *she is*, *it's* for *it is*).

Common Errors: Proofreading the Manuscript

Proofreading is essential for catching typographical, spelling, usage, and grammatical errors. But proofreading can also catch omissions and errors related to the standards and requirements set by the instructor.

1. Complying with the specific requests of the instructor is important for receiving full credit for research and writing efforts.
2. Good writing skills and good presentation skills are not the same.
   - Writing is a creative activity.
   - Good presentation is a mechanical activity—it is simple compliance and attention to detail.
3. Poor presentation of the written material diminishes the quality of the manuscript as a product of the writer.
   - A poorly proofed manuscript impinges on credibility.
   - A sloppy manuscript implies sloppy research as well.
   - Attention to detail implies that the writer is thoughtful and thorough.

Tips on Proofing Papers

Choose someone, preferably from class, to be a draft partner.
- Make a common list of the requirements for the assignment.
- Trade drafts of manuscripts and read them in the presence of one another.

- Check for compliance to the minimum requirements.
- Check the logical development of arguments and presentation of evidence.
- Discuss inconsistencies with each other.

Reread the manuscript as well.
- Address all criticisms by the draft partner.
- Ask the instructor for clarification of requirements and issues on which there is disagreement.

Once the minimum requirements are met, proofread for typographical, spelling, usage, and grammatical errors.

1. *Read the corrected draft aloud.* Typographical, spelling, usage, and grammatical errors are more noticeable when the text is read aloud. Reading the text aloud and from the last sentence to the first sentence (if you can stand it!) allows students to disconnect from the substance of the paper and focus on proper usage, spelling, and grammar.

2. *Spelling is a talent, not a skill.* Those less talented in spelling should take heart from the following comment by Mark Twain and then do the following:

   > To spell correctly is a talent, not an acquirement. There is some dignity about an acquirement, because it is a product of your own labor.... [To] do a thing merely by [grace] where possibly it is a matter of pride and satisfaction,... leaves you naked and bankrupt (Twain 1961, 27).

   Spell checker: When using a word processor, use the spell checker. Spell checkers identify typographical or spelling errors as long as the error is not a real word. Spell checkers are not foolproof, but generally keep writers from making fools of themselves with typographical and spelling errors!

   "i" before "e": The most common spelling error is found in words containing "ei" or "ie," Remember that the letter "i" comes before the letter "e" except when these letters follow the letter "c." The word is spelled with an "ei" when the letter "c" precedes this vowel combination.

   Keep a list of your most common spelling errors: Search the text for these words and double-check the spelling.

   Keep a dictionary and a thesaurus handy: If a dictionary search is unsuccessful, look up a synonym (a word that has a similar meaning) in a thesaurus. Usually, the word will be listed in the thesaurus.

   Spelling aids: For those who have great difficulty with spelling but cannot use a spell checker, there are several handy spelling aids. Buy the following inexpensive tools:

   - A *Bad Speller's* or *Misspeller's Dictionary.* These dictionaries list the words as they are commonly pronounced (or mispronounced) phonetically, or as they are most commonly misspelled; then they provide the correct spelling.
   - A *Word Book* or *Expression Locator.* A *Word Book* is simply a list of words spelled and divided. An *Expression Locator* has the words spelled, divided, and in the context in which they are frequently used.

Ask for help: If none of these tools is available or useful, either ask someone or choose a synonym to replace the word! Do not purposely leave a spelling error uncorrected.

3. *Usage problems are different from spelling problems.* Usage problems are errors in word choice. Also avoid big words when small, common words express ideas clearly. (See *The Elements of Style* by William Strunk Jr. and E. B. White for an excellent discussion.) Listed here are commonly misused words or phrases.

However: For example, the word *however* is often used at the beginning of a sentence and as a substitute for *nevertheless*. This is incorrect. The word *however* should separate two independent clauses and be preceded and followed by a comma.

- *However* is used best as follows: *"Voting is not only a right but it is also a choice. Citizens are, however, losing an important opportunity to shape the policy when they do not vote."*
- *However* is appropriately used at the beginning of the sentence when it means "in whatever way": *"However candidates deliver their messages, they provide voters a perspective on their character."*

Since: The word *since* is often used to suggest a reason and as a substitute for *because*. This is incorrect.

- The word *since* is used to designate a time-dependent or temporal relationship.
- The word *because* is used to designate a causal relationship.

Affect or Effect: *Affect* and *effect* are often used interchangeably. This is incorrect.

- The word *affect* is a verb that means "to influence."
- The word *effect*, as a verb, means "to bring about, to accomplish."
- The word *effect*, as a noun, means "result."

In order to, in order for: The phrase *in order to* is often used instead of a simple *to* or *for*. This is incorrect.

- The phrases *"in order to"* and *"in order for"* include unnecessary words.
- Shorten the phrase from *"He stopped in order to help the woman"* to *"He stopped to help the woman."*

Today, Currently, Presently: These words are often used to indicate that some event is occurring in the present time. This is incorrect.

- The words *today, currently,* or *presently* are colloquial uses of the words and are imprecise references to time; each word implies that the event is happening now, at this moment.
- Avoid the words *today, currently,* or *presently* and provide instead a more direct time reference. Change *"The problem continues today"* to *"Since 1998, there have been no changes in the status of the problem."*

4. *Rewrite passive, negative, vague, and/or ambiguous statements.* As much as possible, write sentences, especially topic sentences, in active voice and make positive assertions phrased in concrete, specific words.

Active versus Passive Voice: The active voice is direct and is characterized by energetic word choice. The passive voice is indirect and leads to lethargic phrasing that connects words by using *to, of, by, was, were, are, has been,* or *there is.* In passive sentences, the action often takes place at the end of the sentence and is not clearly related to the subject.

- Passive voice obscures causation or what happened. Look for ways to formulate the sentence so that the topic of the sentence is at the beginning and the action is clearly focused on the topic directly. Identify what or who is taking action and make that the subject of the sentence, then change the verb to match the action taken by the subject.

- For example, *"The presidential primaries are dominated by southern voters"* can be transformed into an active statement focusing the action at the beginning: *"Southern voters dominate the presidential primaries."*

Negative, noncommittal (vague or ambiguous) language. Avoid evasive language, especially the use of *not,* to avoid asserting the active, positive event. For example, the sentence *"The policy's impact does not seem to create the desired effect"* is negative and vague. Changing the sentence to positive, concrete language creates an assertive statement; for example: *"The goal of the policy was to lower crime, yet the crime rate increased."* The "desired effect" is now a clear statement of the goals and the "impact" is now clearly identified as a crime rate increase.

5. ***Clean up questionable grammar.*** Good grammar is an acquired skill. It is acquired through careful attention to placement of commas, tense agreement, and verb-noun agreement.

Grammar Checker: When using a word processing program, use the grammar checker. Grammar checkers identify usage errors in sentence structure. They are not foolproof but they identify long sentences, wordiness, sentence fragments, improper punctuation, improper word use, and verb-noun disagreements.

- **Caution:** Not every error identified by these programs is really an error. Students must know what is and is not proper usage.

- In general, even when the program identifies a problem in a sentence that is not really a problem, usually some awkward, vague, or ambiguous language triggered the program's response. Take a serious look at any sentence targeted by the program and find a way to rewrite the sentence so that it no longer triggers an error response.

Commas: Commas are required between two or more words modifying a noun, between lists of items in a series, between compound sentences, before and/or after transitional words, and between descriptive phrases.

- A rule of thumb when reading the text aloud: If one pauses in reading the sentence, the sentence probably needs a comma wherever the pause occurred.

- Usage guides typically have sections on rules for commas, periods, and other forms of punctuation. When in doubt, look it up.

Tense: A common problem in writing is switching from the present to the past or future tense in the middle of a sentence or paragraph.

- Use verbs such as *was, is, were, have, had,* and *has* appropriately to agree with the tense chosen for the paragraph or paper.

- Make sure words ending in "-ed" are used appropriately to agree with the tense of the paragraph or paper.

Verb-Noun Agreement: Verb-noun agreement is essential to clarity of expression. Verb-noun agreement requires that the activity associated with the noun is clearly one that can be done by the noun.

- For example, *"our government makes policies . . ."* and *"the institution produced . . ."* are incorrect. Governments and institutions are things that are acted upon; they cannot act. People make policies but policies are made in government institutions.
- A rule of thumb: People act; things and places are acted upon. If the noun is a thing or place, then avoid language that suggests that things and places are responsible for some action.

How to Use a Writing Center

Most universities have a writing center or lab for students who need assistance in completing their writing assignments. Knowing what the writing center can and cannot do helps students use the resource efficiently (Leahy 1990).

What Writing Centers Do

- Writing centers offer limited assistance to students who need help in picking topics and structuring papers.
- Writing centers can help students prepare for research by showing them ways to organize their thoughts.
- Writing centers assist students in the writing process.

What Writing Centers Will Not Do

- Writing center staff are not proofreaders. They can show a student how to proofread but they do not proofread papers.
- Writing centers typically do not offer remedial help for students who lack basic skills. Students with severe writing problems should take remedial classes in basic skills.

Using the Writing Center

All students should use the Writing Center at least once during the writing process. Professors are often too busy or too close to the assignment to give sufficient attention to students' individual writing problems. Students can best benefit when the Writing Center staff is seen as partners in a collaborative learning process.

1. Visit the Writing Center in the discovery phase of the research project. Ask the staff at the Writing Center to give suggestions on how to work through an idea or freewrite about a topic.
2. Construct a thesis sentence. Ask the Writing Center tutor to critique it for focus and specificity.
3. Construct a topic outline. Ask the Writing Center tutor to critique it for logical development.

4. Write a first draft. Ask the Writing Center tutor to critique it for logical development, coherence, and unity.

Online Writing Lab/Centers (OWL)

The Internet hosts numerous sites on writing research papers. Many of these sites are useful for quick information about referencing, usage, grammar, and style, but some are not much more than *fronts* offering term and research papers for "free" or for sale. **Do not use these.** Acquiring a paper from the Internet is inviting a poor grade at best or trouble over plagiarism at worst.

Generic Papers: Instructors will easily spot generic papers. Most instructors have specific guidelines and topics for their assignments.

Custom Ordered: Even papers supposedly "custom ordered" are easy to spot because the context of the research materials and the resulting paper do not reflect the instructor's course-specific context. Because students are taught the course material within the context of the instructor's individual style and perspective, their written papers generally reflect such a style and perspective.

Plagiarism Software: Many instructors are now acquiring software specifically designed to identify Internet plagiarism (cheating). Not only can the software detect plagiarism in commercially produced papers but it can also detect material that has been taken in whole or in part from the Internet.

There are numerous sites offering *ideas* for term and research papers. Be very careful about using these. Ask the instructor *before doing any research* if the topic or idea is appropriate for the assignment. There is nothing wrong with getting ideas from others.

Here are some useful sites for information about writing and editing:

Indispensable Writing Resources: This site provides information about resources on the Net that will help in writing or researching a paper. It includes links to reference materials, writing labs, and related sites. **http://www.stetson.edu/~rhansen/writing.html**

OWL Handouts (listed by topic): OWL handouts are indexed by topic, including one on general writing concerns. They also have information on planning/starting to write, effective writing revising/editing/proofreading, and types/genres of sentences. http://owl.english.purdue.edu/handouts/index2.html

Paradigm Online Writing Assistant: This site provides information about discovering, organizing, revising, and editing. http://www.powa.org/

The Writing Center: This site provides information on writing literature, research, and reviews. http://www.wisc.edu/writing/index.html

What to Do About Writer's Block

Writers of every variety, at one time or another, experience trouble getting started on their manuscripts. Starting the manuscript—putting those first few words on the page—is often a frustrating experience. Here are a few tips for breaking writer's block.

1. **Work with the research materials.**
   - Talk about the research and the topic with a friend.
   - Freewrite about the topic. Do not worry about organization, grammar, punctuation, or style. Write in a stream-of-consciousness style—write anything that comes to mind about the topic.
   - Examine the result of the freewriting. Using a cut-and-paste method, group ideas, arguments, and evidence together into broadly defined categories. Try to identify at least three categories. Often two categories are too broad and more than four are too narrow.

2. **There is no substitute for good research organization.**
   - Using the three or four broadly defined categories from the freewriting exercise, write a scratch outline, then a topic outline, and then a sentence outline.
   - On the sentence outline, match the research notes to the ideas, arguments, and evidence. Write the citation next to each of these.
   - After completing these steps, the materials will have been reviewed, organized, integrated, and synthesized to coordinate with the ideas and arguments.

3. **Now write.**
   - Use the first paragraph to quickly sketch a framework for the thesis sentence.
   - Do not linger over the first paragraph. If necessary, skip it altogether. Write the thesis sentence and begin a new paragraph, the first explanatory paragraph for the body of the work. Always return to the introduction and rewrite it after completing the conclusion.
   - Write without editing and critiquing the work as it progesses. Forget about grammar, structure, usage, and spelling. Concentrate on expressing the ideas.
   - Work as though writing a timed, in-class essay. Do not stop to mull over a point. If stuck on expressing an idea, write a note in the text to address this issue later and continue with the next point.
   - Continue working until completing a draft with a conclusion.
   - If there is enough time between the date of finishing the draft and the date the assignment is due, put the assignment away for at least a day.
   - Examine the research materials and supplement them, if necessary, to address the issues, arguments, and evidence that posed problems.
   - Examine the draft for logical development of ideas, be sure paragraphs exhibit a commitment and response pattern, expand paragraphs that are too short, break up paragraphs that are too long, and then write the introduction.
   - Now correct grammar, usage, and spelling.
   - Using the draft checklist, make sure the instructor's requirements have been fulfilled.
   - Rewrite and revise the second draft copy.

4. **Using the second draft, proofread to prepare the final copy using the tips for correcting for common errors described in the preceding pages.**

CHAPTER 8

MANUSCRIPT FORMAT AND REFERENCING STYLES

Although professors have their own preferences about how a paper should be presented, students should observe a few standards. Students should check their syllabus or hand-out concerning their written assignments for specific details. In general, instructors assign grades on the basis of whether the student met basic requirements for the paper, organization, and quality of sources used in the paper. The following example illustrates a common set of criteria used in an instructor's grading rubric. In addition, the research paper should be professionally presented.

Criteria for Grading a Research Paper

Minimum Requirements for Receiving Credit for the Paper
___ Did the student do the paper as assigned?
___ Did the student do his or her own work—no plagiarism?
___ Did the student meet the deadline for the paper?

Point Assignment for the Evaluation Criteria

Excellent = 5 Good = 4 Adequate = 3 Inadequate = 2 Unacceptable = 1

An A paper will accumulate a range of points from 100 to 90.

A B paper will accumulate a range of points from 89 to 80.

A C paper will accumulate a range of points from 79 to 70.

A D paper will accumulate a range of points from 69 to 60.

An F paper will accumulate a range of points from 59 to 20.

Criteria for Evaluation

___ Format of the manuscript conforms to the instructor's criteria.

___ Manuscript is well organized and well written.

___ Manuscript contains a thorough description of the background or context of the research topic.

___ There is a clear, well-developed thesis statement.

___ Manuscript presents a unique or interesting perspective on the topic.

___ There is a logical development of the argument.

___ Important supporting evidence, arguments, and perspectives concerning research topic are identified.

___ Important evidence and arguments concerning research topic that do not support student's view are identified.

___ All evidence, arguments, and perspectives presented concerning research topic are explained.

___ All evidence, arguments, and perspectives presented concerning research topic are critiqued.

___ Analysis reflects thorough understanding of the topic.

___ Student addressed all issues raised in the analysis.

___ There are no apparent factual errors.

___ There are very few spelling or grammatical errors.

___ Evidence, arguments, and ideas are well documented. If quotes are used, they are used correctly and sparingly.

___ Reference page is complete.

___ References and sources used were clearly relevant.

___ References and sources used were of high quality.

___ References and sources used exhibit depth and breadth.

___ References and sources used exhibit variety.

Standard Presentation of an Assignment

Text: Assignments should be typed, double-spaced, with 1-inch margins.

- Do not justify the right-hand margin. It is difficult to read and distracting.

- Do not double-space between the lines in the bibliography, only between references, unless instructed to do so.
- Each page should be numbered, except the title page, the abstract pages, and the executive summary.

Printing: The paper should look presentable.

- The paper should be printed on white bond paper. Recycled paper is fine as long as it is clean and unused.
- Use a new or full ink cartridge and set the printer on best quality. Do not use colored ink for the text.
- Never purposely turn in an assignment in which the type is barely readable.

Binding: The paper should be bound sensibly.

- The simplest and best method of binding the paper is with a staple in the upper left-hand corner.
- Unless the instructor indicates otherwise, do not use paper clips, folders, multiple staples along the edge, or binders of any kind.

Good Habits:

- **Always always always** make a photocopy of the paper or print an extra copy. Store the computer file on two forms of media (hard drive, USB drive, and/or disk, for example)—papers get lost. When uploading the file to a server, a Web page, or a Web site, make sure to save a copy of any confirmation received of a successful upload. Papers also get lost in this process as well.
- Rewrite at least once before turning in the paper.
- Learn to use a word processing program well.
- Keep all parts of the paper in a single file; students commonly keep title, graphics, and reference pages in separate files and then forget to print all parts of the paper or fail to number their pages coherently.
- **Never never never** wait until the night before to type the paper. Printers fail and computer files get lost at the stroke of midnight; these are common and unconvincing excuses for late papers.
- Avoid overquoting. A rule of thumb: do not use more than two quotes for every ten pages of text.
- Make sure that the work is well documented. A rule of thumb: make sure every paragraph of substantive secondary information has at least two references.

Format and Placement of Items in the Paper or Essay

A description of each of the items below can be found in the following pages. The descriptions of the format and placement of each item reflect the standard form across style guides. Check the style guide preferred or required by the instructor to verify that these suggestions conform to the standards set by the guide.

The Manuscript Should Include the Following Components:

- a title page
- an abstract or executive summary

- table of contents (for long papers)
- list of tables and figures (rarely necessary for short papers)
- headings and subheadings
- an appendix (when necessary)
- tables and figures (when necessary)
- parenthetical (author-date references), footnote, *or* endnote citations
- explanatory notes (when necessary)
- quotations (only when absolutely necessary)
- a bibliography (when using citation footnotes or endnotes, or reference page for author-date referencing)

Placement of Items in the Manuscript:

1. Title page
2. Table of contents and/or list of tables and figures (if required, and beginning on a separate page, not included in page numbering)
3. Abstract page or executive summary (if required, and beginning on a separate page, not included in page numbering)
4. Text (identify parts of text by using headings and subheadings), for example:
   - Introduction
   - Explanation or Background or Literature Review
   - Method or Test of Argument or Reasons
   - Results or Linking of Argument with Evidence
   - Conclusion or Summary
5. Appendix (after last sentence of the body and beginning on a separate page for each type of document, usually labeled Appendix A, Appendix B)
6. Explanatory Notes (beginning on a separate page if using endnote style)
7. References (beginning on a separate page)
8. Tables
9. Figures

Format for the Title Page

1. The title of the paper should be centered and 2 inches above the middle of the page (the title should not be longer than 12 words).
2. The student's name should be 2 inches from the bottom of the page.
3. The course number and professor's name should be under the student's name.
4. The date should be under the professor's name.

Example: Title Page

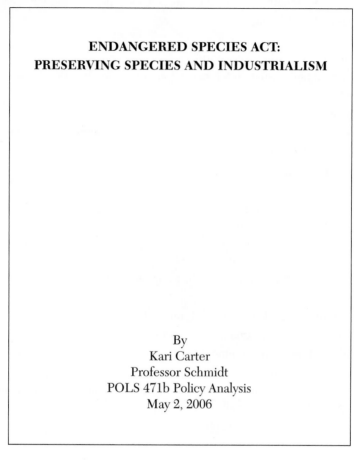

ENDANGERED SPECIES ACT:
PRESERVING SPECIES AND INDUSTRIALISM

By
Kari Carter
Professor Schmidt
POLS 471b Policy Analysis
May 2, 2006

Format for an Abstract

1. The abstract should be on a separate page following the title page.

2. Do not number the abstract page.

3. There are only two parts to an abstract: the title and the text.

4. The word *Abstract* is used as a title and is centered at the top of the page. Double-space before writing the text of the abstract.

5. The abstract should summarize the paper in 150 words or less in one paragraph that is at least four sentences long. (See Chapter 11 for example as part of a paper.)

6. The abstract is not an introduction. It should include, in order:

- A description of the nature of the problem
- A description of the major points and thesis
- A description of the methods or evidence used
- A description of the major conclusions reached

7. The abstract should not contain direct quotations from the text or references.

8. The abstract must use proper sentence structure and grammar.

9. Keep the ideas and main points identified in the abstract in the same order as they are presented in the paper.

10. The abstract may be double- or single-spaced.

Tips for Writing an Abstract

- Read the paper carefully.
- Summarize the focus of the introductory paragraph in one sentence.
- Write down the main points.
- For each point, describe the evidence used to support the point.
- Summarize the focus of the concluding paragraph in one sentence.
- Use this information to write the abstract.
- Use transitions to link the ideas together.

Example: Abstract

Civic engagement as a concept in Political Science courses is intrinsically focused on the study of the politics rather than actions which instill civic responsiveness. This paper examines models for infusing practical civic engagement into learning experiences inside or outside the classroom setting of Political Science students. Using a meta-analysis of different approaches, both theoretical and applied, this research analysis creates a typology of civic engagement models that particularly address issues of building sustainable communities. Notably, this research identifies the relative benefits of different types of approaches for fostering civic engagement. More importantly, this research examines collaborative relationships between the university and community organizations for reinforcing civic responsibility and engagement.

Format for an Executive Summary

1. The executive summary should be on a separate page following the title page.

2. Do not number the executive summary page.

3. There are only four components to an executive summary: the title, the purpose, the methodology, and the findings. (See Chapter 12 for examples.)

4. The words *Executive Summary* are used as a title and are centered at the top of the page. Double-space before writing the descriptions of the purpose, methodology, and findings sections.

5. The executive summary is not an introduction. For a short, simple study, the executive summary should summarize the paper in about a single-spaced page for a short paper. For a short paper, it should include:

- A description of the purpose of the study—about one paragraph
- A description of how the study was conducted—about two paragraphs
- A description of the major findings—a one- to two-sentence generalization with the specific findings *listed with bullets or numbering.*

6. For more in-depth studies, the executive summary should be longer and include headings and subheadings to indicate the different parts of the analysis. Use bullets or numbering to summarize main points and findings in the analysis.

7. The executive summary should not contain direct quotations from the text.

8. The executive summary must use proper sentence structure and grammar.

9. Keep the ideas and main points identified in the executive summary in the same order as they are presented in the paper.

10. The executive summary may be double- or single-spaced. Usually, it is single-spaced.

Tips for Writing an Executive Summary

- Read the paper carefully.
- Summarize the focus of the introductory paragraph in one sentence.
- Describe how the study was conducted.
- For each finding, list the evidence used.
- Summarize the focus of the concluding paragraph in one sentence.
- Use this information to write an executive summary.
- Use transitions to link the ideas together.

Example: Executive Summary

EXECUTIVE SUMMARY

In developing environmental policy, government is faced with balancing the incompatibility of conservation and commerce. Industrialism is known for exploiting the environment at the expense of conservation and accordingly environmentalists strengthen the fight for environmental quality. Environmental quality is a concern for all individuals who desire to preserve a nation of natural amenities for future generations.

The Endangered Species Act (ESA) was developed to reverse the trend of disappearing species as a consequence of economic growth. Protecting endangered species is a valuable goal in the maintenance of ecosystems because biodiversity is an integral component of environmental sustainability. To this end, the ESA provided that a regulatory agency develop the tools necessary to protect endangered species.

The ESA was structured for species protection using the endangered species list, critical habitat designations, and recovery plans. The policy places a low priority on economic considerations for protecting endangered species. Consequently, more than thirty years since it was enacted, the ESA is considered unsuccessful.

- Program tools are not advancing the protection or preservation of species.
- The constraints on commerce and private land owners have generated significant legal litigation.
- The policy does not foster citizen participation in the conservation of species.

Previous attempts to remedy the problem of disappearing species include placing species on the endangered list to track status of species populations and trigger regulatory actions. Additional attempts involve regulatory programs—specifically, recovery plans designed to restore species populations and critical habitat designations to restrict land use activities. All of these remedies revolve around the application of sound science, which is a difficult measure to establish because nature is always changing.

Several alternatives exist for improving the ESA. They range from maintaining the status quo, implementing solutions to reinvent the policy tools, and seeking outside assistance for the development of sound science. A cost/benefit analysis is used to examine the costs and benefits associated with each alternative. The recommendation is to implement the following changes:

- Develop a sound definition of science for species listing.
- Structure recovery plans to include guidelines and timelines for monitoring species status.
- Create incentives for voluntary and cooperative species conservation efforts.

Implementing these recommendations will solve many of the problems with the ESA. First, the species listing process will focus attention on species facing greatest risk of endangerment. Second, guidelines and timelines for recovery plans will promote restoration of species populations. Finally, incentives for public conservation efforts will foster species preservation and greater participation in environmental conservation.

Format for Headings and Subheadings

1. Use headings and subheadings when assignments call for specific information and questions to be answered or when the paper topic is complex. (See Chapter 12 for examples as part of a paper.)

2. There are three kinds:

   - **Major** headings: A major heading should be centered or left-justified (placed at the left margin) and typed in bold and capital letters. These are generally used to identify the major parts of the paper such as the introduction, conclusion, and literature.

   - **Primary** subheadings: A primary heading should be left-justified, typed in bold letters, and have the first letter in each word capitalized. These are used to identify transitions between points or arguments within major parts of the paper.

   - **Secondary** subheadings: A secondary subheading (often referred to as run-in subheading) should be typed in bold italic letters or bold and underlined with only the first letter (and proper nouns) capitalized and a period at the end (sentence style). They are generally the first words in the paragraph; they are usually phrases (not complete sentences) that end in a period. These are used to distinguish between subsections of one of the primary parts of the paper.

3. Double-space between the major heading or primary subheading and the following paragraph.

4. For papers that are twenty pages or less, only major headings and primary headings are used.

5. Major headings should be used when the paper is longer than five pages and develops identifiable points and arguments.

Example: Headings and Subheadings (Abridged and reprinted with permission)

HISTORICAL CONTEXT

The ESEA ensured federal funding for public education institutions to improve low-income facilities and has been slightly altered by Congress every five years (Bailey 1968). President Johnson and Congress agreed that increased funding could provide an equal education to all income levels and racial groups (Bailey 1968, 57). The act still distributes federal funds, but its methods have changed by incremental steps. The latest form of the ESEA, the NCLB, ties student performance on standardized exams to federal funding (Rosenhall 2007).

Legitimization of the NCLB Policy Decision

Legitimization of the NCLB policy decision was based on providing a solution to educational disparity through educator accountability to the federal government and parents, plus local flexibility for spending federal funds (Peterson 2003). President Bush and Congress sought to run education like a business, tracking progress through federal- and state-determined proficiency marks. If adequate progress was not obtained, school sanctions and restructuring would take place (Rudalevige 2003). Education institutions could spend NCLB budget in a variety of ways, so long as an improvement in education was obtained. This local flexibility in spending federal funds disconnected school results from federal government spending requirements.

Use of information. Previous ESEA reauthorizations and information from seventeen states and numerous local governments, already engaged in accountability tactics, contributed to the formation of the NCLB. The importance placed on standards was present in the 1980s but can more readily be seen from the 1994 reauthorization of the ESEA and its companion legislation, the Goals 2000 Act (Peterson 2003). The ability to move to schools within a district and out of a neighborhood—a principle known as school choice—has been present since the Reagan administration and arose again in 1991, 1994, and in the debates of 1999. The flexibility, assessment, and consequent language of the NCLB, have roots in the Clinton administration discussions over the ESEA but were especially present in the efforts to reauthorize the ESEA in the 106th Congress (Mayers 2006). An accountability case study from Chicago, in which educational improvement was achieved by making local schools accountable to the mayor's office, was also used as a template during formation (Peterson 2003).

Format for the Appendix

1. If the paper has an appendix, put it after the last page of text and before the endnotes (if any), the reference page, and any tables or figures.
2. The appendix must be on a separate page.
3. An appendix is used mostly to present background information not presented in tables or figures.
4. An appendix should be identified in the text with a parenthetical reference such as (see Appendix).
5. If there is more than one appendix, identify them as Appendix A, Appendix B, and so on, referenced as (see Appendix A).

Example: Appendix

APPENDIX A: ORGANIZATION AND JURISDICTION OF THE **EEOC**

The U.S. Equal Employment Opportunity Commission (EEOC) is a bipartisan Commission comprised of five presidentially appointed members, including the Chair, Vice Chair, and three Commissioners. The Chair is responsible for the administration and implementation of policy for and the financial management and organizational development of the Commission. The Vice Chair and the Commissioners participate equally in the development and approval of Commission policies, issue charges of discrimination where appropriate, and authorize the filing of suits. In addition to the Commissioners, the President appoints a General Counsel to support the Commission and provide direction, coordination, and supervision to the EEOC's litigation program. A brief description of major program areas is provided on the following pages. When the Commission first opened its doors in 1965, it was charged with enforcing the employment provisions of the landmark Civil Rights Act of 1964.

The EEOC jurisdiction over employment discrimination issues has since grown and now includes the following areas:

- **Title VII of the Civil Rights Act,** which prohibits employment discrimination on the basis of race, color, religion, sex, and national origin.
- **Pregnancy Discrimination Act,** which requires employers to treat pregnancy and pregnancy-related medical conditions as any other medical disability with respect to terms and conditions of employment, including health benefits.
- **Rehabilitation Act of 1973,** which prohibits discrimination on the basis of disability in the federal government.
- **Equal Pay Provisions of the Fair Labor Standards Act,** which prohibits sex discrimination in the payment of wages to men and women performing substantially equal work in the same establishment.
- **Age Discrimination in Employment Act of 1967 (ADEA),** which protects workers 40 and older from discrimination in hiring, discharge, pay, promotions, fringe benefits, and other aspects of employment. ADEA also prohibits the termination of pension contributions and accruals on account of age and governs early retirement incentive plans and other aspects of benefits planning and integration for older workers.
- **Title I and Title V of the Americans with Disabilities Act of 1990 (ADA),** which prohibits discrimination against qualified individuals with disabilities in job application procedures, hiring, firing, advancement, compensation, fringe benefits, job training, and other terms, conditions, and privileges of employment.

Excerpt from U.S. Equal Employment Opportunity Commission. *EEOC Performance and Accountability Report FY 2007.* http://www.eeoc.gov/abouteeoc/plan/par/2007/appendixes.html.

Format for the Table of Contents or List of Tables and Figures

Most students will never use a table of contents or need a list of tables and figures. The table of contents is generally used with papers longer than twenty-five pages, with several parts or chapters. The list of tables and figures is usually used only when the paper has many figures and/or tables embedded in the text of the paper.

1. The table of contents and the list of tables and figures are placed on separate pages before the abstract, executive summary, or introduction.

2. On a page by itself, the table of contents lists all of the headings used in the paper and provides a page number for each heading and subheading. The headings are left-justified and listed in the order they appear in the text. The page numbers where the headings can be found are right-justified (placed at the right margin). It is best to use the leader tab function to format the line with the heading and page number.

3. On a page by itself, the list of tables and figures lists all the tables and figures used in the paper and provides a page number for where each can be found. The table/figure numbers and names are left-justified and listed in the order they appear in the text. The page numbers where the table/figure numbers and titles can be found are right-justified. It is best to use the leader tab function to format the line with the figure or table title and page number.

4. Do not number the table of contents or list of tables pages like the rest of the paper. These pages should be numbered with small Roman numerals and not included in the total number of page numbers in the paper.

Example: Table of Contents

Example: List Table and Figures

Format for Referencing and Placement of Tables and Figures Not Embedded in Text

1. Unless otherwise instructed, place the tables, if any, after the references. (See Chapter 12, "Example of a Policy Recommendation.")
2. Place the figures, if any, after the tables or after the reference page when there is no table.
3. Tables and figures should be numbered separately, placed on separate pages, and fully referenced with a complete citation.
4. The writer should address information found in the table or figure in the text by phrases such as "as seen in Figure 1 . . ." or "as the data in Table 1 show. . . ."
5. After the table or figure has been mentioned in the text, a direct reference to the table or figure is placed on a centered, separate line.

Example: Referencing a Table in the Text

Importantly, as seen in Table 1, most of his nominees were confirmed.

(Table 1 About Here)

The data in the table show that the Democrats' large majorities, ranging from 57 percent to 75 percent in the 73rd–77th Senate, combined with Roosevelt's adherence to traditional selection methods, resulted in very few unconfirmed or rejected nominees.

Format and Placement for Quotations

1. Quotations are sets of information that have been copied verbatim from a source.
2. Quotations should be used *very* sparingly and only when absolutely necessary.
   - **Rule of thumb:** Avoid quotes altogether.
   - **Rule of thumb:** Do not use more than two quotations in every ten pages of text.
3. Quotations must be cited with an exact page number.
4. Quotations that are shorter than three lines long should be placed between quotation marks (at the beginning and the end) with the citation placed after the ending quotation mark.
5. Quotations that are longer than four lines long should be single-spaced and indented ten spaces from the left and right margins. The citation is placed after the last sentence of the quotation.
6. Quotations should never be used as a substitute for writing or synthesizing information.
7. Quotations must be introduced or framed by the text in some way.
   - One way is to identify the author or work directly or indirectly.
   - Another way is to explain why the words that are being quoted are significant.
8. Use quotes:
   - When the exact wording of a statement or point is crucial to the meaning of it.
   - To preserve distinctive phrasing or eloquence of a point.

Example: A Short Quote

Media influence on political behavior has been argued to be minimal until recently.[1] Some scholars argue that news coverage shapes people's attitudes about important political actors as well as people's perspectives on political events. For example, Lipset and Schneider (1987) found that ". . . interest group leaders had an incentive to maintain a high level of criticism . . ." in the media to justify their positions (405). Lipset and Schneider conclude that people have lost confidence in big government, big business, and big labor due to exploitative news coverage about each of them.

---

[1]The major point of debate over how media influences political behavior is over how information is processed. Some studies show that people read selectively and absorb very little of the news. See Graber 1984.

Example: A Long Quote

Media influence on political behavior has been argued to be minimal until recently.[1] Studies show that media is the major source of political information. Lipset and Schneider (1987) suggest that television carries with it a special consideration and influence in providing information to the public.

> The special impact of television is that it delivers the news to a much larger and "inadvertent" audience than was the case before television, when only a limited segment of the population chose to follow news about politics and government. When people read newspapers and magazines, they edit the information by skipping over articles about subjects they are not interested in. Television watchers, however, are exposed to everything (Lipset and Schneider 1987, 405).

They conclude that people's attitudes have changed toward big government, big business, and big labor due to exploitative news coverage about them.

---

[1]The major point of debate over how media influences political behavior is over how information is processed. Some studies show that people read selectively and absorb very little of the news. See Graber 1984.

Format and Placement for Explanatory Notes

1. Explanatory notes are put in the same place as footnotes or endnotes.

2. These are typically used to comment on the context of a fact or opinion, to explain a source, to elaborate on an idea, to define a term, or to provide background on an idea or methodology used.

3. Explanatory notes can be used in papers that have parenthetical citations.

4. If explanations are needed when the paper has footnote or endnote citations, explanatory information can be added after the citation or can stand alone with its own raised number.

5. All endnotes or footnotes must be identified with a raised number in ascending order regardless of whether they are explanatory or merely reference a source.

Example: An Explanatory Note

> Media influence on political behavior has become increasingly noticeable.[1] For example, by analyzing a set of opinion polls, Lipset and Schneider show that news coverage shapes people's attitudes about important political actors as well as people's perspectives on political events. The poll results suggest that people have lost confidence in big government, big business, and big labor due to exploitative news coverage about each (Lipset and Schneider 1987).
>
> ———————
>
> [1]The major point of debate over how media influences political behavior is over how information is processed. Some studies show that people read selectively and absorb very little of the news. See Graber 1984.

Format and Placement for Citations or References

1. Research papers may include footnotes, endnotes, or parenthetical (author-date) references to sources. Unless otherwise directed by the instructor, students should choose one form of citation and stick with it.

2. Parenthetical (author-date), endnote, or footnote citations should be used to identify the source of quotations and all controversial, obscure, or significant facts.
  - **Rule of thumb:** Each paragraph in the body of the paper that deals with evidence or ideas borrowed from others should contain *at least two citations*.
  - **Rule of thumb:** When in doubt, reference the information.

3. All forms of citation must include a specific page number when quoting directly or paraphrasing a fact or data from a source.

4. Each referencing system varies slightly in format from the other. The specifics of each system are explained in detail in the appropriate reference guide book. There are two accepted methods for referencing research materials within the body of a research paper.
  - The first involves using **endnotes** or **footnotes** in combination with a bibliography (see below for examples).
  - The other is referred to as the **"author-date"** system, which involves in-text parenthetical documentation and a reference page.

Structure for Endnote and Footnote Citations

The footnote and endnote system of referencing has a particular style and format.

Usage: Endnotes and footnotes are substitutes for each other and cannot be used together. They differ from each other only by where they are placed.

- Footnotes are placed at the bottom of the page in which they were referenced.
- Endnotes are listed by themselves on a page titled "Notes" centered on the first line of the page. Double-space between the title and the first citation.
- The endnote page is placed after the appendix, or last page of text if there is no appendix.

Text Format: The format for footnotes and endnotes is the same and they are indicated in the text by a raised number.

- Note numbers should be listed in ascending order.
- The endnote or footnote contains all reference information the first time a source is cited.
- Subsequent citations to the same source that *immediately* follow the first citation can be designated by "Ibid." Some style guides suggest that all subsequent citations include the last name of the author and the year, avoiding "Ibid" altogether (check with the instructor or the required style guide).
- Ideas attributed to more than one author are identified by listing both sources/authors, separated by a semicolon.

Reference Format: The reference format for footnotes and endnotes should be left-justified except for the first line, which should be indented five spaces.

Titles: The title of the book, journal, or Internet site must be formatted differently from the rest of the note text. Most often the title is italicized.

No Works Cited or Reference Page: Because footnotes and endnotes must contain, at least in the first citation of the source, complete citation information, papers using them generally do not contain a bibliography, reference page, or works cited page. There are occasions when a bibliography is required. If a bibliography is requested, then the information in the bibliography is basically the same as the information included in the footnotes or endnotes in the first citation of the source, but the format is different. The bibliographic citation begins with the last name, followed by the first name of the author. The remaining information is separated by periods. The sources are listed in the bibliography page in alphabetical order (see *The Chicago Manual of Style* 2003: Section 16.71–16.89).

Content and Punctuation for Footnotes and Endnotes

Footnotes and endnotes should include the following information *separated by commas* (adapted from Kalvelage et al. 1984; Harnack and Kleppinger 1998; *The Chicago Manual of Style* 2003: Sections 17.17, 17.148, 17.234):

Book Footnote or Endnote Information

- the raised number
- the author's full name, first name first
- the complete title (in italics)
- the editor's name (if any)
- the edition (if it is not the first)
- the name and number of the series (if any)
- the place of publication
- the name of the publisher
- the date of publication
- URL for Internet sources
- date of access for Internet sources (Month Day, Year)

Article Footnote or Endnote Information

- the raised number
- the author's full name, first name first
- the title of the article (in quotation marks)
- the name of the periodical (in italics)
- the volume number of the periodical
- the date of the periodical
- the page numbers of the article
- URL for Internet sources
- date of access for Internet sources (Month Day, Year)

Internet Footnote or Endnote Information

- author's name (if available)
- title of the document (in quotation marks)
- title of the complete site (in italics)
- date of the posting or last revision
- volume number (if any)
- URL for Internet sources
- date of access for Internet sources (Month Day, Year)

Examples of Footnotes and Endnotes Used for Reference Citations

Here is a sample of footnote/endnote style formats based on *The Chicago Manual of Style*. The information is separated by commas until the end of the sentence.

Book:

¹Jay M. Shafritz, *The Dictionary of American Government and Politics* (Chicago, IL: Dorsey Press, 1988).

Journal article paginated by volume (page numbers begin at 1 for the first issue and continue in the next issue with the ending page number from the first issue):

²Edmond Costantini, "Political Women and Political Ambition: Closing the Gender Gap," *American Journal of Political Science* 34 (August 1990): 741–70.

Journal article paginated by issue (page numbers begin at 1 for each issue):

³James Coast, "Environmentally Safe Insecticides," *Consumer Digest* 23, no. 2 (1974): 25–32.

Article in an edited book:

⁴Hugh Heclo, "Issue Networks and the Executive Establishment," in *The New American Political System*, ed. Anthony King (Washington, DC: American Enterprise Institute for Policy Research, 1978), 34.

Book with multiple authors:

⁵John Schweller, Christopher Jones, and Timothy Fuller, *Principles of Ecological Wisdom* (New York: Simon and Schuster, 2002), 42.

Multiple works by an author:

⁶John E. Chubb and Terry Moe, "Politics, Markets, and the Organization of Schools," *American Political Science Review* 82 (September 1988): 87–1065.

⁷John E. Chubb and Terry Moe, *Politics, Markets, and America's Schools* (Washington, DC: Brookings, 1990), 70–80.

Government document:

⁸U.S. Congress. House. Committee on Foreign Relations. *Report on Aid to South Africa*, 98th Cong., 2nd sess. (Washington, DC: Government Printing Office, 1985), 1.

Newspaper or magazine article:

⁹Robert S. Greenberger, "Hottest Labor Consultant in Washington Adopts New Right Techniques to Bolster Union's Image," *The Wall Street Journal*, October 23, 1981.

Source with no author:

¹⁰"Dr. King's Widow Testifies in a Civil Trial," *New York Times*, sec. A17, November 17, 1999.

Internet source:

General Web Site Internet Source:

¹¹Raymond Agius, "Quality and Audit in Occupational Health," *Health, Environment and Work*, May 1999, http://www.med.ed.ac.uk.HEW/quality.html (accessed June 8, 1999).

Organizational Web Site Internet Source:

[13]AFL-CIO, "Working Families Need a Voice: Who's Behind It?", January 14, 1999, http://www.aflcio.org/silence/behind.html (accessed July 19, 1999).

Electronic Journal Web Site Internet Source:

[14]"Clinton Proposes Increased Child Care Subsidies," *Amarillo Business Journal*, 3, no. 2 (1999), http://businessjournal.net/stories/020698/child.html (accessed August 25, 1999).

Electronic Magazine Web Site Internet Source:

[15]Debra Rosenberg, "More Than Just a Kiss: Hillary's Conflicted Life as First Lady and Candidate," *Newsweek*, November 22, 1999, http://www.newsweek.com/nw-srv/printed/us/na/a55101-1999nov14.html (accessed November 17, 1999).

Government Site Internet Source:

[16]National Labor Relations Board, "National Labor Relations Board Members," February 17, 1999, http://www.nlrb.gov/members.html (accessed July 14, 1999).

Personal Site Internet Source:

[17]Jon Brown. "Homepage," October 24, 1998, http://www.polsci.swms.edu/brown/personal.html (accessed July 8, 1999).

Electronic news and journal databases:

[18]Jill Schachner Chanen, "Daddy's Home," *ABA Journal* 86, no. 11 (2000): 90, http://www.epnet.com (accessed August 27, 2003).

Personal interviews:

[19]Paul Simon, Personal Interview, August 12, 1998.

Structure for Parenthetical Author–Date Citations System

Styles of parenthetical author-date referencing have a common set of characteristics (see *The Chicago Manual of Style 2003*: Sections 16.107–120).

Format: Parenthetical citations are references to sources that appear in the text between parentheses. This citation system uses a reference that is placed directly into the text, usually after the writer reports information, paraphrases, or directly quotes another writer's material and before the period at the end of the sentence. When the writer is summarizing someone else's conclusion or work, the reference includes the author's last name and the year the work was published; for example: (Jones 2001).

Page numbers: If the material includes specific information or a direct quote from someone else then the reference must include the author's last name, the year the work was published, and the page number where the information can be found. Although *The Chicago Manual of Style* suggests using a comma to separate the year and the page number, some professions prefer using a colon; for example: (Jones 2001, 46) or (Jones 2001: 46).

Placement: The parenthetical citation is generally placed before the period at the end of a sentence.

Reference to same author: Multiple references to the same author are indicated with the same format regardless of how many times the author is cited.

Reference to several works: Ideas attributed to more than one author are identified by listing the references together. The references are separated by semicolons and enclosed by parentheses; for example: (Jones 2001; Brown 1990, 42).

Multiple authors: References to works with multiple authors are listed the first time with all the authors' last names, but the second time only with the first author's name followed by a comma and "et al."; for example: (Smith, et al. 1990).

References with no author: References with titles (no author) should be referenced the way they are listed in the reference page. If the reference is listed by the title, then use an abbreviated title followed by three periods and year of publication; for example: (*How Environments* . . . 2000). If the reference is listed by the source, then use the full name of the source and year of publication; for example: (*New York Times* 2005).

Example: A Parenthetical Citation

The public is primarily exposed to new information about labor unions through the media. Media are generally seen as agenda setters and in some cases actually shape public opinions (Graber 1984; Iyengar 1987). While the citizens' views may come from their considerations of the political environment, the meaning of events tends to be defined for them by the media. In this sense, media act as agenda setters when preexisting attitudes are strong and may change attitudes when preexisting attitudes are weak (Iyengar 1987, 815–20).

Format for the Author-Date Citation System Reference Page

Placement

Place the reference page (entitled **References** or **Works Cited**) after explanatory endnotes or after the last page of text in the absence of an appendix or endnotes.

- A reference page is required for author-date citation systems.
- All sources used for the assignment must be listed on the reference page.

Format

All the sources listed should be typed using a hanging paragraph format.

- A hanging paragraph has the first line flush with the margin (left-justified) and all remaining lines indented five spaces.
- *Microsoft Word* has an autoformatting function for this type of paragraph in the *Format, Paragraph* menu. (Highlight the reference, then use the *Format, Paragraph* menu and look for *Special* and then using the scroll bar, until *Hanging* appears in the box., choose Hanging and click OK.)

Alphabetical Order

Do not separate books from articles or Web references.

- All references should be listed together in *alphabetical* order by the last name of the author.

- *Microsoft Word* has an autoformatting function in the *Table, Sort* menu to alphabetize a list of information. (Highlight all the references, then use the *Table, Sort* menu, and click *OK.*)

Content and Punctuation for Author-Date Reference Page

There are four popular style guides for formatting author-date reference pages for political science manuscripts: *The Chicago Manual of Style*, the *American Political Science Association Style Manual for Political Science Publication, Manual of the American Psychological Association,* and *MLA Handbook for Writers of Research Papers*. **Once a format is chosen, the same format must be used throughout the references**.

Style Guides Used in Political Science

Chicago Manual of Style

Chicago manual of style online. http://www.chicagomanualofstyle.org/home.html.
Chicago manual of style. 2003. 15th ed. Chicago: University of Chicago Press.

APSA

American Political Science Association (APSA). 2006. *The style manual for political science.* Washington D.C.: American Political Science Association.

APA

American Psychological Association. http://www.apa.org.
Publication manual of the American Psychological Association. 2001. 5th edition. Washington, DC: American Psychological Association.

MLA

Modern Language Association (MLA). *Publication Manual FAQ,* http://www.mla. org/style/style_faq/style_faq4.
Modern Language Association. *How do I document sources from the Web in my works-cited list?* (MLA).
Gibaldi, Joseph. 2003. *MLA handbook for writers of research papers.* 6th ed. New York: The Modern Language Association of America.

Stylebooks differ on the order and punctuation of the source information, so check with the instructor for suggestions on which stylebook to use.

- For multiple sources by one author, use a line five spaces in length or a 3-em dash (often available in the *Insert, Symbol, Special Character* menu in *Microsoft Word*) instead of the author's name on the subsequent entry. Some professions prefer to repeat the name in the reference list. Both types of entries are acceptable.
- Citations listed on a reference page must have the following information separated by periods (adapted from Kalvelage, et al. 1984; Harnack and Kleppinger 1998; *The Chicago Manual of Style 2003:* Sections 16.90–106, 17.12, 17.17, 17.148, 17.234, 17.359).

Book Reference Page Information

- author's full name, last name first
- co-authors' full name
- complete title (in italics)
- editor's name (if any)
- edition (if it is not the first)
- name and number of the series (if any)
- place of publication
- name of the publisher
- date of publication
- URL for Internet sources
- date of access for Internet sources (Month Day, Year)

Article Reference Page Information

- author's full name, last name first
- co-authors' full name
- title of the article
- name of the periodical (in italics)
- volume number of the periodical
- date of the periodical
- page numbers of the article
- URL for Internet sources
- date of access for Internet sources (Month Day, Year)

Government Document Reference Page Information

- name of the government (e.g. U.S. or California or Los Angeles, CA or Canada)
- name of the government institution (e.g. Congress or Supreme Court)
- name of any agency or division (e.g. Senate or Office of Civil Rights)
- name of any program or committee (e.g. Appropriations Committee or Endangered Species Program)
- complete title (in italics)
- session (if any)
- report number (if any)
- place of publication (if available)
- name of the publisher (if available)
- page numbers (if any)
- date of publication
- URL for Internet sources
- date of access for Internet sources (Month Day, Year)

Laws, Rules, or Regulations Document Reference Page Information

- complete title of the law, rule, or regulation (in italics)
- name of the document (in italics) (e.g. *Statutes at Large* or *U.S. Supreme Court Reporter* or *Federal Register*
- section number (if any)
- volume number (if any)
- issue date (if any)
- page numbers (if any)
- date of publication
- URL for Internet sources
- date of access for Internet sources (Month Day, Year)

Nongovernmental Organization Document Reference Page Information

- name of the organization (e.g. United Nations)
- name of the institution (e.g. General Assembly)
- name of any agency or division (e.g. Human Rights Council)
- name of any program or committee (e.g. Candidacies)
- complete title (in italics)
- session (if any)
- report number (if any)
- place of publication (if available)
- name of the publisher (if available)
- page numbers (if any)
- date of publication
- URL for Internet sources
- date of access for Internet sources (Month Day, Year)

Internet Material Reference Page Information

- author's name (if available; if not available, then use the name of organization that owns the web site)
- title of the document
- title of the complete site (in italics)
- date of the posting or last revision
- volume number (if any)
- date of access
- URL for Internet sources
- date of access for Internet sources (Month Day, Year)

Examples of Common Author–Date Citation Styles for Reference Page

Chicago Manual of Style Reference Examples

The Chicago Manual of Style has a few distinctive characteristics to its format. The Chicago Manual of Style requires italicized "sentence style" formatting for the title of documents, except for proper names and names of journals, newspapers, etc. Articles in books and journals are *not* italicized or placed in quotes. When there are multiple authors, the first author is listed last name first, first name last. All remaining authors are listed first name last name separated by comma with the final author separated by the word "and".

Multiple works by an author: (*Editor's Note: Multiple works by the same author are listed and organized by year of publication. If the author and the year are the same then the publications for the same author are alphabetized by title and then the year is distinguished by placing an a, b, or c, etc., behind it. While the Chicago Style Manual encourages the use of the 3-em dash, students may use a line five spaces long ending with a period to simulate a 3-em dash. It is also acceptable to repeat the author's name instead of either the line or the dash.*)

Chubb, John E., and Terry Moe. 1988. Politics, markets, and the organization of schools. *American Political Science Review* 82:1065-87.

————. 1990. *Politics, markets, and America's schools.* Washington, DC: Brookings.

Massinga, Ruth. 1999a. Aging out of foster care. *Christian Science Monitor* 91(102): 11.

Massinga, Ruth. 1999b. Statement of Ruth Massinga, Chief Executive Officer Casey Family Program, Seattle, Washington. *Testimony before the House Committee on Ways and Means Subcommittee on Human Resources.* May 13. http://waysandmeans. house.gov/legacy/humres/106cong/5-13-99/5-13mass.htm (accessed October 28, 2005).

Book:

Shafritz, Jay M. 1988. *The dictionary of American government and politics.* Chicago, IL: Dorsey Press.

Book with two authors:

Wilson, Ian, and Stuart I. Morse. 2003. *Law and social change: Civil rights and their consequences.* San Francisco, CA: Munner Press.

Book with three or more authors: (*Editor's Note: By convention if a book has more than six authors only list the first six followed by "et al."*)

Schweller, John, Christopher Jones, and Timothy Fuller. 2002. *Principles of ecological wisdom.* New York: Simon and Schuster.

Article in an edited book:

Heclo, Hugh. 1978. Issue networks and the executive establishment. In *The new American political system*, ed. Anthony King, 51-84. Washington, DC: American Enterprise Institute for Policy Research.

Journal article paginated by volume: (Page numbers begin at 1 for the first issue and continue in the next issue with the ending page number from the first issue. Note: no space after colon.)

Costantini, Edmond. 1990. Political women and political ambition: Closing the gender gap. *American Journal of Political Science* 34:741–70.

Journal article paginated by issue: (Page numbers begin at 1 for each issue. Note: one space after volume number.)

Coast, James. 1974. Environmentally safe insecticides. *Consumer Digest* 23 (2): 25–32.

Government document:

Single Issuing Agency:

General Accounting Office. 2000. *Performance and accountability report.* Washington, DC: General Accounting Office.

Multiple Levels Within Agency:

U.S. Department of the Interior. 2002. U.S. Fish and Wildlife Service. Endangered Species Program. *Recovery report to Congress: Fiscal years 2001–2002.* Arlington, VA: U.S. Fish and Wildlife Service.

Hearings:

U.S. Congress. 2003. House. Committee on Resources. *Abandoned Mine Lands Program.* 108th Cong., 1st sess.

Committee Prints:

U.S. Congress. 2006. House. Committee on Energy and Commerce. *Human tissue samples: NIH research policies and practices.* 109th Cong., 2nd sess. Committee Print.

Reports:

U.S. Congress. 1992. House. *Family and Medical Leave Act of 1992: Conference report (to accompany S.5).* 102nd Cong., 2nd sess. H. Doc 102-816.

Laws and Statutes (Bills or resolutions passed into law can be referenced from the *U.S. Statutes at Large* or the *U.S. Code.*)

Statutes at Large:

Family and Medical Leave Act of 1993. Public Law 103-3. *U.S. Statues at Large* 107 (1993):6.

U.S. Code:

Family and Medical Leave Act of 1993. U.S. Code 29 §§ 2601 et seq.

Legal citations: (*Editor's Note:* The Chicago Manual of Style *provides little guidance for legal citations used in nonlegal writing or general works. It is important that the reference include case names, the year, the volume number of the reporter series, the abbreviated name of the court, and page number. See sections 17.283-17.289 for more examples and details.*)

U.S. Supreme Court Decisions (Decisions are generally referenced from *United States Supreme Court Reports*, unless the decision has yet to be recorded; in that case it is cited from the *Supreme Court Reporter.*)

Reports:
Washington v. Davis. 1976. 423 U.S. 1044.

Reporter:
Washington v. Davis. 1976 96 S.Ct. 2040.

Rules and Regulations:

Federal Register:
Endangered and threatened wildlife and plants: Final rule to list six foreign birds as endangered. 2008. *Federal Register* 73, no. 11 (16 January): *3145-3179.*

Code of Federal Regulations:
Occupational Health and Safety Standards. 2007. *Code of Federal Regulation,* title 29, pt. 1.

State Government and Local Documents:
California. 2002. *AB275 Medi-Cal: Developmentally Disabled: Dental Care.* Chapter 522.
Los Angeles, CA. 1976. *Bicycles and Vehicles: Bicycle Licenses. Municipal Code.* Article 6, Section 26.01.

International Documents:

Laws:
Canada. *Access to Information Act.* 1980-81-82-83, c. 111, Sch. I "1".

Nongovernmental Bodies:
United Nations General Assembly. 2007. *Oceans and the law of the sea: Report of the Secretary General.* Sixty-second Session. Addendum. A/62/66/Add.1.

Newspaper or magazine article: *(Editor's Note: While* The Chicago Manual of Style *recommends against including the page number for a newspaper, it is good practice in academics to include the page number. See Section 17.188.)*
Greenberger, Robert S. 1981. Hottest labor consultant in Washington adopts new right techniques to bolster union's image. *The Wall Street Journal,* October 23, sec. B3.

Newspaper article with no author: *(Editor's Note:* The Chicago Manual of Style *prefers that the reference for newspaper articles begins with the source, not the title of the work. See Section 17.192.)*
New York Times. 1999. Dr. King's widow testifies in a civil trial, November 17, sec. A16.

Source without an author (except for newspapers):
SAS user's guide. 1992. Cary, NC: SAS Institute.

Personal Interviews:
Simon, Paul. 1998. *Personal interview.* August 12.

Online Database: *(Editor's Note: Online databases often provide the user with an option for viewing a PDF or HTML version of the document. A PDF document should be referenced as though it were viewed in its original format because it is just a picture of that material. An HTML version of the material has been reformatted. Because it has been reformatted, it must be referenced as a product of the online service. The HTML reference should include the citation of the main directory of the* *database. Although CMS does not require a date of access, it is good practice to include it in the citation for HTML versions of a document.)*

Chanen, Jill Schachner. 2000. Daddy's home. *ABA Journal* 86(11): 90. http://www.epnet. com (accessed August 27, 2003).

For an Internet Source: *(Editor's Note: When the Internet source does not have a date of publication, the date the site was last updated or created is sufficient. Occasionally, an Internet source will not have any date. In this event, use the abbreviation for no date—"n.d."—in place of the year).*

Organizational Web Site Internet Source:

AFL-CIO. 1999. *Working families need a voice: Who's behind it?* 14 January http://www.aflcio.org/silence/behind.html (accessed July 19, 1999).

Electronic Journal Web Site Internet Source:

Harris, J., 1999. Clinton proposes increased child care subsidies. *Amarilo Business Journal* 3 (2). http://businessjournal.net/stories/020698/child.html (accessed August 25, 1999).

Electric Magazine Web Site Internet Source:

Rosenberg, Debra. 1999. More than just a kiss: Hillary's conflicted life as first lady and candidate. *Newsweek,* November 22. http://www.newsweek.com/nw-srv/printed/us/ na/a55101-1999nov14.htm (accessed November 17, 1999).

Government Site Internet Source:

National Labor Relations Board. 1999. *National Labor Relations Board members.* February 17. http://www.nlrb.gov/members.html (accessed July 14, 1999).

Informally Published Electronic Material Internet Source: *(Editor's Note: Include as much information as possible [author of the content, title or owner of the site, title of the page, URL]. Although* The Chicago Manual of Style *recommends against including the creation date of the Web site, it is good practice to include the creation date and the access date to inform the reader about the currency of the site and its material.)*

Brown, Jon. 1998. *Homepage.* October 24. http://www.polsci.swms.edu/brown/personal.htm (accessed July 8, 1999).

APSA Style Reference Examples

The American Political Science Association style has a few distinguishing format characteristics. The APSA style is created from a combination of two styles found in *The Chicago Manual of Style*. It uses the italicized "headline" format found in the bibliography page style for titles of documents, but uses the sequence for the information found in the reference page format. Titles of articles in books and journals are placed in quotes and in "headline" format. When there are multiple authors, the first author is listed last name first, first name last. All remaining authors are listed first name last name separated by comma with the final author separated by the word "and".

Multiple works by an author: *(Editor's Note: Multiple works by the same author are listed and organized by year of publication. If the author and the year are the same then the publications for the same author are alphabetized by title and then the year is distinguished by placing an a, b, or c, etc., behind it.)*

Chubb, John E., and Terry Moe. 1988. "Politics, Markets, and the Organization of Schools." *American Political Science Review* 82 (August): 1065–87.

———. 1990. *Politics, Markets, and America's Schools.* Washington, DC: Brookings.

Massinga, Ruth. 1999a. "Aging Out of Foster Care." *Christian Science Monitor.* 91 (102): 11.

Massinga, Ruth. 1999b. "Statement of Ruth Massinga, Chief Executive Officer Casey Family Program, Seattle, Washington." *Testimony before the House Committee on Ways and Means Subcommittee on Human Resources.*" May 13. http://waysandmeans. house.gov/legacy/humres/106cong/5-13-99/5-13mass.htm (October 28, 2005).

Book:

Shafritz, Jay M. 1988. *The Dictionary of American Government and Politics.* Chicago, IL: Dorsey Press.

Book with two authors:

Wilson, Ian, and Stuart I. Morse. 2003. *Law and Social Change: Civil Rights and Their Consequences.* San Francisco, CA: Munner Press.

Book with three or more authors: *(Editor's Note: By convention if a book has more than six authors only list the first six followed by "et al."*

Schweller, John, Christopher Jones, and Timothy Fuller. 2002. *Principles of Ecological Wisdom.* New York: Simon and Schuster.

Article in an edited book:

Heclo, Hugh. 1978. "Issue Networks and the Executive Establishment." In *The New American Political System,* ed. Anthony King. Washington, DC: American Enterprise Institute for Policy Research, 51–84.

Journal article paginated by volume: (Page numbers begin at 1 for the first issue and continue in the next issue with the ending page number from the first issue.)

Costantini, Edmond. 1990. "Political Women and Political Ambition: Closing the Gender Gap." *American Journal of Political Science* 34 (July): 741–70.

Journal article paginated by issue: (Page numbers begin at 1 for each issue.)

Coast, James. 1974. "Environmentally Safe Insecticides." *Consumer Digest* 23 (2): 25–32.

Government document:

<u>*Single Issuing Agency:*</u>

General Accounting Office. 2000. *Performance and Accountability Report.* Washington, DC: General Accounting Office.

<u>*Multiple Levels Within Agency:*</u>

U.S. Department of the Interior. U.S. Fish and Wildlife Service. Endangered Species Program. 2002. *Recovery Report to Congress: Fiscal Years 2001–2002.* Arlington, VA: U.S. Fish and Wildlife Service.

<u>*Hearings:*</u>

U.S. Congress. House. Committee on Resources. 2003. *Abandoned Mine Lands Program.* 108th Cong., 1st sess.

Committee Prints:

U.S. Congress. House. Committee on Energy and Commerce. 2006. *Human Tissue Samples: NIH Research Policies and Practices.* 109th Cong., 2nd sess. Committee Print.

Reports:

U.S. Congress. House. 1992. *Family and Medical Leave Act of 1992: Conference Report (to accompany S.5).* 102nd Cong., 2nd sess., H. Doc 102-816.

Laws and Statutes:

Statutes at Large:

Family and Medical Leave Act of 1993. 1993. *Public Law 103-3. Statutes at Large.* Vol.107, sec.10, p. 6.

U.S. Code:

Family and Medical Leave Act of 1993. *U.S. Code* 29 §§ 2601 et seq.

U.S. Supreme Court:

Reports:

Washington v. Davis. 1976. 423 U.S. 1044.

Reporter:

Washington v. Davis. 1976 96 S.Ct. 2040.

Rules and Regulations:

Federal Register:

Endangered and Threatened Wildlife and Plants: Final Rule to List Six Foreign Birds as Endangered. 2008. *Federal Register,* 73, no. 11 (16 January): 3145-3179.

Code of Federal Regulations:

Occupational Health and Safety Standards. 2007. *Code of Federal Regulations.* Title 29, Pt. 1

State government and local documents:

California. 2002. *AB275 Medi-Cal: Developmentally Disabled: Dental Care.* Chapter 522.

Los Angeles, CA. 1976. *Bicycles and Vehicles: Bicycle Licenses. Municipal Code.* Article 6, Section 26.01.

International documents:

Laws:

Canada. *Access to Information Act.* 1980-81-82-83, c. 111, Sch. I "1".

Nongovernmental Bodies:

United Nations General Assembly. 2007. *Oceans and the Law of the Sea: Report of the Secretary General.* Sixty-second Session. Addendum. A/62/66/Add.1.

Newspaper or magazine article:

Greenberger, Robert S. 1981. "Hottest Labor Consultant in Washington Adopts New Right Techniques to Bolster Union's Image." *The Wall Street Journal,* 23 October.

Newspaper article with no author:
New York Times. 1999. "Dr. King's Widow Testifies in a Civil Trial." 17 November.

Source without an author (except for newspapers):
SAS User's Guide. 1992. Cary, NC: SAS Institute.

Personal interviews:
Simon, Paul. 1998. *Personal Interview.* 12 August.

Online database: *(Editor's Note: Online databases often provide the user with an option for viewing a PDF or HTML version of the document. A PDF document should be referenced as though it were viewed in its original format because it is just a picture of that material. An HTML version of the material has been reformatted. Because it has been reformatted, it must be referenced as a product of the online service. The HTML reference should include the citation of the main directory of the database. The APSA style requires a date of access in the citation for HTML versions of a document.)*
Chanen, Jill Schachner. 2000. "Daddy's Home." *ABA Journal* 86 (November): 90. Academic Search (August 27, 2003).

For an Internet source: *(Editor's Note: When the Internet source does not have a date of publication, the date the site was last updated or created is sufficient. Occasionally, an Internet source will not have any date. In this event, use the abbreviation for no date—"n.d."—in place of the year.)*

Organizational Web Site Internet Source:
AFL-CIO. 1999. "Working Families Need a Voice: Who's Behind It?" 14 January. http://www.aflcio.org/silence/behind.html (July 19, 1999).

Electronic Journal Web Site Internet Source:
Harris, J. 1999. "Clinton Proposes Increased Child Care Subsidies." *Amarillo Business Journal* 3 (June) http://businessjournal.net/stories/020698/child.html (August 25, 1999).

Electronic Magazine Web Site Internet Source:
Rosenberg, Debra. 1999. "More Than Just a Kiss: Hillary's Conflicted Life as First Lady and Candidate." *Newsweek,* November 22. http://www.newsweek.com/nw-srv/printed/us/na/a55101-1999nov14.htm (November 17, 1999).

Government Site Internet Source:
National Labor Relations Board. 1999. *National Labor Relations Board Members.* February 17. http://www.nlrb.gov/members.html (July 14, 1999).

Informally Published Electronic Material Internet Source: *(Editor's Note: Include as much information as possible [author of the content, title or owner of the site, title of the page, URL]. The APSA style requires a date of access.)*
Brown, Jon. 1998. *Homepage.* October 24. http://www.polsci.swms.edu/brown/personal.htm (July 8, 1999).

APA Style Reference Examples

The *Publication Manual of the American Psychological Association* style guide is similar to *The Chicago Manual of Style* with a few exceptions. Like *The Chicago Manual of Style*, the APA style requires italicized "sentence style" formatting for the title of documents, except for proper names and names of journals, newspapers, etc. Articles in books and journals are *not* italicized and not placed in quotes. The date is placed in parentheses after the author initial. When there are multiple authors, all authors are listed last name first, first initial (with a period after the initial) last. It is incorrect to say first name. Multiple authors' names are separated by a comma. The final name in the list is separated by an "&".

Multiple works by an author: *(Editor's Note: Multiple works by the same author are listed and organized by year of publication. If the author and the year are the same then the publications for the same author are alphabetized by the title and then the year is distinguished by placing an a, b, or c, etc., behind it.)*

Chubb, J. E., & Moe, T. (1988). Politics, markets, and the organization of schools. *American Political Science Review,* 82, 1065-87.

Chubb, J. E., & Moe, T. (1990). *Politics, markets, and America's schools.* Washington, DC: Brookings.

Massinga, R. (1999a). Aging out of foster care. *Christian Science Monitor,* 91(102), 11.

Massinga, R. (1999b). Statement of Ruth Massinga, Chief Executive Officer Casey Family Program, Seattle, Washington. *Testimony before the House Committee on Ways and Means Subcommittee on Human Resources.* May 13. (Retrieved October 28, 2005, from http://waysandmeans.house.gov/legacy/humres/106cong/5-13-99/5-13mass.htm).

Book:

Shafritz, J. M. (1988). *The dictionary of American government and politics.* Chicago, IL: Dorsey Press.

Book with two authors:

Wilson, I., & Morse, S. I. (2003). Law *and social change: Civil rights and their consequences.* San Francisco, CA: Munner Press.

Book with three or more authors: *(Editor's Note: By convention if a book has more than six authors only list the first six followed by "et al." Style guides differ on the specifics of this policy so check the appropriate style guide.)*

Schweller, J., Jones C., & Fuller, T. (2002). *Principles of ecological wisdom.* New York: Simon and Schuster.

Article in an edited book:

Heclo, H. (1978). Issue networks and the executive establishment. In A. King (Ed.), *The new American political system* (pp. 51–84). Washington, DC: American Enterprise Institute for Policy Research.

Journal article paginated by volume: (Page numbers begin at 1 for the first issue and continue in the next issue with the ending page number from the first issue.)

Costantini, E. (1990). Political women and political ambition: Closing the gender gap. *American Journal of Political Science,* 34, 741–770.

Journal article paginated by issue: (Page numbers begin at 1 for each issue.)
Coast, J. (1974). Environmentally safe insecticides. *Consumer Digest*, 23(2), 25–32.

Single Issuing Agency:

General Accounting Office. (2000). *Performance and accountability report.* Washington, DC: General Accounting Office.

Multiple Levels Within Agency:

U.S. Department of the Interior. (2002). U.S. Fish and Wildlife Service. Endangered Species Program. *Recovery report to Congress: Fiscal years 2001–2002.* Arlington, VA: U.S. Fish and Wildlife Service.

Hearings:

U.S. Congress. (2003). House. Committee on Resources. *Abandoned mine lands program.* 108th Cong., 1st sess.

Committee Prints:

U.S. Congress. (2006). House. Committee on Energy and Commerce. *Human tissue samples: NIH research policies and practices.* 109th Cong., 2nd sess. Committee Print.

Reports:

U.S. Congress. (1992). House. *Family and Medical Leave Act of 1992: Conference report (to accompany S.5).* 102nd Cong., 2nd Sess., H. Doc 102-816.

Laws and statutes:

Statutes at Large:

Family and Medical Leave Act of 1993. Pub. L. No. 103-3. Stat. 107:6 (1993).

U.S. Code:

Family and Medical Leave Act. (1993). U.S.C. 29 §§ 2601 et seq.

U.S. Supreme Court Decisions:

Reports:

Washington v. Davis. 423 U.S. 1044. (1976).

Reporter:

Washington v. Davis. 96 S.Ct. 2040. (1976).

Rules and regulations:

Federal Register:

Endangered and Threatened Wildlife and Plants: Final Rule to List Six Foreign Birds as Endangered. Fed. Reg. 73, no. 11 (Jan. 16, 2008): 3145-3179.

Code of Federal Regulations:

Occupational Health and Safety Standards. (2007). *Code of Federal Regulations* Title 29, Pt. 1.

State government and local documents:

California. (2002). *AB275 Medi-Cal: Developmentally Disabled: Dental Care.* Chapter 522.

Los Angeles, CA. (1976). *Bicycles and Vehicles: Bicycle Licenses. Municipal Code.* Article 6, Section 26.01.

International documents:

Laws:
Canada. Access to Information Act. 1980-81-82-83, c. 111, Sch. I "1".

Nongovernmental Bodies:
United Nations General Assembly. (2007). *Oceans and the Law of the Sea: Report of the Secretary General. Sixty-second Session.* Addendum. A/62/66/Add.1.

Newspaper or magazine article:
Greenberger, R. S. (1981, October 23). Hottest labor consultant in Washington adopts new right techniques to bolster union's image. *The Wall Street Journal,* p. B3.

Newspaper article with no author:
Dr. King's widow testifies in a civil trial. (1999, November 17). *The New York Times,* p. A16.

Source without an author (except for newspapers):
SAS user's guide. (1992). Cary, NC: SAS Institute.

Personal interviews:
Simon, P. (1998, August 12). Personal interview.

Online database: *(Editor's Note: Online databases often provide the user with an option for viewing a PDF or HTML version of the document. A PDF document should be referenced as though it were viewed in its original format because it is just a picture of that material. An HTML version of the material has been reformatted. Because it has been reformatted, it must be referenced as a product of the online service. The HTML reference should include the citation of the main directory of the database. The APA style requires a date of access in the citation for HTML versions of a document.)*
Chanen, J. S. (2000). Daddy's home. *ABA Journal,* 86 (11), 90. Retrieved August 27, 2003, from Academic Search database.

For an Internet source: *(Editor's Note: When the Internet source does not have a date of publication, the date the site was last updated or created is sufficient. Occasionally, an Internet source will not have any date. In this event, use the abbreviation for no date—"n.d."—in place of the year.)*

Organizational Web Site Internet Source:
AFL-CIO. (1999, January 14). *Working families need a voice: Who's behind it?* Retrieved July 19, 1999, from http://www.aflcio.org/silence/behind.html.

Electronic Journal Web Site Internet Source:
Harris, J. (1999). Clinton proposes increased child care subsidies. *Amarillo Business Journal,* 3(2). Retrieved August 25, 1999, from http://businessjournal.net/stories/020698/child.html.

Electric Magazine Web Site Internet Source:
Rosenberg, D. (November 22, 1999). More than just a kiss: Hillary's conflicted life as first lady and candidate. *Newsweek*. Retrieved November 17, 1999, from http://www.newsweek.com/nw-srv/printed/us/na/a55101-1999nov14.htm.

Government Site Internet Source:
National Labor Relations Board. (1999, February 17). *National Labor Relations Board members*. Retrieved July 14, 1999, from http://www.nlrb.gov/members.html.

Informally Published Electronic Material Internet Source: (Editor's Note: Include as much information as possible [author of the content, title or owner of the site, title of the page, URL]. APA style requires a date of access.)
Brown, J. (1998, October 24). Homepage. Retrieved July 8, 1999, from http://www. polsci.swms.edu/brown/personal.htm.

MLA Style Reference Examples

The formats described in *The Modern Language Association Publication Manual* style guide have many distinctive characteristics. The most significant are that the titles of documents are underlined in "headline" format and that the titles of articles in books and journals are placed in quotes and in "headline" format. All titles are listed in a "headline" format and the publication date is placed at the end of the list of information.

Multiple works by an author: *(Editor's Note: Multiple works by the same author are listed and organized by the title.)*
Chubb, John E., and Terry Moe. <u>Politics, Markets, and America's Schools</u>. Washington, DC: Brookings. 1990.
Chubb, John E., and Terry Moe. "Politics, Markets, and the Organization of Schools." <u>American Political Science Review</u> 82 (1988): 1065-87.
Massinga, Ruth. "Aging Out Of Foster Care." <u>Christian Science Monitor</u>. 91.102 (1999): 11.
Massinga, Ruth. "Statement of Ruth Massinga, Chief Executive Officer Casey Family Program, Seattle, Washington." <u>Testimony before the House Committee on Ways and Means Subcommittee on Human Resources</u>. May 13, 1999. 23 October 2005 <http://waysandmeans.house.gov/legacy/humres/106cong/5-13-99/5-13mass.htm>.

Book:
Shafritz, Jay M. <u>The Dictionary of American Government and Politics</u>. Chicago, IL: Dorsey, 1988.

Book with two authors:
Wilson, Ian, and Stuart I. Morse. <u>Law and Social Change: Civil Rights and Their Consequences</u>. San Francisco, CA: Munner, 2003.

Book with three or more authors: *(Editor's Note: By convention if a book has more than six authors, only list the first six followed by "et al." Style guides differ on the specifics of this policy, so check the appropriate style guide.)*
Schweller, John, Christopher Jones, and Timothy Fuller. <u>Principles of Ecological Wisdom</u>. New York: Simon, 2002.

Article in an edited book:

Heclo, Hugh. "Issue Networks and the Executive Establishment." The New American Political System. Ed. Anthony King. Washington, DC: American Enterprise Inst. For Policy Research, 1978. 51–84.

Journal article paginated by volume: (Page numbers begin at 1 for the first issue and continue in the next issue with the ending page number from the first issue.)
Costantini, Edmond. "Political Women and Political Ambition: Closing the Gender Gap." American Journal of Political Science 34 (1990): 741–70.

Journal article paginated by issue: (Page numbers begin at 1 for each issue.)
Coast, James. "Environmentally Safe Insecticides." Consumer Digest 23.2 (1974): 25–32.

Government document:

Single Issuing Agency:
General Accounting Office. Performance and Accountability Report. Washington, DC: General Accounting Office, 2000.

Multiple Levels Within Agency:
United States. Department of the Interior. United States Fish and Wildlife Service. Endangered Species Program. Recovery Report to Congress: Fiscal Years 2001-2002. Arlington, VA: U.S. Fish and Wildlife Service, 2002.

Hearings:
United States. Cong. House. Committee on Resources. Abandoned Mine Lands Program. 108th Cong., 1st sess., 2003.

Committee Prints:
United States. Cong. House. Committee on Energy and Commerce. Human Tissue Samples: NIH Research Policies and Practices. 109th Cong., 2nd sess. Committee Print, 2006.

Reports:
United States. Cong. House. Family and Medical Leave Act of 1992: Conference report (to accompany S.5). 102nd Cong., 2nd Sess., H. Doc 102-816, 1992.

Laws and statutes:

Statutes at Large:
Family and Medical Leave Act of 1993. Pub. L. 103-3. 1993. Stat. 107.6.

U.S. Code:
Family and Medical Leave Act of 1993. U.S. Code 29 SS 2601 et seq.

U.S. Supreme Court Decisions:

Reports:
Washington v. Davis. 423 U.S. 1044. 1976.

Reporter:
Washington v. Davis. 96 S.Ct. 2040. 1976.

Rules and regulations:

Federal Register:

Endangered and Threatened Wildlife and Plants: Final Rule to List Six Foreign Birds as Endangered. Federal Register, 73, no. 11. 16 January 2008. *3145–3179.*

Code of Federal Regulations:

Occupational Health and Safety Standards. Code of Federal Regulations. 2007. Title 29, Pt. 1.

State government and local documents:

California. AB275 Medi-Cal: Developmentally Disabled: Dental Care. Chapter 522. 2002.

Los Angeles, CA. Bicycles and Vehicles: Bicycle Licenses. Municipal Code. Article 6, Section 26.01. 1976.

International documents:

Laws:

Canada. Access to Information Act. 1980-81-82-83, c. 111, Sch. I "1".

Nongovernmental Bodies:

United Nations General Assembly. Oceans and the Law of the Sea: Report of the Secretary General. Sixty-second Session. Addendum. A/62/66/Add.1. 2007.

Newspaper or magazine article:

Greenberger, Robert S. "Hottest Labor Consultant in Washington Adopts New Right Techniques to Bolster Union's Image." The Wall Street Journal 23 October 1981: B3.

Newspaper article with no author:

"Dr. King's Widow Testifies in a Civil Trial." New York Times 17 November 1999: A16.

Source without an author (except for newspapers):

SAS User's Guide. Cary, NC: SAS Institute. 1992.

Personal interviews:

Simon, Paul. Personal Interview. 12 August 1998.

Online database: *(Editor's Note: Online databases often provide the user with an option for viewing a PDF or HTML version of the document. A PDF document should be referenced as though it were viewed in its original format because it is just a picture of that material. An HTML version of the material has been reformatted. Because it has been reformatted, it must be referenced as a product of the online service. The HTML reference should include the citation of the main directory of the database. The MLA style requires a date of access in the citation for HTML versions of a document.)*

Chanen, Jill Schachner. "Daddy's Home." ABA Journal 86.11 (2000): 90. Academic Search. 27 August 2003 <http://www.epnet.com>.

For an Internet source: *(Editor's Note: When the Internet source does not have a date of publication, the date the site was last updated or created is sufficient. Occasionally, an Internet source will not have any date. In this event, use the abbreviation for no date—"n.d."—in place of the year.)*

Organizational Web Site Internet Source:

AFL-CIO. <u>Working Families Need a Voice: Who's Behind It?</u> 14 January 1999. 19 July 1999 <http://www.aflcio.org/silence/behind.html>.

Electronic Journal Web Site Internet Source:

Harris, J., "Clinton Proposes Increased Child Care Subsidies." <u>Amarillo Business Journal</u>, 3.2. (1999). 25 August 1999 <http://businessjournal.net/stories/020698/child.html>.

Electric Magazine Web Site Internet Source:

Rosenberg, Debra. "More than Just a Kiss: Hillary's Conflicted Life as First Lady and Candidate." <u>Newsweek</u>, 22 November 1999. 17 November 1999 <http://www.newsweek.com/nw-srv/printed/us/na/a55101-1999nov14.htm>.

Government Site Internet Source:

National Labor Relations Board. <u>National Labor Relations Board Members</u>. 17 February 1999. 14 July 1999 <http://www.nlrb.gov/members.html>.

Informally Published Electronic Material Internet Source: **(Editor's Note: Include as much information as possible [author of the content, title or owner of the site, title of the page, URL]. The MLA style requires a date of access.)**

Brown, Jon. <u>Homepage</u>. 24 October 1998. 8 July 1999 <http://www.polsci.swms.edu/brown/personal.htm>.

FORMAT AND EXAMPLES FOR ACTIVITIES TO ENHANCE COMPREHENSION AND SYNTHESIS OF CLASS MATERIALS

Enhancing Comprehension and Synthesis of Class Materials

Instructors often require special kinds of assignments to help prepare students for professional research and to develop analytical skills. Rather than simply reading the material and taking a test on the facts, or writing a descriptive term paper or essay, students are asked to process the information in some way that will help them to synthesize the material for use later on. Sometimes the assignments enhance comprehension and understanding of a particular concept or theory. In particular, the assignments are structured to help students develop research and problem-solving skills. Developing such skills encourages students to integrate and synthesize the material in a meaningful and productive way.

Although many of the standards and rules that apply to research papers and essays apply to special assignments, there are some differences. These differences are generally found in the purpose and properties of each kind of activity. The following descriptions encompass a traditional approach to each assignment. Each description is followed by a written example. Be sure to consult the instructor for specific requirements that are in addition to those described in this chapter.

List of special activities described in this chapter:

Analytical Essays

Political Editorials

Analytical Multiple Choice Exams

Essay Exams

Literature Review Presentations

Media Applications

Writing Analytical Essays

Analytical essays are usually very limited assignments. Like essay exam answers, they are meant to be brief but well-reasoned and thorough examinations of some political theory, phenomenon, or behavior. As in a research paper, the evidence used to support an argument in an analytical essay should be source-based. Most often, the instructor will provide source material in a reader or class packet. Sometimes instructors provide students with a particular question to answer or debate using course materials. The students are to take a position and support it using expert opinion. Here is a description of how to construct an analytical essay:

1. **Examine the limits and expectations stated by the instructor for the assignment.**
   - If a particular question must be answered, understand the context, limitations, and focus of the question before researching.
   - If particular readings are required as sources for the essay, read them at least once while focusing on the issues required by the instructor.
   - Before using any materials other than those required or suggested, ask the instructor if it is permissible to include additional sources.

2. **After reading the material, formulate an answer to the question.**
   - Use the introduction to briefly describe the context in which the question is being answered.
   - State the position clearly in a thesis statement.
   - Summarize the answer to the question in one sentence.
   - Be sure that the thesis sentence provides both an answer and a justification or reason.
   - Avoid vague or ambiguous thesis sentences.
   - Be bold, be obvious, be direct, but do not be rhetorical!

3. **Use the assigned material as evidence in support of each reason stated in the position.**
   - Do not outline the articles or materials used as a source.
   - Assert one idea or one justification of the position per paragraph.
   - Use the assigned material to support the assertion.
   - Use the assigned material to provide examples, if necessary.
   - Avoid quoting altogether.
   - Summarize the sources' viewpoints in one or two sentences.

4. Write a conclusion that reasserts the position.

- Briefly review the main reasons why the position is valid.
- Offer some suggestion about the value of examining the issue identified in the assignment or question given by the instructor.

5. A standard two-page analytical essay should be no longer than six paragraphs.

- The essay should have an introduction, an explanatory paragraph for each reason given, and a conclusion.
- Be concise and do not waste words.
- Provide a Reference or Works Cited page for essays using assigned readings. If the readings were taken from only one source (such as a reader or packet), the instructor may want a complete reference only for that source, and then each item referenced from that source can be listed with authors, titles, and page numbers. Check with the instructor for referencing requirements. If the references are from more than one source, students must provide full bibliographic references for each source referenced in the text.

Why Should We Worry About a Judge's Ideology If Judicial Decisions Are Based on Precedent and the Constitution?

An Analytical Essay

By
Jean M. Schuberth
GEB 114, SEC. 3
Professor Schmidt
NOVEMBER 29, 1990
(Reprinted with permission)

Judicial review has been considered a political issue since the framing of the Constitution. Supreme Court Justices interpreted policy and used judicial discretion to define law and to set or overturn precedents. As a nation of people who believe in limited government and equal protection, discretion with which a judge makes decisions is at the source of concern over judicial power. In particular, if well harnessed by an ideological coalition, the act of interpreting law leaves significant opportunity for abuse of judicial power and the introduction of political bias.

Alexander Hamilton believed that the judicial system was the least powerful of the three branches of government. He argued that the court's power did not outweigh the other branches by interpreting the law because it was bound to interpretations that are consistent to the Constitution. Hamilton stated that the legislative branch had controlled the money and "prescribes" the laws and rights of the community (Hamilton 1990, 567). This statement, however, was irrelevant to the power of interpreting law. Interpreting laws prescribes laws and rights to the people, as well as by ruling what can and cannot be done constitutionally. American history reflects an important change in rights and obligations when judicial decisions overrule precedent as being unfair and unconstitutional (Marbury *v* Madison 1990, 573).

A judge's ideology is significant from the standpoint that the Supreme Court makes law. Because judges are empowered to interpret the law, they have the opportunity to substitute their personal interpretation of laws. They control not only how laws are interpreted but also when precedents apply to a case. Only when judicial self-restraint is being utilized for the sake of non-confrontation and non-intervention will a judge's views seem unbiased (Roche 1990, 577). Even then, it is questionable that precedent in this case, as interpreted by Justices, does not exist. Self-restraint allows the opportunity for a coalition of judges to interpret policy again later when a stronger case representing their ideological viewpoints can be used to overturn decisions. A passive attitude by the judiciary can reflect as much ideological input as one which is dominated by an activist court (Roche 1990, 581).

Supreme Court decisions are supposed to be reasoned by precedent and constitutionality. Unfortunately, interpretation of the Constitution depends on individual Justices to put aside their individual perspectives. Justices are obliged to overcome personal needs, use authority responsibly, and at the same time reinterpret, give new definition, reword, and revise the law (Brennan 1990, 583). This is nearly impossible to do. Consequently, judicial decisions reflect a personal ideology based upon individual moral and ethical beliefs experienced as a member of society. Because the role of the Supreme Court judge involves not only interpretation but choosing which issues to try under law (Brennan 1990, 585), the choice and processing of cases often reflect judges' community or environmental experiences. Based upon the legitimate excuse that the thousands of cases received are too many to handle, judicial discretion is necessary for managing and controlling the judicial agenda. In this process, a decision to rule on a case or not will reflect a judge's ideology, if not biases.

The American Constitution, as the law of the land, is a remarkable document with elaborate checks to constrain particular interests abusing power or exhibiting political favoritism at a minority's expense. The judicial branch has no special exemption to these checks. Unfortunately, judicial decisions are as difficult to question as they are to overturn. Individual biases are masked by the aura of an interpreted constitutionality and enhanced by coalitions within the Supreme Court who set, decide, and pursue political agendas reflecting their individual, moral, and political beliefs. A judge's ideology is important to safeguarding political rights and protections because, in coalition, a judge's ideology is the mechanism that helps to define what the Constitution means, as well as what principles and precedents apply to interpreting the Constitution.

REFERENCES

Brennan Jr., William J. 1990. How the Supreme Court arrives at decisions. In *American government: Readings and cases*, 10th ed., edited by Peter Woll, 603–613. Glenview, IL: Scott Foresman/Little, Brown Higher Education.

Hamilton, Alexander. 1990. Federalist 78. In *American government: Readings and cases*, 10th ed., edited by Peter Woll, 566–570. Glenview, IL: Scott Foresman/Little, Brown Higher Education.

Marbury *v* Madison (1803). 1990. In *American government: Readings and cases*, 10th ed., edited by Peter Woll, 571–575. Glenview, IL: Scott Foresman/Little, Brown Higher Education.

Roche, John P. 1990. Judicial Self-Restraint. In *American government: Readings and cases*, 10th ed., edited by Peter Woll, 576–582. Glenview, IL: Scott Foresman/Little, Brown Higher Education.

Writing Political Editorials

Editorials, like analytical essays, are usually very limited assignments. Like analytical essays, editorials are meant to be brief but well-reasoned examinations of some specific phenomenon or behavior. Unlike an analytical essay or a research paper, however, the evidence used to support an argument in an editorial need not be source-based and the tone and language are casual, emotive, and value-laden. Most often, editorials are composed of more opinion than fact in the evidence and reasoning. In other words, they are thoughtful expressions of the author's **views** on political phenomena. The purpose of the editorial is not only to express views but also to persuade others to adopt the same views. Writing editorials, even if they are not published, helps students work on critical thinking and political argument techniques without the constraints of sources and secondary evidence. The students are to take a position and support it using reasons, logic, and, yes, even facts if necessary! Here is a description of how to construct an editorial.

Formulating an Opinion

1. **Identify and research an important salient issue.**
   - The best editorials are those that exhibit knowledge, authority, and passion about an issue.
   - Use course materials for background information.
   - Talk to people and read about the issue in a variety of sources.
   - Gather ideas and viewpoints; analyze them on the basis of credibility.

2. Formulate a reasoned opinion.

- Students must have a reason for every assertion they make in the editorial.
- Every assertion must have a justification.
- Assert one idea or one justification of the position per paragraph.
- Assertions without reasons and justifications can be easily ignored.

3. Keep in mind most editorials are only about 300 to 600 words.

- Use a highly emotive, assertive, active voice with a tone of conviction.
- Avoid jargon and formal language.
- Keep the paragraphs and sentences short and simple.

Format for the Editorial

Although there is no set format for an editorial, most editorials generally follow a pattern. The order and number of the paragraphs can be changed a bit, with the exception of the first and last paragraph. Often, people read only the first and last paragraphs of editorials in the newspaper. Because of this, the first and last paragraphs contain a concise, but compelling assertion about what the issue is (the first paragraph) and what should be done about it (the last paragraph). All the material between these two important paragraphs serves as justification for the assertions.

1. First paragraph:

- Begin the editorial with a controversial or compelling example or comment.
- State succinctly what is wrong or right about a decision made or action taken concerning the issue.
- Tell what should be done.

2. Second paragraph:

- Provide context or background information about the event.
- Focus on what happened before the event.
- State why what happened before was better or worse than the event at issue.

3. Third paragraph:

- Tell how the current situation is in opposition or contrary to the previous situation.
- Explain concisely how the current situation differs from past practices.

4. Fourth paragraph:

- Provide more contextual examples.
- Provide more examples that are illustrative of the issue at its worst.
- Provide a compelling anecdote.

5. Fifth paragraph:

- State strongly why this situation (policy, etc.) is good or bad.
- Provide reasons for the assertions.
- Provide a solution to help resolve the issue.

6. Sixth paragraph:

- Forecast or suggest what will happen because of this situation.
- Tell what the future will look like if the situation is left unchanged.

7. **Seventh paragraph:**
   - Restate why the result of an unchanged situation is good or bad.
   - Provide reasons for why it is good or bad.
8. **Last paragraph:**
   - Restate the issue.
   - Restate the opinion about how to resolve the issue.
   - End with a compelling statement or rhetorical question.

Example: An Editorial

YOUNG VOICES

JUST A HOUSEWIFE? THINK ABOUT IT A BIT LONGER!

What's your impression of this ad? CEO wanted for nonprofit organization: Duties: budget planning and administration, task delegation, scheduling of activities, training and teaching, implementation of the nutrition program, plus miscellaneous duties. Prerequisites: enormous patience, organizational skills, flexibility, ability to handle emergencies efficiently, and an abundance of love and devotion. This position is voluntary, unpaid, and not highly regarded by society.

Who in their right mind would work for no pay? Believe it or not, there are millions of women out there who do this every day. Their title may not be CEO; on the contrary, they all too often refer to themselves as "just a housewife." Why is this honorable profession so terribly underrated in our society? It may just be envy.

Like so many moms on campus, we try to do it all, yet we always feel inadequate. Somehow, it is never enough. Besides, it is very unfashionable to admit that what some of us really want is an old-fashioned style family; it's almost like saying a dirty word.

Women have made great strides for equality and shouldn't face any societal barriers to reaching their full potential. But I think the scale has tipped to where we have to do it all in order to be appreciated.

Just look at the Republican-crafted Welfare Reform Bill. All it accomplishes is forcing mothers out of the home away from small kids who are still in their most impressionable years. Single mothers are mostly affected by this and are not considered in the Republican emphasis on family values.

This implies that it's more acceptable for a mother to have a career than to be a housewife and mother, regardless of marital status. This sentiment even includes men. With few, but very notable exceptions, men on the average don't want to solely provide for a family. It seems to trigger the "fight or flight response," just like the M-word. What contributed to this? Do they feel that women have expectations they can't fulfill?

Maybe we as a group portray that image by chasing after high-paying/high-prestige careers—like the one I am chasing out of pure necessity.

A satisfying career has its definite rewards, but it still falls short of the joys of full-time motherhood. I had a glimpse of that during my maternity leave.

My daughter is now 3 years old and I'm used to this rat race, but I still long for baking cookies with Santa Faces, ironing a crease into a pair of suit pants right where it belongs (I do know how to do that stuff), cooking a meal that appeals to adult taste buds and is not yet another variety of Hamburger Helper, and asking a stressed-out, grumpy, traditional male prototype how his day went.

I'm not advocating the burning of Betty Friedan's "Feminine Mystique," nor have I just discovered that my childbearing years are down to single digits or overdosed on gender studies.

This doesn't come from an escapee from the conservative camp, but from a woman who benches 175 pounds, has fired a machine gun for a living, and hopes for the cloning of Hillary Rodham Clinton. Now that I have confessed and come out of the closet, the National Organization for Women will probably put a contract out on me.

It's just about choices. Choices subtly diminish once the maternal side kicks in, and one soon discovers that the day really has only 24 hours.

I'm far from saying that the three Ks (Kinder, Kueche, and Kirche) are for all women, but defying nature carries a cost that I'm getting tired of bearing.

Christine N. Rueda-Lynn is a columnist
for *The Southwest Standard* at Southwest
Missouri State University.
Reprinted in *Springfield News Leader*
Dec. 1, 1997, p. 8a
(Reprinted by permission)

Analytical Multiple-Choice Exams

Although taking exams is not considered a special assignment, an analytical multiple-choice exam is different from the average multiple-choice exam. To perform well on an analytical multiple-choice exam, students must use the same skills they use in essay writing.

- These exams require knowledge, good reading habits, and critical thinking skills.
- In analytical multiple-choice questions, there are no funny answers, no "all of the above," no "none of the above," and no questions where students must find the wrong answer in the group.
- Students must differentiate between closely related information or concepts.
- Students must understand how information, concepts, and explanations of political behavior or events are influenced by the context in which they are examined.
- The answers to analytical multiple-choice questions can rarely be guessed.
- The answers require well-reasoned responses and rarely exhibit a pattern.

Tips for Answering Analytical Multiple-Choice Questions

The questions used in an analytical multiple-choice exam are typically factual, definitional, conceptual, or practical applications. They are best approached as essay questions! Do the following before answering the question:

1. **Determine what kind of question is being asked.**
2. **Identify the important modifiers and qualifiers in the question.**
   - If writing on the exam question sheet is allowed, underline the key words or concepts and circle the modifiers and qualifiers.

This question asks students to apply what they know about who makes decisions in different kinds of democracies. The important modifiers are "actually make policy choices." The words "elites" and "majority" are not modifiers; they identify who is doing what for whom. The answer requires that the student understand the four terms well enough to apply them. C and D are incorrect because they are different theories of politics; they are not theories of the organization of government and decision-making. Although American government is majoritarian, in a majoritarian government, the majority makes the rules. In the American system, representatives make decisions for the majority. This means B is the answer.

Essay Exams

Many students are uneasy about taking essay exams. Although they may write well, they are reluctant to take essay tests because it may not be clear what is expected. Essay exams are another way of synthesizing information. Here are a couple of suggestions for reading and interpreting an answer to an essay question.

1. **An essay question may contain one or more important terms.** (See "Writing a Thesis for an Essay") For example, here is an essay question concerning the congressional budget process:

   "Describe and analyze the budget process. Provide reasons why each step exists."

   In this case, the student must be careful to address **all** parts of the question. Just listing the information is not enough; the student must also demonstrate knowledge of why each step is important.

2. **Students must be careful, especially when answering questions that ask for criticisms or evaluations, that each assertion (or point) is supported with evidence or examples.**

3. **The question should be answered directly. Underline the key verbs and modifiers that structure or limit the scope of the question.**

4. **The thesis sentence of an answer to this essay question should repeat the key terms of the question and lay out the writer's main points.**
   - In short essays, the thesis sentence should be the first sentence.
   - In longer essays, the thesis should be in the first paragraph.

5. **Address only one idea per paragraph.**
   - Be sure to use a topic sentence, an explanatory sentence, and a summary sentence in each paragraph.
   - Use transitional words, such as *first, second, in addition,* or *thus,* to organize and link ideas from paragraph to paragraph.
   - Most importantly, be obvious—do not be obtuse. Make points clearly, simply, and directly.

6. **Time and space are usually limited during an essay exam so students must use them efficiently.**
   - If each essay contributes equally to the grade, then divide the number of essays by the number of minutes and allot equal amounts to each.

- If each essay does not contribute equally to the grade, determine the amount of time to spend on each by the proportion of each essay's contribution to the grade.

Sample Answer: Essay Test Question
(Reprinted with permission)

GROUP THEORY QUESTION

Group theorists argue that public policy can be defined as the equilibrium that is reached in a group struggle. Explain this theory and offer an alternative, competing explanation of how public policy can be defined. Which one is preferable? Why?

By
Edward Pettit

Pluralist theory is only one of numerous such theories about how public policy is formulated. Though pluralist theory has its strong points, it does not explain how institutional structures constrain possible policy outcomes. Institutions theory offers a competing explanation about how policy is formulated. Unfortunately, institutions theory does not explain why public policy reflects the values of groups who are not part of the policy-making institution. Because of this, institutions theory can be considered less preferable than the pluralist theory for explaining policy making.

Pluralist theory essentially states that group struggle is the central force of politics, and that policies, including the goals, the means, and the outcomes, are directly attributable to group conflict. This theory states that individuals are important only when working in a group. Policy is defined, according to pluralist theory, as the compromise between competing groups and reflects the relative influence of each group. Although it does not account for why policy varies from institution to institution, it does explain why policy content reflects a dominant group's values.

In institutions theory, policy only results when a policy proposal is stated, adopted, implemented, and enforced by an institution. The institution provides a policy with legitimacy, universality, and the coercive force necessary to enforce it equally across the populace. The structure of the policy-making institution provides both the means and constraints to formulating policy responses to public problems.

This policy definition is vastly different from the pluralist view because institutions, not people or groups, legitimize policy. It is, however, deficient because it does not state anything significant about policy content. Because policy content and institutional structure are not logically related, the institutional theory cannot explain why policy content benefits some more than others in society. In pluralist theory, policy content represents group struggle and the dominant group's influence over the policy response and related benefits. Thus, pluralist theory explains variations in policy responses and why some groups benefit at the public's expense.

Both the pluralist and institutional models of policy formulation offer explanations of policy responses, but the pluralist model is more comprehensive because it explains, to a certain extent, not just how policy is made, but why it is made. While the institutional model explains the formal processes of public policy-making, it does not account for variations in policy content. Hence, although the process of policy-making is important, pluralist theory models explain policy outcomes more directly and clearly than the institutional model.

Scholarly Literature Review Presentations

Class presentations on scholarly literature provide students the opportunity to examine different approaches and controversies not covered in the lectures or textbook. Often, the subject of the presentation is a scholarly article or book that provided a path-breaking method or conceptual examination important to building a knowledge community in political science.

Tips for Writing a Literature Review Presentation

1. **A literature review typically includes:**
   - a statement of the author's purpose.
   - an identification of the author's hypothesis.
   - a description of the issue, context, and assumptions.
   - a description of the controversy.
   - an explanation of how the controversy was examined.
   - a description of the author's findings.
   - a concluding statement about the significance of the work.
2. **A literature review presentation is generally graded with the same criteria used to grade written assignments.**
   - Students' grades usually reflect the quality and thoroughness with which they presented the material contained in the categories listed.
   - A literature review presentation is frequently graded on the degree to which the student identified the critical information provided in the scholarly book or article.
   - A solid performance by the student demonstrates depth and breadth of understanding the significance of the work related to the subfield or topic area.
3. **To write the presentation, outline the article or book using the categories above.**
   - The length and degree of detail in the presentation outline will depend on the time allotted for the presentation or the page limit set by the instructor.
   - In general, the outline should be approximately two-and-a-half pages typed in outline form.
4. **Exhibit poise and confidence (try rehearsing).**
   - Be prepared to answer questions of clarification.
   - Vary the voice level, make eye contact with other students, and use gestures.
   - Do not read word for word from the outline. Address the audience in a casual, conversational tone, but avoid rambling from point to point.

Literature Presentation Form

A literature review presentation typically includes the same material as a research presentation, except that the expectation for a clear grasp of the content is somewhat lower than it would be for a description of a student's own research findings.

Purpose: A clear statement of the purpose and focus of the article or book.

Hypothesis: A clear statement of the controversy identified by the author and the hypothesis tested. State the causal relationships clearly in terms of dependent and independent variables.

Background: A brief discussion of the context and background related to the controversy or the assumptions used to justify the model. Note any value assumptions that are controversial.

Method: An explanation of the method used for testing or examining the hypothesis.

- Describe the source materials used.
- Point out any problems identified by the author related to the gathering of data.
- Be sure to relate the data and source materials to the hypothesis.

Results: A summary of the results of the examination or test.

- If data were used, reproduce illustrative charts, graphs, or tables as visual aids.
- Use a table or chart to summarize the author's main points.
- Use an overhead projector to present the material or make copies of a visual aid for everyone.

Conclusion: This statement explains how the goals of the author were accomplished. In particular, this statement summarizes how the results relate to the author's stated goals.

Significance: A statement that applies the results appropriately to an expansion of knowledge about the subject.

AN ARTICLE REVIEW

I. **Purpose:** To review classic innovative article on voting.

 A. **Source:** Gerald Kramer. 1971. "Short-term Fluctuations in U.S. Voting Behavior 1896–1964," *American Political Science Review*, 65: 131–143.

 B. **Author's purpose:** To provide a quantitative analysis of short-term fluctuations in voting share for U.S. House of Representatives elections with respect to the impact of economic conditions, incumbency advantage, and the presidential coattails effect.

II. **Hypothesis:** Tests several competing and complementary hypotheses about influences on electoral outcomes. He argues that economic fluctuations have a greater impact on voting in House elections than political influences, such as coattail effects.

III. **Background:**

 A. Author reviews some of the literature about influence on voting behavior.

 1. Institutional advantage of the incumbent or incumbency advantage theory is problematic. Only an advantage when expectations are low for benefits. Could be a liability if expectations of voters' personal incomes are not realized.

 2. Party popularity may influence outcomes. House races come closest to Downesian model of anonymous candidates competing as members of a common team. Variations in overall popularity of the party could be a major factor in producing fluctuations in short-term voting behavior.

 3. Incumbent party is usually defined as the party of the president because the president's influence over the policy agenda is greater than that of an individual member of Congress.

 4. A vote for the minor party is considered an anti-incumbent vote and is counted as part of the major opposition party vote.

 5. The coattails effect of a presidential race is reflected in the party as a team.

 B. Author makes several assumptions about behavior.

 1. An individual vote represents a choice between teams in the national election.

 2. People base their decisions on past information.

 3. People's expectations are based on the preceding year's events; they are retrospective, not prospective, voters.

IV. **Method:** Uses statistical analysis to test relative impact of different influences on vote choice based on the literature review and methodological assumptions.

 A. Model: States that the Republican party's share of a two-party vote is a function of incumbency, the difference between the actual and the expected performance, and net institutional advantage.

B. Creates a formal, testable model of voting behavior using the following variables.

   1. Dependent variable: Republican party share of votes.

   2. Independent variables: monetary income, real income, unemployment rate, time period, and coattails term.

C. Uses data gathered from 1896–1964.

   1. Data collected from various government documents.

   2. Left out years 1912 (inability to explain progressive votes), 1918, 1942, and 1944 (wartime distortion of income and prices).

V. **Results:** Used six different forms of the model as an equation to test his hypothesis.

A. The variables measuring expected prices and unemployment have an inverse relationship to the dependent variable.

B. All forms of the model explain a large portion of the variance in voting behavior.

   1. Two-thirds of the variance explained by time variable.

   2. Explanatory power of the model is weaker without the time variable. Only half of the variance is explained.

   3. The income variable was significant and powerful in all the equations.

   4. The price variable was only significant with the monetary variable, but not with real income variable.

   5. The unemployment variable was not significant and the direction of influence is counter to theory. Author proposes that unemployment variable is distorted because unemployed people are disproportionately less active politically.

   6. Coattails variable was not significant. Author proposed that result was biased because the minor party vote was included in the measure because of split ticket voting. When minor party vote removed from coattail variable, it became significant.

VI. **Overall finding:** Approximately one-third of the votes gained or lost in a presidential race are carried over into congressional candidate races.

A. Finds limits of the model. Model cannot identify or predict turning points in an election, but can predict Republican vote shares.

B. The most important determinant of vote choice is income not incumbency advantage or coattails effect. A 10 percent decrease in real income will lead to a 4 to 5 percent loss of votes for the incumbent party.

C. Coattails effect helps only when there is a strong presidential candidate. Can increase vote share by 30 percent.

D. The incumbent party only has an advantage when the economy is doing well.

VII. **Significance:**

A. Economic fluctuations are important to congressional elections. An upturn helps the incumbent and a downturn helps the challenger.

B. Found that election outcomes are more responsive to objective changes occurring under the incumbent party than to political changes.

Media Applications Illustrating Course Materials

Audiovisual or multimedia resources, often in the form of educational or popular films, television shows, or broadcasts, enhance understanding of an abstract and conceptual topic. Instructors generally have students listen or view multimedia resources after addressing topics covered in the lectures or textbook. Multimedia resources present alternative ways to think about and approach lecture topics. Although instructors sometimes show or present the multimedia source and then engage the class in discussion, some instructors provide students with assignments whereby they identify media events that exemplify or illustrate the complex conceptual or abstract topics addressed in their textbooks. Applying these concepts to media resources enhances understanding and comprehension of the course lectures and readings.

Tips for Writing a Media Application Paper

The basic skills necessary for addressing media application assignments include identifying examples of a concept and then explaining how that example illustrates the concept. To do this, the student should have studied the course materials, including reading the textbooks and attending lectures, prior to accessing the multimedia resources.

1. **Examine the assignment expectations.**
   - If an analysis is required where particular concepts are to be identified, then be sure to have at least a definition of each concept prior to accessing the media.
   - If a particular question must be answered, be sure to have an understanding of the context, limitations, and focus of the question before accessing the media.
   - If particular readings are required as sources for the paper, be sure to identify and read the sections in the textbook related to the concepts in the assignment.
   - If possible, make a list of components or indicators that characterize the concepts in the assignment from the assigned readings and/or lectures. Place the author and page number or date of the lecture by each component or indicator.
   - Unless required by the instructor, do not use additional materials outside of the course. The focus of the assignment is to assess how well the student can recognize or apply concepts learned in lectures and course texts.

2. **While viewing or listening to the media source, take notes on incidents and/or events that illustrate the assignment concepts.**
   - List the characteristics of the incident/events, including names of people/places, duration of the event, and where the event occurred in the media resource (beginning, middle, end).
   - Link the events to the concepts as much as possible while viewing or listening to the media source.

3. **Organize and classify the incidents/events based on the characteristics or indicators of the concept (see "Classificational Analysis" in Chapter 5).**

4. **Write the paper using the concept names as headings and, depending on the length, the characteristics/indicators of the concept as subheadings.**

- In the introduction, identify the media source and the concepts that will be examined using the media source. If the assignment includes a question, answer the question directly in the introduction.
- In the body, provide discussion of each concept. Make one theoretical assertion per paragraph about the concept. Use additional information about the concept to clarify the position.
- Use the assigned readings as sources for the theoretical assertions. Do not *outline* the articles or materials used as a source.
- After making an assertion and clarifying it, use incidents/events from the media source to provide practical examples.
- Avoid quoting, excessive detail, and overexplaining.
- In the conclusion, briefly summarize why the incidents/events from the media source illustrate the concepts examined in the paper. Offer some insight about the concepts as applied in the media source.
- Provide a reference page listing the media and the textbook sources. Provide full bibliographic references.

Example: Media Application Assignment

Using references to the readings from Denhardt and Denhardt (Chapters 4, 9, 10), Stillman (Chapters 6, 8, 16, and case study 3), and scenes/events from the beginning, middle, and end of the movie, *The Terminal*, provide an analysis (a) identifying types of expected ethical, group dynamic, and leadership behaviors, (b) discussing why violations of these expectations occur, and (c) explaining how scenes/events from the movie are examples of such dysfunctional behavior.

Example: Applying Class Materials to Media

The Terminal: Analysis of Popular Portrayals of Ethical, Group Dynamic, and Leadership Behaviors

By
Alicia Gifford
POLS 460A
Professor Schmidt
November 5, 2006
(Reprinted with permission)

INTRODUCTION

Ethics, group behaviors, and leadership dynamics are fundamental parts of public administration. The behavior of public officials in the movie *The Terminal* (2004) exemplified some of the most serious problems that involve ethics, group behaviors, and leadership by showing ethical conduct and juxtaposing that with unethical behavior. The movie also illustrates several group dynamics throughout the movie and how they came into conflict with one another. Finally, the movie demonstrated contrasting the leadership skills of two different characters, Frank Dixon and Victor Navorski, in managing functional and dysfunctional organizational relationships.

ETHICS

One concern for public officials is maintaining ethical standards. Ethics is the way people deliberate between what is right and wrong in the workplace and to manage human conduct (Denhardt and Denhardt 2006, 155). These are often revealed through actions involving ethical deliberation, whistle-blowing, conflict of interest, inequity of treatment, and irresponsible conduct. Further, public officials are obligated to act in an ethical way according to bureaucratic norms and professionalism. Bureaucratic norms include loyalty, duty, efficiency, effectiveness, and equitable treatment. Moreover, professionalism involves principles that act together to shape the norms of a particular profession (Waldo 2005, 507). Both bureaucratic and professional norms create the standards for ethical behavior.

Ethical Deliberation

Ethical behavior can be interpreted from decisions or deliberations about what is right and wrong. Ethical deliberation is weighing information and making a decision based on this judgment (Denhardt and Denhardt 2006, 129). For example, Victor Navorski refused to break the law by leaving the airport without authorized paperwork even when he was encouraged to do so by others. The clerk who would not give him a pass without this paperwork behaved ethically by adhering to bureaucratic norms, particularly, equitable treatment, even though she felt sorry for Navorski. By the end of the movie, after several people expedited his paperwork, Navorski is permitted to leave the airport to go into New York by the security guards even though Frank Dixon, the supervisor of security, did not want to allow it. The security guards behaved ethically by exhibiting professionalism.

Sometimes ethical behavior may require whistle-blowing. Whistle-blowing is revealing information about fraud, waste, abuse of power, or rule breaking by reporting it to a higher authority to stop the behavior (Denhardt and Denhardt 2006, 147; Montjoy and Slaton 2005, 515–520). Problems arise when no one acts in an ethical manner to "blow the whistle" on rule breaking. Often there are barriers to those that want to stop the rule breaking such as fear of one's career being harmed and being ostracized from the work environment. In the movie, this is seen in the relationship between the security guards and Dixon. There were several times during the movie where the security guards could have reported the maltreatment of Navorski by Dixon. It was clear as the movie progressed that the security guards and other employees were troubled by what they were witnessing, but were afraid to challenge Dixon.

Unethical Behavior

Conflict of interest is a component of deliberate unethical behavior that sometimes occurs with public officials. Conflict of interest is a standard of conduct where public officials benefit personally from policy decisions (Denhardt and Denhardt 2006, 146). An example of a conflict of interest in the movie is when Dixon created a new position within the airport to force Navorski to violate the law and go out of the airport by making it difficult for him to acquire money by returning carts. Dixon abused his power and acted in his own interest by creating the position of Transportation Liaison just so that he could prevent Navorski from returning carts.

GROUP DYNAMICS

Ethical behavior needs a platform and that platform is group dynamics. A group dynamic is when two or more people work together to find a solution to a particular problem. There are advantages and disadvantages to groups. The advantages are that there is more information available with more people working together; synergy is created with a group when the whole is greater than the sum of the parts (Denhardt and Denhardt 2006, 381–383). The disadvantages are that time limits constrain the number of solutions that a group can come up with, it costs more to employ a group than it does a single person. Further, when people feel their ideas are not being recognized, and they are not given the recognition they deserve, their output will tend to be less (Mayo 2005, 160–163).

Communicating

One of the fundamental parts of group dynamics is communication. This includes listening and speaking. There are several key factors to effective listening that include having a reason or purpose, suspending judgment initially, resisting distractions, waiting before responding, rephrasing what you hear into your own words, finding important themes in what people say, and reflecting and finding meaning (Denhardt and Denhardt 2006, 368). Furthermore, speaking is the second part of communicating that needs as much attention as listening. Much of speaking is done in the form of instructions given (Mayo 2005, 161–162). These skills were not employed by Dixon throughout the movie. In the beginning when there was a language barrier between Dixon and Navorski, Dixon did not even attempt to listen to what Navorski was trying to communicate. The group of other employees, the guards, the maintenance workers, and the clerks learned to communicate with Navorski by suspending judgment and finding value in what he said and did and thus were engaged in the group dynamic.

Although communicating is a fundamental part of public administration, this skill, however, is often poorly practiced by people who fail to value or respect others. Communicating in the form of speaking and listening sometimes becomes dysfunctional when the person speaking is not clear or the person listening does not listen clearly to what is being said (Mayo 2005, 161–162). An example of this from the movie occurred when Dixon was telling Navorski that he could not go home, he could not go to New York, and he had to stay in the airport until his country was recognized by the United States. Dixon did not listen to what Navorski was trying to say in his limited English vocabulary and was not communicating with Navorski because of the language barrier. While Navorski was trying to comprehend what Dixon was saying, Dixon was busy eating food and espousing regulations. At no time did Dixon attempt to be clear or coherent for Navorski; it was clear he did not value or respect Navorski.

Inter-group Problem Solving

Sometimes groups also have difficulties solving problems when communication fails. Group problems tend to arise when not everyone agrees on a particular solution to a problem. There are three types of group dynamics that evolve from poor communication:

tribal conceit, learned distrust, and turf wars. Tribal conceit is when people within the group have the mentality that they are better than others. Learned distrust is when people hearing lies over a period of time learn to mistrust the source of information. Turf wars are a fight over territory, capital, or resources (Langewiesche 2005, 168). All three of these types of group dynamics create dysfunctional relationships.

There are examples of each of these group dynamics in the movie. An example of tribal conceit is the separation between the guards, the maintenance workers, and the retail clerks. Each set of people tended to trust only other members of their groups and not people outside their group. In addition, a learned distrust developed between the guards and Dixon because of Dixon's abuse of Navorski. By the end of the movie, even Navorski, who began as a very trusting person, exhibited a learned distrust of anything Dixon had to say. Finally, an example of turf wars occurred at the end of the movie when the security guards went against Dixon's order to keep Navorski in the airport. This shows a turf war between the guards and Dixon. The security guards knew Navorski had permission to leave the airport and asserted their authority by letting him leave even though Dixon had the authority to prevent Navorski from leaving.

LEADERSHIP

Ethical standards and good group dynamics are not the only components of a functional organization. Leadership is also a fundamental part of communicating effectively, motivating others, exercising power, and working well with others. A responsible leader portrays all of these characteristics and is able to achieve goals with the help of others.

Responsible Leadership

It is important that managers engage in responsible leadership when they perform certain tasks such as monitoring the work of subordinates, negotiating, planning, decision-making, and directing subordinates (Denhardt and Denhardt 2006, 337–338; Lindblom 2005, 224–228; Riccucci 2005, 98–100). Problems arise however, when a leader fails to embrace responsible leadership characteristics. For example, Dixon, as a manager, communicated through belligerence and abused his power. This made him a poor leader and thus, his employees were not motivated to help him. Alternatively, Navorski, even though he did not have formal power, exhibited many of these characteristics. He was charismatic, worked well with others, motivated others, and was able to perform tasks that he was given. By the end of the movie, many of the employees from the different groups followed Navorski and helped him achieve his goals.

Irresponsible leadership is often exhibited by dysfunctional behavior (Nagel 2005, 248). Types of dysfunctional behavior include stress syndrome, type A (overly aggressive) behavior, and burnout (Denhardt and Denhardt 2006, 340–343). It was clear from the movie that Dixon was a dysfunctional leader. Dixon exhibited stress syndrome characteristics including stress, defensiveness, alarm, and exhaustion in a variety of scenes when he plotted or discussed his problems with Navorski. He also exhibited defensiveness and alarm when he feared Navorski's plight would interfere in his career advancement plans. In a variety of scenes, Dixon is shown with numerous bottles of stomach medicine that he keeps in his desk. All of these illustrate the pressures of dysfunctional leadership.

Components of Leadership

There are three components to leadership: need for power, need for obedience, and need for political skills (Nagel 2005, 248; Denhardt and Denhardt 2006, 340–343).

Successful leadership is associated with the power to do things, people's willingness to do what is asked of them, and the ability to get people to accomplish goals. For example, in the movie, Navorski had no formal power but through his leadership skills he eventually was able to get people to help him achieve his goal of getting out of the airport. Alternatively, while Dixon had the formal power of his office, over the course of the movie, that power was limited by the lack of motivation of his employees to obey him due to his abusive behavior toward Navorski. To accomplish his goal, to prevent Navorski from leaving the airport, he needed the guards to obey him. While at the beginning of the movie they did, by the end of the movie, they ignored his orders.

CONCLUSION

Throughout the movie the problems facing public officials were exemplified in the areas of ethics, group dynamics, and leadership. This was shown with the relationship between Navorski and Dixon, Dixon and everyone that he worked with, and Navorski and the other employees of the airport. Problems in the workplace occur, but the manner in which they are dealt with is as important as why the problems occur in the first place. To achieve goals, people need to exhibit ethical behavior, minimize group conflict, and embrace responsible leadership. The movie illustrates the way in which these characteristics are exhibited can lead either to success, in the case of Navorski, or failure, in the case of Dixon.

REFERENCES

Denhardt, Robert B. and Janet V. Denhardt. 2006. *Public administration: An action orientation*. 5th ed. Belmont, CA: Wadsworth/Thompson Learning.

Langewiesche, William. 2005. Case study 6: American ground: Unbuilding the World Trade Center. In *Public administration: Concepts and cases*, 8th ed., edited by Richard J. Stillman II, 166–178. Boston: Houghton Mifflin.

Lindblom, Charles E. 2005. Reading 8: The science of "muddling through." In *Public administration: Concepts and cases*, 8th ed., edited by Richard J. Stillman II, 223–233. Boston: Houghton Mifflin.

Mayo, Elton 2005. Reading 6: Hawthorne and the Western Electric Company. In *Public administration: Concepts and cases*, 8th ed., edited by Richard J. Stillman II, 157–165. Boston: Houghton Mifflin.

Montjoy, Robert S. and Christa Daryl Slaton. 2005. Case study 16: The case of the Butterfly Ballot. In *Public administration: Concepts and cases*, 8th ed., edited by Richard J. Stillman II, 514–528. Boston: Houghton Mifflin.

Nagel, Jack H. 2005. Case study 8: The MOVE disaster. In *Public administration: Concepts and cases*, 8th ed., edited by Richard J. Stillman II, 235–253. Boston: Houghton Mifflin.

Riccucci, Norma M. 2005. Case study 3: Dr. Helene Gayle and the AIDS Epidemic. In *Public administration: Concepts and cases*, 8th ed., edited by Richard J. Stillman II, 86–103. Boston: Houghton Mifflin.

The Terminal. 2004. DVD. Directed by Steven Spielberg. Hollywood, CA: DreamWorks Pictures.

Waldo. Dwight. 2005. Reading 16: Public administration and ethics: A Prologue to a Preface. In *Public administration: Concepts and cases*, 8th ed., edited by Richard J. Stillman II, 504–513. Boston: Houghton Mifflin.

FORMAT AND EXAMPLES OF ASSIGNMENTS FOR MANAGING AND PROCESSING INFORMATION

Assignments for Managing and Processing Information

> We start out stupid. All we have at the beginning is the built-in wisdom of the body, which tells us which end to eat with ... and not much more. But we are put here to do battle with entropy, and entropy equals stupidity. Therefore, we are obliged to learn. Our job is to process information and gain control of it: that is to say, to grow wiser as we go along (Silverberg 1986, 225).

As suggested by this quote, the soul of investigation is to control information. It is not enough to collect information for the sake of it. To become professionals, students must acquire the skills necessary for managing and processing information of interest to political scientists. A paper written by someone without a method, without good research skills, without problem-solving skills, or without the ability to synthesize the information available is not much better than amateur journalism.

To prepare students for more complex research, instructors often require them to do special kinds of assignments to help them organize for professional research and develop analytical skills. Rather than simply reading the material and taking a test on the facts or writing a descriptive term paper or essay, students are asked to process the information in some way that will help them synthesize the material for use later on or just to enhance comprehension and understanding of a particular concept or theory. In particular, the assignments are structured to help students develop research and problem-solving skills. More importantly, developing such skills encourages students to integrate and synthesize the material in a meaningful and productive way.

Although many of the standards and rules that apply to research papers and essays also apply to special assignments, there are some differences. These differences are generally found in the purpose and properties of each kind of assignment. The following descriptions encompass a traditional approach to completing each assignment. Be sure to consult your instructor for specific requirements that are in addition to those described in this chapter. Each description is followed by a written example.

List of special assignments described in this chapter:
Annotated Bibliographies

Book Reviews

Research Proposals

Outlines

Research Presentations

PowerPoint Presentations

Annotated Bibliographies

Purpose of an Annotated Bibliography

An annotated bibliography is essentially a list of sources or materials (books, articles, etc.) that have been annotated and that relate to one topic. An annotation is a description of the purpose and significance of a source. More importantly, an annotated bibliography helps the student identify the thesis and the significance of research material in political science. It is often used to help students develop prewriting skills. The research for the assignment should reflect a balance of sources. In addition, it should include scholarly books and articles.

Four Properties of an Annotated Bibliography

This assignment may be double-spaced or single-spaced. In general, the topic paragraph is single-spaced. Students should double-space between sources. The annotation to the reference should be single-spaced.

Title Page: The title page must be inclusive of the topic or subject of the annotated bibliography, the name of the student, the course number, the professor's name, and the date.

Topic Paragraph: On the second page, there must be a paragraph, at least three sentences long, that states the purpose of the annotated bibliography and a general summary of the sources' ideas.

Sources: The sources or entries are constructed with the same information as a standard bibliography, reference page, or works cited page and are listed in alphabetical order.

Annotation: An annotation is placed after the citation (skipping one line) and contains at least two full sentences stating:

- One sentence describing the purpose or thesis of the article or book.
- One sentence describing the significance of the findings and conclusions reached in the book or article.

AMERICANS WITH DISABILITIES ACT
TITLE I: MINORITY ACKNOWLEDGED

By
Noel Adams
POLS 271a Public Policy Formation
Dr. Diane Schmidt
October 30, 2003
(Abridged and Reprinted by permission)

Title I of the Americans with Disabilities Act of 1990 was enacted to eliminate discrimination in employment against individuals with disabilities. This annotated bibliography lists sources that assess the impact of Title I of the ADA and its controversial compliance costs. Overall, this literature shows that Title I of the ADA has improved conditions in employment for Americans with disabilities.

Barnart, Sharon, and Richard Scotch. 2001. *Disability protests: Contentions politics 1970–1999.* Washington, DC: Gallaudet University Press.
Barnart and Scotch discuss and analyze protest concerning people who have physical and mental impairments. The authors found that many groups were involved in the passage of the ADA; these groups were mostly advocacy organizations and members of Congress who were disabled or who had disabled family members.

Davis, Lennard J. 2002. *Bending over backwards: Disability, dismodemism, and other difficult positions.* New York and London: New York University Press.
Davis argues for a reconsideration of the status of disability in the law, in culture, and in society. Davis presents evidence that the actual cost of ADA compliance has been exaggerated by the courts.

Hernandez, Brigida. 2000. Employer attitudes toward workers with disabilities and their ADA employment rights: A literature review. *Journal of Rehabilitation* 66: 4–17.
Hernandez reviews 37 studies regarding the employer's attitudes toward workers with disabilities. The author finds that employers generally support the ADA as a whole, but small companies tend to be less supportive than large companies.

Johnsen, Matthew C., and Kathryn Moss. 1997. Employment discrimination and the ADA: A study of the administrative complaint process. *Psychiatric Rehabilitation Journal* 21: 111–22.
Johnsen and Moss study the employment discrimination complaint process for the ADA. The authors found that discrimination complaints filed under the ADA improved benefit rates by 10 percent more than complaints filed under Section 503 of the Rehabilitation Act.

Stern, Sharon M., and Judith Waldrop. 2003. Disability status: 2000. *Census 2000 Brief.* March, Washington, DC: U.S. Census Bureau.
The authors report data regarding disabled persons. The authors found that disabled persons were less likely than others to be employed.

U.S. Congress. 1990. House. Committee of the Whole House on the State of the Union. *Americans with Disabilities Act of 1990.* 101st Cong., 2nd sess. http://www.lexis-nexis.com (accessed October 1, 2003).
Senator Olin and Senator Bartlett propose amendments to Title I of the ADA that deal with the accommodations employers must make for a qualified disabled person. These proposed amendments provide evidence that the cost of complying with the ADA has been controversial.

U.S. Congress. 1989. Senate. *Americans with Disabilities Act.* 101st Cong., 1st sess. http://www.lexis-nexis.com (accessed September 24, 2003).

Senate members discuss Title I of the ADA prior to its passage. Senator Hatch and Senator Harkin discuss the appropriate interpretation of the "reasonable accommodation" requirement and the "undue hardship" concept.

U.S. Congress. 1990. Americans with Disabilities Act of 1990. *Public Law 101–336.* 101st Cong., 2nd sess. http://www.lexis-nexis.com (accessed September 24, 2003).

Public Law 101–336 is the Americans with Disabilities Act of 1990. This Public Law presents the guidelines for qualifying disabled persons and employers.

Book Reviews

Purpose of Book Review Assignments

- To help students develop analytical skills in reading the primary literature in the field of political science.
- To provide an opportunity for students to identify main ideas of the book and help them examine the author's reasoning and evidence.

How to Write a Book Review

1. **Provide a complete reference, including name, title, place of publication, publisher, and date.**
2. **Describe the subject, scope, and purpose of the book.**
3. **Summarize the author's thesis or hypothesis.**
4. **Identify the evidence used to support the thesis.**
5. **Summarize the author's conclusion.**
6. **Critique the argument.**
   - Is it logically sound?
   - Is there a fair balance of opposing viewpoints?
7. **Critique the evidence.**
   - Is it adequate?
   - Is it factual or merely opinion?
   - Is it based on respected authorities?
   - Is there substantive information?
8. **Critique the author's conclusion.**
   - Does it follow from the evidence presented?
   - Does it generalize beyond the evidence?
9. **Suggest how the book fits into the real world—how does the book relate to current issues or other books on the subject?**
10. **Suggest how the book relates to the material covered in the course—how does it contribute to the body of knowledge in the field?**

Tips for Writing a Book Review

1. Most books assigned in classes for book reviews have already been reviewed by scholars. Read a review or two before reading the book and reference any ideas borrowed from the review. Look in one of these indexes to find a review:
   - *Perspective*
   - *Social Science Citation Index*
   - *The Political Science Reviewer*
   - *Book Review Digest*

2. Look at the table of contents, index, reference pages, preface, introduction, and conclusion carefully before reading the text.
   - Note patterns in the presentation of the ideas.
   - Note the tone of the author.

3. Read with the purpose of answering and fulfilling the requirements of a book review.

4. Assert a perspective or viewpoint about the book, but avoid stating an opinion with shallow words of praise or condemnation.

5. Do not use phrases such as "I think . . ." or "He thinks. . . ." Offer only, as evidence, examples that can be identified explicitly.

6. Be sure to answer any questions the instructor has explicitly asked to be addressed in the book review in addition to the requirements for a book review.

7. For books that include edited works, summarize the focus of the work in general and use specific examples from an individual author's contributions to support particular hypotheses, theories, or arguments that embellish or explain the focus.

Example: A Single Author Book Review

A
BOOK REVIEW
OF
THE POLITICS OF CONGRESSIONAL ELECTIONS

By
Christopher Walka
POLS 318
Professor Schmidt
December 15, 1990
(Reprinted by permission)

The Politics of Congressional Elections, by Gary C. Jacobson (Boston, MA: Scott, Foresman, and Co., 1987), documents the many concerns and corresponding actions candidates undertake to gain political office. The book reduces these myriad factors into three sections: the historical background of the campaign process, the many elements comprising the actual campaign process, and the role of the national party in this election process. Combining statistical tables, graphs, and other informative devices with "real-life" examples candidates have employed, the book balances both parties and their importance to the candidate.

Arguably, the single most important factor to candidates is the electorate. Without their support, the candidate has little or no chance of being elected. Jacobson makes this fact poignantly clear. He provides and explains the uses of a wide range of tactics candidates use to convey their image and issue agenda to the people. Included among these as particularly effective is the use of mass media to emphasize issues important to certain demographic voting areas. Likewise, Jacobson examines incumbency and how it can factor so heavily into the campaign success. Jacobson cites and examines statistics about the re-election rates of particular candidates and corresponding campaign expenditures to show that campaign success heavily depends on incumbency status. He also illuminates efforts of incumbents to quell any challengers, via the use of advertising campaigns well in advance of the traditional election period.

Though advertising serves an important role in the campaign, news coverage is nonetheless important, providing substantive reinforcement to an incumbent's claim of constituency service or ammunition for a challenger's heralding claims that the office holder and the voters are not well matched. Elementary to the media's functioning is that of a watchdog over government. Media serve to help winnow out candidates before the nomination process, as well as serving as the medium by which the candidate's agenda is conveyed to the people. Why Jacobson did not address the "news side" of the media and its relation to the candidate remains unexplained.

Similarly, the issue of campaign finance is also important to the candidate. Jacobson sheds considerable light on this issue, examining funding of both parties, how political action committees factor into this, and how incumbents benefit from prior service. Funding the campaign can be a very demanding venture, both from the generation of those funds and the expenditure of those funds. Jacobson illustrates the fact that campaigns have steadily increased in expense with graphics and statistics. This fact, coupled with regulations concerning contributions to candidates, brings out why campaign finance has dramatically increased in its importance to a campaign's viability.

Jacobson also examines the respective national parties and accompanying benefits available to the candidates recognized by the parties. Party affiliation provides many benefits to the candidate, ranging from resources to constituencies, who identify and vote based on their identification with the party. Definitely not a toothless entity, the party helps lend credence to the campaign and the candidate. Similarly, facilities for the production of campaign literature, and other messages to the electorate, can be produced at substantially less cost than private firms charge. Additionally, Jacobson points out that the party helps establish a candidate to the voters: endorsements from other prominent members of the same party lending valiant support to the candidate. Ultimately, voters believe the candidate to be "for real"—worthy of their attention and worth a vote on Election Day.

Jacobson's book examines many aspects of campaigns. Although the scope is limited to those of congressional positions, it is nonetheless applicable to lesser offices too. The book balances statistics with actual, documented cases to maintain reader interest. Jacobson concludes that the road to election on the federal level is multi-faceted; these facets are as complex as the positions themselves.

THE REAGAN ADMINISTRATION'S POLICIES ON
SOCIAL WELFARE SPENDING:
ADVANTAGEOUS OR OTHERWISE

By
Edward M. Pettit
POLS 324
Professor Schmidt
February 22, 1990
(Reprinted by permission)

Historically, spending for social welfare programs has been the basis for controversy in the political arenas of many countries, especially in the capitalist world. American social spending, and the modern American welfare state in particular, have been no exception to this trend, serving as a solid foundation for debate in the United States for decades. Since the New Deal policies of President Franklin Delano Roosevelt, the controversy surrounding the American welfare state has increased in intensity, placing welfare policies among the more crucial issues in American politics.

One can easily understand, therefore, how the welfare state has come to play such an integral role in the political platforms of many of the recent leaders of the United States. Some presidents, such as Franklin D. Roosevelt (FDR), have sought policies in support of the welfare state, while others, such as Ronald Reagan, have pursued policies to the contrary. Each of these presidents has held strong convictions regarding his stance on the issue, and each has been both praised and criticized for his position. *The Mean Season: The Attack on the Welfare State* (NY: Pantheon Books, 1987), edited by Fred Block, Richard A. Cloward, Barbara Ehrenreich, and Francis Fox Piven, offers numerous criticisms of the Reagan administration's attitude toward the welfare state. Through their individual contributions, the authors provide a variety of criticisms of arguments against the necessity of welfare policy response.

Fred Block offers an interesting perspective to one such criticism when he argues that the Reagan administration's attitude toward the welfare state rests almost predominantly on a blind acceptance of the "realist" view of American politics. Under this notion, Block explains, welfare expenditures are considered to be directly responsible for reducing economic efficiency, and thus weakening our national economy. Block disagrees with this view, claiming that ". . . social justice [welfare expenditures] and the pursuit of economic efficiency are compatible" (Block, 155), and that by strengthening the welfare state, the government of the United States could, in essence, ". . . promote equality, democracy, and a stronger economy" simultaneously (Block, 155). To Block, therefore, the policies of the Reagan administration aimed at reducing welfare spending to insure economic stability were misled and deserving of criticism.

Block's criticism certainly captures one's attention, but in many ways can be considered one dimensional. With regard to the economics in question, however, one person's dimension or perspective is as good as another's. Following from this, then, increasing the purchasing power of the disadvantaged (Block's dimension) might very well turn out to be as healthy for the national economy as providing incentives for increasing big business investment at the expense of the disadvantaged (Reagan's dimension). In this regard, Block's criticism can be considered reasonably relevant, in the abstract, and therefore worthy of further testing.

Barbara Ehrenreich adds an additional criticism of the Reagan administration's attitude toward the welfare state by uncovering what she considers to be its disguised intent. Ehrenreich discusses the Reagan administration's attempts to link the notion of "permissiveness" with the welfare state and its advocates as a means of undermining popular support for social welfare. Ehrenreich contends that by associating social welfare with the notion of "permissiveness" and its connotations of decadence and moral breakdown, the Reagan administration was essentially masking social welfare under the guise of a moral issue. In this regard, she claims the welfare state became shrouded beneath a cloud of value judgments, presenting, to a certain degree, its objective consideration by much of the American populace, and thus undermining its support.

Ehrenreich's criticism, on an ethical level, certainly warrants consideration because associating the welfare state with a moral issue could very well have denied it objective consideration. In reality, however, such clandestine intentions have come to be commonplace in political arenas worldwide, and disguising an issue in such a manner has been a trick of politicians for years. One would imagine that, under scrutinizing observation, similar tactics could most likely be found underlying many American policy issues.

Francis Fox Piven and Richard A. Cloward, however, provide the main focus of the book. They criticize the Reagan administration's attitude toward the welfare state based on its myopic perspective, particularly concerning the societal implications of relief giving. In the opinions of Piven and Cloward, the Reagan administration associated the problems of poverty and the poor directly to welfare programs, contending that welfare choices among the poor are ultimately attributable to material calculations, or the want of money. As such, the authors are quick to point out, Reagan and his subscribers openly neglected ". . . to consider an array of important changes in American Social institutions that ought reasonably to be investigated for their impacts on the lives of the poor" (Piven and Cloward, 83). Such changes, the authors add, might include the impact of the displacement of multitudes of southern agricultural workers during the years following WWII and the more recent impacts of rapid deindustrialization in this country.

In any event, Piven and Cloward continue by stating that by limiting its consideration of the welfare state solely to an economic agenda, the Reagan administration made ". . . the most basic societal processes that affect poverty and the poor seem peripheral" (Piven and Cloward, 73). As such, the Reagan administration created a model of the welfare state, and its relationship between relief giving and social behavior, which was far too simple. Certainly, as a means of criticism, this argument seems quite reasonable, since establishing a simple causal relationship within a complex social and political setting, such as that which the Reagan administration created, is virtually impossible. Therefore, by demonstrating the Reagan administration's negligence in considering numerous significant variables in the relationship between the welfare state and society, other than that of a mere economic calculus, Piven and Cloward, to a certain degree, expose a definite deficiency.

Throughout *The Mean Season: The Attack of the Welfare State*, Block, Cloward, Ehrenreich, and Piven offer numerous different criticisms of the Reagan administration's attitude toward the welfare state. These criticisms themselves, whether accepted or not, represent the long history of controversy which, in recent years, has come to play an increasingly important role in the American political arena. In their approach, these authors may very well be on the forefront of numerous changes in national opinion regarding the welfare state, especially in light of recent changes in the global economy.

The economies of the world are being fueled more and more by human talent. Therefore, investments in social welfare programs, essentially being investments in human capital, will become increasingly vital to the economic self-interests of the countries of the world and especially America. In turn, arguments in support of the welfare state, such as those of the authors of *The Mean Season: The Attack of the Welfare State*, may become increasingly influential. Despite this, however, the dispute over welfare spending will most likely continue to infuse American political discourse for many years to come.

Research Proposals

For upper-level classes, scholarships, grants, and other professional-level work, students may be asked to submit a research proposal. A research proposal is a synopsis of the main elements of a research paper. It should be brief, concise, and specific. This means that students must complete the preliminary research before writing the proposal. The length varies with the research question and design. A research proposal should be no shorter than two typed double-spaced pages and no longer than five typed, double-spaced pages. A research proposal generally includes the following:

A Title Page: Includes the title of the research project and the name of the student.

An Essay: Allocating at least one paragraph to each item, a discussion of the following:

Topic: Describe the focus of the research project, clearly and succinctly.

Purpose: Describe the purpose of the research project.

Hypothesis: Clearly express, in one or two sentences, the question or controversy to be examined. One of these sentences should be the thesis sentence. The thesis sentence may need to be followed with qualifying, explanatory sentences that clarify or propose subhypotheses.

Justification: Provide a discussion of the background, context, or origins of the controversy. This may take more than one paragraph. For complex research topics, include a condensed, but pertinent, literature review on the subject and controversy.

Method: Describe the method and sources used to examine or test the research question.

- Be sure to specify whether qualitative or quantitative (or both) evidence will be used to support the assertions.
- If statistical tools or graphics will be used, be sure to specify the source of the data and how it will be transformed into tables and figures. If survey data are used, be sure to specify the source of the data.
- If the research is based on qualitative evidence, then identify the primary sources, such as scholarly, mass publications, etc.

Expected Results: Describe, based on the preliminary research, what will be found to support the hypothesis. If possible, indicate the strength of that support. Do not overstate.

Expected Significance: Describe what the research will contribute to the body of knowledge on the topic or subject. Be bold, not rhetorical. Avoid saying that the research will enlighten everyone. Keep the assertion carefully and narrowly focused on what can be understood about the subject or topic.

RESEARCH PROPOSAL
DIGITAL MILLENNIUM COPYRIGHT ACT:
OVERLY RESTRICTIVE OR NECESSARY
PROTECTION?

By
Marion Harmon
POLS 300
Dr. Schmidt
September 18, 2003
(Reprinted with permission)

Topic: The topic of this research paper is Public Law 105-304, to amend Title 17, United States Code, to implement the World Intellectual Property Organization Copyright Treaty and Performances and Phonograms Treaty, also known as the Digital Millennium Copyright Act of 1998 (DMCA). The research will focus on the historical context, the legislative process, objectives of the bill, and the policy tools in the bill. It will also focus on support for and opposition to the legislation.

Purpose: The purpose of this paper is to evaluate the effectiveness of the DMCA in dealing with copyright issues related to new technologies. The broad scope of the DMCA has made it a target for criticism since its earliest days. The opposition has criticized decisions interpreting the DMCA as setting copyright law on the path toward eliminating the fair use doctrine and stifling innovation and competition. Civil liberties groups are concerned about the access of the entertainment industry to personal information on those suspected of illegally sharing copyrighted songs online. Supporters point to protecting copyright owners against the circumvention of access and copy controls used in easily copied media.

Hypothesis: The research will test the hypothesis that the DMCA is a necessary yet flawed addition to U.S. copyright law. The DMCA is a necessary component to copyright law because it addresses the problems created through technological change. Yet, the policy is flawed because it can be overly broad in its coverage and infringe on protected rights.

Justification: The DMCA sections appear to be reasonable provisions for digital copyright protections and exemptions. But study of recent news articles reveals interpretations of the DMCA that have led to 12-year-olds being sued for trading music online and librarians calling for "widespread civil disobedience" to fight for digital first sale and fair use doctrines. A bill currently before Congress, the Digital Media Consumers' Rights Act of 2002, proposes to correct some fundamental defects in the DMCA and reestablish the doctrine of fair use, which, its proponents say, has been severely diluted by the application of the DMCA. Copyright protection must be applied to the digital realm, but invading the privacy of individuals and constraining digitized educational information are serious issues deserving serious consideration.

Method: My method of examination will consist mostly of qualitative analysis. First, I will study the legislation and legislative process leading up to the passing of the DMCA using government documents and scholarly research articles. I will also study scholarly and mass publications to learn the arguments of supporters and opponents of the DMCA. Second, I will examine subsequent court cases and related articles to learn about its controversies after it passed. I expect to use a small amount of quantitative data gathered from government documents related to impact of the DMCA. Third, I will examine proposed bills meant to amend the DMCA for their merit in improving the act. Finally, I will determine who benefits most from the DMCA.

Expected Results: The expected results of this research project is a clarification of the issues surrounding the DMCA, as well as a greater understanding of what parts of the law should be amended. The diverse, complex areas of copyright covered by the DMCA are made even more complicated by the many formal arguments of its supporters and opponents. I expect to find valid arguments for amending some sections of the DMCA. Finally, I do not expect to find convincing arguments to completely overturn the legislation.

Expected Significance: The expected significance of the research project is that this evaluation can provide a comprehensive guide to the DMCA and digital copyright issues. I hope to offer insight into whether privacy rights, fair use, and competition are truly threatened by the DMCA, and which proposed legislation makes the most sense to implement to rectify these problems. Finally, I hope to create a clearer picture of which parts of the DMCA deserve further examination and possible amendment.

Constructing Outlines

Purpose

Outlines help to organize ideas, arguments, and evidence into a coherent statement. Ideas must be presented in an ordered sequence. Outlines help writers formulate a controlling pattern for presenting their ideas. Outlines help the writer to:

- order main and minor points.
- balance the introduction, body, and conclusion.
- place arguments with evidence.

Writers use several types of outlines.

Scratch Outlines: a series of ordered notes about how to proceed with the paper.

Topic Outlines: a list of ideas showing the order and relative importance of each idea in brief words or phrases.

Sentence Outlines: a list of ideas showing the order and relative importance of each idea in complete sentences.

How to Construct a Topic or Sentence Outline

1. **Topic and sentence outlines are structured to show relative importance, so before writing the outline:**
   - Write out a thesis sentence.
   - List all the ideas.
   - List all the evidence.
   - Categorize the ideas and evidence so that they form separate chunks of information relating to the points made in the thesis sentence.
   - Order the information by strength and importance.
2. **The parts of an outline are hierarchically ordered.**
   - General ideas precede specific points.
   - Each point should have corresponding evidence.
3. **Each division is numbered in ascending order.**
   - General sections are ordered by Roman numerals.
   - Subsections are ordered by capital letters.
   - Supporting sections are ordered by Arabic numbers.
   - Explanatory sections are ordered by small letters.
4. **Each subsection, supporting section, and explanatory section must have at least two parts.**

Example: A Scratch Outline
(Reprinted with permission)

A POLICY FOR WELFARE REFORM

By
Thomas Mitchell

1. Issue of controlling poverty rate
2. Economic Opportunity Act of 1964
3. Employment conditions in 1964 vs. present
4. Contributing public commentary
5. Cash support programs and controversies
6. Remedial job skill training
7. Programs for children to break poverty at an early age
8. Employment programs for the non-working poor
9. Techniques for measuring success
10. Conclusion

Example: A Topic Outline

A POLICY FOR WELFARE REFORM

By
Thomas Mitchell
(Abridged and Reprinted with permission)

Thesis statement: A multi-generational program that is both curative and remedial in structure will provide training and opportunity to the working poor, the non-working poor, and their families.

I. The Issues
  A. Past Strategies
    1. Preventative, punitive, and alleviating
    2. Goals of each strategy
  B. History of Issue
    1. Economic Opportunity Act of 1964
    2. Employment conditions in 1964 vs. present
    3. Reasons for change in conditions

II. The Goals and Objectives

    A. Goal of Welfare Policy

        1. Security for those deemed worthy

        2. Vehicle to self-sufficiency

        3. Discourage welfare dependence

    B. Demands of the Labor Market

        1. More skills needed presently than ever before

        2. Higher levels of education for even entry-level jobs

III. Past Policy Responses

    A. Cash Support Programs

        1. Examples including OASDI, AFDC, SSI, and GA

        2. Assistance in adding to income level

        3. Controversial due to loss of government authority

    B. Direct Provision of Necessities

        1. Examples including Medicare, food stamps

        2. Political feasibility of direct provision

    C. Preventive and Compensatory Efforts for Children

        1. Rationale for focusing upon education

        2. Problem of equally affordable education

        3. Creation of Upward Bound and Head Start programs

    D. Employment-Related Programs

        1. Explanation of the Family Support Act of 1988

        2. Focus upon JOBS program and its goals

        3. Problems of job creation, costs, and child care

A POLICY FOR WELFARE REFORM

By
Thomas Mitchell
(Abridged and Reprinted with permission)

Thesis statement: A multi-generational program that is both curative and remedial in structure will provide training and opportunity to the working poor, the non-working poor, and their families.

I. As a relative concept, poverty will always exist because inequality is a constant problem.

   A. Welfare policy has traditionally taken one of four forms.

   1. Preventive strategies are designed to ensure that certain groups do not enter poverty.

   2. Alleviating strategies provide assistance to those impoverished.

   3. Punitive strategies discourage assistance to those capable of work.

   4. Curative strategies aim at controlling poverty by attacking its causes.

   B. To comprehend the issue of poverty, one must understand its history.

   1. The Economic Opportunity Act of 1964 attempted to guarantee to everyone the opportunity to live in decency and dignity.

   2. However, the employment conditions that were in existence in 1964 are no longer the same today.

   3. American businesses are now service oriented and demand more skills and education from their laborers.

II. The goals and objective of welfare policy must be considered before constructing a policy.

   A. There are three goals of welfare policy.

   1. Welfare is an attempt to provide some level of security to those deemed worthy.

   2. A lesser goal of welfare is to assist individuals in becoming self-sufficient.

   3. A third goal of welfare policy is to discourage welfare dependence.

   B. Today's labor market is demanding more of its labor force than ever before.

   1. A skilled labor force is necessary in a service sector.

   2. As the need for skilled labor increases, so does the requirement of higher levels of education.

III. Past federal programs in aid of the poor have fallen into four categories.

    A. Cash support programs provide the foundation for federal assistance to the poor.

        1. Two groups included in the Social Security Act were social insurance and public assistance programs.

        2. Because the income of the working poor is often not enough to raise them above the poverty level, cash support programs could add to their income.

        3. Cash support payments are often disliked by policy makers for they have little authority in how the aid is spent.

    B. Welfare policy also includes programs that deliver goods and services directly to the needy.

        1. These programs include Medicare, public housing, and food stamps.

        2. Direct provision of necessities is more politically feasible than cash assistance.

    C. The federal government has focused on protecting children from poverty with preventive and compensatory programs.

        1. Schools play an important role in socializing and educating children for the labor market.

        2. The opportunity for an education is not equally affordable.

        3. Upward Bound was created to motivate and assist poor students early in high school.

    D. In an effort to help the non-working poor, employment programs were created to help them find work.

        1. The Family Support Act of 1988 follows the idea that training and work experience will lead to self-sufficiency.

        2. JOBS programs require states to provide comprehensive education, training, and employment services for welfare recipients.

        3. Employment programs have problems of job creation, costs, and child care facilities.

Standard Research Presentations

Research presentations generally have two purposes. Presentations give students the opportunity to describe their research verbally to their classmates and respond to questions directly. The subject of the presentation is based on the student's research and should follow the organization of the research paper. (This outline style is very similar to the format used for research proposals.)

1. **A standard professional presentation typically includes more than a description of research. It includes:**
   - a statement of the student's purpose.
   - a declaration of the student's position.
   - a description of relevant background on the topic.
   - a description of the controversy.
   - an explanation of how the controversy was examined.
   - a description of the student's findings.
   - a concluding statement regarding the significance of the research project.

2. **A class presentation is generally graded by the same criteria used to grade written assignments.**
   - Students' grades usually reflect the quality and thoroughness with which they presented the material in the presentation categories.
   - Sometimes an instructor will request a copy of the presentation, so write an outline.
   - A quick way to begin writing the presentation outline is to reorganize the topic or sentence outline for the research paper to fit into the presentation categories.
   - The length and degree of detail in the presentation outline will depend on the time allotted for the presentation. Generally, a presentation is two-and-a-half (or fewer) pages typed in outline form.

3. **Class presentations are frequently graded on the degree of professionalism exhibited by the student during the presentation. A solid performance demonstrates depth and breadth of subject area knowledge.**
   - Exhibit poise and confidence (try rehearsing).
   - Answer questions succinctly.
   - Vary the voice level, make eye contact with other students, and use gestures.
   - Do not read word for word from the research paper. Use an outline.

Standard Presentation Form

Purpose: A clear statement of the purpose and focus of the student's research.

Hypothesis: A clear statement of the controversy examined and hypothesis tested. If possible, try to identify the causal relationship between independent and dependent variables.

Background: A brief discussion of the context and background related to the controversy examined and assumptions behind the students' research motives.

- Be sure to present the background so that it supports the purpose and the relationships specified between the variables.
- Work from weakest to strongest assertions.

Method: An explanation of the method or how the hypothesis was tested.

- If quantitative data were used, describe how the data or source materials were collected.
- Fully disclose any problems in information gathering.
- Be sure to relate the data and source materials to the hypothesis.

Results: A summary of the results of the examination or test.

- If data were used, make charts, graphs, or tables to use as visual aids.
- Use a table or chart to summarize the main points.
- Use visual aids for complex material or highly descriptive material. For example, use maps to help the audience understand the context of boundary disputes between nations.
- Use an overhead projector to present the material or make copies of a visual aid for everyone.

Conclusion: This statement explains how the goals of the research were accomplished. In particular, it summarizes how the results relate to the goals of the student's research endeavor.

Significance: A statement that applies the results appropriately to an expansion of knowledge about the subject.

WELFARE REFORM PRESENTATION

By
Thomas Mitchell
POLS 444
Dr. Schmidt
July 1, 1991
(Reprinted with permission)

WELFARE REFORM PRESENTATION NOTES

I. Purpose is to examine manpower programs that are designed to increase the marketability of impoverished citizens and propose a new course of action that will help diminish the number of citizens requiring such aid in the future.

   A. Controversy:

      1. Productivity of American workers stagnant.

      2. The percentage of the population below the poverty level has continued to increase since 1979.

   B. Thesis statement: A multi-generational program that is both curative and remedial in structure will provide training and opportunity to the working poor, the non-working poor, and their families.

   C. Goal: To address the issue of increasing poverty rates, legislative action must be undertaken.

      1. Provide remedial training to the working and non-working poor.

      2. Ensure quality education as a curative strategy to poverty by breaking the cycle of poverty at an early age.

   D. These goals can be achieved through specific policy recommendations.

      1. Continuation of employment programs for the non-working poor.

      2. Provide remedial job skill training and education programs to provide skills to the working and non-working poor and to induce the poor to enter the job market.

      3. Continue to use cash support payments as a means to keep millions of individuals out of poverty.

      4. Create and expand curative programs aimed at high-risk children of all income and educational levels.

II. Brief description of the context or background:

   A. Past strategies.

      1. Preventative, punitive, and alleviating.

      2. Goals of each strategy.

   B. History of issue.

      1. Economic Opportunity Act of 1964.

      2. Employment conditions in 1964 vs. present.

      3. Reasons for change in conditions.

III. Explanation of research method:

   A. Analyzed explicit goals of welfare policies and employment policy.

   B. Examined and evaluated past and present programs used to address goals.

   C. Used secondary sources, primary sources, and expert opinion.

IV. Findings on welfare policies:

    A. Welfare policy goals.

        1. Security for those deemed worthy.

        2. Vehicle to self-sufficiency.

        3. Discourage welfare dependence.

    B. Welfare policy responses—evaluated.

        1. Cash support programs; examples: OASDI, AFDC, SSI.

        2. Direct provision of necessities; example: Medicare.

        3. Preventive efforts for children; example: Head Start.

V. Findings on employment programs:

    A. Goals and problems in labor market.

        1. More skills needed presently than ever before.

        2. Higher levels of education for even entry-level jobs.

    B. Employment-related programs:

        1. Explanation of the Family Support Act of 1988.

        2. Focus upon JOBS program and its goals.

        3. Problems of job creation, costs, and child care.

VI. Recommendations:

    A. Explain multi-generational program.

        1. Provide remedial training to presently impoverished

        2. Create and further educational programs for youth.

    B. Continuation of employment programs.

        1. Need for programs due to welfare stigma.

        2. Poor less able to compete for jobs.

    C. Remedial job skill training programs.

        1. A means of welfare recipients acquiring skills.

        2. Upon completion, recipients enter employment programs.

    D. Continuation of cash support payments.

        1. Allows millions of people to be kept off welfare.

        2. Must participate in skill training to receive cash.

    E. Curative programs aimed at all youth.

        1. Children of various income levels drop out of school.

        2. Children drop out before the legal age.

        3. Head Start, Upward Bound, and elementary programs for all high-risk youth.

VII. Conclusion:

    A. Social condition of poverty.

        1. New demands on labor market.

        2. Resources of workers go untapped.

    B. Past poverty strategies.

        1. Past strategies have been unsuccessful.

        2. Restate thesis.

VIII. Significance:

    A. Summarize four-part recommendation.

    B. Four parts are integrated and mutually reinforcing.

PowerPoint Presentations

Like standard research presentations, PowerPoint presentations provide students the opportunity to share their project results with others. Also like standard research presentations, the subject and organization of PowerPoint presentations are based on the subject and organization of the student's research project. Unlike standard research presentations, PowerPoint presentations have specific formatting structures that require special attention to detail. Importantly, because PowerPoint is a highly visual communication form, students need to include formats that make them accessible to others with visual and cognitive disabilities. This is especially important when the PowerPoint is posted to a common Web site or shared with others in the class. Federal regulations require class materials to be accessible to those with visual, auditory, or cognitive disorders. An excellent source for help in creating effective and accessible PowerPoint presentations is *PowerPoint Magic: Tutorials* (http://pptmagic.com).

Characteristics of Good PowerPoint Presentations

- Readable, simplified text in headline format.
- Organized by headings on each slide.
- Focused on essential information only.
- Graphics used only to enhance comprehension of ideas or data.
- High-contrast slides; consistent formatting across slides.

Characteristics of Poor PowerPoint Presentations

- Overcrowded text on the slide.
- Lots of wrapped sentences or lines of text.
- Inconsistent format with varied fonts and characters.
- Gratuitous graphics and/or multiple graphics on one slide.
- Distracting and/or noisy add-ons.

PowerPoint Presentation: Rules of Etiquette

Effective PowerPoint presentations generally adhere to a set of protocols for communication and slide design that enhance the coherence and visual effectiveness of the presentation. Following these rules will create a powerful presentation while providing the best possible access to other students.

Presentation Style

Students should plan to present approximately one slide per minute in the time allotted for presentation. A 15-minute presentation can support approximately 15–18 slides.

- Students should not read their notes or the slides verbatim to the audience.
- Spoken presentation should match the visual presentation.
- Unless otherwise directed by the instructor, students should focus the presentation for a general audience of intelligent nonspecialists.
- Students should use professional language but speak more conversationally; never use slang or obscene language.

- Students need to make frequent eye contact with the audience.
- Students should gesture to the slides, with a pointer if possible.
- Students should move a bit at least every minute or move a slide every minute or two.

Overall Slide Structure

Use a high-contrast design template (these are generally set up for accessibility).

- Write the presentation in Outline View (text not visible in Outline View cannot be read by screen-reading software).
- Do not use red or green backgrounds (these colors often cannot be seen by those who are color blind).
- Write comprehensive notes with important explanatory details in the Notes pane (this helps deaf students).

Fonts

Fonts should be large, at least 28 points (headings are generally in larger fonts than the text).

- Use fonts consistently (i.e., same font for each heading, same font for each line of text).
- Stick to "standard" fonts (Times, Arial, Symbol, etc.) to avoid having to deal with strange fonts. If the computer used to make the slide presentation is different from the one used in the presentation, the latter computer may not have the particular font set.
- Non-serif fonts (such as Helvetica or Arial) are easier to read than the serif fonts (Times).
- Use bold or color-coded text for aesthetic effects only and not for special emphasis or to convey meaning (visually impaired students will not be able to understand the meaning; do not use red or green fonts at all).

Punctuation

Capitalize the first letter of each word in a heading.

- Capitalize the beginning of each line of text.
- End each line of text with a period (this helps screen-reading software know when the line stops).
- Use other punctuation (such as an exclamation mark) for aesthetic effects only and not for special emphasis or to convey meaning (visually impaired students will not be able to understand the meaning).
- Do not abbreviate or use contractions; acronyms are okay to use, but only after they have been defined.

Text Format

Use one heading per slide.

- Include at least two characteristics or lines of text under each heading.
- Use succinct phrases, not sentences, for text.
- Use no more than three to four lines of text per slide (on average).
- Use no more than five to six words per line per slide (on average; avoid wrapping the text to the next line).
- Use bullets for each line of text after the heading for lists of information that have no rank order; use only one set of bullets per slide.

- Use numbered lists for each line of text after the heading for lists of information that have a rank order.
- Avoid long quotes or paragraphs of text.

Graphics, Images, and Hyperlinks

Use no more than one graphic per slide.

- Keep images and graphics proportional to the other slides.
- Graphics should be fully labeled (captioned) and referenced.
- Describe the image or object in full detail in the Notes panel and in the presentation.
- Each graphic should be tagged with a description of what it is by the Alternative Text (Alt-Text) function for screen-reading software.
- Hyperlinks should be used only if they are accessible and should be captioned.
- Video or audio should be accompanied by a transcript.

Special Effects (animations, slide transition effects, and sound effects)

Be sure not to overuse these effects (animations cannot be seen by the blind, sound effects cannot be heard by the deaf, and elaborate slide transitions distract those with cognitive impairments).

- Avoid red backgrounds, any flashing red letters, and red pictures (these are associated with causing seizures).
- Dark backgrounds should be accompanied by white letters; keep the contrast high.
- Pastel backgrounds are more professional, less harsh, but require high-contrast text.
- Avoid backgrounds with graphics such as clouds or other kinds of objects or characters that overlap the text in any way.
- All transitions should be the same (for all slides).

Example: A Student PowerPoint Presentation File

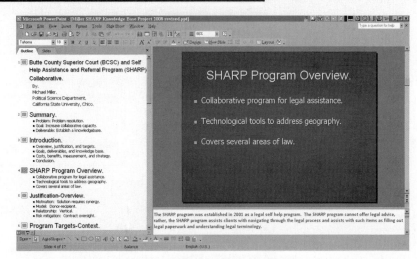

Example: A Student PowerPoint Presentation

(Reprinted in Handout format and grayscale, with permission.)

11

FORMAT AND EXAMPLES OF CONVENTIONAL RESEARCH PAPERS

Formulas for Organizing Standard Research Papers

In the following pages, there are four examples of standard research papers exhibiting a range of writing styles, topics, and research methods.

The First Paper: A Literature Review

"Distributive Justice and Community" is an example of a thematic literature review.

The Second Paper: A Comparative Paper

"The Kennedys and the Rockefellers: Political Dynasties' Effects on the American Electorate" uses qualitative data and is a simple comparative, or case, study.

The Third Paper: An Analysis

"Youth Influence in Political Outcomes," as an example of an analysis, uses a mixture of qualitative and quantitative data to examine the reasons why young people participate in politics and suggests a theory about the impact of this activity.

The Fourth Paper: A Position Paper

"Chief Justice Rehnquist: Does He Lead the Court?" uses empirical research to test a hypothesis using quantitative data and statistical methods. This is an example of a position paper that supports a theory about political influence and leadership in the judicial branch.

These papers exhibit the standard qualities for a research paper in political science where students were not required to address specific criteria or questions. An explanation of the form for each type of paper precedes the examples.

Writing a Literature Review

A literature review is a formal, exhaustive examination of the principal books, articles, and monographs written on a topic. It provides an overview of important scholarly research in the field or subfield. These reviews can be, and often are, inclusive of scholarly research in political science as well as in other fields, such as sociology, economics, or even communications and biology. As such, literature reviews are not limited to one discipline, although the dominant focus for a political science literature review is on scholarly research in the field. Unlike general term papers, students researching and writing a literature review must first locate important pathbreaking scholarly books and articles written about the topic they have chosen, and then they must organize and classify the contributions of this research into a coherent discussion. A literature review synthesizes many different scholarly works in each paragraph (Galvan 2006; Pan 2008).

More specifically, the purpose of a literature review is to:

- Critique scholarly literature.
- Evaluate theories.
- Assess evidence.
- Identify methodological tools.
- Synthesize research across time.

There are three general types of literature review:

- **Chronological:** This type of literature review synthesizes and classifies the changes and similarities in themes, conclusions, and methodologies over time from the earliest scholarly treatment of the topic to the most current studies.
- **Thematic:** This type of literature review identifies similarities and differences in competing themes, theories, and/or perspectives developed for explaining political phenomena.
- **Methodological:** This type of literature review critiques the similarities and differences in methodological approaches to examining and/or measuring political phenomena.

The evidence to collect, compare, and contrast is comprised of:

- Facts accepted as conventional for the field or subfield.
- Primary variables or indicators.
- Characterizations of the relationship between concepts and variables used as measures.
- Limitations or inconsistencies in the findings.
- Methods used to produce findings.
- Controversies in the field or subfield.

Writing a Literature Review

1. Choose a topic and narrow it by a concept and an abstract term (see Chapter 3, "Choosing a Topic"). Choose one type of literature review as the primary organizing structure; do not mix the different types. Students should plan to use headings and subheadings to differentiate the various subcategorizations they discovered in their research.

2. Prepare for research by reviewing textbooks and current research in the field (see Chapter 4, "Locating Research Materials, Using Indexes, Databases, and the Internet").

   - Locate the most current research, and work backward by year.
   - Identify themes used by the authors to justify the purpose of the research.
   - Note other authors' evaluations of the themes and methodological approaches.
   - Establish which authors and which books and/or articles are classics in the field or subfield by keeping track of authors and research that appear often in the bibliographies or reference pages of books and articles.

3. Sort the themes, theories, and methodological approaches according to the principles of classification analysis based on the type of literature review conducted (see Chapter 5, "Creating Evidence with Primary and Secondary Data") and devise a thesis statement.

   - Chronological reviews: cluster the literature into groups by eras.
   - Thematic reviews: cluster the literature into groups by themes or hypotheses.
   - Methodological reviews: cluster the literature by the way in which the authors examined the topic (case studies, cross-sectional analysis, time series, etc).

4. Although there is no rule for how many scholarly books and articles a literature review should include, the expectation is that the student will have exhausted much of the important primary- and secondary-level research in the field or subfield regarding the topic.

   - For a narrow review, students should include up to approximately twenty titles.
   - For a more complex, comprehensive review, the expectation is that the review will cover twenty or more titles.
   - The more complex the review, and the longer the paper, the expectation is the review will cover thirty to fifty sources.

5. The paper should have the following:

   - Title page
   - Abstract (if required)
   - Introduction that provides an overview of the problems or issues existing in the field or subfield and a thesis statement
   - Body with headings (for broad categories) and subheadings (subcategories of evidence)
   - Conclusion that provides an analysis of which set of research is the most convincing and provided the most significant contributions to understanding the problems and issues in the field

DISTRIBUTIVE JUSTICE AND COMMUNITY: A LITERATURE REVIEW

By
Alicia Gifford
POLS 498
Professor Schmidt
December 1, 2007
(Reprinted with permission)

INTRODUCTION

Distributive justice concerns what is just or right with respect to the allocation of goods or services within a society. To understand distributive justice in context to fairness, equality of opportunity is distinguished from equality of outcome. To do so, this literature review examines the theories of distributive justice proposed by John Rawls, Jeremy Bentham, Jean-Jacques Rousseau, John Locke, John Stuart Mills, and Ronald Dworkin as they relate to a community's function in promoting an equitable society.

DISTRIBUTIVE JUSTICE

Distributive justice is related to a society's economy and how justice is understood. In his perspective on societal organization, John Rawls focused on how distributive justice translates to the role of government to create justice in society and how that in turn affects the people in the community. The community provides the social system that shapes the goals of the citizens (Rawls 1971, 229). Under this perspective, distributive justice involves an interpretation of the public good based on how society itself defines justice (Rawls 1971, 229). Justice is described as being in relation to fairness as "justice is fairness" (Rawls 1971, 230). To understand justice as fairness, people must understand two principles: the equal liberty principle and the difference principle.

Equal Liberty Principle

The principle of equal liberty suggests that each individual has the rights that are extended to the society as a whole (Rawls 1971, 65-70). Liberty is explained in reference to three components: "the agents who are free, the restrictions or limitations they are free from, and what it is that they are free to do or not to do" (Rawls 1971, 177). This means that people in society are free, or not, to do anything that is not constrained. So, people are free to do what they want when they are free from certain constraints: written or unwritten. For example, the U.S. Constitution does not explicitly state every right that a person has; some are unstated or are covered as "unalienable rights."

Rawls' view of liberty is not unlike that of Jeremy Bentham, who refers to what is known as negative freedom. This is the view that "liberty is absence of restraint" (Bentham 1789, 20). It is the freedom from external constraint or hindrance. To have liberty one must not have anything or anyone hindering them. This means that distributive justice involves respecting basic liberties. Individuals have the basic liberty to pursue their moral, religious, or philosophical interests without the interference of other people or government. Thus, according to Bentham and Rawls, it is the legal obligation of the government to protect the rights of the people by upholding the rights of liberty and protecting those liberties from obstruction.

Difference Principle

The principle of liberty is further supported by Rawls' second principle, principle of difference. The difference principle states that social and economic inequalities should be arranged so that the greatest benefits go to the most disadvantaged and that the disadvantaged should not be discriminated against (Rawls 1971, 65–70). This means that a community can give projects to some people that will result in more money and power than others as long as the project undertaken is to benefit the people that are disadvantaged. It also suggests that access to the privileged positions or projects is not blocked to the disadvantaged nor are they discriminated against in competition for benefits (Rawls 1971, 65–70).

The critics of the difference principle argue that this perspective suggests redistributing everything to fix inequalities (Meckled-Garcia 2002, 3). Yet, that is not what the difference principle promotes. The difference principle actually shifts responsibility for justice from society to the individual by implying that " individuals should internalize a motivation to be more productive as opposed to accepting that the existing social wealth, or current productive output, should be distributed equally (Meckled-Garcia 2002, 3). According to the difference principle, to promote justice as fairness, there can be inequality; however, those that are not as advantaged cannot be worse off than before and cannot be discriminated against to help those that are advantaged.

UTILITARIANISM

Utilitarianism is a theory where justice is promoted in the form of individual aggregate benefits. The principle of utility is that it "approves or disapproves of every action whatsoever, according to the tendency which it appears to have to augment or diminish the happiness of the party whose interest is in question" (Bentham 1789, 2). Unlike Rawls' perspective, Bentham's argued that it is the moral worth of an action and how useful something or someone is to the end result that determines its utility or value. One critic of utilitarianism argued that this meant that Bentham opposed individual sacrifice for others and even rejected moral rights because they were too subjective (Postema 1998, 1–2). This is a stark contrast with Rawl's conception of liberty and difference; rather than an individual perspective on justice, justice under utilitarianism is viewed from a community perspective.

The concept of utilitarianism was built on and refined by John Stuart Mill. Utilitarianism, as defined by Mill, is that "actions are right in proportion as they tend to promote happiness; wrong as they tend to produce the reverse of happiness" (Mill 1863, 407). Happiness is defined as pleasure and the absence of pain; utility is based on the pursuit of happiness and the deterrence of unhappiness (Mill 1863, 413). Under utilitarianism, rights are contingent on a community's ability to maximize happiness (Postema 1998, 1). Justice in securing those rights is based on internal and external "sanctions." External sanctions involve expectations of approval or disapproval from anything or anyone (Mill 1863, 430). The internal sanction is a moral obligation, personal duty, or conscience (Mill 1863, 431). When this idea is connected to duty it is, in essence, defined as conscience (Mill 1863, 431–432).

Justice and Utility

Based on Mill, distributive justice is relative to an interaction between the individual and the community. From the idea of right and wrong in utility, comes justice. Mill uncovers the connection between liberty, justice, and individual utility by stating what is considered just and unjust within the community. Preserving liberty and promoting justice involves limiting the scope of government while maximizing welfare and preventing harm (Kurer 1999, 201–203). The purpose of justice is to distribute the laws and promote equality, and this is done to prevent the harm of others. There are five criteria for reviewing what is considered just within a community as it relates to individuals. These involve legal rights, deprived rights, contractual rights, equity rights, and deserved rights.

Legal rights. Mill argued that it is considered unjust to deprive anyone of their right to liberty, property, or anything else that belongs to a person by law (Mill 1863, 448). These are legal rights that should be protected and enforced by the community. In Mill's perspective, justice depends on how the community protects these rights. Injustice occurs, in this case, when those who are supposed to have the same rights as others are not afforded those rights. Mill provides the example of slavery; the slaves were theoretically supposed to have the same sacred rights as the masters themselves; however, slave rights were not protected (Mill 1863, 451).

Deprived rights. In Mill's perspective, it is unjust to violate the legal rights of anyone unless the rights are forfeited. The rights that are deprived of the person are rights that he did not deserve to begin with (Mill 1863, 448). Though laws are not meant to be broken or any person to be deprived of any rights, some people deserve to have their rights taken away from them when they deprive another person of a liberty or when the law to begin with was unjust. To support this, Mill argues that to prevent harm "power can be rightfully exercised over any member of a civilized community, against his will" (Mill 1849, 380).

Contractual rights. Mill, however, was very clear concerning contractual relationships. According to Mill, it is unjust to break faith with anyone, or to break an agreement or engagement previously made, either expressed or implied (Mill 1863, 449-450). Although this conception of justice is not an absolute obligation and can be overruled, it does make clear boundaries regarding relationships between individuals in a community.

Equity rights. It is inconsistent with justice to be partial or to discriminate (Mill 1863, 450). Like Rawls, Mill argues that it is fundamental to justice for a community to be equitable, to be impartial, and to deliver fairness in every instance. Impartiality is not regarded as a duty, however, but more of an instrument to carry out communal goals.

Deserved rights. Mill argued that each person should get what he deserves (Mill 1863, 449). This is what constitutes a *just deserts*; this is a person getting what they deserve and deserving what they get (Mill 1863, 449). For example, the United States court system brings charges against those that have murdered or caused harm to another person, though the victims may not be able to speak for themselves. A requirement to bring charges is that there is proof that harm has been done to a person or persons.

Justice and Morality

While it is not clear from Mill how harm is determined, his perspective appears to be based on some kind of community determination of justice based on a conception of public morality. Though morality and justice are often perceived as similar, they are markedly different. Morality is the difference between doing the right thing and the wrong thing based on an individual or community perspective (Mill 1863, 455). Justice is based on the perspective of individual rights; it is a claim on the part of one or more individuals, which the laws give them, to property or other legal rights (Mill 1863, 455). Justice, unlike morality, does not include generosity or beneficence (Mill 1863, 455–456). When generosity and beneficence are included in justice it no longer can be defined as justice and becomes a moral issue. This is because a person does not have to be just to be generous or generous to be just. Justice is defined not only by legal rights but how those legal rights are related to moral perspectives in the community.

NATURAL RIGHTS AND CIVIL SOCIETY

It is clear from Mill, Bentham, and Rawls that an understanding of distributive justice is related to understanding the goals of the community as they relate to individual rights. Other philosophers, John Locke and Jean-Jacques Rousseau, contribute to this understanding through their writings on the natural rights, civil society, and public obligations. Locke's moral and political theory most specifically relates to distributive justice and how that relates and promotes an equitable civil society. Rousseau's perspectives provide a clearer understanding of how civil society incorporates individual rights and promotes justice.

State of Nature and Justice

Even though Lock and Bentham agree that civil society structures justice, Bentham's perspective does not support that there is a state of nature, whereas Locke argues that a state of nature provides the basic foundations for society. Bentham argued that people have always lived in a society, so there can be no state of nature (Bentham 1789, 8). His perspective is that there is a difference between political society and natural society. A natural society has no pretense of equality or structure. Political society is where political power is constantly divided, subdivided, and fought over (Bentham 1789, 8–10). According to Bentham, mankind is governed by pleasure and pain (Bentham 1789, 17–18). Liberty is a "pleasure" and the restrictions on liberty are "pain." Law, as government in a society, is a restriction on liberty and painful for those whose liberty is restricted, but is necessary to maintain social order (Bentham 1789, 112–113). The state limits the rights of the individual to promote liberty for all of its citizens. The government's purpose is to protect the rights of its individuals and promote economic and personal goods (Bentham 1789, 82). A stable society can provide the security, lessen the pain, and increase the pleasure; this is the main purpose of a supportive society (Rosen 1998, 136).

To counter Bentham's arguments, Locke argued that the state of nature was a period of time prior to the creation of governments where people lived in unstructured communities (Locke 1690, 8–14). Under this conception, human nature is characterized by "freedom, equality, and reason" (Locke 1690, 8–14). Locke identifies three laws of nature. The laws are "Preserve yourself. Do not harm others. Help others if possible" (Locke 1690, 8–14). So opposed to Bentham, Locke's perspective is that the laws of nature provide the basis for government.

To understand the foundations of society, Locke contrasted civil society with an uncivilized condition of humans in a state of nature (Rowley 1998, 412). Not only does human nature contribute the challenges of creating an equitable society but in structuring the role of the government. Locke argues in the *Second Treatise of Government* for the support of the "rule of law and rightful politics, not only in the fundamental legislation that is the constitution but also in the regular governance of the legislature" (Mattie 2005, 77–78). The rule by legislation preserves the society and supports the state of nature with the involvement of government (Mattie 2005, 78–82).

The nature of the state is to help the citizens rather than deter their natural rights. Locke argued that the "authority of any government is conditional on its performing the functions for which it was entrusted with power" (Locke 1690, 10). According to Locke, governments are formed because people want to entrust power in them for protection against "annoyances" (Locke 1690, 8–14). The annoyances are the result of individuals acting irrationally and against the laws of nature. Government is created by the people when "individuals come together and give clear, direct, explicit consent to the formation of the state" (Locke 1690, 8–14). When the laws of nature are followed by all citizens of the state, then government intervention will be minimal; mostly the state will provide public services and safety. The most important responsibility of the state is to protect the rights of life, liberty, and property with the laws that are enforced. The state has these responsibilities as long as the government does not encroach on the natural rights of the citizens. Natural rights are protected by giving the state power over "only those who freely give their direct consent to the state are considered citizens of the state . . . so no one's natural freedom is violated" (Locke 1690, 8–14). This provision protects any dissenters in a state that do not agree with the government or wish not to partake in it.

Social Contract and Civil Rights

Understanding the role of the "social contract" helps to further understand the nature of the state and justice, according to Rousseau. The public agreement between a community, the social contract, is derived from the public and individuals who draw together for a common purpose. According to Rousseau, "each individual, in making a contract, as we may say, with himself, is bound in a double capacity; as a member of the Sovereign he is bound to the individuals, and as a member of the State to the Sovereign" (Rousseau 1778, 184). For society to operate successfully, individuals and the state must work in conjunction with one another to achieve the goals of society.

The theory of a social contract can be examined from a consensus viewpoint, much like Locke's perspective. According to the consensus view, a social contract is a shared body of laws and institutions which are structured, ordered, and regulated for creating a society (Affeldt 2000, 570). The way in which a society forms is central to the functioning of the society for three reasons. First, whether a group constitutes a society is influenced by the laws, institutions, and customs previously established (Affeldt 2000, 570). Second, the nature of the origin of a society is a historical matter, which occurs gradually over time (Affeldt 2000, 570). Third, each society has a specific origin during a specific historical period (Affeldt 2000, 570).

Yet, unlike Locke, Rousseau's conception of civil society constrains natural rights, and therefore justice based on those rights. With the social contract, a man loses "his natural liberty and an unlimited right to everything he tries to get and succeeds in getting; what he gains is civil liberty and the proprietorship of all he possesses" (Rousseau 1778, 188). Natural liberty is "bound only from the strength of the individual" and civil liberty is "limited by the general will" (Rousseau 1778, 189). As long as the state is sovereign, equitable society is promoted through the social contract, not by protecting natural rights.

EQUITY AND CIVIL SOCIETY

While protecting natural rights may or may not be essential to a definition of distributive justice, it is clear that equity is fundamental to the promotion and success of civil society. According to Ronald Dworkin, no government can be legitimate that does not show equal concern for the fate of all of its citizens that claim citizenship (Dworkin 2000, 1–3). Two fundamental humanist principles are founded on equity: the objective that all human lives flourish and each person is responsible for the success and flourishing of their lives (Dworkin 2000, 92–95). The laws enacted by the government, when favoring certain parts of the public over others, go against equality and knowingly worsen the lives of some citizens. Like Rawls and Mills, Dworkin's perspective identifies equity or equal treatment, as a critical component to creating a civil society.

Equal Welfare vs. Equal Resources

While justice depends on equity, there is no universal equality. People in a single society can be equal in some ways and in other ways are not. Theoretically, according to Dworkin, people can differ on the basis of equality of welfare and equality of resources (Dworkin 2000, 11–12). The equality of welfare involves fulfilling goals and ambitions while equality of resources would involve equal resources (Dworkin 2000, 17). The equality of resources, then, is the equality of whatever resources are owned privately by individuals (Dworkin 2000, 65). For example, two people may be equal in income (equal resources), but may not be equal in job satisfaction (equal welfare). For the most part, equality of welfare involves public funds and equality of resources involves private funds.

Societal Resources

Like Rawls, Dworkin's perspective of distributive justice involves both welfare and resources. Dworkin defines a just distribution by using the envy test as a criterion. Based on this criterion, an unjust distribution occurs when, after a distribution of societal resources, one person envies another person's share of the resources (Dworkin 2000, 67–68). Dworkin's perspective is not quite the same as Rawls' though. Dworkin's viewpoint is based on the notion that by creating an opportunity for equal initial resources, citizens would have an equal chance of competing for community resources through an auction (Christofidis 2004, 270–274). Alternatively, Rawls argues against committing community resources to some unless it benefits the least advantaged.

CONCLUSION

Distributive justice is the allocation of justice and how that pertains to society. Clearly, understanding justice based on laws and protection of natural rights is easier than understanding justice through the distribution of welfare and resources. Justice as defined by equal liberty and equal opportunity to have natural and/or legal rights enforced is basically supported by political theorists Rawls, Bentham, Rousseau, Locke, Mills, and Dworkin. But distributive justice as defined by perceptions about what is public and private resource allocations, as well as arguments about the role of the community in determining these allocations, differ vastly among these theorists. Private resource protection as a natural right may or may not be subject to distributive justice depending on how the role of civil society is defined. As a social contract, resource distribution is based on public agreement, not natural rights. Alternatively, civil society, as based on a foundation of natural rights, is limited by a duty to protect ownership of those resources. In sum, while there is little disagreement that distributive justice depends on equitable protection of rights afforded to each member of the community, how public and private resources are impacted by the definition and value placed on those rights depends on the role of civil society in defining those rights.

REFERENCES

Affeldt, Steven G. 2000. Society as a way of life: Perfectibility, transformation, and the origination of society in Rousseau. *Monist* 83 (4): 552–607.

Bentham, Jeremy. 1789. Mill, John Stuart. 1863. *The Utilitarians*. Garden City, NY: Doubleday and Company, Inc. repr., 1961.

Christofidis, Miriam Cohen. 2004. Talent, slavery and envy in Dworkin's equality of resources. *Utilitas* 16 (3): 267–287.

Dworkin, Ronald. 2000. *Sovereign virtue: the theory and practice of virtue*. Cambridge, MA: Harvard University Press.

Kurer, Oskar. 1999. John Stuart Mill: Liberal or utilitarian? *The European Journal of the History of Economic Thought* 6 (2): 200–215.

Locke, John. 1690. *Second treatise of government*. Cambridge, MA: Hacket Publishing Company, Inc. repr., 1980.

Mattie, Sean. 2005. Prerogative and the rule of law in John Locke and the Lincoln presidency. *Review of Politics* 67 (1): 77–111.

Meckled-Garcia, Saladin. 2002. Why work harder: Equality, social duty, and the market. *Political Studies* 50: 779–793.

Postema, Gerald J. 1998. Bentham's equality-sensitive utilitarianism. *Utilitas* 10 (2): 144–158.

Rawls, John. 1971. *A theory of justice*. Cambridge, MA: Harvard University Press.

Rosen, F. 1998. Individual sacrifice and the greatest happiness: Bentham on utility and rights. *Utilitas* 10 (2): 129–143.

Rousseau, Jean-Jacques. 1778. *The social contract*. New York City, NY. Oxford University Press. repr., 1947.

Rowley, Charles K. 1998. One the nature of civil society. *Independent Review* 2 (3): 401–423.

Writing a Comparative Study

In many political science courses, especially in comparative politics or international relations, instructors will ask students to compare government responses to issues, problems, or political phenomena. Comparison papers may use qualitative evidence, quantitative evidence, or a mixture of both. Here are three simple frameworks with which to organize research and ideas (Lester 1990, 74).

Comparative Papers on Two or More Objects or People

1. In the introduction, briefly identify and compare the items.
- State the central point of the comparison.
- In the thesis sentence, present the relevance of the comparison or why the comparison is important.

2. In the body:
- Examine the first item's characteristics thoroughly.
- Next, examine the second item's characteristics thoroughly.
- Next, identify characteristics that are similar and offer an explanation/evidence of why they are similar.
- Next, identify characteristics that are different and offer an explanation/evidence of why they are different.

3. Discuss the significant differences and similarities. Suggest why it was important to identify these differences and similarities.

Comparative Papers on Two or More Ideas or Theories

1. In the introduction, briefly identify and compare the items.
- State the central point of the comparison.
- In the thesis sentence, present the relevance of the comparison or why the comparison is important.

2. In the body:
- To start, identify characteristics that are similar and offer an explanation/evidence of why they are similar.
- Next, identify characteristics that are different and offer an explanation/evidence of why they are different.
- Next, discuss and evaluate the central issues or characteristics that differentiate the items.
- Present arguments that rank one item over the other.

3. Reiterate the major differences and strong points of each item.
- Suggest why it was important to identify these differences and similarities.
- Conclude by identifying and supporting the reason why one item is preferable to another.

Papers That Compare Responses to Issues by Two Subjects or Objects

1. **In the introduction, briefly identify and compare the items and the issues.**
   - State the central point of the comparison.
   - In the thesis sentence, present the relevance of the comparison or why the comparison is important.

2. **In the body:**
   - Identify the first issue. Discuss the differences and similarities between the treatments of the issue. Present arguments about why the differences and similarities exist.
   - Identify the second issue. Discuss the differences and similarities between the treatments of the issue. Present arguments about why the differences and similarities exist.
   - Identify the third issue. Discuss the differences and similarities between the treatments of the issue. Present arguments about why the differences and similarities exist.
   - Present arguments that rate one treatment over the other.

3. **Reiterate the major differences and similarities in each treatment of the issue.**
   - Suggest why these differences and similarities exist.
   - Conclude by identifying and supporting the reason why one treatment is preferable to another.

Example: A Comparative Paper

THE KENNEDYS AND THE ROCKEFELLERS: POLITICAL DYNASTIES' EFFECTS ON THE AMERICAN ELECTORATE

By John T. Sullivan
POLS 318
Professor Schmidt
December 1, 1988
(Reprinted with permission)

ABSTRACT

One of the most intriguing phenomena in American politics is that of the so-called "dynasty" and its effects on the voters. These political dynasties appear to create irrational tendencies in voting patterns. The dynasty also appears to be akin to a candidate-centered campaign on a greater magnitude. In particular, a political dynasty is an unpredictable anomaly on the political scene, but it is relatively easy to identify. The specific examples of the political families, the Kennedys and the Rockefellers, provide evidence that political dynasties influence the careers of family members and give them extra political influence.

INTRODUCTION

The political dynasty, in the American context, is an organization usually centered on a family which transcends traditional campaign and voter perception. By transcending these norms, the dynasty develops the image of American "royalty." The Kennedy and Rockefeller families have evolved as the most dominant examples of political dynasties in the twentieth century. The phenomena, as evidenced in these examples, appear to center around one individual and build from there. Once established, this mutation of American politics becomes its own organization, nearly independent of its respective parties in power and strategy (Salmore and Salmore 1989, 39). Even though the later elements of the dynasty benefit from their link to the overall public perception, they are, at times, mistakenly associated and credited with the dynasty's accomplishments as well (Granberg 1985, 504–516).

Each political dynasty, however, is different; each dynasty has its own dynamics that separate it from the rest of the political community. The Kennedys, for example, are a nationally recognized political family, although the family center or core is in Massachusetts. The Rockefellers, while equally nationally known, have spread their political dominance over the governor's mansions in New York, Arkansas, and West Virginia (Salmore and Salmore 1989, 125). While both families exhibited a drive for dominance, the political bases of their influence span the spectrum from highly centralized to decentralized (Clinch 1973, x).

THE KENNEDY DYNASTY

The Kennedys and their episodic saga in American politics are the premier political dynasty in evidence. The roots of the Kennedy dynasty began with John F. Fitzgerald, who was the mayor of Boston and a U.S. Congressman (Davis 1984, 41). The figure who is the symbol of the Kennedy mystique, however, is John F. Kennedy (JFK), 35th president of the United States. JFK's popularity and successful election have created a standard by which the Kennedy heirs were measured. Because of JFK's success and characteristic demeanor, Kennedy heirs were perceived as intellectually keen, eloquent, and youthful (Wills 1982, 153). Those virtues were even more firmly associated with the Kennedy family due to efforts by his successor, Lyndon Johnson, to immortalize Kennedy in public for political purpose to gain public support for the presidential agenda (Schuyler 1987, 503–504).

The first tests of the Kennedy dynasty's effects on the electorate came soon after JFK's assassination. In 1964, Robert F. Kennedy (RFK), brother of the former president, challenged President Johnson and the Democratic Party regulars for the presidency. RFK sought to build on the foundations of residual grief over his slain brother. In particular, RFK promised to return to the values and programs of JFK. RFK became a rallying symbol for disenfranchised party opposition to Johnson (Halberstam 1968, 5). Johnson feared, as did other Democratic party leaders, "that the country would turn to Robert Kennedy... as the successor to the throne, as the rightful heir to the Kennedy tradition..." (Schuyler 1987, 506). Even though the Kennedy campaign started late, party supporters won their first primary with the help of the Kennedy family "machine," which used its own network and popularity to sidestep the party apparatus (Halberstam 1968, 161).

The reincarnation of the Kennedy dynasty had dramatic effects, as fate again lent a hand. RFK, broadening the reformist, intellectual style of the Kennedys (Halberstam 1968, 162), contributed his final piece to the puzzle as he was assassinated following a crucial 1968 California primary. Until his death, RFK's candidacy was gaining momentum by the day. Voters, especially young people, flocked to his campaign. There is little doubt that such voting behavior was caused by the Kennedy dynasty; RFK was a late entry, a freshman senator, and opposed to the policies of his own incumbent president. These factors would destroy other contenders for the oval office.

RFK's assassination event merely further magnified the Kennedy mystique as the promises of two Kennedy family politicians would go unfulfilled (Halberstam 1968, 209). Because of this, the public looked to the last heir—apparent in Senator Edward M. Kennedy. The subsequent trials of Ted Kennedy are the best examples of the Kennedy dynasty. Because the Kennedy image had been firmly entrenched by liberals in the original Kennedy administration (Matusow 1983, 153) and enhanced by the revival of that liberalism by RFK's run, much was expected of Ted Kennedy. Despite a divorce and a highly controversial accident in which a woman he was with died, Ted Kennedy had been easily reelected to the Senate and was a serious candidate for the presidency. His past electoral successes and near success for president occurred in part because of the Kennedy name. In addition, he has forged an impressive senatorial record in keeping with family tradition, and he has echoed the rhetoric of his deceased brothers at two national conventions (Wills 1982, 294).

Even with the Kennedy's success, the "ghosts" of the Kennedy family's past have forced Ted Kennedy into ill-fought contests for the presidency (Wills 1982, 295). The public's perception of him is still linked to the Kennedy legacies. Ted Kennedy's popularity is due in part to a public perception that he is more liberal than his record indicates (Granberg 1985, 504–516). The public has a rigid perception of the Kennedy dynasty that is evident in the emerging popularity of a new Kennedy. Joseph P. Kennedy III, oldest son of Robert, is running for his third term in Congress as he and the Kennedy machine reclaimed the seat held by his great-grandfather, uncle, and former House Speaker Tip O'Neill. Young Joseph Kennedy defeated a field of 10 candidates to win the seat ("Liberals Rebuffed" 1986, 28). Thus, the Kennedy dynasty continues with young Joe, 37 years old, maintaining and rejuvenating the family.

THE ROCKEFELLER DYNASTY

Like the Kennedy dynasty, the reign of the Rockefellers in the United States has been one of philanthropy and public service. The Rockefellers are presently in their fourth generation of public service. The Rockefeller dynasty began with the billions of dollars made by John D. Rockefeller in the late nineteenth century and early twentieth century through his success in founding Standard Oil (Ensor Harr and Johnson 1988, xiii).

Unlike the Kennedys, the Rockefellers established themselves as a political dynasty more through philanthropic causes than public service (Lundberg 1975, 329). Although the Rockefellers' public image is associated with being ruthless businessmen (Collier and Horowitz 1976, 4), it is estimated that by the third generation of Rockefellers, a staggering 5 billion dollars was donated to the philanthropic causes by John D. Sr., John D. Jr., and John D. Rockefeller III (Lundberg 1975, 329).

More importantly, the Rockefeller dynasty has produced one vice-president and former governor, a U.S. senator and a former governor, and another governor—all from different states (Salmore and Salmore 1989, 125; Ensor Harr and Johnson 1988, 8–9). The Rockefellers first entered the political arena in 1958. Nelson Rockefeller (Nelson), son of John D. Rockefeller Jr., ran for and won the governor's seat in New York (Collier and Horowitz 1976, 330). From there, Nelson used his reputation as a base to run for the presidency. In 1968, Nelson ran for the nomination of the Republican party without entering the primaries (Halberstam 1968). He used polls to boost his popularity and bypass any losses in primaries that would diminish his chances of success. Although Nelson lost to Nixon, the Rockefeller machine continued to churn.

In 1964, Winthrop Rockefeller, brother of Nelson, ran unsuccessfully for the governor of Arkansas, but he won in 1966 and 1968 (Lundberg 1975, 285). Winthrop reshaped the new Rockefeller political mold by supporting issues important to blacks and impoverished citizens. Likewise, Nelson was very popular with black voters in his campaign for president. Winthrop became Arkansas' first Republican governor in a century (Lundberg 1975, 285). Winthrop, long regarded as the "black sheep" in the family, retired from the governor spot when his term ended in 1970 (Ensor Harr and Johnson 1988, 5).

The Rockefeller political spotlight has also shone on the nephew of Nelson and Winthrop. John (Jay) D. Rockefeller IV has gone where no Rockefeller has gone before. Though Nelson was appointed as vice-president for the troubled Ford administration, no Rockefeller had served in Congress. Jay, following two terms as the Democratic governor of West Virginia, ran and won a senate seat in 1984 ("King of the Hills and Hollers" 1984, 22–24). Although the Rockefeller dynasty has been accused of buying elections (Salmore and Salmore 1989, 125), with the election of "J.D. IV," the Rockefeller name has secured its place in the elite American political arena.

CONCLUSION

The success of the Kennedy and the Rockefeller families as two prime examples of American dynasties exemplifies the primary political dynamics that are essential to being part of American political life. These dynamics are instant name recognition for family members, instant empathy from the electorate for the family member's position on issues, nonrational voting behavior based on residual biases associated with the family, and ability to exhibit independence from party politics. The practical effects of establishing a political dynasty are political survival. The societal effect is much less noticeable; political dynasties package political change as familial continuity and thus provide for the survival of their family's influence, as well as goals for society. Because of this, political dynasties built in the past shape present political life and have uncommon influence over America's destiny.

246 Chapter 11 ■ Format and Examples of Conventional Research Papers

REFERENCES

Clinch, Nancy Gager. 1973. *The Kennedy neurosis*. New York: Grosset & Dunlap.

Collier, Peter and David Horowitz. 1976. *The Rockefellers: An American dynasty*. New York: Holt, Rinehart and Winston.

Davis, John H. 1984. *The Kennedys: Dynasty and disaster 1848–1983*. New York: McGraw-Hill Book Company.

Ensor Harr, John and Peter J. Johnson. 1988. *The Rockefeller century*. New York: Charles Scribner's Sons.

Granberg, Donald. 1985. An anomaly in political perception. *The Public Opinion Quarterly* 49: 504–16.

Lundberg, Ferdinand. 1975. *The Rockefeller syndrome*. Secaucus, NJ: Lyle Stuart Inc.

King of the hills and hollers. 1984. *The Economist*, October 20.

Halberstam, David. 1968. *The unfinished odyssey of Robert Kennedy*. New York: Random House.

Liberals rebuffed. 1986. *The Economist*, September 20.

Matusow, Allen J. 1983. John F. Kennedy and the intellectuals. *The Wilson Quarterly* (Autumn): 140–53.

Salmore, Barbara G., and Stephen A. Salmore. 1989. *Candidates, parties, and campaigns*. Washington D.C.: Congressional Quarterly Inc.

Schuyler, Michael W. 1987. Ghosts in the White House: LBJ, RFK, and the assassination of JFK. *Presidential Studies Quarterly* 49: 503–18.

Wayne, Stephen J. 1990. *The road to the White House*. New York: St. Martin's Press.

Wills, Garry. 1982. *The Kennedy imprisonment*. Boston: Little, Brown and Co.

Writing an Analysis

In some courses in political science, instructors ask students to examine political events or phenomena critically. An analysis of an event is part descriptive, part historical, part journalistic, and part imagination! It involves identifying and differentiating between relevant and irrelevant information and is specifically focused on the causal relationship between variables. In other words, an analysis provides an examination of the causes of political events. It involves asking not just who, what, when, and where, but also who benefited politically, who paid the political costs, what were motivations or incentives, and when the impact of the event was realized. An analysis is typically, but not always, supported with both qualitative and quantitative evidence. Here is a standard formula for political event analysis (Lester 1990: 73).

1. **Describe the event. In particular, briefly describe the context in which the event occurred.**
   - Identify specific activities that led up to the event.
   - Identify any perceived reactions to the event or arguments about its impact.
   - State a thesis about why the event occurred.
   - Be sure the thesis sentence clearly identifies the important causal variables associated with the event.
2. **For the body, using the thesis sentence as a guide:**
   - Examine critically all important activities preceding the event.
   - Using evidence, show how each activity is linked to the event.
   - Rank or order the events by importance to the outcome. Support this ranking with evidence.
   - Provide evidence that describes the political consequence of the event or outcome.
3. **Summarize the causal relationships and emphasize the important determinants of the event or outcome.**
   - Show how the evidence supported the thesis sentence.
   - Reaffirm the explanation of the event's impact on politics in society.

YOUTH INFLUENCE IN POLITICAL OUTCOMES

By
Patrick J. Brown
POLS 318
Professor Schmidt
October 9, 1990
(Reprinted with permission)

ABSTRACT

The youth in this country have had a direct influence on electoral outcomes by adding new voters to the voting block in 1972 and by taking part directly in the electoral process. Volunteering time to a candidate is the best way to get directly involved in an election. Also, if the youth vote in an election, they can add millions of votes to the outcome. In addition, if the majority of the youth movement is voting for a particular candidate, they can really make a difference in the election results. Although voter turnout of the youth has always been the lowest of the voting blocks, the youth movement can still make a difference. A good example of this occurred in the presidential election of 1968. The youth in the 1980s identified with the Republicans and in the 1970s with the Democrats. This report will show that when the youth coalesce, they can make a difference in electoral outcome.

INTRODUCTION

According to the Twenty-sixth Amendment to the Constitution of the United States, citizens eighteen years of age or older have the right to vote. This Amendment was the turning point of the youth movement of the late 1960s. Since then, the youth of the United States can not only protest against their government, they can vote to change the representatives who govern it. Even before 1972, when the Amendment was approved, the youth (ages 18–24) in the United States had made a difference in the electoral process and the outcomes. The youth can and have made a difference on electoral outcomes by adding a new voting block, with millions of new voters, and by taking part directly by working and volunteering for candidates.

TRENDS IN STUDENT ACTIVISM

In the 1960s, young people all over the world, particularly in the United States, seemed to develop a distinctive style of political dissent. Newspaper coverage about some youth organization holding a protest or political rally became increasingly frequent. According to Anthony Orum, there are three important conclusions that emerge from observing youth and their politics in the United States through historical perspectives. The conclusions are: the United States was not the first nation to experience vigorous political activity, it was uncommon to experience large-scale political activity by American youth until the 1960s, and most of the youth activists were well educated and wealthy.[1] A study of accredited four-year universities during the 1967–68 academic year found that only about 2 percent of the student population belonged to leftist student organizations and that an additional 8–10 percent were strongly sympathetic with the movement for social change and were capable of temporary activism, depending on the issues.[2]

The activism of the 1960s had its origins in Berkeley, California, when in 1964 student activists were banned from political activities in an area of campus where they were formerly allowed. When the American involvement in Vietnam escalated, student unrest on campuses often became violent. According to Robert K. Landers:

> Student activists, to make a distinctive mark on their time, must overcome the thinness of their ranks and assert a plausible claim to represent in essence, the future. Hence, they must somehow arouse the sympathies of—and get occasional demonstrations of support from—the mass of students. During the 1960s, activists were able to accomplish this, but during the 1980s, they had been far less successful.[3]

The protests and the Vietnam War were both fought by young people. The unpopular war called more attention to the impact of government than any other event in this century.[4] Those who wanted to make a change had some alternatives. Some activists called for a revolution; however, others called for a non-violent means of expression.

TRENDS IN YOUTH VOTER TURNOUT

One alternative to revolution was to exercise the power of voting. Importantly, the Twenty-sixth Amendment, lowering the voting age to eighteen in 1972, created a potential new influence on the outcome of elections. In addition, the post–World War II "baby boom" also resulted in many new voters entering the electorate in the late 1960s and early 1970s. Both of these factors drastically changed the electorate in this country. There were approximately 25 million new voters.[5] Many of these voters were more inclined to be less partisan and vote more along the lines of the issues.

Disappointing Youth Voter Turnout

There was, however, a surprise to those who advocated the Twenty-sixth Amendment: the trend of a declining youth turnout. In 1972, only about 48.3 percent turned out and voted. Although voting can be a powerful force for the youth agenda, only about 45.6 percent of that same group four years later voted.[6] Further, in the 1972 election, the percentage of 18–20-year-olds who were not registered was 41.9 percent and for 21–24-year-olds who were not registered was 40.5 percent.[7]

Nonetheless, in terms of non-voters, young people tend to be more interested in politics than older Americans. Among the population as a whole, older persons are more interested than the youth. The voting turnout by age characteristics of 18–20-year-olds from the 1972 election to the 1984 election was considerably low compared with the rest of the voting classes. Since 1972, Democrats have outnumbered Republicans in terms of new voters by more than two to one.[8] The major reason was the Democrats' opposition to the war in Vietnam. Unfortunately, the Democrats, more than the Republicans, are inclined to not vote in an election. Together with youth identification with the Democratic Party, this characteristic might help explain the low youth turnout.

More importantly, the tendency of the youngest voters to identify with the Republican Party may offer the greatest hope of increasing the size of the GOP. Although youth generally identify with the political party of their parents, increasingly young voters are aligning with the Republican Party, regardless of their parent's party identification.[9] This change could help the party grow generational replacement. For example, in the 1984 election, the younger voters supported the reelection of Ronald Reagan. This was a big change since the first youth election in 1972. The cause of this shift was not a move to the right among college students, but rather a shift to the middle ground or moderate positions in 1984.[10] Further, according to a *New York Times–CBS News* poll, Ronald Reagan won the support of full-time students by a margin of 51 to 48 percent. Again in the 1988 election, George Bush defeated Michael Dukakis in the youth category 52 to 47 percent.[11]

Inducing Youth Turnout

Although young people vote less than any other category, there are opportunities to change this trend. To induce voting among youth, candidates must advocate what young people perceive as their needs. In addition, the parties must change structurally to be more appealing and inclusive of young people. Finally, voting must result in identification benefits to youths.[12] Youth need to feel something when they vote. Young people must be persuaded to find efficacy and clear reasons for participating.[13] The foremost obstacle to increasing voting participation among youth is persuading them that their votes count.

Nonetheless, students and young people participate. Many of these activists volunteer in political campaigns because they feel strongly about the issues and candidates and because they want to make a difference. In conservative terms, there is a word to describe the effort of youth activism on college campuses to participate in the electoral process. The term is referred to as the Mass-Based Youth Effort.[14] The school that a potential activist can attend is called the Morton Blackwell Leadership Institute.[15] Based in Virginia, the Institute holds training seminars in central locations throughout the U.S. During this two-day seminar, activists learn how to conduct a canvas of the university's student population. Once activists locate the strong supporters for their candidate, they remind their supporters to go to the polls and vote. These activists also learn how to identify unregistered voters who agree with their party and how to register them to vote. Youths are taught how to get active and directly involved in the electoral process, while showing young people how the election directly concerns them.

Another youth-based set of groups which mobilize students are the College Republicans and the College Democrats. Both the College Republicans National Committee and the Young College Democrats planned massive voter registration drives in the 1984 and 1988 elections. The Republicans concentrated on all fifty states, compared with the seventeen-state effort in 1980. The College Democrats, for the first time in 1984, worked in thirty states.[16] The College Republicans have a full-time staff in Washington, D.C., and they have an annual budget of $250,000. The College Democrats have only a $12,000 budget and lack any central office or staff.[17] The main reason for the difference is that Morton Blackwell used to be the Executive Director of the College Republican National Committee, and the mass-based youth effort concepts are used by the National Committee. The College Republicans now hold their own leadership training schools.

Impact of Youth Mobilization Programs

These youth movements have made a difference in electoral outcomes. In 1984, some 35,000 new student voters in Ohio helped to defeat three statewide referendums that would have raised the drinking age and cut education funding.[18] Also, in New Orleans, at Xavier University in 1984, 98 percent of the students were registered to vote.[19] Top priority was finally placed on voter registration by youth groups in 1984. Since then, efforts are still going strong on campuses all over the country.

Students were also actively involved in Gary Hart's campaign for president in 1984. The students are credited with Hart's win in the New Hampshire primary because of the student canvassing effort. The students canvassed 90 percent of the precincts in the state.[20] The New Hampshire win placed Gary Hart in the race as a major contender. Many students joined the campaign as full-time staff for the rest of the way. About half of Gary Hart's volunteers were students, compared with a third working for Jesse Jackson, and a fourth working for Walter Mondale.[21] All of the Democratic candidates made numerous campus campaign stops in 1984, because they believed that students could make a difference in many ways.

Probably the best example of a direct youth influence on the outcome of an election happened in the presidential election of 1968. Senator Eugene McCarthy was an early Democratic candidate for president of the United States. As president, Lyndon Johnson was favored in the race. The vote predictions in the New Hampshire primary by Gallup Polls had predicted, in January, that McCarthy had only 12 percent of the vote. When it was all over in March of 1968, McCarthy received 42.4 percent of the vote.[22] The students, most of whom could not even vote yet, came to New Hampshire from Michigan, Wisconsin, Yale, and Harvard to work for their candidate, Eugene McCarthy. McCarthy gave the students the inspiration to care about politics and the presidency. He also promised to end the war in Vietnam. It was estimated that as many as five thousand students campaigned on weekends and two thousand were full-time.[23]

In particular, an important campaign stop for the Eugene McCarthy Campaign was in Wisconsin. Theodore H. White sums up what happened next during that visit:

> Student headquarters for McCarthy at the Wisconsin Hotel, a mile away, was explosive in contrast—eight thousand students were now roving over Wisconsin. Every town of five thousand had its student platoons, sleeping at friendly homes, in church basements, and still, on this Saturday they were pouring in, eight hundred from Michigan alone—and now the students were veterans—volunteer specialists had broken the lists down into streets, blocks, and districts—assigned eighty calls to each volunteer. By two o'clock in the morning, Sunday, student headquarters were sending back the other busloads because they could not be used.[24]

When the votes were counted, Eugene McCarthy had 56.2 percent to Lyndon Johnson's 34.6 percent and Robert Kennedy's 6.3 percent.[25] Later, President Johnson gave a speech in which he withdrew his name from the electoral process and did not seek another term. The students in Eugene McCarthy's campaign worked many tasks, from administrative to the most menial kinds of campaign work. The allure of the McCarthy campaign primarily centered on the treatment of youths in his campaign organization. His campaign staff did not distinguish between adults and the youth movement. They all worked together for a common cause.

CONCLUSION

The youth in the United States, in terms of voting, have always had the lowest turnout. Nevertheless, youth can still make a difference in electoral outcomes. Youth groups' major influence comes because of the new voting block of 1972 and the impact of the numbers of "baby boom" votes cast in the elections. The candidates in the 1972 election had to appeal to American youth. Because young people were protesting government policies, it was difficult to win over the youth vote in the late 1960s and the early 1970s. Most of those who were mobilized attached themselves to the Democratic Party. This continued to be the case until 1984, when the young people realigned to the Republican Party during the reelection of Ronald Reagan. The youth vote has been largely Republican since that time. Part of the reason was a shift to more moderate positions by the youth and because of the Republicans' youth effort to attract votes, volunteers, and registration of new young voters in this country.

Perhaps the lowering of the voting age in this country did not have the impact in terms of increasing the number of young people that actually voted. It did, however, give millions of young people an incentive to use a nonviolent means of expressing opinions about policy decisions that impact them the most. Hard-working mass-based youth movements can make a difference in this country like they did in the election for president in 1968. Theodore H. White describes that remarkable event in 1968 that best summarizes the potential impact of youth voting participation:

> It was not part of the script of history that Lyndon Johnson of the Pedernales should be brought down by a poet from Watkin, Minnesota. Hard-working college students, in nine weeks, had brought down not a dean, not a president of a university, but the President of the United States.[26]

NOTES

[1]Anthony M. Orum, *The Seeds of Politics* (New Jersey: Prentice-Hall, Inc., 1972), 2.

[2]Richard E. Peterson, "The Scope of Organized Student Protest," in *Protest! Student Activism in America*, eds. Julian Foster and Durward Long (New York: Morrow, 1970), 78.

[3]Robert K. Landers, "Student Politics 1980s Style," *Editorial Research Reports*, 1986, 661; see also Louis M. Seagull, *Youth and Change in American Politics* (New York: Franklin Watts Inc., 1977).

[4]William C. Mitchell, *Why Vote?* (Chicago: Markham Publishing Company, 1971), 8.

[5]Ibid, 8; see also M. Kent Jennings and Richard G. Niemi, *The Political Character of Adolescence* (New York: Princeton University Press, 1974).

[6]David Hill and Norman Luttbeg, *Trends in American Electoral Behavior* (Itasca, IL: F.E. Peacock Publishers, Inc, 1980).

[7]William J. Crotty, *Political Reform and the American Experiment* (New York: Thomas J. Crowell Co., 1977), 54; see also Stanley Kelly, Richard E. Ayres, and William G. Bowen, "Registration and Voting: Putting Things First," *American Political Science Review* (June 1967): 61.

[8]William H. Flanigan, *Political Behavior of the American Electorate* (Boston: Allyn and Bacon, Inc., 1972), 26.

[9]Everett Carl Ladd, "On Mandates, Realignments, and the 1984 Presidential Election," *Political Science Quarterly* (Spring 1985): 18; see also M. Kent Jennings and Richard G. Niemi, "The Transmission of Political Values from Parent to Child," *American Political Science Review* (March 1968): 171.

[10]Landers, 613; see also Frank J. Sorauf and Paul Allen Beck, *Party Politics in America* (Glenview, IL: Scott, Foresman, 1987).

[11]Larry J. Sabato, *The 1988 Election in America* (Glenview, IL: Scott, Foresman, 1989), 32.

[12]Curtis Gans, "Why Young People Don't Vote," *Educational Digest* (February 1989): 40.

[13]Gans, 43.

[14]This information is based on my field observation of the institution. See Morton Blackwell, *Leadership Source Manual*, mimeo (Springfield, VA: Morton Blackwell Leadership Institute, 1990).

[15]Blackwell 1990.

[16]Donna St. George, "Students Bone up on Art of Politics," *National Journal* (April 7, 1984): 667.

[17]Larry J. Sabato, *The Party's Just Begun* (Glenview, IL: Scott, Foresman, 1988), 81.

[18]St. George, 665.

[19]Ibid.

[20]Ibid.

[21]Ibid.

[22]Eugene J. McCarthy, *The Year of the People* (New York: Doubleday and Company, Inc., 1969), 89; see also Arthur Herzog, *McCarthy for President* (New York: Viking Press, 1969).

[23]McCarthy, 70.

[24]Theodore H. White, *The Making of the President 1968* (New York: Atheneum Publishers, 1969), 120.

[25]McCarthy, 108.

[26]White, 125.

BIBLIOGRAPHY

Blackwell, Morton. *Leadership Source Manual*. Mimeo. Springfield, VA: Morton Blackwell Leadership Institute, 1990.

Crotty, William J. *Political Reform and the American Experiment*. New York: Thomas J. Crowell Co, 1977.

Flanigan, William H. *Political Behavior of the American Electorate*. Boston: Allyn and Bacon, Inc., 1972.

Gans, Curtis. "Why Young People Don't Vote," *Educational Digest* 54 (February 1989): 40–43.

Herzog, Arthur. *McCarthy for President*. New York: Viking Press, 1969.

Hill, David, and Norman R. Luttbeg. *Trends in American Electoral Behavior*. Itasca, IL: F.E. Peacock Publishers, Inc, 1990.

Jennings, M. Kent, and Richard G. Niemi. *The Political Character of Adolescence*. New York: Princeton University Press, 1974.

_____. "The Transmission of Political Values from Parent to Child." *American Political Science Review* 62 (March 1968): 168–84.

Kelly, Stanley, Richard E. Ayres, and William G. Bowen, "Registration and Voting: Putting Things First." *American Political Science Review* 61 (June 1967): 359–79.

Ladd, Everett Carl. "On Mandates, Realignments, and the 1984 Presidential Election." *Political Science Quarterly* 100 (spring 1985): 1–25.

Landers, Robert K. "Student Politics 1980s Style," *Editorial Research Reports* 2 (1986): 609–628.

McCarthy, Eugene J. *The Year of the People*. New York: Doubleday and Company, 1969.

Mitchell, William C. *Why Vote?* Chicago: Markham Publishing Company, 1971.

Orum, Anthony M. *The Seeds of Politics*. New Jersey: Prentice-Hall, Inc., 1972.

Peterson, Richard E. "The Scope of Organized Student Protest." In *Protest! Student Activism in America,* edited by Julian Foster and Durward Long. New York: Morrow, 1970.

Sabato, Larry J. *The 1988 Elections in America.* Glenview, IL: Scott, Foresman and Company, 1989.

_____. *The Party's Just Begun.* Glenview, IL: Scott, Foresman and Company, 1988.

Seagull, Louis M. *Youth and Change in American Politics.* New York: Franklin Watts Inc., 1977.

Sorauf, Frank J., and Paul Allen Beck. *Party Politics in America.* Glenview, IL: Scott, Foresman and Company, 1987.

St. George, Donna. "Students Bone Up to Art of Politics." *National Journal* 16 (April 7, 1984): 665–68.

White, Theodore H. *The Making of the President 1968.* New York: Atheneum Publishers, Inc., 1969.

Writing a Position Paper

Instructors in some upper-level political science classes may assign a research paper that requires the student to do more than just research what other people say about a topic or controversy. A position paper takes the research process one step further than simple comparison or analysis. In a position paper, the student is required to construct a theory or position about an event, problem, or controversy and defend that theory or position using evidence. Position papers include, at minimum, scholarly qualitative evidence. Quantitative evidence and statistical methods are often used to provide further support for the writer's theory or position. Here is a standard formula for writing a position paper.

1. **Describe a problem, event, or controversy. In particular, briefly describe the significance of the item.**
   - Identify alternative explanations about why the problem/controversy exists or the event occurred.
   - In the thesis sentence, state a unique perspective about why the event occurred or why the problem/controversy exists.
   - Be sure to clearly separate the paper's perspective from the others described.
   - Be sure the thesis sentence clearly identifies the important causal variables associated with the event, controversy, or problem.

2. **Trace the evolution of the event, problem, or controversy.**
   - Describe the context in which the event, problem, or controversy occurred.
   - Analyze the details, major identifiable issues, and minor underlying issues connected with the event, problem, or controversy.

3. **Identify the arguments or different important perspectives that have been used to explain the event, problem, or controversy.**
   - Be sure to justify why these perspectives are important.
   - Differentiate between the alternative explanations. How are they different? How are they similar?
   - Criticize the alternative explanations for errors in reasoning, omissions, and/or facts.

4. **Describe the paper's competing theory or position and justify it with evidence.**
   - State clearly how the paper's perspective is different or corrects errors identified in other explanations.
   - Present evidence that strongly supports the paper's theory or position.
   - Identify any evidence that appears to refute the paper's theory or position. Explain why this evidence is not valid or how the paper's theory must be adjusted to address the evidence, if it is valid.

5. **Restate the theory or position and provide a concluding statement.**
   - Defend the theory or position by briefly recalling the evidence that supports the paper's explanation, and not the alternative explanations.
   - Make sure the analysis and arguments support this defense.
   - If possible, suggest a course of action on how the event, problem, or controversy could be addressed better in the future.

CHIEF JUSTICE REHNQUIST: DOES HE LEAD THE COURT?

By
Chris Kozenski
POLS 435
December 7, 1989
(Reprinted with permission)

INTRODUCTION

The Chief Justice, as the head of the Supreme Court, is in both a good and bad position to lead and influence the members of the Court. There are two limitations of power facing the Chief Justice. As Laurence Baum (1986) indicates in his book *The Supreme Court*, the first limitation is that the Chief Justice is burdened with more administrative duties than ever. As the head of the federal court system, the Chief serves both a powerful ceremonial and bureaucratic role, which keeps him very busy. According to Baum, one observer of the Court, Jeffery Morris, states that the Chief "may well stand at a relative disadvantage . . ." in the writing and arguing over opinions "because of the unique demands upon his time" (1986, 153).

The second limitation of the power of the Chief Justice is that present day Justices are strong-minded, skilled individuals who are not likely to be controlled. Chief Justice John Marshall, in the early 1800s, had substantial control over his Court as seen by his writing of the Court's opinion in almost all cases. Rarely under Marshall did another Justice's views win out over the Chief Justice. Yet, Chief Justice Rehnquist would never be able to lead the Court as strongly (Baum 1986; Steamer 1986).

But the position of Chief Justice also has formal powers that strengthen his position as the leader of the Court. In particular, there are three formal powers which can be quite important: (1) presiding over oral argument and conference, (2) creating the discuss list, and (3) opinion assignment (Baum 1986). By presiding over conference, the Chief Justice opens the discussion on a case, summarizes it, and then gives his personal opinions on the case. He can also end discussion on the case. In this way, it might be possible for the Chief to "frame alternatives, thus helping to shape the outcome of the discussion" (Baum 1986, 153).

The discuss list is a set of petitions that will receive group judgment by the Court. The Chief Justice has the duty to make the first informal version of the list. By doing this, the Chief plays an important role in determining which cases will be heard and decided on by the group (Baum 1986; Chaper 1987; Cannon and O'Brien 1985).

OPINION ASSIGNMENTS IN THE REHNQUIST COURT

The Chief Justice's third power—opinion assignment—is by far his strongest leadership tool. The Chief Justice is, by position, the Justice who assigns the writer of the Court's majority opinion. If the Chief is not in the majority, then the next senior-most Justice in the majority assigns the opinion (Baum 1986; Chaper 1987). What makes this power so important is that it is in these majority opinions where the Supreme Court establishes "controlling constitutional principles" and where "broader policy objectives beyond the immediate case are fashioned" (Slotnick 1978, 219). So by assigning the opinions to the Justice of his choice, the Chief is in a good position to alter, even frame, the public policies that result from Supreme Court decisions.

Because of the importance of opinion assignment, it should be shown that certain factors do come into play when the Chief Justice makes an assignment. There are four factors, in particular, that have influence on the Chief Justice's assignment. The first is the equality of distribution. This means that the Justices should have relatively equal workloads and if the Chief assigns opinions disproportionately, he will upset those Justices who do not have an equal share of the workload, and therefore an unequal share of opinions (Slotnick 1978; 1979). Ability and expertise are also important factors the Chief takes into consideration when assigning an opinion (Brenner and Spaeth 1986; Spaeth and Michael 1985). The fourth factor is the importance of the decision. If a decision is considered important, often the Chief will self-assign the opinion. This is traditionally an unwritten norm of the Court. As the "first above equals" the Chief lends his prestige to a decision when he is the author of the opinion (Slotnick 1978).

Still, there are four other things the Chief Justice must take into consideration when making an assignment. David Danelski suggests that whomever the Chief Justice designates to speak for the Court may be highly influential in:

1) determining the precedent value of a decision (because the Justice who authors the opinion often decides the grounds for the decision).

2) making the decision as publicly acceptable as possible.

3) holding a majority together when it is a close vote.

4) and minimizing the number of dissenting and concurring opinions (Danelski 1986).

Often, the assigner of the opinion will choose the Justice who stands in the middle of the voting coalitions to gain support for the majority decision. For example, if a particular decision has the court divided, the Chief must choose the Justice with a moderate view to gain votes from the dissenting side of the court (Danelski 1986).

Equality of Assignments

There are two ways in which equality of opinion assignment can be examined. The first way is through measuring absolute equality; this is simply the equality of caseloads between the Justices. Another way to examine equality is to look at it conditionally; this means that equality is based on the frequency of times a Justice is available to write the opinion (Altfeld and Spaeth 1984, 300).

To see how fairly Chief Justice Rehnquist assigned opinions, I examined majority opinion assignments from both viewpoints of equality (Altfeld and Spaeth 1984, 299–304) the same way Harold Spaeth studied Court decisions.[1] Absolute equality was examined for the 1986, 1987, and 1988 terms. Table 1 displays the number of opinions that each Justice wrote per term, regardless of who made the assignment or how often the Justice was in the majority. It was measured using a mean (which is simply the average number of times a Justice wrote an opinion for that year), a standard deviation (Std. Dev.), and a coefficient of relative variation (CRV) which standardizes a set of deviations based on different means.

(TABLE 1 ABOUT HERE)

Because the Chief Justice assigns a majority of cases, it was up to Rehnquist to assign fairly and equally if he wanted a record of distributive equality in opinion assignments. Table 1 shows an impressive equal distribution of opinion writing between the Justices. Treating the terms as a whole ('86–'88) each Justice wrote an average of 15.8 opinions. The number of times a Justice varied by more than three assignments from the term average is only three (two occurring in 1986, Powell and Scalia; one occurring in 1988, Scalia). Rehnquist's CRVs are low in all three terms (1986, CRV .15; 1987, CRV .13; 1988, CRV .13).

---

[1]Opinion Assignment Ratio (OAR) was used here in order to compare with Spaeth's findings of Burger and Warren. (The overall OARs are as follows: Rehn. = 14.0, Bren. = 17.3, White = 14.8, Mar. = 16.1, Blac. = 13.6, Pow. = 15.8, Stev. = 15.8, O'C = 14.2, Sca. 11.1, Ken. = 12.6.)

Comparing Rehnquist to other Chief Justices only enhances his record of absolute quality. Rehnquist has an overall CRV of .12, while Burger's overall CRV is .179, and Warren's was .24. Stone, Vinson, Taft, and Hughes are all at least twice as high as Burger, which makes Rehnquist's CRV the best of the last six Chief Justices of the Supreme Court (Spaeth 1984; Goldberg 1986).

Rehnquist has a very good overall distribution record, but what happens when conditioned equality of assignments is looked at? To study this, opinion assignment ratios were used to see the overall picture. Again following Spaeth's study, Rehnquist's equality of assignments in "important" cases was compared to that of Burger and Warren. It is in these "important" cases where major public policy is made. To test whether Chief Justice Rehnquist is leading the Court's public policy, it is necessary to look at his opinion distribution practices in these important cases.

There have been many methods employed to define important cases. Sidney Ulmer deems a case important by the amount of times the "court cites the case within five years of the decision" (Altfeld and Spaeth 1984, 303). This cannot apply here because of the recent data being used. Another approach uses constitutional casebooks, and if the case is discussed in several of these books, then it is considered as important. But because both of these methods have come under fire for various reasons, Spaeth's method was used. Spaeth's method defined a case as important if it appears within a rectangle on the front cover of the Lawyers' Edition of *U.S. Reports*. Of these important cases (47 in all between 1986 and 1989) Rehnquist assigned 72 percent of the opinions. (He assigned 50 percent in 1986, 80 percent in 1987, and 82 percent in 1988.)

As a norm of the Court, the Chief Justice is expected to disproportionately assign important decisions to himself, being the "first above equals." Yet Rehnquist's patterns of opinion assignments in important cases show huge disparities. Using an opinion assignment ratio (OAR), each Justice was given a ratio for the '86–'88 terms. The OAR is "simply the percentage of times a given Justice is assigned the majority opinion when he is in the Court's majority" (Slotnick 1979, 63). Measuring a Justice's OAR is important because "it is more sensitive than a simple average would be when dealing with a Justice who is in dissent [or not sitting] a great deal of the time" (Altfeld and Spaeth 1984, 304).

According to their OARs, as seen in Table 2, three Justices had very high OARs and were at least 13.6 points above the mean; these Justices were Rehnquist with an OAR of 29.4, White with an OAR of 37.9, and Powell with an OAR of 42.9.

(TABLE 2 ABOUT HERE)

There were also three Justices who had OARs of zero, meaning that no time in the 1986, 1987, or 1988 terms did Chief Justice Rehnquist assign them an "important" opinion to write. These Justices were Brennan, Marshall, and Stevens. Blackmun also had a relatively low OAR of 6.7. The standard deviation is 15.1 and the CRV = .96. This is a tremendously high CRV, which shows that there are great differences in the number of opinions each Justice wrote.

Comparing Rehnquist to other Chief Justices shows to what degree Rehnquist unequally assigned cases. Burger's overall CRV of important cases was .47 (Altfeld and Spaeth 1984, 304). Stone's CRV was .40, Vinson's CRV was .55, and Warren's CRV equaled .44 (Altfeld and Spaeth 1984, 304). Even if Slotnick's rule is followed, which excludes those Justices who are available in less than ten cases (Brennan and Powell), Rehnquist's CRV is still .80, while Burger's declines to .34 (Altfeld and Spaeth 1984, 304).

In sum, these results show that Rehnquist unequally assigned the opinions of important cases. In particular, he especially favored those Justices who fit his ideology. Further, according to the data reported, his distributive inequality is the largest of the last five Chief Justices.

Self-Assignment

To see if this inequity came from Rehnquist's self-assignment practices, his OARs were compared to the average OAR of the Court. Following Slotnick's (1978) study, Tables 3 and 4 show the results of the comparison.

(TABLES 3 AND 4 ABOUT HERE)

Rehnquist has a lower OAR than the Court average in the case universe, which means he writes .5 fewer opinions than does the average Justice on the court when considering all cases. Only when important decisions are examined does Rehnquist's OAR exceed the Court average by 13.6.

Table 4, however, shows that it is the norm for the Chief Justice's OAR to be substantially above the Court average. This confirms Slotnick's (1978) findings. Rehnquist is only 1.5 above the total for all Justices from Taft to Burger. Thus, these findings suggest Rehnquist's unequal distribution of opinion assignments in important cases is not due to his self-assignment practices.

IDEOLOGIES ON THE REHNQUIST COURT

To further test these findings on Rehnquist's leadership practices, the Justices' judicial perspective was evaluated on an ideological spectrum. To address this same issue Harold Spaeth and David Rohde examined the conflicts between the liberal and conservative positions on the Court (Baum 1986). Rohde and Spaeth break these issues of conflict down into three categories: (1) freedom, (2) equality, (3) New Dealism. Using these categories, it is easy to rank the Justices on an ideological spectrum.

To confirm that Rehnquist is leading the Court, evidence is needed to show that he is assigning those opinions of important cases disproportionately to those who are most like him. In a study on the 1986 term, Rohde and Spaeth looked at the voting patterns on "freedom" cases in 58 non-unanimous decisions. Freedom cases are defined as involving "conflicts between individual freedoms and governmental action" (Baum 1986, 138). They found that some Justices were prone to vote liberally and others were prone to vote conservatively. This comes as no surprise. By using a scalogram, Rohde and Spaeth were able to rank the Justices according to their number of liberal votes.

In 1986, according to the scalogram, Marshall, Brennan, and Stevens, in that order, had the most liberal votes. Blackmun also voted liberally more than conservatively. On the other end of the spectrum, Rehnquist, O'Connor, White, Scalia, and Powell had the most conservative votes.

Looking at the interagreement among Justices, Baum (1986) uses a table for the median percentage of cases in which pairs of Justices supported the same opinion as in the 1985 and 1986 terms. Unlike the Rohde and Spaeth study, this table includes all cases in all issue areas. Baum finds that Rehnquist agrees with Powell 87 percent of the time, and White and O'Connor 81 percent and 85 percent of the time. Rehnquist had the lowest rates of agreement with Marshall, 39 percent; Brennan, 42 percent; and Stevens 49 percent of the time. This interagreement, along with the findings of Spaeth and Rohde, makes a very clear picture. These findings also clearly support the assertion that Chief Justice Rehnquist assigns important opinions to Justices who will fulfill his policy objectives; these Justices often include Powell, White, and the Chief Justice himself.

DISCUSSION AND CONCLUSIONS

So far, this study has shown that Chief Justice Rehnquist has a fair overall opinion assignment rate. More importantly, this study has shown that Rehnquist has an unfair opinion assignment rate in important cases where most public policy is made. In particular, the findings show that Rehnquist favors conservatives, like himself, by giving them more politically significant opinions to write. Yet, it is important to mention that Rehnquist only assigned 73 percent of the total important cases in the three terms studied. Brennan assigned the other 27 percent of the cases, except for one assigned by Marshall. Thus, Justice Brennan appears to have assigned cases just as unfairly as Rehnquist did.

The OAR ratio should be used to examine the relative assignment behavior more closely. But because the numbers were so low, actual percentages of times Brennan assigned opinions to each Justice is an adequate and meaningful substitute for an OAR ratio. Brennan self-assigned the opinion exactly 50 percent of the time. Stevens, Marshall, and Blackmun were each assigned 10 percent. Brennan only assigned 10 important cases in all, so of the 10, he assigned 80 percent (or 8) of them to liberals on the Court.[2] Both O'Connor and Powell were assigned one opinion. From these numbers it is plain to see that Brennan uses the 27 percent of the cases he assigns to promote liberal public policies. In this way he, too, is a leader of the Court; although he is not as powerful as the Chief Justice. Thus, this suggests that although the Chief Justice has a normal self-assignment rate, he self-assigns cases less than the average Justice overall and is similar to the higher OAR ratio Chief Justices in self-assignment on important cases.

FINAL REMARKS

Earlier in this paper, many different factors were mentioned, each having a possible effect on opinion assignment practices. Among the more important factors mentioned were expertise and holding the majority vote together. It is true that these factors work together and produce an effect on the Chief Justice's decision. Yet, it is apparent that Chief Justices, through the use of their power of assignment, also have wide discretion in pursuing their own public policy ideals (Slotnick, 1979). Chief Justice Rehnquist is no exception; in fact, he was shown to have possibly the widest discretion of the more recent Chief Justices. It will be interesting to see if this trend continues in his future terms as Chief Justice.

---

[2]The case of K-Mart vs. Cartier was not included because of the plurality of opinions.

REFERENCES

Altfeld, M.F. and H.J. Spaeth. 1984. Measuring influence on the U.S. Supreme Court. *Jurimetrics Journal* 24: 236–247.

Baum, L. 1986. *The Supreme Court.* 3rd ed. Washington, D.C.: Congressional Quarterly.

Brenner, S. and H.J. Spaeth. 1986. Issue specialization in majority opinion assignment on the Burger court. *Western Political Quarterly* 39: 520–527.

Cannon, M.C. and D.M. O'Brien. 1985. *Views from the bench*. Chatham, NJ: Chatham House.

Chaper, J.H. 1987. *The Supreme Court and its Justices*. Chicago: American Bar Association.

Danelski, David. 1986. The influence of the decisionmaking process. In *Courts, judges, and politics*, edited by W.F. Murphy and C.H. Pritchett. New York: Random House.

Goldberg, A.J. 1986. The Rehnquist Court. *Hastings Constitutional Law Quarterly* 14: 21–24.

Slotnick, E.E. 1978. The Chief Justices and self-assignment on majority opinions: A research note. *Western Political Quarterly* 31: 219–25.

———. 1979. Who speaks for the Court? Majority opinion assignment from Taft to Burger. *American Journal of Political Science* 23: 60–77.

Spaeth, H.J. 1984. Distributive Justice: Majority opinion assignments in the Burger court. *Judicature* 67: 299–304.

Spaeth, H.J. and F.A. Michael. 1985. Influence relationships within the Supreme Court: A comparison of the Warren and Burger courts. *Western Political Quarterly* 38: 70–83.

Steamer, R.J. 1986. *Chief Justice*. Columbia: University of South Carolina Press.

Table 1: Distribution of Opinions and Judgments of the Court

JUSTICE	TERM		
	1986	1987	1988
Rehnquist	17	15	16
Brennan	16	16	17
White	16	20	18
Marshall	15	15	15
Blackmun	13	15	15
Powell	20	—	—
Stevens	15	19	15
O'Connor	18	16	13
Scalia	12	16	11
Kennedy	12	7°	16
Mean	15.78	16.50	15.11
Std. Dev.	2.43	2.17	1.97
CRV	.15	.13	.13

Mean: the average number of times a Justice wrote an opinion. Std. Dev: standard deviation from the mean. CRV: a coefficient of relative variation that standardizes a set of deviations based on different means.

° Kennedy did not participate in the entire '87–'88 term, so he was excluded from the mean, Std. Dev., CRV. If Kennedy was included, the following data apply: mean = 15.44, Std. Dev. 3.44, CRV = .22.

Source: *Supreme Court Reporter* 1986, 1987, 1988.

Table 2: Rehnquist's Assignees and Their Opinion Assignment Ratios in "Important Cases"

Assignees	Number of Assignments	Times Available	OAR
Rehnquist	10	34	29.4
Brennan	0	9	0
White	11	29	37.9
Marshall	0	10	0
Blackmun	1	15	6.7
Powell	3	7	42.9
Stevens	0	14	0
O'Connor	2	18	11.1
Scalia	4	29	13.8
Kennedy	3	19	15.8

Mean (for the court) = 15.8
Std. Dev. (for the court) = 15.1
CRV (for the court) = .96
Source: Lawyers' Edition, *U.S. Reports*, 1986, 1987, 1988.

Table 3: Self-Assignment Rates v. "Other" Assignment

Unit	Rehnquist's OAR	OAR for Court
Case Universe	14	14.5
"Important" Decisions	29.4	15.8

Table 4: Self-Assignment v. "Other" Assignment

	Case Universe		"Important" Decisions	
Chief Justice	*Self-Assign OAR*	*Court OAR*	*Self-Assign OAR*	*Court OAR*
Taft	16.3	11.1	38.2	10.2
Hughes	15.5	11.8	34.8	10.8
Stone	16.4	13.0	19.4	13.7
Vinson	12.1	14.6	24.6	13.1
Warren	13.0	14.0	19.0	13.5
Burger	13.7	14.5	25.7	12.9
TOTAL	14.8	12.6	24.8	12.7
Rehnquist	14.0	14.5	29.4	15.8

FORMAT AND EXAMPLES OF ASSIGNMENTS REQUIRING SPECIAL TECHNIQUES

Assignments Requiring Special Analytical Techniques

This chapter includes nine examples of highly specialized research papers that exhibit a range of writing styles and topics where students apply concepts, theories, and accepted wisdom in political science to real-life experiences. These papers build on the students' training and knowledge in a subfield. Such assignments provide students with the opportunity to collect information, manage it, and make it useful by writing about it. As in standard research papers, the ideas in the papers develop from a thesis sentence and present an argument about the significance of the findings. Unlike standard research papers, these papers require a special analytical structure to be considered complete. As in standard research papers, these techniques are not specific to the study of American government. The study of comparative public policy and international agreements requires the same attention to the processes and details of making and implementing public policy. These papers exhibit the standard form and degree of thoroughness necessary for studying different kinds of topics. The explanation and form for each type of paper precedes the examples.

First Paper: Analytical Case Study

"Dysfunctional Behavior in the FBI," examines the organizational practices of the Federal Bureau of Investigation. As a case study of administrative behavior, the paper focuses on the historical and contemporary organizational relationships among staff, administrators, and the public.

Second Paper: Problem-Solving Case Study

"Building Inspection Expense Analysis: Building Inspection Department" is a policy memorandum that provides a highly condensed analytical summary of budget expenditures and budget recommendations.

Third Paper: An Analysis of Legislation

"Foster Care Independence Act of 1999: A Coordinated Effort" uses government documents and is limited to examining the initiation phase of public policy making.

Fourth Paper: A Policy Evaluation

"The No Child Left Behind Act of 2001: Accountability, Standardization, and Federal Sanctions" uses a variety of sources, from political science to scientific research reports. It is limited to examining the initiation and expansion phase of public policy making.

Fifth Paper: A Policy Recommendation

"Preserving Endangered Species" uses a variety of literature and some statistical information to propose an evaluation and formulation of environmental reform. This paper analyzes the entire policy life cycle from the initiation to the expansion to the reformulation stages.

Sixth Paper: Writing a Policy Memo

"Reciprocity in Collaboratives" combines the skills of policy analysis with a professional memorandum format used in the public, nonprofit, and private sectors for communicating with decision-makers. In this type of assignment, students are challenged to identify problems, issues, and solutions briefly and succinctly. Students may use this type of memo for communicating with supervisors or superiors in their jobs or internships.

Seventh Paper: Participant Observer/Internship Report

"Internship Report: Campaign Volunteers: VIPs or Peons?" provides an introspective view of the relevance of fieldwork to theoretical constructs learned previously in the classroom. This assignment requires the student to identify where theory and practice conflict or agree. The work is performed outside the classroom setting.

Eighth Paper: Grant Writing

"SHARP Knowledgebase Project" provides an example of a grant application for foundation funding of a simple project that a student working for an organization can propose. It combines the skills required for a policy recommendation with those for writing proposals for a research project. This type of assignment requires students to pay attention to the details of the application and specify how tasks are to be accomplished. It also requires a firm grasp of cost/benefit analysis where the real costs of accomplishing tasks are associated with the real expected benefits.

Ninth Paper: Writing a Project Report

"Knowledgebase Project Collaboration Between the Butte County Superior Court and the Self Help Assistance and Referral Program (SHARP): Interim Report" provides an example of a report that a student may need to write to communicate the results of a civic engagement, service learning, or experiential education project. As an illustration, it also demonstrates the kind of report a student may have to write if that project was funded by a grant. The skills required for students to complete the report include descriptive analysis as well as qualitative and quantitative analytical skills for managing and presenting project results.

Analytical Case Study

Analytical case studies provide students with the opportunity to apply theories learned in class to practical situations. The goal of an analytical case study is to examine behavior related to political decision making and explain why and how that behavior influenced political outcomes. Importantly, the reason for doing case studies is to learn something about how the political *system* works by examining how a *component* of the system works.

- The usefulness of case studies is that the research provides intricate details about the structure of organizations, the strategies used by decision-makers, and the behavior of individuals.
- The problem with analytical case studies is that they are not often generalizable across the political spectrum.

The best analytical case studies focus on aspects of political behavior that are applicable to the broader political spectrum while providing a compelling story about the idiosyncratic aspects of the subject being studied. At the end, the reader should know some interesting contextual information about the subject of the case study and understand more about the effect of particular structures and behavior on political outcomes.

How to Write an Analytical Case Study

1. **Title Page**
2. **Executive Summary**
   - Use bullets to highlight the key problems.
   - Summarize the conclusions.
3. **Narrative of Historical Context**
   - Write the thesis as a statement of the specific objective of the case study (i.e., what is to be explained and how).

- Identify when the organization was formed (cultural and political context).
- Identify why the organization was formed (goals, mission).
- Describe the structure of the organization.
- Describe the external political pressures on the staff from interest groups, Congress, the president, other agencies, or courts.
- Describe the internal political pressures on the staff from standard operation procedures, agency structure, distribution of authority, or agency missions.

4. Problem Identification

- Write this section in short-story form with descriptive and compelling language.
- Identify no more than four problems.
- If more than four problems exist, then classify or cluster the problems together into categories.
- Rank-order the problems from most compelling to least compelling.
- Describe the most compelling problem first and then the rest in rank order.
- Provide an illustrative, compelling, descriptive example for each problem identified.
- Identify the characters involved in the problems.
- Describe how the characters are involved in controversy and/or conflict.

5. Analysis of the Problem

- Suggest how the problems identified influenced political outcomes.
- Suggest how individual behavior influenced the problems and the outcomes.
- Suggest how organizational structure influenced the problems and the outcomes.
- Identify any attempts to solve the problems.
- Suggest why attempts to solve the problems failed.
- Identify any solutions available but untried.
- Suggest why some available solutions have not been, or cannot be, used.

6. Conclusion

- Restate the problems.
- Restate the effect of the problems on political outcomes.
- Identify new knowledge about the organization resulting from the analysis.
- Identify new knowledge about how the political system works resulting from the analysis.

DYSFUNCTIONAL BEHAVIOR IN THE FBI

By
Steve Goard
POL 260A
Professor Diane Schmidt
December 1, 1998
(Reprinted with permission)

EXECUTIVE SUMMARY

The primary mission of the Federal Bureau of Investigation (FBI) is to investigate federal violations, such as bankruptcy fraud, antitrust crimes, and neutrality violations. The FBI, since the J. Edgar Hoover administration, has chosen the path of bureaucratic effectiveness over efficiency and equity. Though Congress granted authority to the FBI to investigate violations, the FBI became a bureau of corruption because of:

- unchecked personal power.
- corrupt standard operating procedures.
- legislative collusion.
- presidential collusion.

Within the context of these problems, the FBI became an effective agency in achieving more authority, creating fear, and ruining individuals. The lack of responsible oversight and accountability that was pervasive during the Hoover administration continues to taint the image of the FBI and the credibility of its agents.

ORIGINS OF THE FBI'S POWER

In July of 1907, the American-born grandnephew of Napoleon I, Charles J. Bonaparte, approached Congress with the idea of creating a permanent detective force within the Department of Justice (DOJ). In July of 1908, upon authority of the United States Congress, the Federal Bureau of Investigation (FBI) was established. In 1910, Congress passed the Mann Act to help curb prostitution. The act inadvertently expanded the authority of the FBI and enabled the FBI to develop dossiers on criminals, elected officials, and wealthy socialists. During the World War I era, Congress gave the FBI the responsibility to investigate espionage, sabotage, and draft violations. At this point, the FBI demonstrated their crude tactics on monitoring and catching such violators. During this period, the FBI extended their perimeter of censorship and continued to violate more civil liberties. For example, German teachers and German music composers were prohibited from teaching and performing (Gentry 1991).

PROBLEMS IN THE FBI

In December of 1924, the young J. Edgar Hoover was appointed as the director of the FBI. Hoover's appointment was to correct the bureau's reputation as a corrupt national law enforcement agency (Turner 1970). Hoover acknowledged the orders from Congress publicly, but some historians contend that Hoover and the FBI never intended to correct, but to continue, the pre-1924 intelligence activity (Croog 1992).

Unchecked Personal Power

Faced with a corrupt FBI, Hoover publicly accepted the challenge and vowed to restore the values of the FBI. December of 1924 marked the beginning of a new era under the control of Director J. Edgar Hoover. Upon Hoover's appointment, the FBI's authority was limited to federal violations only (Charles 1997). But in 1934, FBI agents were given the power to make arrests and to carry firearms (Feinman 1991). This grant of authority prompted Hoover to create more government files on United States citizens.

Further, in 1936 the FBI was given the far-reaching authority to investigate possible Nazis. This authority, however, was quickly abused by the Hoover administration (Felt 1979). Not surprisingly, the FBI's focus centered on radical activists, organizations, and even influential personalities ranging from famous author Ernest Hemingway, civil rights activists Martin Luther King Jr. and Malcolm X, and even went so far as to investigate First Lady Eleanor Roosevelt (Theoharis 1993).

Hoover, an influential and persuasive person himself, conned and convinced Congress into believing his investigations were needed to protect national security. Yet, many believe that the primary motivation for the investigations was more related to controlling and containing dissent than it was to promote the public interest (Theoharis 1993).

Corrupt Standard Operation Procedures

To continue such illegal investigation, Hoover and the FBI created the "secret file" system. The norm for the FBI was that agents would relay all information to the heads of the administration; they in turn would review the information and debrief the White House. The "secret file" system was a carefully calculated technique to keep some illegal investigations from being exposed (Powers 1987). All information known to be sensitive would be labeled "personal and confidential." All information that entered the FBI with that label would end up on Hoover's desk. Hoover would then review all the information and would file it away for safekeeping (Jung and Thom 1997). The "secret file" procedure kept all illegal politically motivated reports out of the FBI's central records system. This technique allowed Hoover to safely sidestep the Attorney General's ban and continue to investigate and monitor political activities (Theoharis 1993).

Perhaps there was an intended coincidence in the name of the "secret files"; it is everything the name implies. The FBI investigated and kept information on influential individuals, radicals, and anyone thought to be a communist. The investigative approach the FBI took involved the gathering of information using sex as a tool. The FBI used the prostitution ring and other sexual decoys to infiltrate specific groups and sometimes individuals (Marx 1992). In New York City, for instance, the FBI financed the making of pornographic films and had policewomen direct the on-camera sex acts.

Hoover's bulging files on individuals contained information on more than just sex and other improper acts (Marx 1992). In another example, the FBI came upon information that, in Chicago, there was a link between the organized crime ring and prostitution. Federal agents took over a credit card processing company and over a four-year period processed $30 million in customer payments for sexual services. These transactions were recorded on credit card receipts as food, beverages, and office supplies, which could be taken as business tax reductions. The FBI-run agency paid, out of the FBI's bank account, for sex clubs. It provided $100,000 to bribe the local police agencies in order to stay open. The investigation did not lead to any arrests, but helped the FBI collect information on high-profile individuals and political leaders who received bribes (Marx 1992).

All of this was in pursuit of information. Hoover was adept at this. The information gathered implied the threat of public ruin, threat of exposure, all which was used as a political tool. But the outlandish investigations did not stop there. Sex was used as an investigative tool, as well as other inappropriate methods, in order to gather new information. The bureau investigated the sexual habits and many other elements of a person's private life. For example, the FBI investigated the Church Committee, instructing the informant to sleep with as many wives as possible (Croog 1992). The tactic here was to break up marriages and gather information.

The FBI's approach was to gather information and control that individual with the threat of public humiliation (Croog 1992). One clear example of the FBI's approach was the case involving a rather noninfluential gossip columnist, Inga Arvad. Arvad became the target of an intensive FBI investigation due to her political views and employment by the *Washington Times-Herald* (Theoharis 1993). Arvad was a target due to the FBI's tainted and overexpanded definition of "communist." The FBI approached Arvad's place of employment and demanded an investigative interview. For fear of the public discovering that the *Washington Times-Herald* employed a communist, the *Washington Times-Herald* complied. When the interview turned up nothing, the FBI stepped up the investigation by adding wiretaps to Arvad's personal telephone. Although the investigation turned up nothing, Hoover used his persuasive tactics to convince the Attorney General to continue the investigation. After years of harassment, the FBI discontinued the investigation. With the information gathered, the FBI discovered that Miss Arvad was a strong isolationist, but held nothing that reflected pro-axis or anti-axis information.

Legislative Collusion

The FBI's jurisdiction and authority is directly granted by legislation. The president, Attorney General, and Congress all decide the authority the FBI is given. Glancing back at the events described earlier, it appears that the FBI expands its authority and jurisdiction by creating and implementing new policy within the FBI.

For example, the FBI, with this new secret policy, avoided being limited by legislation. During the 1950s, the Cold War hit its fevered pitch. Senator Joseph McCarthy and the House of Un-American Activities Committee (HUAC) alerted the nation to the serious threat of a communist takeover in the United States (Moore 1990). Congress granted the FBI the authority (known as the Responsibilities Program) to investigate communist subversives in the government. Hoover, the FBI, along with the president and Congress, used the Responsibilities Program to go after suspected communists, influential people, organizations, political opponents, and even people they plainly disliked (Jung and Thom 1997). With the Responsibilities Program safely intact, the FBI created a very broad definition of communist.

Although this was the first time that legislation gave the FBI the authority to investigate suspected communists, the truth of the matter was the FBI had been conducting these types of investigations since the 1930s (Feinman 1991). The FBI's definition of "communist" included almost any left-wing activity that could be interpreted as subversive. The Responsibilities Program was designed to investigate possible communist subversives employed in the government and public services (Croog 1992). All information was reviewed and the FBI secretly supplied governors and high-level municipal authorities with any information about the individual being investigated. The immediate problem with the program was confidential leaks. The Responsibilities Program quickly devolved into a systematic tool of harassment providing irrelevant information on perceived subversives, which lead to many terminations of employment, particularly those in education.

To maximize total control of the new program, Hoover and the FBI insisted that FBI headquarters alone be the ones to determine the information to be divulged.

This response was due to the questionable legality of the FBI's investigative techniques. The FBI established a plan in which FBI agents would see to it that those terminated from employment were not rehired somewhere else.

The fall of the Responsibilities Program came in the late 1950s. Some historians contend that the techniques employed by the FBI caused the destruction of the program. The confidential leaks to the media exposed some awful truths about the FBI's illegal investigations. There were 794 individuals investigated; 429 were employed in education. Hoover claimed the FBI was effective in finding and removing communists that were in the position to poison the minds of the youth of this country. Of the 429 suspected communists employed in education, 429 were terminated from educational employment (Jung and Thom 1997). The FBI made it clear that they were outraged that those individuals who leaked this information could be retained in government employment.

There was a point in the FBI's history where Hoover ignored legislation and implemented his own program of continuing his secret policies. During the Ford administration, Hoover created an execution squad. The squad's job was to cause the permanent disappearance of individuals the FBI believed would never be brought to justice, if proper policy and procedure were followed. The squad members consisted mostly of organized crime families, but also included military personnel and local police (Marx 1992). Hoover believed the squad would be more effective if the FBI and its agents were not directly involved.

The squad was considered a special force of assassins to take out any individuals the FBI named. Although there has been no official recognition of the squad, some historians contend some of the squad's victims included KGB agents, former Japanese officers, and Nazi war criminals. Some historians claim the squad offers some insight into the relationship that the FBI had with famous organized crime families (Turner 1970). The squad gives even further insight into why the FBI was so reluctant in going after organized crime families.

Presidential Collusion

The FBI was more than just an asset to the nation's people; the FBI was a political tool for several politicians. The FBI was the mortal enemy of anyone being investigated. The FBI demonstrated its bureaucratic survival skills and capacity to manipulate the press, Congress, and the President of the United States without revealing its hand. The majority of the authority and jurisdiction the FBI was awarded can be directly attributed to the relationship the FBI had with the presidential administration. Presidents Roosevelt, Nixon, Carter, Ford, and Johnson all had a personal stake in the FBI.

With Roosevelt's election in 1932, the FBI no longer had to be so circumspect. In 1934, Roosevelt secretly ordered the FBI to investigate and monitor the activities of American Nazis and Nazi sympathizers. Between 1934 and 1936, the president requested investigative reports on all right-wingers. By 1939, Roosevelt ordered the FBI to conduct widespread surveillance on political opposition and critics of presidential policy (Jung and Thom 1997). During the Roosevelt administration, the FBI's illegal investigations primarily focused on foreign policy critics. The FBI had a favored relationship with the Roosevelt administration. Roosevelt supported the New Deal crime-control program, which gave the FBI more authority to go after "bad guys" without regard to personal and civil rights. The FBI investigated the lives and activities of political organizations, political opponents of the president, and critics of administrative policy. The FBI consistently sought potentially damaging information on individuals' personal lives (Feinman 1991). Carefully cultivated informants would relay sensitive information back to FBI headquarters (due to the FBI's secret file system, the information landed directly on Hoover's desk). Hoover would then leak this damaging information on to friendly journalists, presidents, and other politicians for the multiple purposes of destroying and discrediting those individuals.

The FBI's hit list included several members of the American Civil Liberties Union (ACLU), Charles Lindbergh, and several political opponents. Although several presidents used the FBI in their favor to achieve personal success, Hoover and the FBI were a feared bureaucracy (Watters and Gillers 1973). The FBI flexed its bureaucratic muscle by turning the game against those who played it. President Nixon publicly praised the FBI and Hoover for making the FBI the defender of Americans' precious right to be free from fear. But fear is what the FBI brought to President Nixon. Recorded on the White House tapes, Nixon expressed his concern about the FBI files and how the FBI had secret files on everyone, including him. Nixon feared the information the FBI collected on him. Nixon feared that the FBI could bring down the Nixon administration if Nixon ever restricted the FBI's authority.

Fear and the FBI's blackmail controlled several politicians and the way policy was enacted. While several people were successfully blackmailed, those who refused to submit were often ruined by mysterious, and sometimes false, FBI press leaks. Some historians would contend death resulted for a few who refused to comply with the FBI. With Hoover as the head of the country's chief law enforcement agency, the president could investigate, monitor, and potentially destroy political opponents. Since 1936, the FBI catered to each of the succeeding administrations, proving the FBI's political worth (Charles 1997).

EVALUATION OF PROBLEMS IN THE FBI

The secret investigations gave the FBI some persuasive power when it came to American politics. The secret files and the secret files system helped the FBI to become a powerful and experienced agency, an agency led by those committed to effectiveness. The unstoppable behavior of the FBI was directly influenced by the FBI's authority and secret power to control high-profile figures, including presidents of the United States. Despite so many obvious violations of civil liberties through illegal investigations, the FBI continued to operate under a crime-control fashion.

The secret file system, in particular, proved to be an asset for the FBI and the way Hoover ran the agency. The illegal investigations included wiretaps, prostitution, physical assaults, and blatant violations of constitutional rights. These investigations even sought out the individuals who controlled the FBI (i.e., the president, Attorney General, and Congress). The FBI collected such a massive amount of damaging information on high-profile figures that the threat of exposure kept the FBI's authority from being limited. The FBI became an effective agency in achieving more authority, creating fear, and ruining individuals. The FBI created several programs on its own authority and kept these programs centralized. These tactics employed by the FBI kept presidents and Attorneys General ignorant, allowing the FBI to elude investigations into its own activity.

While the FBI initiated several of these programs on its own authority, it would be wrong to conclude that the FBI was the only factor in their creation. Hoover and the FBI took advantage of the times. The Cold War, the threat of communism, and the civil rights demonstrations created an awkward tension between political freedoms and the right to rid the United States of the communist agents. At those times, Hoover led the FBI on his own personal beliefs, convincing the appropriate people and manipulating them into believing there was a need for programs (Gentry 1991).

With Hoover as the director, the FBI became the bully agency that mastered the science of manipulation and used it in its favor. While following secret orders of the president to investigate his opposition and critics, the FBI secretly investigated those giving the orders. The FBI's investigations generally uncovered damaging information, which caused fear among those expected to control the FBI. With the threat of exposure, very few would monitor the activities of the FBI. The FBI acted like a pack of hyenas, seeking out and destroying whatever they desired. Some historians have reached various conclusions that the creation of programs like the Responsibilities Program and the execution quad was a direct result of the inadequate supervision of the FBI (Jung and Thom 1997).

The threat of communism, the civil rights demonstrations, and the subversive press were situations where the FBI manipulated the minds of members of Congress, the president, and the public. Situations described in the examples earlier demonstrate how the FBI took the opportunity to abuse and expand the FBI's power. Consequently, the FBI gained more power and authority, while the monitoring of the FBI decreased substantially. This is just what Hoover and the FBI wanted—no restriction and no limits.

CONCLUSION

Upon the authority of Congress, the United States in 1908 received its first permanent detective force, the Federal Bureau of Investigations. Charles Bonaparte succeeded with his idea and the FBI was granted the authority to investigate federal law violations. It was soon after the FBI's creation when the FBI began using illegal investigative tactics to gather information. Every time America was faced with a threatening situation, the FBI would receive greater jurisdiction and authority. The World War I era gave the FBI greater jurisdiction to investigate sabotage, espionage, and draft violators. With insurmountable power and authority the FBI continued to ignore the intended purpose of the FBI. The wave of corruption quickly spread throughout and consumed the FBI. The FBI continued to use illegal tactics that violated due process, civil liberties, and most of all, frayed the fabric of the FBI.

Faced with a corrupt law enforcement agency, the administration was pressured to make a change. With the appointment of J. Edgar Hoover, the problems became worse. Hoover publicly acknowledged the FBI's problems and vowed to restore the FBI's dignity. Privately, Hoover's plans were to ignore efficiency and equity while rebuilding the FBI's reputation. Hoover wanted an effective agency and believed the only way to achieve complete effectiveness was to attack with full force.

Using these tactics, the FBI quickly confirmed its political worth. Deception and manipulation achieved effectiveness. The FBI created the secret file system and began the onslaught of investigations. The FBI investigated a broad spectrum of individuals, including the president's wife. The secret file system allowed the FBI to continue the hundreds of illegal investigations. The system's policy required all reports that included sensitive information to be labeled "personal and confidential." Those reports fell directly on the director's desk, avoiding the FBI's central records system.

This paper clearly demonstrates, through examples, how the FBI chose bureaucratic effectiveness over efficiency and equity. The FBI currently continues to repair the reputation of a corrupt agency. Although death ended the career of the infamous Hoover, scandals like those of Ruby Ridge and The Branch Davidians in Waco continue to raise the ghost of Hoover's FBI. Some historians will contend there was a sigh of relief when Hoover's era ended. Yet, under the specter of great Hoover's legacy, the FBI continues to receive more jurisdiction and authority, while still conducting investigations that remain "personal and confidential."

REFERENCES

Charles, Douglas M. 1997. FBI political surveillance and the Charles Lindbergh investigation. *The Historian* 59 (4): 831.

Croog, Charles. 1992. FBI political surveillance and the isolationist-interventionist debate, 1939–1941. *The Historian* 54 (3): 441–458.

Feinman, Ronald L. 1991. The rise and fall of domestic intelligence. *Presidential Studies Quarterly* 21 (1): 174.

Felt, Mark W. 1979. *The FBI pyramid: From the inside*. New York: G.P. Putman's Sons.

Gentry, Curt. 1991. *J. Edgar Hoover: The man and the secrets*. New York: Diane Publishing Co.

Jung, Patrick, and Cathleen Thom. 1997. The Responsibilities program of the FBI, 1951–1955. *The Historian* 59 (2): 347–361.

Marx, Gary T. 1992. Under-the-cover undercover investigations: Some reflections on the United States use of sex and deception in law enforcement. *Criminal Justice Ethics* 11 (1): 13.

Moore, Richter H. Jr. 1990. United States: Politics and public policy. *Perspectives on Political Science* 23 (2): 109.

Powers, Richard G. 1987. *Secrecy and power: The life of J. Edgar Hoover*. New York: MacMillan Inc.

Theoharis, Athan. 1993. The FBI, the Roosevelt administration and the 'subversive' press. *Journalism History* 19 (1): 3.

Turner, William W. 1970. *Hoover's FBI: The men and the myth*. Los Angeles, CA: Kingsport Press, Inc.

Watters, Patty, and Stephen Gillers. 1973. *Investigating the FBI: A tough fair look at the powerful bureau, its present and its future*. New York: Library of Congress.

Problem-Solving Case Studies

Unlike analytical case studies, problem-solving case studies provide students with the opportunity to go beyond problem identification to recommending a course of action. Importantly, the main reasons for doing problem-solving case studies are to identify a problem, to provide reasons for how the problem occurred, and to provide suggestions for resolving the problem most efficiently. Problem-solving case studies are no less than one page and no more than five pages.

- For narrowly defined problems, the case study report is a highly condensed, concise description of the problem, the causes, and recommended solutions, of approximately two pages.

- For broadly defined or complex problems, the case study report is condensed into an executive summary, with supporting material attached, of approximately five pages.

The best problem-solving case studies focus on aspects of decision making that are internal and specific to the target of the study. External factors are only important if they are responsible for influencing the target's decisions. At the end, the reader should know what the problem is, what possibly caused the problem, and what can be done to resolve the problem.

How to Write a Problem-Solving Case Study

1. **Identify the target of the case study.**
2. **Identify the objective of the case study.**
   - Summarize the problem in one or two sentences.
   - Write concisely, clearly, and assertively.
3. **Provide a brief review of:**
   - General conditions.
   - Specific conditions.
4. **Identify the major problems and their causes.**
   - Rank-order the problems.
   - Investigate and report possible causes or causal relationships.
5. **Identify possible solutions for each problem identified.**
   - Rank-order the solutions for each problem.
   - Identify the benefits, costs, and unintended consequences of applying a solution.
6. **Make a recommendation.**
   - Choose a solution for each problem identified.
   - Suggest how the solution can be implemented.
7. **Attach any data, supporting evidence, and references for additional information.**

(Reprinted with permission)

MEMORANDUM

To: City Department Manager
From: Annette Allison
Date: October 5, 1999
Re: Building Inspection Department Expense Analysis

Objective:

This report analyzes the city's Building Inspection Department Budget to identify which expenditure items are responsible for budget increases. These increases have resulted in the department being over budget for two years. The report provides a recommendation for either budget allocation increases and/or reduction of spending in discretionary budget categories. Decisions to decrease spending should be based on further investigation of the relative spending efficiency in categories showing significant increases.

1. **How well did the department spend what was actually budgeted?**
   - FY I was under budget by 9%.
   - In FY II & III the budget was within 1% of its targets.
   - FY IV & V were both well over the budget targets (31% & 7%, respectively).

2. **Major spending categories over five-year period:**
   - <u>Salaries</u> (158,712 in FY V) are the *largest* spending category during all five years.
   - <u>Capital improvements</u> (9,795 in FY V) are the *second largest* spending category during all five years and show significant increases in the last two years.
   - Travel expenses category shows significant increases in the past two years.
   - Smaller spending categories are office supplies, training, and dues and subscriptions.

3. **Major variances (dollar and percent changes) from year to year:**
   - The total spent budget increased by 31% from FY III to FY IV.
   - The total spent budget increased 23% from FY IV to FY V.
   - <u>Capital improvements</u>, <u>printing</u>, and <u>travel expenses</u> were major spending categories during FY V.

4. **Line-item changes and changes in budget shares over time:**
   - <u>Salaries</u> account for the *largest share* of the spent budget. During the past five years, salaries have accounted for between 81%–86% of the total spent budget.
   - <u>Travel expenses</u> accounted for the *second largest share* of the total spent budget in both FY IV & V, accounting for 9% in those years.

- <u>Capital improvements</u> was the ***third largest share*** of the spent budget.
- <u>Car allowance</u> and <u>office supplies</u> are also ***large shares*** of the spent budget.

5. What changes are revealed when inflation is taken into account?

- When inflation is taken into account, the spent budget still reveals that there has been a steady increase in the total spent budget over the past five years, with a sizable increase within the past two years.
- Although salaries have been steadily increasing over the past five years, employees are making much less over the past four years when inflation is taken into account.

6. What else might account for the specific changes?

- The larger salary, training, and travel expenditures over the past five years might indicate the hiring of more staff.
- The large amounts spent on capital improvements might indicate that the building inspection department is growing and requires new or additional facilities.

7. Impact of spending trends on next year's budget:

- Since the building inspection department has been over budget the past two years, it may reflect a need for more budget allocations for the following budget year.
- Capital improvements and travel expenses should be looked at closely when allocating the following year's budget, however, because these services may not be needed.

8. Ratio analysis:

- Based on the per capita ratio in FY V, each resident spends approximately $4.27 to support the building inspection department.

Recommendation:

The results of this analysis suggest that while ***salaries are the largest spending item, they are not responsible*** for the department being over budget in the last two years. Increases in expenses related to ***capital improvements, travel, and office supplies significantly contributed to the increases*** in the spent budget. This report recommends scrutiny of these expenditures particularly as they relate to the purposes and necessity for continued increased spending in each of these categories. Based on the results of an evaluation of these expenditures, the city should either increase the budget allocation and/or reduce spending on capital improvements, travel, and office supplies to reduce the likelihood of the department being over budget in the future.

Attachments: Expense Analysis

Building Inspection Department
Building Inspection Expense Analysis (Excerpt)

Expense	Yr 1 Spent	Yr 1 Constant	Yr 2 Spent	Yr 1–2 $ Diff	Yr 1–2 % Change	Yr 2 Constant
Salaries	$90,340	$90,340	$99,830	$4,375	5%	$94,715
Truck & car repairs	$4,286	$4,286	$1,732	$(2,643)	−62%	$1,643
Travel expenses	$546	$546	$612	$35	6%	$581
Supplies	$1,092	$1,092	$1,242	$86	8%	$1,178
Office supplies	$3,400	$3,400	$5,500	$1,818	53%	$5,218
Street lighting	$208	$208	0	$(208)	−100%	$—
Telephone	$146	$146	$330	$167	114%	$313
Gas & oil	0	$—	0	$—		$—
Equipment repairs	0	$—	0	$—		$—
Tools & supplies	0	$—	0	$—		$—
Christmas lights	$944	$944	$6,662	$5,377	570%	$6,321
Real property lights	$1,170	$1,170	$840	$(373)	−32%	$797
Education & training	$224	$224	$1,190	$905	404%	$1,129
Dues & subscriptions	0	$—	0	$—		$—
Utilities	$1,736	$1,736	$1,400	$(408)	−23%	$1,328
Printing	$236	$236	$134	$(109)	−46%	$127
Capital improvements	$270	$270	0	$(270)	−100%	$—
Communications	0	$—	0	$—		$—
Total	$104,598	$104,598	$119,472	$8,753	8%	$113,351

Analysis of Legislation

Purpose of an Analysis of Legislation

Analyzing a congressional bill helps the student understand more about the legislative process. Unlike other policies, which can be custom, rulings by courts, regulations written by bureaucrats, or executive orders, legislation is made in Congress. To examine the legislative process, students need to identify the context within which the legislation was introduced, the goals of the legislation, the supporters, the opponents, and the problems in passing the bill. (For more information, see Robert U. Goehlert and Fenton S. Martin, *Congress and law-making: Researching the legislative process.* 2nd ed. Santa Barbara, CA: ABC-CLIO, 1989. See the section on tracing legislation, pages 53–59.)

Writing an Analysis of a Legislative Bill

1. **Choose a statutory law.**
   - Find the public law number.
   - Choose one that is at least a year old.
2. **Identify where the idea for the bill originated—Congress, bureaucracy, interest groups, or the executive office.**
   - Sometimes an idea or draft has more than one source.
   - Find out who introduced the bill.
   - Examine the hearings.
3. **Identify the objectives, targets, or goals of the bill.**
   - What was the legislation supposed to do exactly?
   - Who was supposed to benefit?
   - Does the bill expand or correct other policy action by government?
4. **Identify the means or policy instruments used to achieve the goals or objectives.**
   - How was the legislation supposed to achieve its goals?
   - Policy tools—transfers? regulation? subsidy? spending?
5. **Identify who supported and who opposed the bill.**
   - Was it a partisan bill?
   - Did support come from an ideological coalition?
6. **Examine the bill's success in passing.**
   - What constraints prevented it passing easily?
   - What kind of problems did it encounter?
7. **Write with the following structure.**
   - Include an introduction, a description of the origins of the bill, the objectives, and the tools used to achieve the objectives.
   - Compare and contrast the various political arguments and forces supporting and opposing the bill.
   - Relate these political problems to any problems in passing the bill. Separate the political problems from institutional or structural problems that may exist and then provide a conclusion.

Analysis of Legislation Guide and Check-off Sheet

A. Origins of the Legislation

  1. Identify the exact title of the bill that produced the law; find the public law number.

  2. Identify where the idea for the bill originated. Sometimes an idea or draft has more than one source.

- *Source:* Congress, bureaucracy, interest groups, and/or the executive office.
- *Who Introduced:* Find out who introduced the bill (and cosponsors); examine the hearings.
- *Problems Identified:* List the problem(s) or issue(s) that government is being asked to solve. Be specific.

B. Objectives and Tools

  1. Identify the objectives, targets, and/or goals of the bill.

- *Goals:* What was the legislation supposed to do exactly? Relate each objective to a problem/issue identified in the bill's origins.
- *Objectives:* Which problems/issues are targeted by the bill? Are all the problems/issues identified above addressed by the legislation? Are there other problems/issues addressed in the legislation that were not identified by those who brought it to the agenda? Are there problems/issues identified by those who brought it to the agenda that were not addressed/ignored in the legislation?
- *Targets:* Who was supposed to benefit? Who was supposed to pay the cost (experience adverse action)?
- *New, Expanded, or Reformulated:* Is it a new activity for government or does the bill expand or correct other policy action by government?

  2. Identify the means or policy instruments used to achieve the goals or objectives.

- *Relate Each Tool to Each Objective:* How was the legislation supposed to achieve its goals?
- Policy tools—transfers? regulation? subsidy? spending? taxing?
- How was each tool supposed to solve the problem/issue identified in each objective?

C. Passing the Bill (Formulation)

  1. *Drafting/Presentation:* Identify who supported and who opposed the bill.

- Was it a partisan bill?
- Did support come from an ideological coalition?

  2. *Mark-Up:* Examine the bill's success in passing in the committee.

- What constraints (such as timing, budget problems, competing legislation, etc.) prevented its passing easily?
- What kind of problems did it encounter in the process of passing and how did it change as a result?
- Which objectives had the most support and from whom and why?
- Which objectives had the most opposition and from whom and why?

- Which tools had the most support and from whom and why?
- Which tools had the most opposition and from whom and why?

3. ***Floor Vote:*** Examine the bill's success in passing on the floor.
   - What constraints (such as timing, budget problems, competing legislation, etc.) prevented its passing easily?
   - What kind of problems did it encounter in the process of passing and how did it change as a result?
   - Which objectives had the most support and from whom and why?
   - Which objectives had the most opposition and from whom and why?
   - Which tools had the most support and from whom and why?
   - Which tools had the most opposition and from whom and why?

4. ***Conference Committee and Final Floor Vote:*** Examine the bill's success in conference committee and the final floor vote.
   - What constraints (such as timing, budget problems, competing legislation, etc.) prevented its passing easily?
   - What kind of problems did it encounter in the process of passing and how did it change as a result?
   - Which objectives had the most support and from whom and why?
   - Which objectives had the most opposition and from whom and why?
   - Which tools had the most support and from whom and why?
   - Which tools had the most opposition and from whom and why?

5. ***Presidential Support:***
   - Did the president sign it? veto it?
   - If vetoed, what kind of problems did it encounter on the floor before passing?

FOSTER CARE INDEPENDENCE ACT OF 1999: A COORDINATED EFFORT

By
Alyssum Root
POLS 600
American Institutions and Public Organizations
Professor Schmidt
November 1, 2005
(Reprinted by permission)

ABSTRACT

The Foster Care Independence Act of 1999 (FCIA) was signed into law on December 14, 1999. The passage of this law was likely due to its symbolic features and the efforts of key political players to reach compromises. The diverse target populations of the FCIA, emancipated foster youth and Filipino veterans, were characterized as symbols of vulnerable citizens who both needed and deserved help. Although First Lady Hillary Clinton was among the earliest political figures involved as political advocates for emancipating foster youth, highly visible members of Congress from both parties were critical sponsors, negotiators, and defenders of the bill. The bill involved not only creating opportunities for serving the needs of foster youth, it also created a cost savings by expanding rights for Filipino veterans. The bill also provided for a redistribution of funding to support benefits for foster youth. Although the bill received popular support in the House, it was stalled in the Senate. Senator Chafee's death midway through the process inspired the renaming of Title I of the FCIA in his honor and added another popular symbol to the bill. The legislation, with Chafee's name in place, was reintroduced as H.R.3443 and passed without opposition. President Clinton was the final political figure to support the FCIA, as the legislation reflected what his own policy agenda symbolized.

INTRODUCTION

Key components of the successful passage of *H.R.3443: The Foster Care Independence Act of 1999* (FCIA) included its symbolic merit and influential political players. More specifically, the goals of the FCIA symbolized popular ideals and helped the FCIA to pass with bipartisan support. The diverse issues addressed in the FCIA included negative outcomes for foster youth after leaving the child welfare system and the loss of dignity experienced by Filipino veterans of World War II. These issues affected young people who were characterized as vulnerable and elderly veterans who were characterized as vulnerable, lonely, forgotten heroes.

While the goals of the legislation were important to its passage, the coalition of political players was also important to the passage of the FCIA. One of these players was First Lady Hillary Clinton, who helped the social problems associated with foster care become political issues. Representatives Nancy Johnson (R-CT) and Benjamin Cardin (D-MD) were also important, as they collaborated to author, introduce, amend, and defend the FCIA. Once the bill had been introduced, opposition arose about a provision to repeal a law giving states federal funding to supplement child support payments. Representatives Johnson and Cardin worked in the mark-up session of the bill and during the debate, however, to effectively neutralize the controversy. Senator John Chafee (R-RI) was also influential as the sponsor of the Senate companion bill, S1327. Title I of the FCIA was named in Chafee's honor after his death partway through the process, and the bill was reintroduced as H.R.3443. Finally, President Clinton was influential as a strong supporter via his policy agenda. Helping to improve the lives of elderly veterans and abused children, who symbolized vulnerable and deserving citizens, supported the president's agenda in his budget proposal.

ORIGINS OF THE LEGISLATION

The FCIA addressed issues that had been present for several years but given minimal attention by policy makers. Challenges foster youth faced during emancipation were first addressed through federal law in 1986. Few reputable studies were available to examine the life of young adults after emancipation from the foster care system. It became clear, however, that foster youth commonly experience significant negative outcomes, including homelessness, incarceration, and unemployment, as well as special challenges. Policy makers remained uninvolved until First Lady Hillary Clinton became aware of the problems, and the FCIA was introduced. Likewise, Filipino veterans had been concerned about unfair benefits since 1946, but their issues were just becoming salient in 1996. The issues of both these populations were relatively unaddressed until the introduction of the FCIA.

Foster Youth Face Challenges

Prior to the introduction of the FCIA, few clearly understood the severity of problems associated with emancipated foster youth. Foster youth face challenges that make it difficult for them to successfully transition into adulthood. Some of these barriers were: insufficient life skills, lack of healthy connections, mental health problems, and lack of knowledge about available resources. These factors often caused foster youth to struggle during the process of emancipation (Massinga and Pecora 2004, 15; Shirk and Stangler 2004, 10 and 12; *USA Today* 2005; Cook and Sedlak 1995).

Though studies were limited, they consistently showed significant trends among foster youth involving negative outcomes. To clearly identify the depth and breadth of these outcomes, Representative Johnson commissioned a report from the General Accounting Office (GAO) prior to hearings about the FCIA. The GAO reviewed available studies and concluded that negative outcomes for former foster youth remained serious. The GAO identified several common outcomes, including homelessness, poverty, unemployment, incarceration, and others (U.S. General Accounting Office 1999a, 1999b). The GAO report concluded that significant negative outcomes for former foster youth were consistent findings among studies. These studies gave conclusive evidence that foster youth face special challenges after leaving the foster care system.

In addition to the GAO findings, the Westat study was one of the most comprehensive research projects addressing alumni of foster care and also found that negative outcomes were a significant trend for alumni of foster care. This study was completed in 1991, followed eight hundred and ten youth two-and-a-half to four years after leaving foster care, and covered eight different states (Loman and Siegel 2000). Further, the Westat study provided evidence that foster youth are likely to experience homelessness, poverty, unemployment, and incarceration, among others. This research concluded that forty-six percent of former foster youth did not complete high school, fifty-one percent were unemployed, and twenty-five percent had experienced homelessness (U.S. General Accounting Office 1999a). The Westat study provided significant evidence that negative outcomes were problematic for emancipated foster youth. The Westat study determined that poor education, homelessness, and unemployment, among others, were common experiences for emancipated foster youth.

Developing Political Salience

The FCIA began as an amendment to Title IV-E of the Social Security Act in 1986, was addressed briefly in 1993 out of necessity, and then did not receive political attention until four years later. Title IV-E of the SSA was first amended for the purpose of assisting older foster youth in 1986 and has continued to evolve for this reason. The amendment, The Independent Living Initiative, was the first attempt at policy designed to decrease negative outcomes experienced by former foster youth. This bill was permanently authorized in the 1993 Omnibus Budget Reconciliation Act, and funding was increased to seventy million dollars per year. This occurred because the original legislation required reauthorization at the end of 1992 (*CQ Weekly* 1993). Research continued to show significant levels of negative outcomes, including homelessness, poverty, and incarceration for alumni of foster care (Child Welfare League of America 1999a, 1999b).

The FCIA was introduced in 1999 to further address this problem. Like its predecessors, the FCIA amended Title IV-E of the SSA. Support for the FCIA began to build political saliency in 1997 when First Lady Hillary Clinton became involved (Clinton 2005). First Lady Clinton had been a strong supporter of the Adoption and Safe Families Act of 1997 (ASFA). She met with a group of seven foster youth prior to a speech about ASFA (McBroom 1999). Though First Lady Clinton planned to talk with the youth about ASFA, the discussion repeatedly turned to the stories of youth and the challenges of emancipation (Perez n.d.). It became evident that ASFA left a gap in meeting the needs of foster youth who were not adopted prior to aging out (*U.S. Newswire* 1999). As First Lady Clinton became more involved, she asked foster youth to tell their stories at well-publicized hearings (Mendel 2005).

Momentum for the bill increased because First Lady Clinton remained involved in foster youth legislation. In November of 1998, she wrote a column addressing the challenges foster youth face as they age out of foster care, and in January of 1999, she hosted an event dedicated to calling attention to these issues. First Lady Clinton invited youth to speak at the event, as well as large nonprofit organizations, and the Secretary of Health and Human Services (Petrie 1999). During this event, the First Lady announced that President Clinton's budget proposal allocated money to assist emancipating foster youth (Clinton Foundation 1999; U.S. Executive Office of the President 1999b). The following month First Lady Clinton wrote an article devoted to building support for this budget proposal. In this article, through the stories of foster youth, The First Lady reemphasized the need for the proposed funding (Clinton 1999).

Filipino Veterans of World War II

The FCIA also served to recognize unrelated problems that were becoming issues after decades of their existence as problems. The FCIA included a response to political awareness of Filipino veteran's issues after many years of activism. Though largely symbolic, provisions in the FCIA were meant to acknowledge a larger problem of inequity for Filipino veterans of World War II after years of political inactivity. The problems of Filipino veterans took nearly fifty years to begin receiving political attention. These veterans first experienced inequity in 1946 due to the Rescission Act. In 1996, they finally began to be recognized, due in large part to publicized protests. Legislation to address issues of inequity for Filipino veterans also took several years, though it began to gain political support in 1996 and continued largely as a symbolic gesture.

Filipino veterans of World War II received fewer benefits than other American veterans due to the Rescission Act of 1946. In 1942, these veterans were given American citizenship and promised the same benefits as other United States veterans, because they had been drafted to fight for the United States. The Rescission Act changed their status, however, and many Filipino veterans lost their right to benefits (Cabotaje 1998; Dijamco 1996). In response, advocacy groups arranged for public protests, and Filipino veterans' issues began to receive unusual public and political attention. In 1996, several members of The National Coalition for Filipino Veterans and Representative Bob Filner chained themselves to the White House garden fence (Satoshi 2004). In San Francisco, Filipino veterans protested by camping in a place they called Equity Park. In the same city, an art show featuring photographs of Filipino veterans titled "Unfinished Mission: The American Journey of Filipino WW II Veterans" was well publicized (Green 1998).

Though legislation about Filipino veteran's equity issues was initially unsuccessful, it was gaining popularity. During the 105th Congress, the Filipino Veterans Equity Act had 209 cosponsors, but was stalled in the Senate Committee on Veterans Affairs. In 1998, the Chairman of the House Veteran's Affairs scheduled a hearing to address the bill, even though he personally did not support the legislation (Cabotaje 1998; Filipinas 1998; U.S. Congress 1998). The bill was reintroduced in 1999, but again failed to pass, this time due to budgetary constraints. When it became clear that legislation directly addressing equity issues and that also cost money would not pass, Representative Gilman introduced H.R. 26, the Veteran's SSI Extension Act. H.R. 26 became the basis for Title II of the FCIA, Benefits for Certain World War II Veterans. This legislation allowed veterans to leave the U.S. and still receive a percentage of their SSI benefits. While the bill was considered a compromise by some Filipino veterans' advocates, the need to pass legislation of some kind was becoming more urgent. The population of Filipino World War II veterans had declined from two hundred thousand veterans to seventy thousand (Dijamco 1996; Lachica 1999; Satoshi 2004, 19; U.S. Congress 1998; U.S. Congress 1999h).

OBJECTIVES AND TOOLS

The FCIA encompassed goals that were largely symbolic. Issues faced by both older foster youth and Filipino veterans were acknowledged in similar ways through the FCIA. The objectives of the FCIA were primarily symbolic ideals to which funding was allocated. The reduction of negative outcomes for foster youth coupled with increased funding and without quantified expectations typified the FCIA. Similarly, the goal to afford Filipino veterans the dignity of a reasonable standard of living among family in their native land is qualitative in nature. Titles II and III are tools themselves, as the decrease in spending and increase in revenue generated by these titles was used to justify spending on Title I. The FCIA's tools appeared to center around funding these symbolic objectives.

Goals

The goals of the FCIA were both functional and symbolic. Goals regarding foster youth were to address the negative outcomes experienced by foster youth after emancipation. This legislation was also designed to restore dignity and acknowledge Filipino veterans' issues through the legislative process. Most importantly, the FCIA was written in part to address negative outcomes older foster youth face as they transition into adulthood.

This legislation lists negative outcomes to be addressed through this bill, including poor education, unemployment, dependency on public assistance, homelessness, non-marital childbirth, incarceration, and high-risk behaviors. Furthermore, the FCIA requires that states certify they will encourage youth participation, coordinate agencies, and train foster parents (U.S. Congress 1999d; P.L. 106–169 1999).

This bill was also designed to recognize the service provided by Filipino veterans and the issues regarding veterans' benefits. When it became clear that the Filipino Veterans SSI Extension Bill would not be passed in 1999, it was included in an early version of the FCIA, H.R.1802, as Title II, Benefits for Certain World War II Veterans (U.S. Congress 1999h). Advocates saw this as a way to pass legislation regarding Filipino veterans' issues (Lachica 1999). Benefits for Certain World War II Veterans did not address issues of equity for Filipino veterans. The FCIA allowed Filipino veterans of World War II to return home to their families without a complete loss of benefits. This provision, therefore, only affected those veterans who already had benefits (Chao 1999; P.L. 106–169 1999).

Objectives

The FCIA's objectives were not based on benchmarks. Specifically, the objectives of the FCIA were qualitative in nature, and there were no quantifiable expectations set by the policy. Independent Living Programs (ILPs) were required to improve, while addressing negative outcomes and staying within budgetary constraints. Title II met the goal of restoring dignity and recognizing Filipino veterans' issues by allowing eligible veterans to return home if they wished. To address the issue of negative youth outcomes, a major objective of the FCIA was to improve ILPs. The legislation requires that ILPs be held accountable for improvement, or lack thereof. Furthermore, the bill stated expectations that ILPs address the negative outcomes listed in the FCIA (Collins 2004; P.L. 106–169 1999). There were no specified expectations in levels of improvement; however, there was just the requirement that some improvement be evident through data about ILP participants. Furthermore, spending is not expected to reflect services (Nixon 2005).

Like foster youth issues, Title III offers opportunity for veterans but does not set quantitative expectations. Veterans are afforded dignity and acknowledgement of their concerns through this policy. Though the Congressional Budget Office estimated that seven thousand eligible veterans would choose to return home, it was used in regards to financial estimates (Ganio 1999).

Targets

The FCIA primarily addressed the issues of two different populations who were characterized as needy and deserving of help. Older foster youth and young adults who had emancipated from foster care were the recipients of services provided by ILPs. These youth were described as vulnerable and young. Conversely, Filipino American veterans of World War II were depicted as elderly, lonely, and as the forgotten heroes of America.

Foster youth. ILPs are designed to assist foster youth throughout the process of their transition into adulthood. Services begin before the youth emancipates (also commonly referred to as "aging out"). Foster youth typically emancipate on their eighteenth birthday or high school graduation. As young adults become legally responsible for their own care upon emancipation (County of Sacramento 2001), they have access to ILP services, which often include case management, transitional housing, life skills training, connections with other community resources, and counseling. These services address the significant challenges foster youth face before, during, and after they age out (State of California 2004). Improving these services is one focus of the FCIA.

Supporters of the FCIA relied on the emotions that emerged when faced with the plight of foster youth, who are often characterized as vulnerable, victimized, and as having special needs. One of the bill's major advocates was Terry Harrak, who told her life story, highlighting personal experiences of abandonment, homelessness, and illness (English and Grasso 2000; *Focal Point* 2001). Youth and representatives for nonprofit agencies testified at hearings such as the Johnson-Cardin Independent Living Bill hearing for the Subcommittee on Human Resources. During their testimony, they told stories about themselves, their siblings, and other foster youth (Block 1999; Bowie 1999; Kroner 1999; Massinga 1999a, 1999b; McCaffrey 1999; Matheny 1999). Also, often associated with youth aging out of care is poor mental health caused by experiences of mental stress before, during, and after entering the child welfare system (Foster 2001, 13–14; Nelson 2001).

Filipino World War II Veterans.   Like foster youth, supporters encouraged specific characterizations of the second group targeted by the FCIA. Descriptions of Filipino World War II veterans usually portrayed them as elderly, heroic, and lonely. During hearings and in publications, emphasis was placed on Filipino veterans' heroism in the war and their experiences during the Battle of Bataan and the subsequent death march. Patrick Ganio, president of the American Coalition for Filipino Veterans, shared a story about a Filipino nurse's assistant who served during World War II, later became a citizen of the United States, developed heart problems and leukemia, and had to stay so that she could receive medical care paid for with her SSI. These veterans were described as lonely and desperate to reunite with their families before they died (Dijamco 1996; *Filipino Reporter* 1999; Ganio 1999).

The FCIA officially recognized the issues concerning emancipated foster youth and Filipino veterans of World War II, who were portrayed as needy and deserving of help. The stories of abused foster youth were highlighted, as were the heroic exploits and suffering of Filipino World War II veterans. These veterans were often described as lonely in the United States, and many wished to return to their families in the Philippines before their death. These two specific populations were the targeted recipients of the FCIA.

Policy Tools

The FCIA included both an expansion of preexisting legislation and new legislation. Although the FCIA's objectives are qualitative and symbolic in nature, funding was used as a primary tool for achieving the FCIA's objectives. Interestingly, the improvement of ILPs was funded by Titles II and III, which include reallocations of funding and authority. More specifically, H.R.3443 is an amendment to Title IV-E of the SSA, which makes changes to the previous initiative regarding ILPs. Title IV-E of SSA was both an expansion of Title I and a new introduction of Title II. SSA attempted to resolve issues faced by emancipated foster youth prior to H.R.3443; the 1999 amendment was designed to improve on that prior legislation. The new changes allow for increased funding and flexibility for states to improve the 1993 legislation (Collins 2004; Nixon 2005). Title II, however, was a new policy about an issue which had been acknowledged three years earlier as uniquely different legislation. H.R.3443 amended Title IV-E to expand Title I and introduced new policy for Filipino veterans. Prior to the FCIA, veterans had to give up their SSI to move out of the United States (Lachica 1999). Thus, the action allowed through the FCIA was a new attempt to meet the objective of recognizing Filipino veterans.

Increased funding. The primary policy tool used to achieve the objectives of the FCIA centered on providing funding. To improve ILPs, the FCIA increased funding for the program and allowed states to have more flexibility in spending the FCIA allotment. ILP program funding doubled, and Titles II and III were used to justify spending on Title I. Funding for ILPs increased from seventy million dollars per year to one hundred forty million dollars per year and was directed towards improving the original 1986 ILP legislation (Kellam 1999). Up to thirty percent of this funding could be used to provide room and board for emancipated foster youth (American Psychological Association 2005). Furthermore, eligibility for services was expanded to include all foster children likely to age out of care (Kessler 2004, 5), and data collection to improve ILPs was a main feature of Title I subsection A (Juvenile Law Center 2005; Nixon 2005). As such, the FCIA funding was designed to provide flexibility in improving ILPs.

Alternatively, the FCIA made it possible for veterans to continue to receive a portion of their SSI, and thereby made moving back to their native country affordable. Veterans who chose this option, however, would lose twenty-five percent of their usual SSI payment. Furthermore, this reduction in SSI, coupled with increased federal revenue from Title III, was a tool to fund increased allocations for ILPs. More specifically, to achieve the objective of affording Filipino veterans the opportunity to move back home, the FCIA provided them with the financial means to return to their families before they died. Prior to FCIA, elderly veterans who wanted to return home had to choose between staying in America and having an income or living with family again and having no income (*Filipino Reporter* 1999). Seventy-five percent of usual SSI payments were considered a reasonable income because of the high value of the American dollar in the Philippines. Thus, the expectation was that veterans who were lonely could return to their families in the Philippines while maintaining a dignified standard of living (Lachica 1999).

Redistribution of costs. Both Titles II and III were significant sections of the FCIA, in part because they helped to save the government money through redistribution of costs, and were used as a tool to fund Title I of the same bill. Title II was expected to reduce Social Security Income fraud, while putting new mechanisms in place to effectively reclaim overpayments from recipients. Title III repealed the hold harmless provision for child support, entitling most states to less federal funding than they had been previously guaranteed (U.S. Congress 1999d). Additionally, the provision allowing veterans to move out of the United States and retain seventy-five percent of their SSI was estimated to save the government about thirty million dollars over a five-year period. These savings were often used as supporting arguments for the FCIA when the bill was introduced and during related hearings. Titles II and III of the FCIA were used to justify the increase in funding for ILPs.

FORMULATION

Collaboration among key political players contributed significantly to the FCIA's successful passage through Congress. Representatives Johnson, Cardin, and Gilman were responsible for introducing key components of the FCIA and then combining them into

H.R.1802, the first version of the FCIA. The opposition H.R.1802 encountered was ineffective due to Johnson and Cardin's proactive defense during the debate. Senator Chafee's death inspired a renaming of Title I of the bill, and the FCIA was introduced as H.R.3443. H.R.3443 passed quickly in both chambers of Congress and received strong support from the Clinton administration as it was compatible with his policy agenda.

Drafting/Presentation

The introduction of this bill involved a team of key players. Representatives Johnson and Cardin initially introduced bills that were incorporated into H.R.1802. Representatives Cardin and Johnson worked as a bipartisan team on the FCIA. Representative Cardin was a Democratic leader who introduced the Transition to Adulthood Act. He cosponsored H.R.1802 with Representative Johnson and has since been formally recognized for his work helping families and children (Maryland n.d.). Representative Cardin's Republican counterpart in the House of Representatives was Nancy Johnson, who sponsored H.R.1802, and H.R.3443. She was also the chair of the Committee on Ways and Means Subcommittee on Human Resources, where the bill was referred (Johnson 2005). Though these two politicians belonged to different political parties, they worked together to support the FCIA.

The work of Representatives Cardin and Johnson was supplemented by that of Representative George Gilman (R-OR), whose legislation was also included in H.R.1802. First, H.R.26, The Filipino Veterans SSI Extension Act, was introduced by Representative Gilman on January 1 (U.S. Congress 1999d). This legislation was incorporated into H.R.631, the SSI Fraud Prevention Act sponsored by Johnson. H.R.631 was followed by H.R.671, The Transition to Adulthood Program Act sponsored by Cardin (*GovTrack* n.d.; U.S. Congress 1999c, 1999k). These three bills were combined into H.R.1802, which was introduced by Representative Johnson and cosponsored by Representative Cardin, as well as fourteen other Democrats and five Republicans. Between three authors, members of the House thus wrote and began the legislative process of the FCIA during the 106th Congress.

Less than one week after the passage of H.R.1802, S1327 was introduced by the popular Senator John H. Chafee, who helped to inspire support for the FCIA. Chafee had a reputation for supporting foster youth, and among the Filipino community was depicted as an honored and friendly veteran (Lachica 1999). Senator Chafee was the only Republican to represent Rhode Island in sixty-eight years and was described as a liberal Republican with a moderate voting record. He had been appointed once and re-elected four times (U.S. Congress 1999a).

Mark-Up

Limited time caused most of the work to be done in the House, where the bill originated. H.R.1802 was introduced in May and referred to the Subcommittee on Human Resources where changes were made to accommodate concerns from states and meet administrative requirements. During the roughly six weeks this version of the FCIA spent in the House, one change was made due to prohibitive costs and administrative policy. A decision not to require states to provide Medicaid was reluctantly made in this committee because Congress could not comply with the Pay-As-You-Go-Rule (California Institute for Federal Policy Research 1999; U.S. Congress 1999c), which would have required that Congress find funding for an estimated four hundred million dollars to finance the Medicaid provision over a five-year period (Allred 1999; Beadle 1999). Because the 106th session was near an end while the companion bill was still in a Senate subcommittee, there was little time to complete the process and H.R.3443 was introduced.

Opposition. Opposition was addressed during the mark-up of H.R.1802 in the House of Representatives, and the mark-up was not completed in the Senate due to time constraints. Title III of the bill was a source of opposition. Representative Gerald D. Kleczka from Wisconsin noted that some states, including his, gave most of the money collected from child support back to families leaving welfare. He argued that repealing the hold harmless provision meant his state would also lose funding, despite efforts to comply with the intent of Congress that child support impact families directly (U.S. Congress 1999d). Additionally, the National Governor's Association (NGA) wrote a letter asserting the organization's opposition to both repealing the hold harmless provision and increasing the state's share of costs for required paternity testing in child support cases. The letter explained that these reductions were inappropriate ways to fund the FCIA. Similarly, the American Public Human Services Association (APHSA) officially opposed the FCIA because of Title III, Child Support (National Governor's Association 1999).

The Subcommittee on Human Resources wrote a series of amendments to help appease the opposition to Title III. The provision that would have required states to pay twenty-four percent more of the cost of paternity testing was removed (California Institute for Federal Policy Research 1999; Kirchhoff 1999a, 1999b). Furthermore, states who returned at least fifty percent of child support payments to families leaving welfare could still receive some funding from the federal government for child support.

Time constraints. Work on the FCIA primarily occurred in the House Ways and Means Subcommittee on Human Resources due to concerns about limited time. Though H.R.1802 was introduced in May, there were concerns about passing the bill by November, when Congress was scheduled to recess. On June 25, H.R.1802 was discharged from the Committee on Commerce and referred to the Committee of the Whole House to help accelerate the FCIA's progress. Members of the Committee on Commerce made this agreement with the understanding that they would still be able to participate in the conference committee (U.S. Congress 1999d).

The FCIA was still in the Senate Committee on Finance in October, when House members encouraged the speedy passage of the bill during hearings. Representatives Cardin, Johnson, and Thomas DeLay (R-Texas) all testified at the Senate Committee on Finance Subcommittee on Health Care hearing on Foster Care and Children's Health. During their testimony, Representatives Cardin and Johnson briefly mentioned key differences between S1327 and H.R.1802 and encouraged the Senate to pass S1327 quickly. They assured members of the subcommittee that differences could be resolved during the conference committee. Likewise Representative DeLay urged quick passage during his testimony at this hearing. Using his own experience as a foster parent to emphasize the problems with the previous ILP legislation, Representative DeLay connected the need for quick passage of the FCIA to the urgency of improving the 1993 ILP initiative (Bailey 1999; Cardin 1999; U.S. Congress 1999j; DeLay 1999; English 1999; Ganio 1999; Johnson 1999; McGeady 1999).

House and Senate Floor Vote

After a successful mark-up session in the House Ways and Means Subcommittee on Human Resources, H.R.1802 was scheduled for a floor vote in the House. There was little time remaining before the end of the congressional session, and the companion bill in the Senate was still in the Subcommittee on Finance. Although the Senate companion bill was expected to pass once it was reported out of committee, the mark-up session for S1327 was never completed.

House floor vote. H.R.1802 was readily accepted and passed in the House of Representatives. During the debate on June 25, opposition to H.R.1802 was ineffective. Both Representatives Cardin and Johnson announced early in the debate that the letters APHSA sent contained inaccurate statements. Later Johnson responded to concerns caused by the letters during the debate. Members of Congress appeared to accept Johnson's rebuttal to the opposition without any argument, as they replied by thanking Johnson and confirming their support for the FCIA. Additionally, Kleczka offered his support, noting that the hold harmless provision had been adjusted to meet the needs of his state (U.S. Congress 1999b, 1999c, 1999d, 1999e).

Following the debate in the Committee of the Whole, H.R.1802 passed with a majority vote (U.S. Congress 1999f, 1999g;). Three hundred and eighty-five members voted for the FCIA, and six voted against the bill. Members of the House of Representatives appeared to pass H.R.1802 almost without reservation. All six of the nay votes were from Republican representatives; however, many supporters considered this vote to be evidence of bipartisan support (Cardin 1999; Johnson 1999; Lachica 1999; U.S. Congress 1999i).

Senate action, Senator Chafee's death, and introduction of H.R.3443. S1327 was still in the Senate Committee on Finance when Senator Chafee died on October 24. Supporters of the FCIA were concerned that S1327 would not complete the process in time because the Senate did not have a strong enough Republican leader who supported the bill. In response, key members of both chambers worked together to create a compromise bill, H.R.3443, to replace H.R.1802 and halt the process of S1327. The vote on H.R.3443 circumvented the process of S1327. As a result, members of the Senate did not vote on S1327 (Croll 2002; Malinowski 1999).

Conference Committee and Final Floor Vote

The combination of the short time frame for deliberation and passage of a compromise bill between H.R.1802 and S1327, as well as the untimely death of a key Senate sponsor, resulted in the unusual and expedited introduction and replacement of the two bills by the compromise bill, H.R.3443. The introduction of H.R.3443, coupled with a change in the name of a key component of the legislation, helped to move the FCIA beyond procedural obstacles and served the additional purpose of honoring the late Senator Chafee (Croll 2002; Malinowski 1999; Way 1999). H.R.3443 was introduced to both chambers with its passage prearranged. Senator Johnson explained that the House and Senate had been working together to write H.R.3443 and that the language in this version of the FCIA had already been agreed upon by both groups (U.S. Congress 1999c, 1999h). Importantly, this final version of the FCIA included a name change of Title I of the bill, designed to honor the late Senator Chafee. H.R.3443 did not meet any opposition during the final floor vote and passed quickly. H.R.3443 was introduced and passed in the House of Representatives on November 18, and followed by the Senate on November 19, the final day of the 106th Congressional session (Child Welfare League of America 1999a, 1999b).

Presidential Support

Presidential support was assured because the FCIA was symbolic of the Clinton administration's philosophy. Importantly, the FCIA was compatible with President Clinton's policy agenda and as such received executive branch support. More specifically, H.R.3443 complemented Clinton's focus on increasing funds for foster youth legislation (U.S. Congress 1999j). The president's proposal appropriated two hundred eighty million dollars, a forty percent budget increase, to The Transitional Living Program, which was similar to ILPs (Clinton Foundation 1999; Massinga 1999; U.S. Congress 1999l). The FCIA is clearly related to the types of programs targeted in the administration's budget proposal and as such enjoyed fiscal support. Furthermore, President Clinton added the passage of this bill to his list of accomplishments (Clinton Foundation 1999; U.S. Executive Office of the President 1999c).

Attendees of the signing ceremony were people who symbolized the goals of the FCIA. Ten Filipino veterans, alumni of foster care, and Senator Chafee's son were at the ceremony (Malinowski 1999). Reports depicted the veterans as proudly saluting President Clinton (Lachica 1999; Satoshi 2004). The ceremony also included speeches by former foster youth, who emphasized the personal value of the FCIA, and representatives of several large organizations who had testified at various hearings. During his speech, President Clinton thanked Lincoln Chafee for attending on his father's behalf (U.S. Executive Office of the President 1999a; U.S. Congress 1999i; Perez 1999; *Bangor News Daily* 1999; *U.S. Newswire* 1999). These symbolic participants represented the most popular aspects of Public Law 106-169.

CONCLUSION

The FCIA passed successfully due to effective symbols and the efforts of several key political players. The targeted populations were foster youth and elderly veterans who symbolized vulnerable and deserving citizens. The bill began and ended with significant executive support, primarily from First Lady Hillary Clinton, who worked to facilitate a status change of the problems faced by emancipating foster youth to the level of a politically salient issue. Other players included Representatives Cardin and Johnson, who authored, introduced, amended, and defended both H.R.1802 and H.R.3443. Senator Chafee was also influential as a popular politician, a strong Republican voice in support of the FCIA, and the sponsor of the Senate companion bill S1327. The strategic compromises between Representatives Cardin, Johnson, and Gilman created the unique pairing of foster youth and Filipino veterans as the targets of the bill. These members of Congress created a bill that not only authorized services for foster youth but used savings from newly created pension rights for Filipino veterans to create the foundation for funding foster youth services. While its passage was mostly unopposed, time constraints and the untimely death of Senator Chafee increased the saliency of the bill and triggered increased efforts by supporters in both chambers to compromise and assure passage. Importantly, Chafee was the honoree of the final version of this legislation H.R.3443 after his death on October 24. Using this bill to memorialize a respected member of Congress became symbolic as well. Finally, President Clinton supported the FCIA, which was compatible with his policy agenda. On December 14, 1999, amid a ceremony featuring symbolic players, Clinton signed P.L. 106-169 into law.

REFERENCES

Allred, Victoria. 1999. Senate clears foster child assistance bill. *CQ Weekly* November 27: 2844.

American Psychological Association. 2005. *Congress passes the Foster Care Independence Act*. http://www.apa.org/ppo/issues/pfosterkids.html (accessed August 9, 2005).

Baily, Percy. 1999. Prepared testimony by Percy Baily, St. Louis, Missouri, before the Senate Committee on Finance Subcommittee on Health Care. *Federal News Service*. October 13. http://www.lexisnexis.com (accessed October 29, 2005).

Bangor Daily News. 1999. Senator Collins attends signing of foster care bill, December 20, 1.

Beadle, Andrew. 1999. House subcommittee votes to double foster care grants, enhance states' flexibility. *CQ Weekly* May 22: 1214.

Block, Kelli Sutton. 1999. Statement of Kelli Sutton Block People Places of Charlottesville, Charlottesville, Virginia. *Testimony before the House Committee on Ways and Means Subcommittee on Human Resources*. May 13. http://waysandmeans.house.gov/legacy/humres/106cong/5-13-99/5-13bloc.htm (accessed October 28, 2005).

Bowie, Montrey. 1999. Statement of Montrey Bowie, High School Student, Our House Program, Elliot City, Maryland. *Testimony before the House Committee on Ways and Means Subcommittee on Human Resources*. 13 May. http://waysandmeans. house.gov/legacy/humres/106cong/5-13-99/5-13bowi.htm (accessed October 28, 2005).

Cabotaje, Michael A. 1998. Equity denied: Historical and legal analyses in support of the extension of U.S. veteran's benefits to Filipino World War II veterans. *Asian Law Journal* 6. http://www.asianlawjournal.org/Volume_6/vol6_articles.html (accessed November 7, 2005).

California Institute for Federal Policy Research. 1999. Foster Care Independence Act continues to progress. *California Capitol Hill Bulletin* 6 (18). http://www.calinst.org/bulletins/bull618w.htm#_1_9 (accessed August 9, 2005).

Cardin, Benjamin. 1999. Prepared testimony of Benjamin Cardin Third District Maryland before the Senate Finance Committee Subcommittee on Health Care. *Federal News Service*. October 13. http://www.lexisnexis.com (accessed October 29, 2005).

Chao, Julie. 1999. Filipino veterans make first step toward WW II benefits the president signs a bill allowing survivors who receive SSI to return home and get 75% of the funds. *San Francisco Examiner*, December 21, sec. A10.

Child Welfare League of America. 1999a. *CWLA testimony submitted to the Senate Finance Subcommittee on Health Care for the Hearing on Health Care Needs of Children in the Foster Care System*. October 13. http://www.cwla.org/advocacy/indlivtest991013.htm (accessed October 29, 2005).

Child Welfare League of America. 1999b. *Foster Care Independence Act of 1999*. November 23. http://www.cwla.org/advocacy/indlivhr3443.htm (accessed June 5, 2005).

Clinton Foundation. 1999. *President Clinton signs landmark law to help foster care youth prepare for independent living.* http://www.clintonfoundation.org/legacy/121499-fact-sheet-on-foster-care-independence-act.htm. (accessed October 30, 2005).

Clinton, Hillary. 1999. *Talking it Over.* February 3. http://clinton4.nara.gov/WH/EOP/First_Lady/html/columns/hrc0203993.html (accessed November 6, 2005).

Clinton, Hillary. 2005. *Senator Clinton highlights pressing needs of youth aging out of foster care. Hillary Rodham Clinton.* October 19. http://Clinton.senate.gov/news/statements/details.cfm?id=247432 (accessed October 28, 2005).

Collins, Mary Elizabeth. 2004. Enhancing services to youths leaving foster care: Analysis of recent legislation and its potential impact. *Children and Youth Services Review* 26 (11): 1051–1065.

Cook, Ronna, and Andrea Sedlak. 1995. National evaluation of independent living programs. In *Preparing foster youths for adult living: Proceedings of an invitational research conference,* edited by Edmund V. Mech and Joan R. Rycraft, 19–26. Washington DC: Child Welfare League of America.

County of Sacramento. 2001. Grand Jury. *Transitional assistance for aging out foster children.* http://www.sacgrandjury.org/reports/00-01/fosterchildren-AgingOut.asp (accessed September 30, 2005).

CQ Weekly. 1993. Special report: 1993 Budget reconciliation summary 1993 Budget Reconciliation Act. December 18: 31.

Croll, Adrienne. 2002. Legislative history of Title VIII of the Social Security Act. *Social Security Bulletin.* Spring. http://www.findarticles.com/p/articles/mi_m6524/is_1_64/ai_86196011 (accessed June 25, 2005).

DeLay, Tom, and Nancy Johnson. 1999. Foster independence. *Washington Times,* June 25, sec. A19.

DeLay, Tom. 1999. Prepared testimony of Tom DeLay before the Senate Committee on Finance Subcommittee on Health Care. *Federal News Service.* October 13. http://www.lexisnexis.com (accessed October 29, 2005).

Dijamco, Kathleen M. 1996. Fighting the good fight: Filipino veterans helped win the war, but they are losing their battle for civil rights. *The Filipino Express* 10 (21): 15.

English, Abigail, and Kathi Grasso. 2000. The Foster Care Independence Act of 1999: Enhancing youth access to health care. *Journal of Poverty Law and Policy.* July–August. http://www.abnet.org/child/englishgrasso.pdf (accessed June 5, 2005).

English, Abigail. 1999. *Prepared testimony of Abigail English, J.D., Director Center for Adolescent Health and the Law before the Senate Committee on Finance Subcommittee on Health Care. Federal News Service.* October 13. http://www.lexisnexis.com (accessed October 29, 2005).

Filipinas. 1998. Community news and events. May 30: 35. http://www.proquest.com. (accessed October 29, 2005).

Filipino Reporter. 1999. War vets favored by house unit bill. June 3. 26 (23): 5. http://www.proquest.com. (accessed October 29, 2005).

Focal Point. 2001. The human face of foster care in America: Terry Harrak 15 (1): 25–26.

Foster, Lisa K. 2001. *Foster care fundamentals: An overview of California's foster care system.* Sacramento, CA: California Research Bureau. California State Library.

Ganio, Patrick Sr. 1999. Prepared testimony of Patrick Ganio Sr. ACFV president before the Senate Committee on Finance Subcommittee on Health Care. *Federal News Service.* October 13. http://www.lexisnexis.com (accessed October 29, 2005).

GovTrack. n.d. *H.R. 631[106]: SSI Fraud Prevention Act of 1999.* http://www.govtrack .us/congress/bill.xpd?bill=h106-631 (accessed October 28, 2005).

Green, Stephanie.1998. Unfinished mission: S.F. exhibit examines Filipino WW II vets' lives. *Asian Week.* July 9–15. http://www.asianweek.com/070998/a_e.html (accessed November 4, 2005).

Johnson, Nancy. 1999. Prepared testimony of Representative Nancy Johnson before the Senate Finance Committee Subcommittee on Health Care. *Federal News Service.* October 13. http://www.lexisnexis.com (accessed October 29, 2005).

Johnson, Nancy. 2005. *About Congresswoman Nancy L. Johnson.* June 4. http://house .gov/nancyjohnson/bioweb.htm (accessed June 4, 2005).

Juvenile Law Center. 2005. *Foster Care Independence Act.* n.d. http://www.jlc.org/ home/legaldevelopmemts/fcia.php (accessed August 9, 2005).

Kellam, Susan. 1999. *Clinton signs foster care independence act.* Connect For Kids. http://www.connectforkids.org/node/157 (accessed June 7, 2005).

Kessler, Michelle. 2004. *The transition years: Serving current and former foster youth ages eighteen to twenty-one.* Tulsa, OK: University of Oklahoma.

Kirchhoff, Sue. 1999a. Bill to help foster children make transition to adult life heads to house floor. *CQ Weekly*, May 29: 1275.

Kirchhoff, Sue. 1999b. House votes to expand aid to combat problems of youths as they move off foster care. *CQ Weekly*, June 26: 1554.

Kroner, Mark. 1999. Statement of Mark Kroner, Director Self-sufficiency Services, Lighthouse Youth Services. *Testimony before the House Committee on Ways and Means Subcommittee on Human Resources.* May 13. http://waysandmeans.house. gov/legacy/humres/106cong/5-13-99/5-13kron.htm (accessed October 28, 2005).

Lachica, Eric. 1999. *Media advisory. American Coalition for Filipino Veterans, Inc.* http://pinoytexas.com/veteransbill.html (accessed October 28, 2005).

Loman, Anthony L., and Gary L. Siegel. 2000. *A review of literature on independent living of youths in foster and residential care. Report, the Institute of Applied Research.* St. Louis, MO: The Institute of Applied Research. http://www.iarstl.org/ papers/IndLivLit.pdf (accessed October 9, 2005).

Malinowski, Zachary W. 1999. Clinton signs Chafee foster-care bill. *The Providence Journal,* December 15, sec. B08.

Massinga, Ruth, and Peter J. Pecora. 2004. Providing better opportunities for older children in the child welfare system. *The Future of Children* 14 (1): 15–16. http://www .futureofchildren.org/usr_doc/14-1_syn8.pdf (accessed August 24, 2005).

Massinga, Ruth. 1999a. Aging out of foster care. *Christian Science Monitor* 91 (102): 11.

Massinga, Ruth. 1999b. Statement of Ruth Massinga, Chief Executive Officer Casey Family Program, Seattle, Washington. *Testimony before the House Committee on Ways and Means Subcommittee on Human Resources.* May 13. http://waysandmeans.house. gov/legacy/humres/106cong/5-13-99/5-13mass.htm (accessed October 28, 2005).

Matheny, Sonja. 1999. Statement of Sonja Matheny, student North Carolina Central University and Center of Keys for Life Program, Temple Hills, Maryland. *Testimony before the House Committee on Ways and Means Subcommittee on Human Resources.* May 13. http://waysandmeans.house.gov/legacy/humres/ 106cong/5-13-99/5-13math.htm (accessed October 28, 2005).

McBroom, Patricia. 1997. *Mrs. Clinton: Shorten foster care time.* University of California at Berkeley. n.d. http://www.berkeley.edu/news/berkeleyan/1997/1203/ Clinton.html (accessed November 4, 2005).

McCaffrey, Eileen. 1999. Statement of Eileen McCaffrey Executive Director, Orphan Foundation of America. *Testimony before the House Committee on Ways and Means Subcommittee on Human Resources*. May 13. http://waysandmeans.house.gov/legacy/humres/106cong/5-13-99/5-13mcca.htm (accessed October 28, 2005).

McGeady, Mary Rose. 1999. *Prepared statement by Sister Mary Rose McGeady, D.C, President Covenant House before the Senate Committee on Finance Subcommittee on Health Care. Federal News Service*. October 13. http://www.lexisnexis.com (accessed October 29, 2005).

Mendel, Dick. 2001. Fostered or forgotten? *AdvoCasey*. Fall 2001. http://www.aecf.org/publications/advocasey/fall2001/fostered.htm (accessed July 3, 2005).

National Governor's Association. 1999. *Letter*. June 24. http://www.nga.org/nga/legislativeUpdate/1,1169,C_LETTER%5ED_1545,00.html (accessed June 4, 2005).

Nelson, Douglas W. 2003. Gratified but not satisfied on foster care independence. *AdvoCasey* 3 (2): 2–3.

Nixon, Robin. 2005. *Frequently asked questions III*. National Foster Care Coalition. http://www.casey.org/NR/rdonlyres/E8E5EC9B-2C0B-496B-A165-5A55D2F793A5/457/ChafeeFAQIII1.pdf (accessed June 20, 2005).

Perez, Alfred. n.d. *Alfred Perez: A national advocate*. http://www.fyi3/Independent/success/perez.cfm (accessed November 4, 2005).

Petrie, Laurie. 1999. Safety net for teens honored. *Cincinnati Post*, February 1, sec. A1.

Rovner, Julie. 1991. Children in crisis overwhelm foster care. *CQ Weekly*, March 30: 795.

Satoshi, Nakano. 2004. *The Filipino World War II veterans' equity movement and the Filipino American community*. Prepared for the 7th International Phillippine Studies Conference. International Institute of Asian Studies, Leiden.

Shirk, Martha, and Gary Stangler. 2004. *On their own: What happens to kids when they age out of the foster care system*. Boulder, CO: Westview Press.

State of California. 2004. California Department of Social Services. Children and Family Services Division. *Chafee Foster Care Independence Program state plan for fiscal years 2005–2006 in California's Title IV-B Child and family services plan*. http://www.childsworld.ca.gov/res/pdf/IV-BPlan.pdf (accessed September 30, 2005).

U.S. Congress. 1998. House of Representatives Committee on Veteran's Affairs. *Benefits for Filipino veterans*. http://commdocs.house.gov/monnittees/vets/hvr072298.000/hvr072298_0HTM (accessed November 11, 2005).

U.S. Congress. 1999a. *Biographical directory of the United States Congress*. Scribner Encyclopedia of American Lives; U.S. Congress Memorial Tributes. Washington, D.C.: Government Printing Office. http://bioguide.congress.gov/scripts/biodisplay.pl?index=c000269 (accessed November 9, 2005).

U.S. Congress. 1999b. Foster Care Independence Act of 1999. 106th Cong., 1st sess. *Congressional Record* 145, no. 164.

U.S. Congress. 1999c. House. Committee of the Whole. Foster Care Independence Act of 1999. 106th Cong., 1st sess. *Congressional Record* 145, no. 92.

U.S. Congress. 1999d. House. Committee on Ways and Means. *Foster Care Independence Act of 1999*. H. Rep. 106-182, Part 1. http://www.lexisnexis.com (accessed October 24, 2005).

U.S. Congress. 1999e. House. Foster Care Independence Act of 1999. 106th Cong., 1st sess. *Congressional Record* 145, no. 92. http://ww.lexisnexis.com (accessed October 24, 2005).

U.S. Congress. 1999f. House. Foster Care Independence Act of 1999. *Bill Tracking Report*. http://ww.lexisnexis.com (accessed October 23, 2005).

U.S. Congress. 1999g. House. *Fraud Prevention Act of 1999. Bill Tracking Report*. http://ww.lexisnexis.com (accessed October 24, 2005).

U.S. Congress. 1999h. House. H.Res. 221. *House Calendar* No. 75. http://ww.lexisnexis.com (accessed October 24, 2005).

U.S. Congress. 1999i. House. Office of the Clerk. *Final vote results for roll call 256*. http://clerk.house.gov/evs/1999/roll256.xml (accessed October 28, 2005).

U.S. Congress. 1999j. House. The Filipino Veterans SSI Extension Act, H.R. 26. *Congressional Record-Extensions*. http://ww.lexisnexis.com (accessed October 24, 2005).

U.S. Congress. 1999k. Senate. Finance Committee Subcommittee on Health. Kit Bond Senate finance health care foster care and children's health. *Federal Document Clearinghouse Congressional Testimony*. October 13. http://ww.lexisnexis.com (accessed October 29, 2005).

U.S. Congress. 1999l. Transition to Adulthood Program Act. 106th Cong., 1st sess. *Congressional Record* 145, no. 24.

U.S. Executive Office of the President. 1999a. Office of Management and Budget. *H.R. 1802–Foster Care Independence Act. Statement of administrative policy*. Washington DC. http://clinton2.nara.gov/OMB/legislative/sap/HR1802-h.html (accessed October 30, 2005).

U.S. Executive Office of the President. 1999b. White House Office. *Foster care transitioning event remarks by first lady Hillary Rodham Clinton*. http://clinton4.nara.gov/WH/EOP/First_Lady/html/generalspeeches/1999/19990129.html (accessed November 6, 2005).

U.S. Executive Office of the President. 1999c. White House Office. President Clinton: *Helping foster care youth prepare for independent living*. The White House at Work. http://clinton3.nara.gov/WH/Work/121499.html (accessed November 4, 2005).

U.S. General Accounting Office. 1999a. Challenges in helping youths live independently. *Testimony before the House Subcommittee on Human Resources, Committee on Ways and Means*. http://www.gao.gov (accessed October 22, 2005).

U.S. General Accounting Office. 1999b. *Effectiveness of Independent Living Services unknown*. http://www.gao.gov (accessed October 22, 2005).

U.S. Newswire. 1999. Transcript of remarks by the president and first lady at a foster care event today. December 14: 1.

USA Today. 2005. Hardship follows children after foster care. April 7: 08d. http://www.proquest.com (accessed August 9, 2005).

Way, Kathy. 1999. *Washington update*. Evan B. Donaldson Adoption Institute. http://www.adoptioninstitute.org/policy/polupd1199.html (accessed November 9, 2005).

Policy Analysis: Evaluation or Recommendation

Purpose of a Policy Analysis

A policy analysis examines the impact of a public policy on the political environment in which it was or is to be implemented.

- Not all public policies are made by Congress.

- Policies can be customs, rulings by courts, regulations written by bureaucrats, or executive orders.
- An examination of a public policy is intended to identify the goals, the tools, and the outcomes to evaluate whether it was or is a successful and worthwhile intervention by government.

Formats for a Policy Analysis

Policy analysis usually takes one of two formats:

Policy evaluation is limited to evaluation of past or present policies. This type of analysis entails examining the characteristics of a current or past policy—its origins, its goals, who benefits, the instruments used to implement the goals, and its perceived or actual impact.

Policy recommendation involves proposing a new solution to a new or existing problem. This type of analysis may or may not involve an analysis of a current policy. A policy recommendation must first evaluate current policy responses to the problem or to similar problems but then take the analysis one step further to argue for the adoption of a new solution to the current problem. It provides both the rationale for the solution and a description of how it would be implemented, who it would benefit, who is likely to oppose it, and how to evaluate its progress toward solving the problem.

Researching and Writing a Policy Evaluation

1. **Identify a social problem or social condition.**
   - Look in the newspaper for ideas.
   - Choose something of particular interest and state clearly why it is of interest.
2. **Identify indicators of the social condition.**
   - Find one relevant quantitative indicator from each of the following:
     - An almanac.
     - A statistical yearbook.
     - *American Statistics Index.*
   - Locate sources related to the topic or problem using a computer search system, the library catalog, abstracts, and indexes.
     - Obtain two books on the subject.
     - Locate five scholarly journal articles.
     - Locate two articles from quality publications.
     - Locate two articles from mass publications.
   - Locate one government publication related to the topic or problem from each of the following:
     - *Congressional Information Service Index.*
     - *Monthly Catalog of U.S. Publications.*
     - *Congressional Record.*

3. **Identify the nature of the problem.**
   - Describe the problem.
     - Explain clearly what the problem is.
     - Explain clearly why the problem is of public concern.
   - Present evidence of the existence of the problem.
     - Quantitative (statistical or numerical) evidence.
     - Qualitative (expert opinion, examples) evidence.
   - List the factors underlying the problem.
     - Identify the broad underlying factors.
     - Identify the specific underlying factors.
4. **Find the public policy (if available) dealing with the problem.**
   - Describe the different solutions proposed or available and the solution adopted.
   - Identify where the public policy originated—custom, Congress, bureaucracy, judicial, or executive policy.
     - Examine how and where the policy was initiated.
     - Sometimes a policy has more than one source.
   - Identify five important political actors or players who either supported or opposed the solution adopted.
     - State the issue position of each player.
     - State the power of each player.
     - Identify at least two reasons why each player is important.
     - Rank-order the players by importance to implementing the solution.
   - Identify whether the policy been expanded or adjusted over time.
     - State the conditions for the change.
     - State the reasons for the change.
5. **Identify the objectives, targets, or goals of the policy.**
   - What was the policy supposed to do exactly?
     - What target population was supposed to benefit?
     - Is the solution curative? preventative? remedial?
   - What were the means or policy instruments used to achieve the goals or objectives?
     - How was the policy supposed to achieve its goals?
     - Policy tools—transfers? regulation? subsidy? tax?
6. **Analyze who or what benefited and or was hurt by the policy.**
   - Who seems better off? who is worse off?
   - Who paid the cost? who benefited?
7. **Evaluate the success of the policy by examining whether the goals or objectives were achieved.**
   - Match the goals with the outcomes.
   - What are the signs the policy is working?
   - Did the targets benefit as expected?
   - What constraints prevented it from working well?
   - What do the experts say about the policy?

8. Include a discussion, in order, of the following:

- An introduction that includes:
  - A brief description of the social problem.
  - The context.
  - Solution adopted to solve the problem.
  - A statement that assesses the usefulness of the solution for solving the problem.
- Subheadings identifying the discussion of:
  - The issue.
  - The historical context or background.
  - The objectives of the solution with justification.
  - The critique of the policy response in meeting the objectives, with justification.
  - An assessment with a cost/benefit analysis.
- A conclusion that restates briefly the context of the social problem and the justification for the critique of the solution.
- A list of sources for all borrowed ideas, arguments, and data. Use tables, charts, and graphs to illustrate data where necessary.

Policy Evaluation Guide and Checkoff Sheet

Executive Summary

- Identify the policy.
- Objectives of the policy (should include bullet points).
- Policy evaluation's major findings (should include bullet points).

Brief Description

- Identify the policy.
- Summarize its implied and/or expressed goals in concise detail.

Problems and Issues Identified

- Describe the social problem thoroughly.
- Describe how the problems were identified.
- Describe how the problems became issues.

Historical Context

- Identify and explain, chronologically, the who, what, where, when, how, and why (politics) related to getting the problem/issue on the governmental/decision agenda.
- Describe the process and circumstances of the formulation of the policy decision.
- Describe the legitimization of the policy decision.
- What kind of policy process was involved in passing this policy?
- Specifically, what types of individuals supported or did not support the proposed response to the problem/issue?
- Describe how information was used in formulating a solution.

Objectives of the Solution

- Describe the purpose of the tools or instruments used as policy responses to the problems/issues.
- Do the goals of the policy solution directly relate to the identified problems/issues? Why or why not?
- Specifically, what goals, problems, and/or issues are these tools supposed to address, remedy, fix, or resolve?
- Particularly, who are the targets of these tools?
- Explain why these tools were chosen over others.

Critique of Policy Response in Meeting Objectives

- Based on research, do the policy responses adequately address the identified problems? Why or why not?
- Are there unresolved problems or issues that have been identified but not addressed by the policy response?
- Specifically, what criteria and/or data are supposed to measure the policy's success?

Assessment, Cost/Benefit Analysis

- Based on research, was the policy outcome worth the costs associated with the policy response?
- What are the barriers to measuring whether or not the policy outcomes reflect success?
- What intervening events or unexpected circumstances influenced the policy outcomes positively or negatively?
- Were there budget or implementation problems that constrained policy success?
- Did pluralist forces help or hinder the implementation process?

Conclusions About the Problem and Critique of Solution

- Identify important findings from the evaluation.
- Was the policy proposal a good proposal with carefully built structures of support?
- What is the value of this evaluation to understanding public policy formation related to the policy domain?

**POLICY EVALUATION
THE NO CHILD LEFT BEHIND ACT OF 2001:
ACCOUNTABILITY, STANDARDIZATION, AND FEDERAL SANCTIONS**

By
Joshua Ford
POLS: 668
Dr. Schmidt
April 30, 2007

for students of different racial and economic backgrounds needed to be addressed as a civil rights issue (Bailey 1968, 42). As such, the Civil Rights Movement provided visible participants, heightening the public awareness of disparity in public programs and resulting in a policy window for the ESEA.

HISTORICAL CONTEXT

With the Brown decision, and the passing of the Civil Rights Act of 1964, equality issues were in the forefront of the American political agenda (Peterson 2003). The Civil Rights Movement and the Brown decision compelled national and local education bodies to address disadvantaged students and communities in an effective and timely manner (Bailey 1968). The ESEA was designed to distribute federal resources to education institutions who served low income residents, therefore promoting educational equality. Inadequacies in the ESEA, particularly in closing the achievement gap, created further pressure for additional reform through regulatory mandates and benchmarks to help close the achievement gap. The latest form of the ESEA, the NCLB, ties student performance on standardized exams to federal funding as a way to achieve objectives unmet by previous attempts to close the achievement gap (Rosenhall 2007).

ESEA: The Foundation of NCLB

As a result of heightened saliency of educational disparities in the Civil Rights Movement, Commissioner of Education Francis Kappel designed the ESEA at President Johnson's request. Upon completion of the design, President Johnson sought congressional deliberation and support for his educational reforms (Bailey 1968, 55). The ESEA was introduced to Congress in January of 1965 and was passed in April of 1965. President Johnson and Congress agreed that increased funding could provide a basis for an equal education to all income levels and racial groups (Bailey 1968, 57). The ESEA ensured federal funding for public education institutions to improve low income facilities and has been slightly altered by Congress every five years (Bailey 1968). The act still distributes federal funds, but its methods have changed by incremental steps.

The 106th Congress was scheduled to reauthorize the ESEA, but an agreement could not be reached and the previous reauthorization was rolled over for another year (Peterson 2003). Then, Texas Governor George W. Bush, as well as Vice President Al Gore, promoted education reform during their 2000 presidential election campaigns. Bush characterized himself as a "compassionate conservative"; that is, he was "compassionate" for low income students in underfunded schools and "conservative" for emphasizing individual parental choices and local flexibility in spending federal funds (Rudalevige 2003, 74).

The NCLB Policy Decision

Upon election, George W. Bush called a meeting in Austin, Texas, with both Republican and Democratic leadership to discuss education reform. The meeting was attended by Republicans, including Representative John Boehner (R-OH), Senator Judd Gregg (R-NH), and Senator James Jeffords (R-VT). It was also attended by Democrats, including Senator Evan Bayh (D-IN), Representative Tim Roemer (D-IN), and Senator Zell Miller (D-GA) (Peterson 2003). By including perspectives from a variety of ideological positions from those present in the Austin meetings, President-elect Bush created a Republican-New Democrat coalition. The willingness of these notable legislators to work together almost ensured that legislation would pass. Senator Jeffords introduced the ESEA reauthorization S1 in the U.S. Senate on May 3, 2001, closely followed by H.R.1, introduced by Representative Boehner in the U.S. House of Representatives on May 15, 2001 (U.S. Congress 2004). These legislative proposals provided the basis of the NCLB.

Legitimization of NCLB.   Legitimization of the NCLB policy proposal was based on providing a solution to educational disparity through educator accountability to the federal government and parents, plus local flexibility for spending federal funds. (Peterson 2003). President Bush and members of Congress sought to run education like a business by tracking progress through federal- and state-determined proficiency benchmarks. If adequate progress was not obtained, school sanctions and restructuring would take place (Rudalevige 2003). Further, education institutions could spend the NCLB budget in a variety of ways, so long as an improvement in education was obtained. This local flexibility in spending federal funds disconnected school results from federal government spending requirements.

Use of information.   Previous ESEA reauthorizations and information from seventeen states and numerous local governments, already engaged in accountability strategies, contributed to the formation of the NCLB. The importance placed on standards was present in the 1980s but can more readily be seen from the 1994 reauthorization of the ESEA and its companion legislation, the Goals 2000 Act (Peterson 2003). The ability to move to and from schools within a district, and out of a neighborhood, is a strategy known as school choice. School choice as an educational reform has been present since the Reagan administration and arose again in 1991, 1994, and in the debates of 1999. The flexibility, assessment, and consequence language of the NCLB has roots in the Clinton administration discussions over the ESEA but was especially present in the efforts to reauthorize the ESEA in the 106th Congress (Mayers 2006). An accountability case study from Chicago, in which educational improvement was achieved by making local schools accountable to the mayor's office, was also used as a template during formulation of the objectives and tools of the policy reform (Peterson 2003).

NCLB political support and opposition.   School accountability to the federal government through fiscal policy was widely supported in both chambers of Congress. Republicans and New Democrats both supported the bill, and primarily only party extremes and state officials opposed it (Rudalevige 2003). Democrats viewed the loose definition of accountability as a way to receive a return on the federal investment in education. Republicans saw accountability as a way to limit expenses by granting funds based on improvement (Peterson 2003).

Although both Democrats and Republicans realized the ESEA needed reauthorization, private school choice, the changed federal government role in education, and the language surrounding Annual Yearly Progress (AYP) reports created some disagreement (Peterson 2003). Senator Paul Wellstone (D-MN) argued that the NCLB was not a true commitment to education and that the increase in standards would hinder progress. Senator Wellstone called for his fellow senators to vote against the bill. During legislation, governors also pressured Congress to lower AYP requirements present in the bill (Rudalevige 2002). Senator Jeffords agreed with the governors and provided analyses suggesting that the current AYP would cause the majority of schools to fail. The AYP language was altered, and the new AYP required a one percent improvement in the test scores for each year in the disaggregated groups, but the progress would be assessed during a three-year time span.

In addition, private school choice as an option in the NCLB proposal was split between party lines. Republicans primarily agreed with private school choice as a way to create incentives for public school improvement. Yet Democrats felt that it would undermine accountability because private schools were not public organizations (Rudalevige 2002). In particular, some opponents argued that school choice would increase inequities between schools and students, as those who could afford to leave the neighborhood schools do so, resulting in fewer federal dollars for improving the neighborhood school.

Legislative Highlights

The U.S. Senate's Health, Education, Labor, and Pensions (HELP) committee and the House of Representative's Education and Workforce Committee added to the NCLB blueprint to get a bill to both chamber floors (U.S. Congress 2004; U.S. Congress 2004b). On March 8, 2001, the HELP committee approved S.1 for the Senate floor by a vote of 20–0. On June 14, 2001, the amended text of S.1 passed the Senate floor by a vote of 91–8 (U.S. Congress 2004b). The Education and Workforce committee approved H.R. 1 on March 14, 2001, which was passed by the House on June 16, 2001. The conference report was accepted by the House on December 13, 2001, by a vote of 381–41 (U.S. Congress 2004a) and in the Senate on December 18, 2001, by a vote of 87–10 (U.S. Congress 2004b). On January 8, 2002, President George W. Bush signed the NCLB into law.

OBJECTIVES OF THE NCLB SOLUTION

The NCLB is a mixed regulatory and distributive policy, in which the federal government requires a school to participate in several mandates to receive NCLB funds. Once a school meets federal mandates, it must show enough proficiency progress to continue receiving federal funds and avoid restructuring sanctions (NEA 2004a). The NCLB regulatory factors, as established by the federal government, allow federal control over institutions receiving Title I funds (Peterson 2003). The NCLB policy objectives were chosen because they held educators accountable and were believed by legislators to increase the policy's chances of reaching its goal. The policy's five performance-based objectives, designed for increasing accountability, improving student performance, and enhancing learning environments, are:

- All students will reach high standards, at a minimum attaining proficiency in reading, language arts, and mathematics by the 2013–2014 school year.
- All limited English proficiency students will become proficient in English, with a minimum attaining proficiency in reading, language arts, and mathematics by the 2013–2014 school year.
- All students will be taught by highly qualified teachers by 2005–2006.
- All students will be educated in learning environments that are safe and conducive.
- All students will graduate from high school.

NCLB Tools Addressing Educational Disparity

The policy objectives of the NCLB were aligned with regulatory tools used by the federal government to control education institutions and assess educational proficiency (U.S. DOE 2004). The NCLB contains four performance-based regulatory policy tools

(U.S. DOE 2005; U.S. DOE 2006b) for increasing accountability, performance, and learning environment quality. These regulatory tools include:

- State-administered and NAEP federally administered standardized exams.
- Required sanctions placed on underperforming education institutions.
- Public school choice for students in underperforming schools.
- Highly qualified teachers using proven teaching methods.

These tools support one or more of the five NCLB performance objectives and the overarching expressed goal of the NCLB, to close the achievement gap between students of different financial, ethnic, social, and disabled status (U.S. DOE 2006a).

Standardized tests. National Assessment of Education Progress (NAEP) exams are formal checkups on states, ensuring that state-administered assessments are accurately judging student progress (U.S. DOE 2005). The results from state-administered assessments, as well as NAEP assessments, are divided into different groups and subgroups of students based on race, financial, and disability status (Jennings and Retner 2006). Each state sets its own proficiency mark and must show a one percent increase per group and subgroup of students towards AYP. This division of results by group and subgroup is intended to limit educational disparity by determining if it is taking place, and if so, by placing sanctions on schools to ensure that the educational disparity ceases.

The state-administered assessments and NAEP assessments to determine student proficiency relate to directly measuring the performance objectives of the NCLB for improving student proficiency levels in specific subjects and the standards of the English language (Mayers 2006). The policy states that, by the 2013–2014 school year, all students will attain at least proficiency in reading, language arts, and mathematics (U.S. DOE 2004). By setting an objective for all students to reach high standards, these performance objectives address the problem of educational disparity in academic subjects. In addition to every student reaching minimum performance standards, the policy also requires that all limited English proficiency students reach proficiency in English (U.S. DOE 2004). By setting an objective for a minority group to reach a proficient standard, this performance addresses the problem of educational disparity between native speakers and non-native speaking groups. The division of the results by group and subgroup pertains to the English proficiency objective, while overall school results pertain to the objective for all students reaching proficiency in reading, language arts, and math.

Sanctions on failing schools. The policy establishes funding sanctions as tools to create incentives for achieving proficiency and safety standards, as well as to hold schools accountable for not reaching those standards. Essentially, the NCLB creates a set of sequential sanctions designed to achieve all five of the performance-based objectives. Under the provisions of NCLB, schools receiving Title I funds can fail to achieve standards for two consecutive years before having to participate in NCLB sanctions. Upon the third consecutive failing year, the school must have a school improvement plan put in place and must offer school choice to continue receiving funds (N.H. DOE 2003). In the fourth consecutive failing year, the school must still offer school choice, along with Supplemental Education Services (SES) (N.H. DOE 2003). In the fifth consecutive failing year, the school must offer school choice, SES, and must choose one corrective action.

The corrective actions include: replace school staff, institute a new curriculum, decrease management authority in school, appoint outside experts, extend the school year or day, or restructure the school's internal organization (N.H. DOE 2003). In the sixth consecutive failing year, the school must offer school choice, SES, and plan to restructure (N.H. DOE 2003). Plans to restructure require the school to choose one of the following courses of action: reopen as a public charter school, replace all or most of staff, or enter into a contract with a private entity that is effective in school management. Finally, in the seventh consecutive failing year, the school implements its restructuring plan under an Alternative Government Arrangement (NCREL 2003).

The targets of these regulatory sanction tools are the educators, administrators, and students (Neel 2006). If students remain in failing schools, with no alternative action being taken to remedy the problem, then students would be less likely to reach proficiency requirements of the NCLB. Educators are expected to be accountable for student performance, and administrators are held responsible for the performance of their educators. If improvement is not obtained, the federal government will remove educators and administrators (McCall, Kingsbury, and Olson 2004).

School choice. Public school choice as a regulatory policy tool supports performance objectives of the NCLB for providing high learning environments and improving graduation rates. If a student attended a school that had not reached AYP for two years, then the student has the option of transferring to a school that is reaching AYP (Jennings and Retner 2006). This addresses the problem of disparity in education and attempts to remedy it by allowing a student to change schools when the school they are attending is deemed failing (AFT 2004a). If that environment is absent, students may leave the school for one that has an environment conducive to learning. This, in turn, is supposed to improve student chances to graduate from high school.

Highly qualified teachers. NCLB policy makers emphasized highly qualified teachers and scientifically based teaching methods as tools for improving educational effectiveness. Legislators reasoned that highly qualified teachers promoted an equal education to all students (Jennings and Retner 2006) and imposed a requirement that all teachers shall be highly qualified by the 2005–2006 school year (Neel 2006). The targets of this tool are educators. Educators must meet the highly qualified benchmarks, and students shall be instructed by highly qualified teachers using scientifically based teaching methods.

CRITIQUE OF POLICY RESPONSE IN MEETING NCLB OBJECTIVES

Based on performance data and as implemented, the NLCB objectives and regulatory tools designed to reach those objectives have been problematic and difficult to achieve at best and have had negative, unintended consequences of reducing the quality of public education at worst. The U.S. DOE's performance data is a collaborative effort performed by EDFacts. EDFacts provides a centralized tool that collects, assesses, and uses educational data to determine improvement in schools. The data serves a two-fold purpose: to assess NCLB effectiveness relevant to educational improvement and to assess the performance of the states to NCLB standards (U.S. DOE 2005). Yet, it was educators and students that were first to identify the problems inherent in NCLB (AFT 2004b). For each of the problems, the U.S. DOE has either not responded or its response has been unsatisfactory towards reaching a solution. The problems identified in the current policy are the following:

- The AYP formula does not give schools sufficient credit for student improvement.
- If a single subgroup fails to meet AYP, the entire school is labeled as failing and subject to federal sanctions.
- Criteria relating to highly qualified teachers are inapplicable and inappropriate to certain teachers.
- Public school choice is poorly designed and undermines schools.
- Many NCLB mandates are funded by state not federal dollars.
- Unrealistic/unattainable expectations for attaining proficiency in reading, language arts, and mathematics.
- Unrealistic/unattainable expectations for attaining English language proficiency for ESL learners.

Annual Yearly Progress Unaddressed Problems

The Government Accountability Office (GAO) and the Office of Inspector General (OIG) both performed studies regarding the relevance of the nominal level measurements used by the U.S. DOE to build its data regarding AYP (U.S. DOE 2006a). AYP is used to determine schools at risk. It examines percentages of students reaching a minimum level for each grade tested in the school. If the percentage is high enough for each group and subgroup, the total student body is classified as proficient and not at risk (Neel 2006). Both studies found that measurement levels used by the U.S. DOE were not judging growth, but only proficiency levels (U.S. DOE 2006a). The GAO recommended that the U.S. DOE experiment with growth models. The U.S. DOE agreed with the GAO's findings and initiated a pilot program in seven states using growth models to judge performance (U.S. Congress 2006). The U.S. DOE has not posted results regarding its pilot program, but Secretary of Education Margaret Spelling expressed concern that the use of growth models would destroy the educator accountability currently present under the NCLB (U.S. Congress 2006).

Labeling Failing Schools

Unexpectedly, schools across the nation with sound, strong track records of performance are considered failing (CEP 2007). For example, King Philip Middle School in West Hartford, Connecticut, is considered failing, even though eighty percent of its students reached proficiency in math and eighty-eight percent in reading (Fusarelli 2004, 84). Only forty-one percent of King Philip Middle School's forty-five special education students attained math proficiency on the Connecticut Mastery Test. The failure of eight special education students to attain proficiency in math caused the entire school to fail. In another example, Durant Middle School in Wake County, North Carolina, also failed to meet AYP requirements under the NCLB. The school fell short in both reading and math for ESL students. Durant Middle School reached twenty-seven of twenty-nine proficiency goals but is considered failing and subject to federal sanctions because five ESL students did not reach AYP (Fusarelli 2004).

Specifically, two testing provisions under the NCLB encourage subgroup failure on assessments. First, as soon as ESL students become proficient in English, they are no longer considered ESL students (Fusarelli 2004). This encourages failure on NAEP exams for the remaining subgroup of ESL students. As noted above, failure for only one subgroup of students results in the entire school being labeled as failing. Reassigning students from ESL to the general student population is causing ESL subgroups to be more likely to fail. Second, according to NCLB provisions, ninety-five percent of students in each subgroup, in each grade, must be tested. Students being absent on a test day can result in the entire school being listed as in need of improvement (Jehlen 2007). For example, in Georgia, 536 of 846 schools (sixty-three percent) failed to make AYP because they could not test ninety-five percent of their students in every subgroup (Fusarelli 2004).

Highly Qualified Teachers

NCLB policy formulators failed to consider that mandating the use of highly qualified teachers would not necessarily or adequately remedy identified problems (AFT 2004a). The means of becoming highly qualified are present in teaching credential programs for new teachers, but the policy lacks measures to ensure that veteran teachers are also highly qualified. The U.S. DOE indicates veteran teachers can demonstrate their highly qualified status by a High Objective Uniform State Standard Evaluation (HOUSSE) means test (U.S. DOE 2006b). The U.S. DOE, however, did not require states to develop a HOUSSE means assessment and many states have not; this oversight has resulted in fewer certifications of highly qualified teachers (AFT 2004a).

As indicators of the pervasiveness and impact of HOUSSE testing, the U.S. DOE gathered data regarding the effects of teachers with HOUSSE elementary math certificates on elementary math students. As seen in Figure 1, in 2003 the average fourth-grade student being taught by a HOUSSE certified elementary math instructor received a scale score of 226 on the NAEP exam, while the average fourth-grade student being taught by a non–HOUSSE certified elementary math instructor received a score of 223 (U.S. DOE 2006a).

(FIGURE 1 ABOUT HERE)

In states that did not have HOUSSE means assessments, the average 2003 fourth-grade math NAEP score was 228 (U.S. DOE 2006a), two points higher than the average 2003 NAEP score from fourth-grade students being taught by a HOUSSE certified instructor. The data indicate that HOUSSE certification had very little, if any, meaningful impact on proficiency scores.

Public School Choice

Two unanticipated problems that pertain to public school choice have been identified but remain unaddressed within the NCLB provisions. These problems involve earmarking a portion of the funding and burdens on high-capacity schools. First, school districts are required to put twenty percent of their Title I funds in a reserve to pay for school choice related transportation and supplemental services (Mayers 2006). Title I funds pay for school choice transportation fees as opposed to investing twenty percent of the Title I funds back into the failing schools (Mathis 2003). In addition, capacity problems are also not addressed regarding public school choice (U.S. GAO 2006). Students have used public school choice to transfer to schools that are above their capacity, resulting in a higher student-teacher ratio and less personal instruction time.

Unfunded Requirements Have Impact on Federal Mandates

The NCLB requires states to develop accountability measures and assessment standards to receive NCLB funds but fails to provide the funding for developing and processing these assessment measures. For example, in 2007, Texas expects to underwrite $1.2 billion for NCLB accountability standards (Mathis 2003). Likewise, the State of Connecticut expects to pay $42 million in 2008, which is compounded by Connecticut school districts paying $700 million locally for developing these measures (NEA 2004a). As such, these requirements have the impact of an unfunded federal mandate even though provisions of the NCLB specifically prohibit mandated spending for compliance. Section 9527 of the NCLB states:

> Nothing in this Act shall be construed to authorize an officer or employee of the Federal Government to mandate, direct, or control a State, local educational agency, or school's program of instruction, or allocation of State or local resources, or mandate a State or any subdivision thereof to spend any funds or incur any costs not paid for under this Act (Public Law 107-110).

The language of Section 9527 caused the National Education Association (NEA) to file a court case against the U.S. Department of Education because the impact of the mandated assessment tools to receive funding effectively creates an unfunded mandate. Recently, though, the GAO issued a report stating that NCLB did not meet the Unfunded Mandates Reform Act's definition of a mandate (Williams 2005). The GAO stated that the NCLB federal requirements placed on states are a condition of federal financial assistance and the states are not forced to comply. As such, states are free to forgo the funding should they decide not to invest in assessment measures.

Unrealistic Objectives

The proficiency objectives of the NCLB, that all students reach proficiency in their grade level for math and reading by the 2013–2014 school year and that all ESL students reach proficiency in their grade level by the 2013–2014 school year (NEA 2004a), are unrealistic and essentially unattainable statistically. With all American public education students subjected to standardized exams, the normal distribution will spread out in a bell-shaped curve around the mean. The mean represents the norm, or average, and for this purpose it represents grade level. Sixty-seven percent of students will reach a level within one standard deviation either up or down from the mean, ninety-five percent of students will reach a level within two standard deviations either up or down from the mean, and ninety-nine percent of students reach a level within three standard deviations either up or down from the mean. For each student to reach proficiency, the bell curve would need to split, or the grade level would have to be extremely low, including three standard deviations up and down from the mean, encompassing ninety-nine percent of students. This would leave one percent of students behind, and creates a sub-par proficiency level for each grade (Brulle 2005).

NCLB COST AND BENEFIT ANALYSIS

The purpose of the NCLB is to increase accountability, improve student performance, and enhance learning environments through mandating or requiring that schools, teachers, and students demonstrate pre-established levels of proficiencies. The U.S.

DOE claims that NCLB has produced four benefits related to these objectives (U.S. DOE 2004). The U.S. DOE claimed benefits are:

- Schools are accountable to the federal government to ensure that all students are learning.
- Student proficiency amounts have improved in mathematics and reading.
- Teachers utilize assessment data and scientifically based teaching methods to improve classroom instruction.
- Parents are now given unprecedented information and options to ensure that their children are in a conducive learning environment.

Yet, these perceived benefits have unintended costs, including detrimental effects on teachers and students such as "creaming" students for improving assessment measures. These costs outweigh the benefits such that it is an ineffective, inefficient, and inequitable public policy (Brulle 2005).

Accountability Provisions Create Creaming Effect

While schools are being held accountable to the federal government under the NCLB, it has not done so effectively because the policy has not ensured all students are learning. One of the costs of determining accountability based on growth measures is for schools to refocus or target students who can demonstrate growth. Essentially, teachers are "creaming" students. This involves teachers focusing their attention on a particular group of students rather than all students. Currently, AYP counts the number of students identified as proficient. Teachers have been focusing their efforts on students that are performing directly below proficiency standards, also known as cusp (borderline) students, to statistically show the highest level of improvement (Kingsbury, Olson, and McCall 2004). Educator interviews supported by the drastic increase in U.S. DOE proficiency data support this. During the first years of the NCLB, there was a significant increase in proficient status in mathematics and reading. This was a result of educators directing lesson plans to cusp students (McCall, Kingsbury, and Olson 2004).

Such refocusing has also had an inequitable impact on different types of students. Advanced students receive less attention because they are above the proficiency mark, and students that are grossly below the proficiency mark are neglected because they are the least likely to reach proficiency (McCall, Kingsbury, and Olson 2004). Further, the number of cusp students has been decreasing as a result of such targeting. In turn, U.S. DOE scores on NAEP exams have began to decline as the pool of these students declined. In 2006, the U.S. DOE reported its first overall decline in educational proficiency; the number of proficient students in both math and reading fell by 1.4 percent for fourth-grade reading, and 2 percent for fourth-grade mathematics (U.S. DOE 2006a).

Learning Environments Disrupted

Two components of the NCLB were designed to address the learning environment: teachers were mandated to improve classroom instruction by using scientific-based teaching methods and, should they fail to do so, parents are supposed to be given the opportunity for choosing another school. Yet, these mandates created unintended incentives for constraining curriculum, as well as inefficiencies in school funding. As such, while the benefits of school choice and scientific-based curriculum may induce improvement, the cost of such requirements has been detrimental to students, teachers, and schools.

Public school choice reallocates funding inefficiently. Under NCLB, schools must allow school choice and pay transportation fees if one subgroup fails to meet AYP. The federal government requires that schools receiving Title I funds keep twenty percent in reserve to pay for school choice transportation costs (LAE 2005). Transportation funds for school choice primarily come from a reserve of Title I funds (Jenner and Retner 2006). This takes money away from schools needing improvement and by doing so undermines the overarching goal of NCLB, making the policy inefficient. For example, districts like Broward County in Florida spent $1.5 million of its 2004 Title I money for school choice transportation costs, and Santa Ana County, California, spent $3 million of its Title I funds for the same (LAE 2005).

Standardized tests dictating teaching curriculum. Although the NCLB provides strong incentives for improving curriculum, critics claim that a cost of the NCLB is that tough mandates and standards on federal tests encourage educators to teach to assessment instruments. In essence, such mandates and standards create incentives to "teach to the test" instead of adapting state-of-the-art broad-based curriculum. For example, a Firestone 2001 study found that educator curriculum was driven by test material in regard to Elementary School Performance Assessments (ESPA) (Fusarelli 2004). The study found that ESPAs encourage educators to use scientifically based teaching methods and to allow more time for math and reading studies. Students are, however, losing valuable information regarding subjects not tested on NAEP and state-administered exams (Brulle 2005). Also, music, science, and social studies programs are being cut from schools to allow more time and funding for NAEP and state-administered exam subjects (Fusarelli 2004).

Improved Student Performance Questionable

The overarching goal of the NLCB is to close the achievement gap through mandating proficiencies. Measures of successfully accomplishing these objectives demonstrate, on face value, that proficiencies in mathematics and reading have improved since the NLCB implementation. Yet, there is increasing evidence that not only do these outcome measures fail to directly gauge improvement, they obscure the impact of accountability requirements and learning requirement mandates on student performance. As such, there is mounting evidence that the NCLB is ineffective in improving student performance and has actually created greater inequities by widening the achievement gap.

What rising state test scores represent. Rising state test scores are a result of additional time being spent on math and reading curriculum and instructors teaching to standardized tests (Rosenhall 2007). As shown in Figure 2, twenty-seven percent of schools significantly reduced social studies instruction to dedicate more class time to math and reading.

(FIGURE 2 ABOUT HERE)

In a continuing trend, twenty-two percent of schools reduced science instruction, twenty percent of schools reduced art and music instruction, and ten percent of schools reduced physical education instruction to make additional time for math and reading based instruction (CEP 2005). In a Wisconsin state survey, sixty-two percent of educators felt that the NCLB testing mandates required additional time spent on mathematics and reading and that the only way to accomplish that additional time was to cut other subjects (Zellmer, Frontier, and Pfeifer 2006, 45). In the same survey, eighty percent of educators felt that they were no longer teaching children how to think, but instead how to take standardized exams.

NCLB growth data misrepresents benefits. The Northwest Evaluation Association (NWEA) compiled assessment data from twenty-two states to determine if the NCLB AYP requirements were adequately assessing academic growth. NWEA assessments were primarily reading and math based and tracked individual student growth in ten of the twenty-two states. The data showed that some schools deemed proficient displayed small growth, while some schools deemed failing had high growth. The NWEA also found that students were performing better on NAEP standardized exams than they were on NWEA exams, which were broader exams (McCall, Kingsbury, and Olson 2004). While the U.S. DOE claims the achievement gap has narrowed, the NWEA study found that Hispanic, African American, and Native American students had less growth than Asian and White students during the 2003 school year (Kingsbury, Olson, and McCall 2004).

The NWEA consensus was that the NCLB did not have any positive effects on student growth (McCall, Kingsbury, and Olson 2004). The NWEA study contained four conclusions on the effects of the NCLB on students:

- State-level tests tend to improve observed achievement, although on broader exams student scores are falling.
- The NCLB has improved student achievement on standardized reading and mathematics assessments.
- Since the NCLB's enactment the achievement gap has been increasing.
- Students in ethnic groups that have shown achievement gaps in the past grow less under the NCLB, compared both with their own ethnic group and White students (Cronin, Kingsbury, McCall, and Bowe 2005).

Ethnic students left behind. Students with the same initial NAEP scores demonstrated different amounts of growth under the NCLB (Kingsbury, Olson, and McCall 2004). Although White students are among the highest achieving, achievement levels among Hispanic, African American, and Native American students grew noticeably less than White students. This was seen in grades three through eight and across all subject areas. The NWEA uses the RIT scale, which calculates growth relating to students yearly starting points. In the 2003–2004 school year for third-grade reading, Hispanic students beginning at 159, the lowest score on the RIT scale, increased fourteen points; White students increased their score by sixteen points. Hispanic students beginning at 212, the highest score on the RIT scale, increased two points, while White students increased four points (McCall, Kingsbury, and Olson 2004). Throughout the data, White students are increasing their RIT scores by two points more than Hispanic, African American, and Native American students. This expresses that the achievement gap under the NCLB has remained the same, making the NCLB ineffective (McCall, Kingsbury, and Olson 2004).

The U.S. DOE claims that the education gap is narrowing, but their data suggests that the education gap persists and, in some cases, is increasing when examining racial differences (U.S. DOE 2006b). As seen in Figure 3, for 2003 fourth-grade NAEP reading scores, the White student average was 287, while the average African American students received a score of 252.

(FIGURE 3 ABOUT HERE)

The education gap between the two groups of students was thirty-five points on the NAEP score. For 2005 fourth-grade reading NAEP scores, the average White student received a score of 288, while the average African American student received a score of 253. The education gap between the two groups of students is again thirty-five, expressing that four years after the enactment of the NCLB, the education gap between these two groups of students is the same as it was two years after NCLB enactment (U.S. DOE 2006a). The education gap between White and Hispanic students has been increasing; growing four points between 2003 and 2005. This suggests that the NCLB is inequitable; certain student groups, such as Hispanic and African American students, are not displaying growth equal to that of White students.

Barriers of Measuring the NCLB Policy Outcomes

In essence, while the NCLB has identified some policy success, critics have found much contrary and conflicting data to suggest that the policy is, at best, creating more problems than it has resolved. Some of these conflicting results could be related to the reliability of testing tools, variation in state measurement instruments, insufficiency of time to identify success, and/or budgetary constraints. These measurement problems create clarity issues for assessing the overall impact of the policy in reducing the achievement gap.

Statistically unreliable testing tools. The primary barrier to measuring NCLB success involves test score reliability. Test scores under the NCLB are not reliable, and three years prior to the passage of the law, a study found that seventy percent of year-to-year test score alteration is random variation (Mathis 2003). The alterations in the student body, especially when combined with random error, present substantial barriers to measuring the true educational benefits of the NCLB. A study of Massachusetts schools found that all schools with high testing gains one year did not have them the next year (Lee 2004). The same results were present in Florida, where sixty-nine percent of schools posting first-cycle testing gains had lost the testing gains by the second testing cycle (Mathis 2003).

State-determined proficiency marks. Each state determines its own proficiency mark, and the continuing trend is for states to lower their proficiency mark to obtain the objectives of the NCLB (Hoff 2002). Louisiana is one such state. If states set a proficiency mark too high, they begin with a great number of schools labeled as failing and will lose Title I funding (Hoff 2002). This is what led to sixteen states diluting proficiency standards after the enactment of the NCLB. Doing so makes it hard to measure improvement because, prior to the NCLB, many states held students to a higher expectation and standard (Kingsbury, Olson, and McCall 2004).

Rapidly placed sanctions. Sanctions placed on schools happen rapidly, which many school administrators argue do not give schools adequate time to address problems or show improvement (Rosenhall 2007). With annual sanctions, school administrators are forced to work with difficult sanction requirements, as opposed to focusing on educational improvement. For example, officials with the Grant School District in Lake Tahoe, California, have made alterations in local schools as a result of federal sanctions but argue that the pace of the changes is too quick to assess the effectiveness of previous sanctions (CEP 2007).

NCLB budget constraints.   Federal financial support to states for education is lower than what was authorized under the NCLB. As shown in Figure 4, for fiscal year (FY) 2003, $16 billion was authorized under the NCLB for Title I appropriations; however, only $11.4 billion was requested by President Bush, and only $11.7 billion was authorized by Congress (NEA 2004b).

(FIGURE 4 ABOUT HERE)

The NEA performed a study regarding NCLB objectives and the required financing and determined that in FY 2003, forty-three percent more funding was needed for Title I appropriations to reach NCLB objectives. The FY 2004 budget cut Title I funds by $6.15 billion, $81 million from Teacher Quality State Grants, $88 million in math-science partnerships, $15 million from advanced credentialing, and $63 million from Preparing Tomorrow's Teachers to Use Technology (PTTUT) (LAE 2005).

CONCLUSION

The NCLB is not an effective, efficient, or equitable public policy. The policy tools and objectives increased the achievement gap, school compliance is expensive, and the five performance-based objectives have not been accomplished. The major findings from this policy evaluation are:

- Annual Yearly Progress (AYP) does not measure student growth or educational quality.
- English as second language (ESL) student provisions and ninety-five percent student testing provisions are unrealistic.
- Educators structure their lessons towards mid-range students, resulting in an increasing achievement gap.
- Educator curriculum is directed towards standardized exams.
- Less class time is being spent on non-tested subjects, resulting in a less broad education.
- States have lowered expectations to comply with federal proficiency standards.
- States and localities spend their own money to meet NCLB federal mandates.
- The achievement gap between different subgroups of students is persisting, and in certain groups increasing.
- Policy success is difficult to measure because of test score reliability.
- The funding authorized under the NCLB has not been delivered.

The regulatory policy tools used by the U.S. DOE have impeded the ability of the NCLB to reach any of its performance-based objectives and its overarching goal to close the achievement gap. The NCLB does hold educators accountable, but the accountability standard is not defined, the means to measure progress are inadequate, and testing scores are unreliable. Educators are forced to restructure lesson plans towards NAEP-tested subjects and towards students who can statistically show the most improvement. This diminishes educational subject content and furthers the education gap between certain groups of students, most significantly ESL students.

The NCLB was not a commitment by the federal government to invest in education, but an attempt to force educational improvement through accountability and standardization. Accountability and standardization were not an effective means for educational improvement and have hindered progress. Education is a large policy domain in which there are numerous differentiating factors between groups that education serves. By holding educators accountable to sanctions, the federal government is forcing educators to use discriminatory teaching methods to show statistical improvement. This makes the NCLB inequitable; the most statistical improvement can be gained from teaching to cusp students. The NCLB testing requirements and data collection mandates make the policy inefficient for localities and states; the federal mandates are expensive and are not beneficial to students. The achievement gap persists and in some cases is increasing between certain student groups and subgroups, making the NCLB inequitable and ineffective.

REFERENCES

American Federation of Teachers (AFT). 2004a. *NCLB: Its problems and promises.* http://www.aft.org (accessed February 21, 2007).

American Federation of Teachers (AFT). 2004b. *New NCLB rules: Half-measures put schools at risk.* http://www.aft.org/pubs-reports/american_teacher/2004/mayjune/nclb.html (accessed September 17, 2006).

Bailey, K. Stephen, and Edith K. Mosher. 1968. *ESEA: The office of education administers a law.* Syracuse, NY: Syracuse University Press.

Brulle, Andrew. 2005. What can you say when research and policy collide? *Phi Delta Kappan* 86 (6): 433–437. http://www.ebsco.com (accessed April 17, 2007).

Brunner, Borgna, and Elissa Haney. 2006. *Civil rights timeline: Milestones in the modern civil rights movement.* Upper Saddle River, NJ. Pearson Education. http://www.infoplease.com/spot/civilrightstimeline1.html (accessed March 1, 2007).

Center on Education Policy (CEP). 2005. *NCLB: Narrowing the curriculum.* Washington, DC: CEP Publications.

Center on Education Policy (CEP). 2007. *Number of schools facing restructuring, No Child Left Behind Act's last consequence increases sharply.* Washington, DC: CEP Publications.

Cronin, John, Gage Kingsbury, Martha McCall, and Branin Bowe. 2005. *The impact of the No Child Left Behind Act on student achievement and growth.* Lake Oswego, OR: NWEA Growth Research Database.

Fusarelli, Lance. 2004. The potential impact of the No Child Left Behind Act on equity and diversity in American education. *Educational Policy* 18 (1): 71–95. http://www.ebsco.com (accessed March 2, 2007).

Hoff, David. 2002. States revise the meaning of proficient. *Education Week* 2 (4): 110–112. http://www.ebscohost.com (accessed February 21, 2007).

Jehlen, Alain. 2007. Testing how the sausage is made. *NEA Today* 25 (7): 29–37.

Jennings, Jack, and Diane Rentner. 2006. How public schools are impacted by No Child Left Behind. *Education Digest* 72 (4): 4–9. http://www.ebscohost.com (accessed February 14, 2007).

Kingsbury, Gage, Allan Olson, and Martha McCall. 2004. *Adequate yearly progress using the hybrid success model: A suggested improvement to No Child Left Behind.* Lake Oswego, OR: NWEA Growth Research Database.

Lee, Jaekyung. 2004. How feasible is adequate yearly progress? Simulations of school AYP uniform averaging and safe harbor under the No Child Left Behind Act. *Education* 12 (14): 112–132.

Louisiana Association of Educators (LAE). 2005. *ESEA/NCLB funding facts.* http://www.lae.org/legislative/esea_funding.html (accessed February 14, 2007).

Mathis, William. 2003. NCLB costs and benefits. *Phi Delta Kappan* 84 (9): 679–687. http://www.ebscohost.com (accessed April 17, 2007).

Mayers, Camille. 2006. Public Law 107-110 No Child Left Behind Act of 2001: Support or threat to education as a fundamental right? *Education* 3 (126): 449–461. http://www.ebscohost.com (accessed February 11, 2007).

McCall, Martha, Gage Kingsbury, and Allan Olson. 2004. *Individual growth and school success.* Lake Oswego, OR: NWEA Growth Research Database.

National Education Association (NEA). 2004a. *Maze of education regulations produces bizarre results.* http://www.nea.org/lawsuit/absurdities.html (accessed February 18, 2007).

National Education Association (NEA). 2004b. *No Child Left Behind: The funding gap in ESEA and other federal education programs.* http://www.nea.org (accessed April 26, 2007).

Neel, Richard. 2006. Consider the opportunities: A response to No Child Left Behind. *Education and Treatment of Children* 29 (4): 533–547. http://www.ebscohost.com (accessed February 3, 2007).

New Hampshire Department of Education (N.H. DOE). 2003. *No Child Left Behind Act of 2001.* New Hampshire, Government Printing Office. http://www.ed.state.nh .us/education/index.html (accessed February 28, 2007).

North Central Regional Education Laboratory (NCREL). 2003. *Resources for implementing the NCLB.* Naperville, IL: Learning Point Associates. http://www.ncrel. org/policy/feature/nclbresources.html (accessed February 20, 2007).

Peterson, Paul, and Martin R. West, ed. 2003. *No child left behind? The politics and practice of school accountability.* Washington, DC. Brookings Institution Press.

Public Law 107-110. *No Child Left Behind Act of 2001.*

Rosenhall, Laurel. 2007. *Big changes seen under No Child Left Behind.* Sacramento, CA: Sacramento Bee Publications.

Rudalevige, Andrew. 2002. *Accountability and avoidance in the Bush education plan: The No Child Left Behind Act of 2001.* Cambridge, MA: Kennedy School of Government. http://www.eric.ed.gov (accessed October 31, 2006).

Rudalevige, Andrew. 2003. The politics of the No Child Left Behind Act: Did the need to build consensus give too much leeway to state capitals? *Education Next* 4 (11): 62–81.

U.S. Congress. 2002. House of Representatives. Committee on Education and the Workforce. *Implementation of the No Child Left Behind Act.* 107th Cong. 2nd Sess. Washington, DC: Government Printing Office.

U.S. Congress. 2004a. House of Representatives. *107 bill tracking of H.R. 1.* 107th Cong. 1st Sess. Washington DC: Government Printing Office. http://www.lexis-nexis.com (accessed September 20, 2006).

U.S. Congress. 2004b. Senate. Committee on Health, Education, Labor and Pensions. *107 bill tracking of S.1.* 2001. 107th Cong. 1st Sess. Washington, DC: Government Printing Office. http://www.leisnexis.com (accessed September 21, 2006).

U.S. Congress. 2006. House of Representatives. Committee on Education and the Workforce. *No Child Left Behind: Can growth models ensure improved education for all students?* 109th Cong. 2nd Sess. Washington, DC: Government Printing Office.

U.S. Department of Education (U.S. DOE). 2004. *Paige details No Child Left Behind implementation progress.* Washington, DC: Government Printing Office. http://www.ed.gov/print/news/pressreleases/2004/02/02242004.html (accessed February 14, 2007).

U.S. Department of Education (U.S. DOE). 2005. *No Child Left Behind: A road map to state implementation.* Washington, DC: Government Printing Office. http://www.ed.gov (accessed February 12, 2007).

U.S. Department of Education (U.S. DOE). 2006a. *2005 assessment results: The nation's report card.* Washington, DC: Government Printing Office.

U.S. Department of Education (U.S. DOE). 2006b. *Fiscal year 2006 performance and accountability report.* Washington, DC: Government Printing Office.

U.S. Government Accountability Office (GAO). 2004. *Unfunded mandates: Analysis of reform act coverage.* Washington, DC: Government Printing Office.

U.S. Government Accountability Office (GAO). 2006. *No Child Left Behind Act: Education actions needed to improve local implementation and state evaluation of supplemental educational services.* Washington, DC: Government Printing Office. http://www.lexisnexis.com (accessed February 14, 2006).

Williams E. Mary. 2005. *Education: Opposing viewpoints.* Detroit, MI: Greenhaven Press.

Zellmer, Michael, Anthony Frontier, and Denise Pheifer. 2006. What are NCLBs instructional costs? *Educational Leadership* 64 (3): 43–46. http://www.ebsco.com (accessed April 17, 2007).

Figure 1: Average 4th-Grade Students Mathematics NAEP Scores Between HOUSSE Certificated Instructors, Non-HOUSSE Certified Instructors and States Not Offering HOUSSE Certification

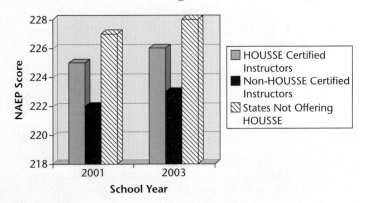

Data taken from the Institute of Education Sciences and the National Center of Education Statistics as part of the United States Department of Education. 2006. *2005 assessment results: The nation's report card.* Washington, DC. Government Printing Office. Graph created by Joshua Ford.

Figure 2:   Percentage of Districts That Have Reduced Instructional Time in Some Subject Areas to Make More Time for Reading, Mathematics, and Language Arts

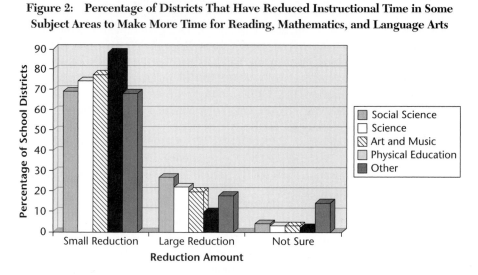

Data taken from the Center for Education Policy (CEP). 2005. NCLB: Narrowing the curriculum. Washington, DC: CEP Publications. Graph created by Joshua Ford.

Figure 3:   Average 4th-Grade Student Scores on the Reading NAEP Exam by Racial Group 1990–2005

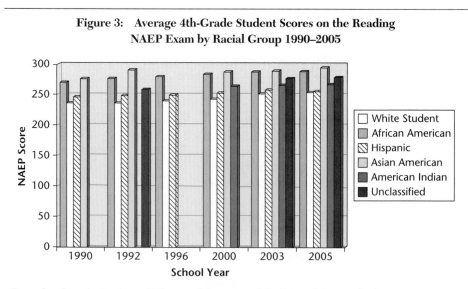

Data taken from the Institute of Educational Sciences and the National Center of Education Statistics as part of the United States Department of Education. 2006. 2005 *Assessment results: The nation's report card*. Washington, DC: Government Printing Office. Graph created by Joshua Ford.

Figure 4: NCLB Title I Funding for Fiscal Year 2003 and 2004 by Amount Authorized by the NCLB, Amount Requested by the Executive Office, the Amount Appropriated by Congress, and the Amount Needed for Schools to Reach NCLB Objectives

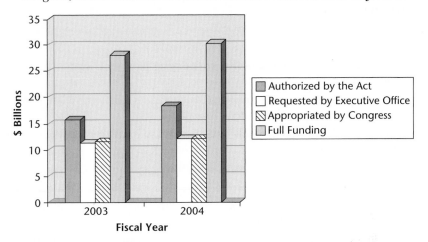

Data taken from the National Education Association (NEA). 2004. *No Child Left Behind: The funding gap in ESEA and other federal education programs*. Annapolis Junction, MD: NEA Publications. Graph Created by Joshua Ford.

Researching and Writing a Policy Recommendation

1. **Identify a social problem by examining newspapers or observing your environment.**
   - Choose a new problem (e.g., AIDS).
   - Or choose an old problem (e.g., homelessness).
2. **Conduct an evaluation of a policy addressing problems similar to the problem identified.**
   - For new problems, examine policies closely related to the problem or that indirectly address the problem identified.
   - For old problems, examine policies currently enforced that directly or indirectly address the problem.
   - Be sure to identify the inadequacies of existing government policies examined.
     - This step will aid in avoiding proposing a policy solution that is already in force.
     - This step provides the depth and breadth necessary to recommend policy solutions.
3. **Identify the goals or objectives to be achieved in an ideal solution to the problem.**
   - What is to be done about the problem?
   - What do experts say should be done about it?
   - Rank the objectives by order of importance.
   - What desired outcome is most important?
4. **Identify alternative solutions proposed to solve the problem.**
   - What public actions do experts propose to deal with the problem?
     - Identify at least three alternatives.
     - Know the position and qualifications of each source.
   - Identify which alternatives address the objectives and outcomes stated as being most important.
     - Clearly distinguish between each alternative's objectives.
     - Be sure to identify undesirable objectives stated by the experts that are supplemental or complementary to those that are desirable.
   - What are the proposed outcomes of the alternative solutions?
     - Identify the expected outcomes of each alternative.
     - Clearly distinguish between outcomes that are desirable and undesirable.
     - Match up the stated objectives with the outcomes from each alternative.
   - Rank-order the alternatives by preferred objective and outcome.
     - Be able to justify which alternative best fits the objectives and outcomes preferred.
     - Clearly distinguish between objectives and expected outcomes.
5. **Who do experts say should perform the actions?**
   - Identify the level of government that will be responsible for the policy.
   - Identify the government agency that will implement the policy.

6. Identify the costs and benefits of each alternative.

- Examine all the real and implied costs.
  - Describe how the costs will be measured.
  - Identify the data source used to measure costs.
  - Identify and justify three real costs.
  - Identify and justify three implied costs.
- Examine all the real and implied benefits.
  - Describe how the benefits will be measured.
  - Identify the data source used to measure benefits.
  - Identify and justify three real benefits.
  - Identify and justify three implied benefits.

7. Recommend the alternative that provides the greatest benefit for the least cost.

- Decide which benefits are necessary.
- Be able to justify all acceptable costs to achieve the benefits.

8. Identify at least five important political actors or players who are likely to either support or oppose the solution.

- Be sure to identify some players who are supporters and some who are part of the opposition.
- Identify the issue position, the power, and the priority of each player listed.

9. When writing the recommendation, include a discussion, in order, of the following:

- An executive summary that includes:
  - A brief description of the social problem.
  - The context.
  - Previous attempts to solve the problem.
  - The recommendation.
- Headings identifying the discussion of:
  - The issue.
  - The historical context/previous or current policy responses.
  - Evaluation (critique and assessment) of previous policy responses.
  - The objectives of the ideal solution with justification.
  - The critique of available alternatives with comparative cost/benefit analysis.
  - The complete recommendation with justification.
  - A conclusion that restates briefly the context of the social problem and justification of the solution.
- A list of sources for all borrowed ideas, arguments, and data. Use tables, charts, and graphs to illustrate data where necessary.

Policy Recommendation Guide and Checkoff Sheet

Executive Summary
- Identify the policy problem (should include bullet points).
- Summarize previous attempts to remedy the problem.
- Summarize the recommendations (should include bullet points).

Problems and Issues Identified
- Describe the social problem thoroughly.
- Describe how the problems were identified.
- Describe how the problems became issues.

Historical Context/Previous Policy Responses
- Identify and explain, chronologically, the who, what, where, when, how, and why (politics) related to getting the problem/issue on the governmental/decision agenda.
- Specifically, what types of individuals supported or did not support a response to the problem/issue?
- Describe the purpose of the tools or instruments used as policy responses to the problems/issues.
- Do the goals of the policy solution directly relate to the identified problems/issues? Why or why not?
- Specifically, what goals, problems, and/or issues are these tools supposed to address, remedy, fix, or resolve?
- Particularly, who are the targets of these tools?
- Explain why these tools were chosen over others.

Evaluation (Critique and Assessment) of Previous Policy Responses
- Based on the research, do the policy responses adequately address the identified problems? Why or why not?
- Are there unresolved problems or issues that have been identified but not addressed by the policy response?
- Based on the research, was the policy outcome worth the costs associated with the policy response?

Ideal Solution
- What problems or issues still need remedial action?
- What do experts or targets say is the most desired outcome?

Cost/Benefit Analysis of Available Alternative Solutions
- How does each alternative solution address (or not) the unresolved problems or issues identified?
- Compare the expected benefits of each proposed solution to the ideal solution.
- Compare the costs of each proposed solution to the ideal solution.

Recommendations

- State specifically what actions are recommended.
- Identify which problem/issue is resolved by each action.
- Provide a justification for each action chosen.
- Provide a cost/benefit analysis with suggestions for how success will be measured.

Conclusions About the Problem and Justification of the Proposed Solution

- Identify important inadequacies of the past or current policy responses.
- Restate why these inadequacies must be addressed.
- Summarize the reasons why the recommendations are the best way to address these inadequacies.

POLICY RECOMMENDATION: PRESERVING ENDANGERED SPECIES

By
Kari Carter
POLS471B
Public Policy Analysis
Dr. Schmidt
May 2, 2006

EXECUTIVE SUMMARY

In developing environmental policy, government is faced with balancing the incompatibility of conservation and commerce. Industrialism is known for exploiting the environment at the expense of conservation and, accordingly, environmentalists strengthen the fight for environmental quality. Environmental quality is a concern for all individuals who desire to preserve a nation of natural amenities for future generations.

The Endangered Species Act (ESA) was developed to reverse the trend of disappearing species as a consequence of economic growth. Protecting endangered species is a valuable goal in the maintenance of ecosystems because biodiversity is an integral component of environmental sustainability. To this end, the ESA provided that a regulatory agency develop the tools necessary to protect endangered species.

The ESA was structured for species protection using the endangered species list, critical habitat designations, and recovery plans. The policy places a low priority on economic considerations for protecting endangered species. Consequently, more than thirty years since it was enacted, the ESA is considered unsuccessful. ESA problems include:

- Program tools are not advancing the protection or preservation of species.
- The constraints on commerce and private land owners have generated significant legal litigation.
- The policy does not foster citizen participation in the conservation of species.

Previous attempts to remedy the problem of disappearing species include placing species on the endangered list to track status of species populations and trigger regulatory actions. Additional attempts involve regulatory programs that specifically involve recovery plans designed to restore species populations and critical habitat designations to restrict land use activities. All of these remedies revolve around the application of sound science, which is a difficult measure to establish because nature is always changing.

Several alternatives exist for addressing the problems of the ESA. They range from maintaining the status quo by leaving the policy as it is, implementing solutions to reinvent the policy tools, and seeking outside assistance for the development of sound science. Based on a cost/benefit analysis of each of these alternatives, the following changes are recommended:

- Develop a sound definition of science for species listing.
- Structure recovery plans to include guidelines and time lines for monitoring species status.
- Create incentives for voluntary and cooperative species conservation efforts.

Implementing these recommendations will solve many of the problems with the ESA. First, the species listing process will increase efficiency by focusing attention on species facing greatest risk of endangerment. Second, guidelines and time lines for recovery plans will improve effectiveness by promoting restoration of species populations. Finally, incentives for public conservation efforts will foster species preservation and greater equity in participation in environmental conservation.

PROBLEMS AND ISSUES IDENTIFIED

The Endangered Species Act (ESA) was signed into law by President Richard M. Nixon in December 1973. This act amended the Endangered Species Preservation Act of 1966 and the Endangered Species Conservation Act of 1969 (Smith n.d., 2). The ESA strengthened federal species protection programs incorporating land use restrictions and increased penalties for displacing endangered species (U.S. Fish and Wildlife Service 2005). ESA funding authorization expired on October 1, 1992 and Congress has continued funding for species protection programs through the discretionary budget (Buck, Corn, and Baldwin 2002, 1).

Description of Environmental Problem

Public concern for species preservation is tied to the larger issue of environmental conservation (Congress and the Nation 1969, 784). Economic growth is poisoning animals and humans, compromising atmospheric conditions, producing cancer causing pollutions, and destroying land and species in the process (Congress and the Nation 1977, 288). Industrialists and private land owners have been sufficiently constrained by land use restrictions imposed by the ESA and seek relief through the judicial process (Committee on Resources n.d., 1).

Environmentalists were the most highly visible critics of the impact of growth on the environment and have routinely brought the problem to the attention of policy-makers and the public. Environmentalists are concerned about land consumption because natural habitats are being disrupted and certain species are facing extinction (Sierra Club n.d.). Once a species becomes extinct it ceases to be available for human enjoyment or as raw materials used to develop medicinal remedies, and ecosystems are potentially irreversibly imbalanced (Myers 1976). The concern for endangered species extends to concern for human species and the ability to sustain a quality environment for future generations (National Wildlife Federation n.d., 4).

Species Extinction as a Political Issue

While environmental protection has clearly been on the governmental agenda for some time, support for addressing species extinction is related to recent changes in the rate of extinction. The rate of species extinction is at the highest level ever recorded (National Academy of Sciences 1995, 1). Species extinction is believed to threaten overall environmental diversity. Protecting species promotes environmental sustainability because disruption of biodiversity in one species intrinsically leads to disruption of biodiversity in species further up the food chain (Center for Biological Diversity n.d.a, 1).

HISTORICAL CONTEXT AND PREVIOUS POLICY RESPONSES

The ESA has its origins in the environmental movement, but its legitimacy as a policy has its foundations in the mid- to late-1960s executive and congressional initiatives. Its goals of species preservation are clearly linked with the problem associated with increasing rate of species extinction. The policy provisions, notably land use restrictions and penalties for species disruption, are enforceable regulatory tools for minimizing the impact of economic growth on endangered species.

Environmental Agenda Setting

Environmental issues were gaining national importance from the mid-1960s through the 1970s, particularly in presidential administrations. Environmental preservation was on presidential agendas and was the focus of presidential initiatives. For example, in 1965, President Johnson presented a platform that valued the relationship between humankind and the environment (Congress and the Nation 1969, 476). In addition, during the first Nixon administration and with his support, Congress demonstrated federal commitment to environmental protection by enacting the National Environmental Policy Act of 1969, Clean Air Act of 1970, Federal Environmental Pesticide Control Act of 1972 and the Marine Mammal Protection Act of 1972 (Stathis 1992, 277–285).

During the second Nixon administration, government trust was eroded by the Watergate scandal and the criminal investigation of Vice President Spiro Agnew (Welch, Gruhl, Comer, and Rigdon 2005). The pessimistic political climate, combined with the American death toll from the Vietnam War, a national energy crisis, and a deepening economic recession, created a dismal national climate (Stathis 1992, 287). In an attempt to appease the American public, President Nixon responded with a request for further legislation to protect endangered species.

Political Support for Protecting Endangered Species

With the support of President Nixon, and mounting congressional support for addressing environmental protection issues, the ESA was drafted and introduced into Congress. The origins of the ESA began with the U.S. Senate passing S1983 by a unanimous vote, which also contained amendments exempting Alaskan Natives because requiring species protection would present a risk to human survival (United States Code 1973a, 994). The House of Representatives cleared S1983, attaching HR37 to discourage the destruction of critical habitat (*Congressional Quarterly* 1974, 672). Consensus was reached in the conference bill that included these critical components, clearing the way for congressional approval and the president's signature.

Tools Used as Policy Responses

The goal of the ESA is to protect endangered species in a variety of ways. The goal of species protection is tied to species preservation and the larger issue of environment conservation. The ESA strengthened federal species protection programs through land use restrictions and increased penalties for displacing endangered species. The regulatory provisions or tools authorized in the policy are designed to address the impact of increases in economic growth on species preservation. According to a Natural Resources Conservation Service (NRCS) report there was a 23 percent increase in land development for the ten-year period from 1987 to 1997 (U.S. Department of Agriculture 2000, 7). Land use restrictions are extended to private land owners who possess habitat where endangered species are found (U.S. Department of Agriculture 1997, 1–3). The disappearance of land represents a loss of species habitat, a primary concern for endangered and threatened species.

More specifically, the policy authorizes a variety of provisions for monitoring and tracking endangered species. In particular, the U.S. Fish and Wildlife Service (USFWS) functions as the regulatory agency for ESA administration for implementing regulations and tracking compliance for species protection (U.S. Fish and Wildlife Service 2005). Species protection is accomplished through the endangered and threatened species listing process, critical habitat designations provide a safe haven for species preservation, and recovery plans are designed to stabilize species populations (U.S. Fish and Wildlife Service 2005). To monitor compliance, the USFWS uses an endangered species list as the primary policy instrument to identify and track endangered species (United States Code 1973b, 3002). Subsequent policy responses to further species protection include critical habitat designations, species recovery plans, and the addition of threatened species to categories protected by the ESA (U.S. Fish and Wildlife Service 2005).

Finally, a biological assessment is required to list species; listing triggers critical habitat designations and recovery plan development (Buck, Corn, and Baldwin 2002, 8). Performing biological assessments, in consideration of individual species needs, establishes the scientific basis for species programs (Marano and Lieberman 2005, 1).

Targets of the Policy

The ESA targets any person or organization involved in land use activities negatively affecting species populations (Sierra Club 2006, 2). Industrial land owners are a central target for land development and private citizens are targeted for general land use because the largest percentage of endangered species exist on private land (U.S. Department of Agriculture 1997, 1). In addition, government at all levels is a target for public land management practices (National Wildlife Federation n.d., 1). Specifically, the USFWS is a target for the burden of ESA implementation (Environmental Defense 2004, 2).

Why Regulation?

To resolve the conflict of administrative agency regulatory responsibility and provide tools for ESA implementation, Congress prescribed specific agency duties and appropriated substantial funding to support additional government activities (United States Code 1973b). Regulatory and management jurisdiction over marine species was delegated to the Department of Commerce to coincide with agency authority granted in the Reorganization Plan No. 4 of 1970 (National Oceanic and Atmospheric Administration 1994, 1). Other fish and wildlife species regulation and management resides with the Department of Interior to utilize the endangered species list framework established in earlier 1966 and 1969 legislation (United States Code 1973b, 3002).

The endangered species list is used to track the number of species needing protection (National Wildlife Federation n.d., 1). The Interior Secretary is afforded discretion in endangered species listing and delisting processes to prevent species extinction (United States Code 1973a, 982). ESA tools were structured to give the regulatory agency enormous power over protecting endangered species, and economic considerations are secondary (Association of Consulting Foresters 2004, 1). To strengthen regulatory activities the USFWS created critical habitat designations to restrict land use activities where endangered species are found and crafted recovery plans to promote long-term species protection (Center for Biological Diversity n.d.c, 2).

EVALUATION OF PREVIOUS POLICY RESPONSES

The ESA policy responses promote and encourage the protection of species with few limits to the number of species that can be listed (Smith n.d., 3). Emphasis is placed on policy violations, not provisions, to encourage a proactive approach to species protection (U.S. Congress 1995, 11). Intuitively, policy success is primarily measured by species delisting. Another measure of success is to prevent species from being placed on the list because they do not need protection (DeAlessi n.d., 3).

ESA Policy Failures

The main goal of the ESA is to preserve and protect endangered species. To accomplish the goal, the policy authorizes species evaluations, placement of a species on endangered lists, and enforcement of compliance with protections. Yet, because the process is not linked to scientific measures, the policy is inadequate in species protection.

Subjectivity of listing. The ESA does not specify scientific standards for species evaluations; scientific findings are left to agency discretion (United States Code 1973b, 2991). Species listing can involve submitting a petition accompanied by a scientific case for listing, an agency request for species review, or an emergency request indicating a species is threatened or endangered (Small Business Administration n.d., 1–2). As a result, environmentalist groups have effectively diverted government resources away from species protection programs and onto responding to legal litigation for determining the criteria (Marano and Lieberman 2005, 2).

More importantly, because the evaluation is subjective and species tend to be listed according to regulatory agency preferences, the list has grown exponentially (Brown and Shogren 1998, 7). For example, the number of the listed species has grown to nearly 1,300 due to the vague standard of scientific data used to classify endangered and threatened species (Marano and Lieberman, 2005, 1). The data in Figure 1 illustrates growth of the endangered species list from 1980–2005.

(FIGURE 1 ABOUT HERE)

The number of species on the endangered list has grown from 281 in 1980 to 1,272 in 2005 (U.S. Fish and Wildlife Service 2006, 2). The positive linear trend is strong through the year 2000. Figures indicate a 36 percent increase in listed species from 1980 to 1985, a 55 percent increase from 1985 to 1990, and a 61 percent increase from 1990 to 1995. The increase is less, 29 percent, for the period between 1995 and 2000 and drops to 2 percent between 2000 and 2005. Albeit species listing has slowed, the list is still growing and there are a significant number of species to manage.

Lack of emphasis on species recovery. When a species is placed on the endangered list, fear of extinction triggers critical habitat designations and the development of a recovery plan. The ESA is well structured for species protection but fails to place adequate emphasis on species recovery as a means for species preservation (Smith n.d., 2). Recovery plans are supposed to ensure species populations are stabilized. Recovery plans exist for approximately 80 percent of species, yet only twelve species have been delisted (Environmental Defense 2004, 2). Delisting occurs when species populations have recovered sufficiently. Species are not benefiting from recovery plans; 39 percent are classified with unknown status, 21 percent are marked with declining status, and 6 percent of species are categorized as improving (Marano and Lieberman 2005, 1). In addition, recovery plans lack tracking mechanisms, making it difficult to evaluate respective performance in promoting species recovery (National Wildlife Federation n.d., 2–3). Finally, recovery plans lack time lines for species recovery and are not required in certain circumstances (Buck, Corn, and Baldwin 2002, 4).

Absence of incentives for compliance. Finally, the absence of incentives for species protection does not encourage compliance with the ESA (Committee on Resources n.d., 6). Incorporating incentives to promote ESA compliance reduces resistance to regulatory activities and fosters public willingness to control the use of natural resources (Smith n.d.). This problem is critical in that species listing triggers the designation of critical habitat (Brown and Shogren 1998, 8). Critical habitat designation places restrictions on land use, which results in a restriction of activities of land owners in restricted areas that feature physical or biological characteristics essential to species preservation (Ryan and Schuler 1998, 4). This, in essence, creates disincentives for compliance.

Importantly, designations of critical habit create inequities between land owners. Ideally, land owners are affected equally, but land possessed by private owners contains 90 percent of species listed as endangered or threatened (Brown and Shogren 1998, 3). With the largest percentage of endangered species residing on private property, private citizens have the most to lose in complying with the ESA (Brown and Shogren 1998, 3). Yet, private citizens owning property for aesthetic purposes make stronger candidates for species preservation (Environmental Defense 2004). Statements taken before the Task Force on Endangered Species Act suggest constituent interest in species protection is likely to wane as mitigating circumstances create economic hardships for land owners (U.S. Congress 1995). Unless the ESA is restructured to alleviate such unintended consequences, it is not likely to accomplish the original intent of species preservation.

Unresolved Problems with Species Protection

In addition to failing in setting attainable and measurable goals for species protection, the ESA encompasses a couple of problems not resolved by current legislation. These problems involve cross-jurisdictional inconsistencies and provisions that are overly broad. As a result, the ESA has created ambiguity and confusion in species protection.

Inconsistent evaluative measures. The USFWS and National Marine Fisheries Service (NMFS) determine sufficient circumstances for species listing, yet the agencies define a candidate species differently. The USFWS defines a candidate species by the amount of species evidence they have received and the NMFS defines a candidate species as one with which they are concerned, but require more information before listing (Ryan and Schuler 1998, 1-2). The criteria for establishing a species as endangered or threatened need to be consistently evaluated against the biological needs of individual species (National Academy of Sciences 1995, 2).

Overly broad preservation objectives. Scientists acknowledge the value of species preservation and maintaining ecosystem balance to advance public health, and at the same time, they propose it is impossible to save every living thing (U.S. Congress 1995, 166). Critics of the policy indicate that objective criteria for determining which species to preserve are important for creating balance. The wide use of critical habitat designation is not required to preserve species as long as a core area is reserved to protect endangered species through recovery plans (National Academy of Sciences 1995, 2). Recovery plans are effective tools to promote sustainability as long as they include objective, measurable criteria that lead to species recovery (Marano and Lieberman 2005, 3).

Value of ESA Outcomes Compared to Its Costs

The primary outcome of the ESA is that species protection has been provided for a greater number of species as the endangered species list grows larger. List size has increased significantly as a result of citizen environmental organizations mobilizing to address environmental problems exacerbated by economic growth (Fowler and Shaiko 1987, 487). In that sense, the policy has provided the expected benefit of species preservation. Yet, a larger endangered species list has led to an expanded restriction of land use. Costs associated with restricted land use can be expressed in terms of the reduced productivity of land and its uncompensated financial burden on private citizens (U.S. Congress 1995, 4). As such, policy implementation has been hindered by compliance costs borne by private individuals and oversight costs and problems in administrative agencies (Brown and Shogren 1998).

IDEAL SOLUTION

The ESA has created complex problems through efforts to protect threatened and endangered species, yet the ESA is needed for promoting environmental conservation (National Wildlife Federation n.d., 2). A reauthorization of the policy is appropriate provided that species programs are improved to align the methods and management of species preservation with overall conservation efforts. Particularly, the infusion of reasonable scientific guidelines into species protection programs is essential for achieving ESA objectives (National Academy of Sciences 1995, 2). Some of these reforms are already on the congressional agenda, while others still need to be addressed.

Improving Methods and Management: TESRA

The most important goal is to protect endangered species (Committee on Resources n.d., 1). Statements before the Task Force on Endangered Species Act reflect that members of the House of Representatives generally support species protection (U.S. Congress 1995). Environmentalists are adamant that strict land use regulation is essential to retard species extinction (Center for Biological Diversity n.d.a). Scientists agree that species protection contributes positively to biodiversity and environmental preservation (U.S. Congress 1995).

In response to these testimonies, Resources Chairman California Republican Richard Pombo sponsored H.R.3824: Threatened and Endangered Species Act of 2005 (TESRA), which the House passed on September 29, 2005 (Congressional Research Service 2005a, 1). TESRA proposes to enhance species protection by applying scientific guidelines to the species listing process, creating objective and measurable species recovery plans, compensating land owners for loss of land use, developing cooperative recovery agreements, and reducing the use of critical habitat designations (Congressional Research Service 2005b). Former Chairman of the U.S. Senate Committee on Environment and Public Works, Idaho Republican Senator Michael Crapo, sponsored Senate bill S.2110 as joint legislation supporting TESRA; the bill was read twice and remains on referral to the Committee on Finance (Library of Congress 2005, 1).

Stabilization of Species

While TESRA addresses the problems of inconsistency in methods and management in ESA, it does not directly address the problem of promoting species stabilization. A thorough reform of the ESA would create recovery programs that promote stabilization of species populations (Dalmia 2005, 1). Scientific experts suggest responsive species protection involves establishing recovery plans in a timely manner and preserving a core habitat supporting species survival for a period of twenty-five to fifty years (National Academy of Sciences 1995, 2). The Bald Eagle Act of 1940 preceded the ESA in species conservation efforts and more than sixty-five years later the bird is under consideration for delisting from the endangered species list due to positive species management practices (U.S. Fish and Wildlife Service n.d., 1). The process, designed to foster preservation of a national symbol, has taken longer than the average expected recovery plan of forty-two years (Center for Biological Diversity n.d.d, 1).

Linking Designations to Recovery Plans

While TESRA reduces the use of critical habitat designation, it is important that reforms retain the authority for these designations. Critical habitat designations are an important component for achieving preservation goals. These designations are problematic because they are not linked to a plan. In fact, courts ruled critical habitat designations unlawful because the practice does not consider species recovery (Buck, Corn, and Baldwin 2002, 3). Recovery plans are an effective tool to promote sustainability as long as they include objective, measurable criteria that lead to species recovery (Marano and Lieberman 2005, 3). Linking critical habitat designations to a species recovery plan creates greater opportunity for coherent integration of land constraints and species preservation.

COST/BENEFIT ANALYSIS OF ALTERNATIVE SOLUTIONS

Reforms to ESA need to create a balance of interests and improve coherence in the provisions designed for species preservation; anything less would not resolve existing problems in protecting endangered species. Yet, balancing interests and improving coherence has varying costs and benefits. The difficulty in addressing interests and coherence is that environmental value is incalculable, according to Brown and Shogren (1998, 4), and the legislative intent of the ESA is to arrest and reverse the rate of species extinction at any cost (National Academy of Sciences 1995, 3). As such, reforming ESA may not be as well supported as simply leaving it as is.

Based on this perspective, there are three competing alternatives for addressing problems related to the ESA involving balancing interests and improving coherence. The first alternative, *Maintaining the Status Quo*, is to continue the current policy. Leaving the ESA unaltered continues a policy that is unsuccessful in recovering species (Marano and Lieberman 2005, 1). The second alternative, *Adopt TESRA Reforms*, is to amend the ESA with recommendations proposed in TESRA. Amending the ESA with TESRA recommendations is a responsive solution because it requires consistent scientific criteria for species listing, objective and measurable recovery plans, rewards for cooperative conservation efforts, and reductions in critical habitat designations (Congressional Research Service 2005b, 1). It solves most of the management and methods problems associated with the ESA. The third alternative, *TESRA Plus Guidelines*, is to amend the ESA with recommendations proposed in TESRA, but have the scientific guidelines for implementing the policy developed outside of the administering regulatory agencies. This would fully address the management and methods problems associated with the ESA and improve the scientific coherence of its provisions by obtaining scientific guidelines from a panel of experts outside the regulatory agency.

Evaluating alternatives for addressing ESA problems requires an examination of benefits and costs expected by each alternative on the basis of internal and external, tangible and intangible, primary and secondary expected impacts from each choice. Internal and external benefits refer to costs and benefits that have an impact within or outside the target area of species preservation. Tangible and intangible costs and benefits are those impacts which are directly measurable in concrete terms related or indirectly measurable in abstract terms. Finally, primary and secondary costs and benefits are first intended consequences and second-order unintended consequences.

Expected Benefits of Proposed Alternatives

The expected benefits of each alternative are compared in Table 1.

[TABLE 1 ABOUT HERE]

Maintaining the status quo. As shown in Table 1, leaving the ESA unaltered provides an internal benefit for species by designating more land for protection and an external benefit to humanity because more land is available for human activities (National Wildlife Federation n.d., 1). In addition, weakly defined scientific data for species provide a tangible benefit for environmentalists to protect more species and an intangible benefit for the regulatory agency given latitude in species listing (Congressional Research Service 2005b, 1). Finally, critical habitat designations are a primary benefit to species by forcing land use conservation and a secondary benefit for humanity, increasing environmental sustainability (Center for Biological Diversity n.d.c, 1).

TESRA amendments. Table 1 illustrates that amending the ESA with TESRA provides an internal benefit for species preservation through structured recovery plans and an external benefit promoting environmental conservation (Environmental Defense 2004, 1). Likewise, private land owners receive tangible benefits through compensation for loss of land use; environmental conservation is an intangible benefit of greater public involvement (Dalmia 2005, 1). Correspondingly, the primary benefit of this alternative is the importance given to protect most endangered species; the secondary benefit is certain species preservation is more likely to occur (National Academy of Sciences 1995, 3).

TESRA plus guidelines. Table 1 depicts that amending the ESA with TESRA and scientific guidelines developed outside regulatory agency jurisdiction offers the greatest number of benefits. Initially, internal benefits of improved recovery programs are complemented by regulatory agency benefits of focusing on recovery programs as science definition is defined elsewhere (Dalmia 2005, 1). Secondly, external benefits of expertly defined science provide better guidelines for judicial rulings (National Academy of Sciences 1995, 3). This alternative also adds an intangible benefit; regulatory agencies gain in autonomy from science decisions (Center for Biological Diversity n.d.b, 1).

Expected Costs of Proposed Alternatives

The expected costs of each alternative are compared in Table 2.

[TABLE 2 ABOUT HERE]

Maintaining the status quo. As shown in Table 2, leaving the ESA unaltered has internal costs to private owners for loss of land use, and externally land use is restricted for all human activity (Ryan and Schuler 1998, 4). In addition, tangible costs include increased litigation, and intangible costs include government time spent on litigation (Buck, Corn, and Baldwin 2002, 3). Furthermore, the primary cost is land use restrictions for all human activity and the secondary cost is private land owners undermining species protection goals.

TESRA amendments. Table 2 illustrates that amending the ESA through TESRA proposals increases internal government costs for revising species programs and externally reduces money available for other environmental conservation programs

(Congressional Budget Office 2005, 4). Secondly, tangible costs include compensating land owners for land use loss and compensation presents an intangible cost because species protection is not guaranteed (DeAlessi n.d., 5). Moreover, primary costs are possible loss of threatened species as recovery programs target endangered species; secondary costs include any loss of species that threatens environmental sustainability (Center for Biological Diversity n.d.a, 1).

TESRA plus guidelines. Table 2 depicts ESA amendments using TESRA proposals and scientific guidelines developed outside regulatory agency jurisdiction, which adds internal and external costs to government. Primarily, internal costs involve loss of control over scientific definitions (Center for Biological Diversity n.d.b, 1); external costs include less cooperation with program implementation. Additionally, tangible costs include funding an outside source to develop science definition; intangible costs concern the problem that loss of land use does not guarantee species preservation. Further, the primary cost is time required for agency coordination of scientific findings (U.S. Senate Committee of Environment and Public Works 2004, 1), whereas the secondary cost is any loss of a species threatens environmental sustainability.

RECOMMENDATIONS

ESA revisions will inevitably be contentious because commerce and conservation have different goals (Brown and Shogren 1998, 4). While the alternative that combines TESRA proposals with scientific guidelines created outside represents the optimal solution, it is not likely to garner necessary political support. The Department of Interior will not want to relinquish control of the scientific definitions because regulatory authority would be diminished. Yet, the current problems with the ESA are costly enough to warrant some revisions. Accordingly, the policy recommendation is to amend the ESA with TESRA proposals.

Recommended Action

Amending the ESA with TESRA proposals adequately solves ESA problems and possesses the highest level of political support because legislation has already passed the House of Representatives. The TESRA proposal recommends applying current scientific data to species listing, developing structured recovery plans, and providing incentives for species recovery and preservation activities (Congressional Research Service 2005b, 1). At the center of each of the actions is establishing the best available science (National Academy of Sciences 2003, 1–4).

These reforms directly address the critical failings of the ESA. First, the application of the best available science for species listing will ensure most important species receive greatest protection and reduce the subjectivity of the process (National Academy of Sciences 1995, 3). Second, the reforms increase the emphasis on species recovery by developing specific guidelines for species recovery plans; this improves species preservation by providing clear recovery time lines and measurements for species target populations (Dalmia 2005, 1). Third, the reforms support sparing use of critical habitat designations to help resolve the problem of land owners practicing land sterilization to avoid land use restrictions (Smith n.d., 3). Fourth, the reforms create consistent methods and management standards for evaluations. Finally, the reforms help create a balance of interests by narrowing the preservation objectives.

Justification for Adopting TESRA Objectives

TESRA reforms enhance the efficiency, effectiveness, and equity of the ESA for a number of reasons. First, structured recovery plans are more effective in preventing species extinction and lead to improvements in environmental conservation (Environmental Defense 2004, 1). Second, reducing critical habitat designations in favor of cooperative conservation is more equitable in balancing the burden of environmental conservation on land owners (Dalmia 2005, 1). Finally, applying the best available science to the species programs promotes efficiency in regulatory activities by directing attention to species in greatest need (National Academy of Sciences 1995, 3).

More specifically, incorporating scientific criteria costs more for government to revise current programs but ensures attention is directed to aid most endangered species (Brown and Shogren 1998, 8). Alternatively, rewards for cooperative conservation and land owner compensation increase program costs, yet it is responsive to species preservation and environmental conservation (Environmental Defense 2004, 1). Further, TESRA reforms create measurable data for monitoring the impact of the policy reforms on species preservation, as well as the public. The primary indicators demonstrating policy effectiveness of ESA amendments are reductions in species listings, recovery plans existing for all species, and more species being removed from the endangered list because they no longer need protection.

CONCLUSION AND JUSTIFICATION

The ESA has been structured to protect all species for environmental value. While the value of all species is not known, certain species have provided important public health benefits. Due to the uncertainty of which species will provide benefits, some feel it wise to keep all options open. To keep all options open for species requires that some options be removed for certain citizens.

Important Inadequacies of Past Policy Responses

By indiscriminately focusing on species preservation at all costs, the ESA has created some complex problems and issues within communities. Although the ESA treats all land owners equally by restricting land use, the practice of designating critical habitat has proven to be the least effective practice in protecting endangered species. Further, the ESA has shifted species preservation into redistributive economics by placing the burden of environmental conservation on land owners. Finally, the lack of applied science in ESA programs has created extensive litigation to resolve policy intentions due to the subjectivity of its definitions and measures.

Even at its best, the ESA has failed to address growing discontinuities in implementation. Polarization over ESA has diminished overall public concern for environmental conservation. The ESA tools place emphasis on protecting and preserving species; however, only 1 percent of endangered species have been delisted. Either the ESA failed to protect species or it has failed to engage in species recovery. ESA practices have created incentives for noncompliance; landowners retaliating against severe land restrictions have resorted to covert practices to ensure land remains free of listed species.

Why TESRA Reforms Will Work

Although current implementation costs exceed current costs for species protection, amending the ESA with TESRA proposals is the best alternative for improving the ESA. Foundationally, this policy recommendation balances competing interests of environmentalists and land owners, and at the same time, it structures species protection programs to promote the reversal of species extinction. These reforms also improve policy coherence necessary for resolving the inadequacies of the ESA by pursuing scientific criteria for administrative decision-making and enhancing the focus on measurable impacts. Furthermore, creating collaboration between species conservation and land owners is likely to hasten species recovery time by reducing resistance and promoting compliance with ESA policy goals for species preservation.

REFERENCES

Association of Consulting Foresters of America, Inc. 2004. *ACF position statements: Reauthorizing the Endangered Species Act.* February 7. http:www.acf-foresters.com/position4.cfm (accessed November 5, 2005).

Brown Jr., G., and Jason F. Shogren. 1998. *Economics of the endangered species act. The Journal of Economic Perspectives* 12 (3). http://www.jstor.org/ (accessed September 25, 2005).

Center for Biological Diversity. n.d.a. *The extinction crisis.* http://www.biologicaldiversity.org/swcbd/aboutus/index.html (accessed March 25, 2006).

Center for Biological Diversity. n.d.b. *Stop H.R. 3824 Rep. Pombo's anti-endangered species bill.* http://www.biologicaldiversity.org/swcbd/Programs/policy/esa/CBD-TESRA.pdf (accessed March 18, 2006).

Center for Biological Diversity. n.d.c. *An analysis of H.R. 3824 Rep. Pombo's anti-endangered species bill as passed by the House September 29, 2005.* http://www.biologicaldiversity.org/swcbd/Programs/policy/esa/CBD-ANALYSIS.pdf (accessed March 18, 2006).

Center for Biological Diversity. n.d.d. *Measuring the success of the Endangered Species Act.* http://www.esasuccess.org/reports/main1.html.

Committee on Resources. n.d. Committee on Resources members. http://resourcescommittee.house.gov/issues/more/esa/whitepaper.htm (accessed February 11, 2006).

Congress and the Nation. 1969. *Chronology of legislation on conservation.* Washington, DC: Congressional Quarterly Inc.

Congress and the Nation. 1977. *Chronology of action on the environment.* Washington, DC: Congressional Quarterly Inc.

Congressional Budget Office. 2005. Congressional Budget Office members. September 27. http://www.cbo.gov/showdoc.cfm?index=666&sequence=0 (accessed March 18, 2006).

Congressional Quarterly. 1974. *93rd Congress, 1st session 1973.* Washington, DC: Congressional Quarterly Inc.

Congressional Research Service. 2002. *Endangered species: Difficult choices.* October 4. http://www.policyalmanac.org/environment/archive/crs_endangered_species.shtml (accessed March 18, 2006).

Congressional Research Service. 2005a. *H.R. 3824: Threatened and Endangered Species Recovery Act of 2005.* September 30. http://www.govtrack.us/congress/bill .xpd?bill=h109-3824 (accessed February 11, 1006).

Congressional Research Service. 2005b. *H.R. 3824: Threatened and Endangered Species Recovery Act of 2005.* September 30. http://www.govtrack.us/congress/bill. xpd?tab=amendments&bill=h109-3824 (accessed February 11, 1006).

Congressional Research Service. 2005c. *H.R. 3824: Threatened and Endangered Species Recovery Act of 2005.* September 29. http://www.govtrack.us/congress/bill.xpd? tab=summary&bill=109-3824 (accessed February 11, 2006).

Dalmia, S. 2005. *Endangered species act needs a dose of sanity.* http://www.reason.org/ phprint.php4 (accessed February 11, 2006).

DeAlessi, M. n.d. *Conservation through private initiative: Harnessing American ingenuity to preserve our nation's resources.* http://reason.org/ps328polsum.prd (accessed February 11, 2006).

Environmental Defense. 2004. *An interview with environmental defense wildlife expert RobertBonnie.* May 3. http://www.environmentdefense.org/print_article.cfm? ContentID=3708&displaymode=p (accessed February 18, 2006).

Fowler, L., and Ronald G. Shaiko. 1987. *The grass roots connection: Environmental activists and senate roll calls. American Journal of Political Science* 31 (3). http://jstor.org/ (accessed September 25, 2005).

Library of Congress. 2005. S.2110 summary. December 15. http://thomas.loc.gov/cgi-bin/ bdquery/z?d109:SN02110:@@@L&summ2=m& (accessed March 28, 2006).

Marano, N., and Ben Lieberman. 2005. *Improving the Endangered Species Act: Balancing the needs of landowners and endangered wildlife.* September 23. http:// www.heritage. org/Research/EnergyandEnvironment/wm861.cfm (accessed February 19, 2006).

Myers, N. 1976. *An expanded approach to the problem of disappearing species. Science* 193 (4249). http://jstor.org/ (accessed September 25, 2005).

National Academy of Sciences. 1995. *Science panel recommends changes to improve implementation of Endangered Species Act.* May 24. http://www4.nationacademies. org/news.nsf/isbn/0309052912?OpenDocument (accessed March 26, 2006).

National Academy of Sciences. 2003. *Broader approach needed for protection and recovery of fish in Klamath River Basin.* October 22. http://www4.nationalacademies. org/news.nsf/isbn/0309090970?OpenDocument (accessed March 26, 2006).

National Oceanic and Atmospheric Administration Library. n.d. *Reorganization Plan No. 4 of 1970.* http://www.lib.noaa.gov/edocs/ReorganizationPlan4_1986.html (accessed November 4, 2005).

National Wildlife Federation. n.d. *The Endangered Species Act: Safety net for wildlife.* http://www.nwf.org/wildlife/esa/safetynet.cfm (accessed March 6, 2006).

Ryan, P., and Galen Schuler. 1998. *The endangered species act: A primer.* http://www.mrsc.org/subjects/environment/esa/esaprime.aspx?r=1(accessed February 18, 2006).

Sierra Club. n.d. *Land protection: Kempthorne factsheet.* http://www.sierraclub.org/ wildlands/kempthorne/ (accessed March 26, 2006).

Sierra Club. 2006. *The latest.* March 26. http://www.sierraclub.org (accessed March 26, 2006).

Smith, R. n.d. The Endangered Species Act: Saving species or stopping growth? *Regulation: The Cato Review of Business & Government.* http://www.cato.org/pubs/regulation/reg15n1-smith.html (accessed September 25, 2005).

Stathis, Stephen W. 1992. *Landmark legislation 1774–2002.* Washington, DC: CQ Press.

United States Code Congressional and Administrative News. 1973a. 93rd Congress. 1st sess., Vol. 1. St. Paul, MN: West Publishing Co.

United States Code Congressional and Administrative News. 1973b. 93rd Congress. 1st sess., Vol. 2. St. Paul, MN: West Publishing Co.

U.S. Congress. 1995. House. Committee on Resources. *The impact of the Endangered Species Act on the nation.* 104th Cong., 1st sess. Washington, DC: Government Printing Office.

U.S. Department of Agriculture. 1997. Northeastern Area Forest Service. March. http://www.na.fs.fed.us/spfo/pubs/wildlife/endangered/endangered.htm (accessed February 18, 2006).

U.S. Department of Agriculture. 2000. Natural Resources Conservation Service. December. http://www.nrcs.usda.gov/technical/NRI/1997/summary_report/table1.html (accessed February 18, 2006).

U.S. Fish and Wildlife Service. n.d. *U.S. Fish and Wildlife members.* http://www.fws.gov/ (accessed March 18, 2006).

U.S. Fish and Wildlife Service 2005. *The Endangered Species Program.* http://www.fws.gov/endangered/. (accessed November 4, 2005).

U.S. Fish and Wildlife Service. 2006. *U.S. Fish and Wildlife members.* http://ecos.fws.gov/tess_public/TESSBoxscore (accessed March 6, 2006).

U.S. Senate Committee on Environment and Public Works. 2003. *Hearing statements: Senator Michael D. Crapo, of Idaho.* April 10. http://epw.senate.gov/hearing_statements.cfm?id=213421 (accessed March 26, 2006).

U.S. Senate Committee on Environment and Public Works. 2004. *Hearing statements: Statement of Julie MacDonald, Deputy Assistant Secretary for Fish and Wildlife and Parks.* August 20. http://epw.senate.gov/hearing_statements.cfm?id=225434 (accessed March 26, 2006).

Welch, Susan, John Gruhl, John Comer, and Susan M. Rigdon. 2005. *Understanding American government,* 8th ed. Belmont, CA: Wadsworth Publishing.

Table 1: Cost/Effectiveness Analysis Comparing Benefits for ESA Policy Alternatives

Benefits	Internal (a) External (b)	Tangible (a) Intangible (b)	Primary (a) Secondary (b)
Alternative 1 No ESA amendments	a. More land available for species preservation.[1] b. More land available for human activities.[1]	a. Ambiguous definition of science creates more opportunity for environmentalists to dispute government actions.[2] b. Government has more latitude with ambiguous science language.[2]	a. Forces land use practice towards conservation.[3] b. Increases environmental sustainability.[3]
Alternative 2 Amendments proposed by TESRA	a. Better species recovery programs improve species preservation.[4] b. Species preservation improves environmental conservation.[4]	a. Includes economic consideration in species preservation.[5] b. Money spent compensating loss of land use encourages greater public involvement with overall environmental conservation.[6]	a. Most important species get greatest attention.[7] b. Preservation of certain species is more likely to occur.[7]
Alternative 3 Amendments proposed by TESRA Plus Guidelines	a. Better species recovery programs improve species preservation.[4] Agency resources focus on recovery programs.[6] b. Species preservation improves environmental conservation.[4] Judiciary has better guidelines for rulings.[7]	a. Includes economic consideration in species preservation.[5] b. Money spent compensating loss of land use encourages greater public involvement with environmental conservation.[6] Agency gains autonomy from science decision-making.[8]	a. Most important species get greatest attention.[7] Agency spends less time negotiating science definition.[7] b. Preservation of certain species is more likely to occur.[5]

[1]National Wildlife Federation. *The Endangered Species Act: Safety Net for Wildlife*. n.d. http://www.nwf .org/wildlife/esa/safetynet.cfm (accessed March 6, 2006).

[2]Congressional Research Service. H.R. 3824: *Threatened and Endangered Species Recovery Act of 2005*. September 29 2005b. http://www.govtrack.us/congress/bill.xpd?tab=summary&bill=109-3824 (accessed February 11, 2006).

[3]Center for Biological Diversity. *An analysis of H.R. 3824 Rep. Pombo's Anti-Endangered Species Bill as Passed by the House September 29, 2005*. n.d. http://www.biologicaldiversity.org/swcbd/Programs/policy/esa/CBD-ANALY-SIS.pdf (accessed March 18, 2006).

[4]Environmental Defense. *An Interview with Environmental Defense Wildlife Expert Robert Bonnie*. May 3, 2004. http://www.environmentdefense.org/print_article.cfm?ContentID=3708&displaymode=p (accessed February 18, 2006).

[5]E. Buck, M. Lynne Corn, and Pamela Baldwin. *Endangered Species: Difficult Choices*. October 4, 2002. http://www.policyalmanac.org/environment/archive/crs_endangered_species.shtml (accessed March 18, 2006).

[6]S. Dalmia, *Endangered Species Act Needs a Dose of Sanity*. October 5, 2005. http://www.reason.org/phprint.php4 (accessed February 11, 2006).

[7]National Academy of Sciences. *Science Panel Recommends Changes to Improve Implementation of Endangered Species Act*. May 24, 1995. http://www4.nationacademies.org/news.nsf/isbn/0309052912?OpenDocument (accessed March 26, 2006).

[8]Center for Biological Diversity. *Stop H.R. 3824 Rep. Pombo's Anti-Endangered Species Bill*. n.d. http://www.biologicaldiversity.org/swcbd/Programs/policy/esa/CBD-TESRA.pdf (accessed March 18, 2006).

Table 2: Cost/Effectiveness Analysis Comparing Costs for ESA Policy Alternatives

Costs	Internal (a) External (b)		Tangible (a) Intangible (b)		Primary (a) Secondary (b)	
Alternative 1 No ESA amendments	a.	Loss of land use for private land owners.[1]	a.	Ambiguous definition of science increases litigation.[2]	a.	Restricts land use for human activity.[1]
	b.	Loss of land use for all human activity.[1]	b.	Government spends more time on litigation and less on species.[2]	b.	Private land owners undermine the goal of species protection.[1]
Alternative 2 Amendments proposed by TESRA	a.	Increase in government costs to revise proposed species protection programs.[4]	a.	Increase in government costs to compensate land owners for loss of land use.[4]	a.	Cost of losing threatened species as recovery programs target endangered species.[5]
	b.	More money spent on species preservation reduces money available for other environmental conservation programs.[4]	b.	Money spent on loss of land use does not guarantee species preservation.[8]	b.	Any loss of species is a threat to environmental sustainability.[6]
Alternative 3 Amendments proposed by TESRA plus science definition developed outside of regulatory agency	a.	Increase in government costs to revise proposed species protection programs.[4] Loss of government control over definition of science.[7]	a.	Increase in government costs to compensate land owners for loss of land use.[4] Government funding assistance to outside source for developing science definition.	a.	Cost of losing threatened species as recovery programs target endangered species.[6] Time required for regulating agency to coordinate science findings.[3]
	b.	More money spent on species preservation reduces money available for other environmental conservation programs.[4] Less cooperation with program implementation.[7]	b.	Money spent on loss of land use does not guarantee species preservation.[8]	b.	Any loss of species is a threat to environmental sustainability.[6]

[1] P. Ryan and Galen Schuler. *The Endangered Species Act: A primer*. 1998. http://www.mrsc.org/subjects/environment/esa/esaprime.aspx?r=1 (accessed February 18, 2006).

[2] E. Buck, M. Lynne Corn, and Pamela Baldwin. *Endangered Species: Difficult Choices*. October 4, 2002. http://www.policyalmanac.org/environment/archive/crs_endangered_species.shtml (accessed March 18, 2006).

[3] U.S. Senate Committee on Environment and Public Works. *U.S. Senate Committee Members*. August 20, 2004. http://epw.senate.gov/hearing_statements.cfm?id=225434 (accessed March 26, 2006).

[4] Congressional Budget Office. *Congressional Budget Office Members*. September 27, 2005. http://www.cbo.gov/showdoc.cfm?index=666&sequence=0 (accessed March 18, 2006).

[5] Congressional Research Service. *H.R. 3824: Threatened and Endangered Species Recovery Act of 2005*. September 29 2005b. http://www.govtrack.us/congress/bill.xpd?tab=summary&bill=109-3824 (accessed February 11, 2006).

[6] Center for Biological Diversity. *The Extinction Crisis*. n.d. http://www.biologicaldiversity.org/swcbd/aboutus/index.html (accessed March 25, 2006).

[7] Center for Biological Diversity. *Stop H.R. 3824 Rep. Pombo's Anti-Endangered Species Bill*. n.d. http://www.biologicaldiversity.org/swcbd/Programs/policy/esa/CBD-TESRA.pdf (accessed March 18, 2006).

[8] M. DeAlessi. *Conservation Through Private Initiative: Harnessing American Ingenuity to Preserve Our Nation's Resources*. n.d. http://reason.org/ps328polsum.prd (accessed February 11, 2006).

Figure 1:   U.S. Species Listed per Calendar Year 1980–2005

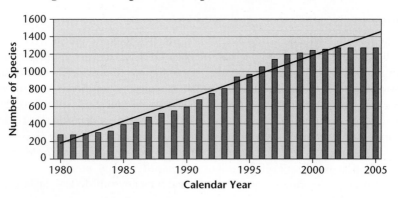

U.S. Fish and Wildlife Service. 2006. *U.S. Fish and Wildlife Members.* http://ecos.fws.gov/tess_public/ TessBoxscore (accessed March 6, 2006).

Writing a Policy Memo

Purpose

Policy memos are frequently used in common practice to communicate essential information briefly and succinctly to decision-makers. Decision-makers in public, nonprofit, and private sector organizations depend on these memos to provide them with substantive information in a concise, accessible format. A typical policy memo requires as much research and analysis as any other form of policy communication, yet it is designed to convey only the essential information necessary for making a decision. (For additional discussion, see www.skillsheets.com/docs/SkillSheets_aanvulling_E1h.pdf; www2.eastwestcenter.org/research/popcomm/pdf/8_Writing_a_Decision_Memo_and_Giving_a_Policy_Briefing/Policy_memorandum.pdf; *Policy memos* n.d.) To see a professional example, view www.science.calwater.ca.gov/pdf/dv/DV_healey_mount_levee_memo_112407.pdf.

How to Construct a Policy Memo

- Policy memos are generally short; they are usually one to one-and-a-half pages (single spaced, one-inch margins, 12-point font), are professionally presented, and use an organization's letterhead. Policy memos are rarely longer than three pages.
- The audience level is intelligent nonspecialist. The writing style is direct, using short words, very little, if any, jargon, and short sentences. The paragraphs should be no shorter than three sentences, but no longer than five sentences. The policy memo will generally take at least five paragraphs to complete.
- Policy memos generally do not have verbatim quotes, contractions, or personal references (no "I, me, you, we," etc.). They also do not include references; however, some decision-makers may ask for references.
- Policy memos include a formal memo heading and require topic headings throughout the document.
- Policy memos may include a table or graph if necessary. The tables and graphs are usually embedded in the text.
- Policy memos may include bulleted or numbered lists.

Structure of a Policy Memo

Policy memos have a distinctive structure. They always include a topic, background, issues, alternatives, and a recommendation. A standard format for a policy memo includes the following, in order and with headings where indicated:

- Memo Heading (TO, FROM, DATE, SUBJECT).
- *Summary:* This is the opening paragraph (usually has no heading, or may use "Summary" or "Introduction" as the heading). This section contains the main message of the memo. The paragraph includes a brief summary of the issue and what should be done. It specifies the issue succinctly, identifies the focus of the information contained in the memo, and states the recommended action.
- *Context:* This section provides the context or background of the problem and usually includes a very brief evolution of the problem that is chronologically organized.

- *Issues:* This section provides a brief identification of the issues and controversies. In general, no more than three issues should be discussed. This section also includes an identification of positions on the issues held by stakeholders involved in the controversy.

- *Options*: This section discusses available options or tasks for solving the problem and resolving the issues. It includes a tightly focused discussion or analysis of how the problem can be solved, the pros and cons of each option, and the risk or opposition associated with each option for the decision-maker.

- *Recommendation*: This section identifies what the reader should do and what evidence or arguments support this course of action.

Example: A Policy Memo

To: Dennis Beardsley
        Interim Assistant City Manager/General Services Director
        City of Chico
From: Rebekah Funes, Student Assistant
Date: March 11, 2008
RE: Reciprocity in Collaboratives

Adopting a framework for collaboration between the City and participating organizations and between partner organizations has potential to greatly enhance efficacy of project implementation and a sustainable management strategy for the Park. In advance of adopting a framework for collaboration, the City should consider methods to avoid potential conflicts between the partnership and current City organizational culture. As with any successful collaboration, participating organizations, and particularly accountable governments, need to seek greater education on the principles and methods of collaboration and the role of effective leadership within a collaborative. The concept of collaborative action conflicts with the prevailing work culture that leaders and governments have the "best" answers and that "people" must be actively managed and controlled if the organization is to fulfill its goals. Thus, developing a collaborative is as much about developing a culture of collaboration as it is determining the mission and strategy the collaboration will employ.

Context.   The City is a core constituent in the partnerships as it retains legal authority over implementation and future management of all Park projects, possesses legitimacy in enacting policy solutions, and is capable of providing key information and financial backing to approaching and solving problems. Participating organizations are important to integrated program success as they bring technical expertise, as well as financial and human resources, to the table and are capable of encouraging and leveraging even greater community investment. The City, however, has utilized a bureaucratic chain of command and ad hoc and permanent committees for a number of years in its traditional approach to natural resource management. It is a common perception for agencies to be concerned about the loss of authority or legitimacy when delegating responsibility to external organizations or the community.

Issues.   True collaborations and networks seek to accommodate all participants despite the presence of legitimate policy makers; however, there is common concern that collaborative decisions will run contrary to governmental interests. A number of groups and individuals participating in the development of the Natural Resource Management Plan for inclusion in the City's Bidwell Park Draft Master Management Plan had an experience that ran contrary to the principles of collaboration and discouraged individuals from continuing to invest in the Vegetation Management Partnership. After numerous hours of study, meetings, and document preparation/editing, a substantial piece of work was submitted to the City but was extensively edited. The City initiated and supported this multi-organizational effort, yet was selective about the information it published and adopted. Feedback of that nature would be less damaging to the principles of collaboration if done during the development process, not after.

Options.   In collaborative management structures, authority is based on expertise and legitimacy in the ability to reach collective agreement. Although all organizations work towards problem identification and solutions, the City is an essential constituent, retaining legal authority, possessing legitimacy in developing policy, providing key information, and carrying the repercussions of the final decision. Acceptance of collaborative decisions carries greater "moral authority" than do authoritative decisions; they have the backing of a network of practice, which encourages continued community investment. If it is the City's interest to convene and leverage technical expertise and human resources through a sustainable collaborative, the City must invest in a reciprocal relationship with the group by way of greater leadership and involvement during the project development process. This would bring greater legitimacy, effectiveness, and sustainability to the group.

Recommendation.   Collaborative management, when new to organizations or divisions, can pose an issue because it challenges the status quo. City leadership needs to acknowledge and accept the responsibility of reciprocity to continue to leverage community, as well as human and financial, resources in joint projects to manage Bidwell Park. In acknowledging the need for collaboration, the City will begin to effectively utilize community resources by broadening critical participation.

Participant Observation and Internship Report

An internship is a special course that many political science departments offer. Internships usually involve fieldwork in a governmental agency, a political party, an interest group, or some other public agency. The purpose of an internship is to give students the opportunity to combine their academic and fieldwork experiences. Usually, internship students are required to have a faculty and a fieldwork supervisor who will be responsible for co-directing the internship. In most cases, the student is responsible for producing a field report that relates a set of theoretical concepts particular to a subdiscipline of political science to what the student has observed, participated in, and experienced in the field.

Guidelines for an Internship Report

1. **Get a detailed job description of duties and of faculty and field supervisors' expectations for the fieldwork.**
   - Make sure to achieve the goals set by both the faculty and field supervisors.
   - Make sure to conduct the work in a responsible and professional manner.
2. **Keep a detailed log of the day's activities.**
   - Be sure to differentiate between significant and insignificant details in the log.
   - Describe experiences in detail and include facts and measurements.
   - Be sure to get permission from the field supervisor to record any data that might be considered classified or personal.
   - Depending on the work assigned, keep a tally or list of the number of times the same type of duty was assigned or task was repeated.
   - Put the date and time worked on each new entry.

3. **Annotate each entry, writing for at least 10 minutes. If necessary, use a "stream-of-consciousness" writing style. Freewrite as much as possible.**
   - Pose questions about why some condition exists or what purpose a particular task served.
   - Draw some conclusions about the significance of the observations and experiences.
   - Describe feelings about what was observed, experienced, or participated in when it was happening.
   - Describe current feelings about what was observed, experienced, or participated.
   - Make some connections between knowledge gained from academic training and what was observed, experienced, or participated in.

4. **At the close of the internship, conduct a content analysis of the log.**
   - To conduct a content analysis of the log, create a typology of the types of phenomena observed, types of situations experienced, and types of activities participated in listed in the log.
     - A typology is a set of distinct categories of information.
     - In this case, one category would be observation, one category would be experiences, and one category would be activities.
   - Label each item in each category by some ranking method. Try the following, but be prepared to justify the designation given to each item:
     - Significant or insignificant.
     - Conforms or does not conform to theory.
   - Identify the frequency (how many times or how often) with which each item in the typology occurred.
     - Was there any pattern in the time, place, or context in which an event occurred?
     - How many times did the same type of event occur?

5. **Using the typology, prepare a report that compares theories about political phenomena or behavior with the events observed, experienced, or participated in during the internship.**
   - The format for the report should be similar to an analytical essay.
     - The report should not be purely descriptive.
     - Describe the goals and expectations associated with the fieldwork.
     - Describe the context of the fieldwork.
   - Assert in the thesis statement whether the observations, experiences, or activities support or cast doubt on these theories.
     - Identify a theory or parts of theories about political phenomena or behavior that are the focus of the report.
     - Suggest whether they are valid or not valid based on the fieldwork.
   - Compare and contrast theory and practice.
     - Begin the comparison by briefly describing the theory or theories in question.
     - Use the events that occurred during the fieldwork as evidence to support or cast doubt on the theory or theories.

■ Clearly separate what was observed from what was experienced and from what was actually participated in.

6. **After comparing and contrasting theories with the field events, write a conclusion.**
   - Summarize the goals of the fieldwork.
   - Review briefly the incidences where the theory was confirmed by the fieldwork.
   - Review briefly any discrepancies between theory and practice.
   - Suggest how the fieldwork expanded knowledge or awareness of political phenomena or behavior. Was this experience beneficial? How?

7. **Include in an appendix of the report a copy of a letter or internship evaluation form that is signed by the field supervisor. The letter should contain an assessment of the quality of your performance related to the following:**
   - Dependability.
   - Initiative.
   - Cooperation.
   - Thoroughness.
   - Professional attitude.
   - Assertiveness.
   - Professional strengths.
   - Professional weaknesses.
   - Overall quality of fieldwork completed.
   - Number of hours worked.

The intern should be sure to ask for an evaluation of his or her work. It is best, even if an evaluation sheet similar to the one on the following page must be used, to ask for a letter on the organization's stationary. This letter, if the student has done a good job in the internship, can be placed in a professional portfolio and sent with a career file for job interviews.

Many internship programs have evaluation forms for assessing an intern's work in the field. In the event that one is not available, the student should ask the faculty advisor what is necessary for evaluation and then ask the field supervisor for a letter assessing the work and a more detailed evaluation according to the standards set by the faculty advisor. The one following can be used as a guide. This evaluation, together with a letter and good fieldwork, will provide credentials for future employment.

Sample: Intern Evaluation Form

A. On the following scale, please rank your intern's performance:
5 = Excellent 4 = Good 3 = Average 2 = Poor 1 = Unacceptable

a. _____ Dependability

b. _____ Initiative

c. _____ Cooperation

d. _____ Thoroughness

e. _____ Professional attitude

f. _____ Assertiveness

g. _____ Professional strengths

h. _____ Professional weaknesses

i. _____ Overall quality of fieldwork completed

j. _____ Number of hours worked

B. What were the intern's major strengths?

C. In what ways could the intern improve?

D. What is your overall assessment of the intern's performance?

E. Were the number of hours worked equivalent to the number agreed on at the beginning of the internship?

Please sign your name to verify this assessment.

(Name)_____ (Title)_____ (Date)_____

INTERNSHIP REPORT
CAMPAIGN VOLUNTEERS: VIPs OR PEONS?

By
Caryn M. Cieplak
POLS 395
Professor Diane Schimdt
November 23, 1988
(Reprinted with permission)

INTRODUCTION

I have had the unique opportunity to work for a politician that has served in a vast and diverse number of elected positions. Harry "Bus" Yourell has been in public office for close to 35 years. Harry "Bus" Yourell is a very well-known political figure in Cook County. His experience ranges from local trustee positions to his newly elected position of Commissioner of the Metropolitan Sanitary District–Cook County. His recent exit from his position as Cook County Recorder of Deeds was to give him the county experience needed to run for this new position. The new position will take him out of the limelight because he will be sharing it with two other people newly elected to the position. This will give him the incentive to adopt necessary changes within the scope of this office.

In his new position, Bus will be dealing with issues such as building dams, water pollution, and air pollution. My fieldwork was conducted during Bus's campaign for Commissioner. I was expected to help in the election activities. I was particularly interested in studying the role of campaign volunteers and constituency targeting election techniques. My experiences as a volunteer in Bus's campaign support the theories of incumbency advantage through constituency service, name recognition, and local party support. In particular, my experiences in working with him have inspired me to run for a local office someday.

FIELDWORK TASKS

Before my internship, my knowledge of politics was limited to what I could understand from the conversations around me and what I learned from class. Because of my inexperience, one of my main duties was to help with his election to Commissioner by being an envelope stuffer. Stuffing envelopes, though tedious, is something that every campaign headquarters must engage in and is probably one of the most effective ways to reach constituents. Through periodic mailings, constituents are given the opportunity to "get to know the candidates" by reading about their backgrounds and past records in politics. Not only does it clearly define the stances that the particular candidate takes, it provides some humor when the candidate's literature criticizes the opponent(s). Further, mailings are vital in order to effectively and efficiently reach the entire area (on a local level). Walking the precincts can be effective, but it is much easier to reach people through the mail.

One interesting finding from my fieldwork relates directly to the source of the mailings. None of the mail was sent out for Bus's personal benefit. The Cook County Democratic Headquarters covered the county candidates through their mass mailings. The mail sent from Bus's office consisted mainly of literature that promoted the township candidates, the State Representative, and United States Representative. The literature, i.e., personal bibliographies, sample ballots, etc., were all signed by Bus because he is the Committeeman of Worth Township. It was apparent from this literature that Bus was closely aligned with his party.

Not only did I stuff envelopes but I answered the telephone as well. An important part of a volunteer's job in a township office is manning the telephones when constituents call to question a candidate's position on certain issues. Again, this is not a glamorous job, but it is a very important one. When constituents call to clarify a candidate's position, it is a chance to capitalize on the possibility that the person does not know enough about the candidate. If this is true, then it may be possible to convince the person to vote for your candidate.

For example, it is very common for one out of every two telephone calls to Bus's office to be from a senior citizen. They need to be dealt with very lightly and very carefully. Senior citizens are very powerful people in Worth Township and although Bus never uses his age as a way to relate to this segment, they realize that he is 69 and has been in local politics for almost 35 years. Anyone who is going to answer these types of phone calls needs to be well versed in not only the candidate's position but in what certain segments of the constituency want to hear.

Past records of the candidate play a very important role when trying to convince undecided voters to vote for a candidate. For instance, one day while I was manning the telephones, a constituent called and asked me exactly what Bus had done for them in the past that should make them vote for him in a new position. Taxes at the local level are always a major concern to taxpayers. Knowing this, I was able to tell the voter something that he did not know. Bus, as the Cook County Recorder of Deeds, was able to computerize his entire office at absolutely no cost to the taxpayer and therefore enable more efficient work output to the public. Bus also managed to increase his budget by less than 1 percent over the four years he was in office. Success like this can only come from years of experience. The voter on the other link of the telephone was very pleased to hear this and thanked me repeatedly for my time.

APPLICATIONS OF THEORY TO PRACTICE

This leads me to another point that is important—experience. When it came time for Bus to run for the Commissioner of the Metropolitan Sanitary District, it was clear that the position was something new to him. As a representative serving in the Illinois State Legislature for nine terms, Bus has dealt with local pollution topics before, whereas the other nine candidates in the running for this position had minimal exposure to this subject. His experience qualified him for this position.

Knowing of his experience, however, I was able to address many of the questions people had, but not all of them. Because I was ignorant of the duties he would take over as Commissioner, I could not adequately answer some questions at first. I was uncomfortable about not knowing the answers so I read everything I could find about the Sanitary District. After researching the Commissioner's role in the Sanitary District, I felt much more confident in my discussions with constituents and candidates.

In a way, volunteering can create loyal party members and can serve as a recruiting device. For example, it is clear that as a volunteer, feeling ignorant and ineffective in helping constituents provided me with incentives to become more educated about the issues in local politics. Once I became informed, I experienced a great sense of efficacy. Researching the Commissioner's role in the Sanitary District gave me more confidence in what I know about local political offices. More importantly, it has provided me with a foundation to collect information and the confidence to effectively address public problems with confidence when I run for office.

Not only do the personal contacts with volunteers help a candidate secure a loyal inner circle of trusted campaign workers, another great asset that an experienced politician can use to his advantage is the personal contacts that he has made over his years of public service. These personal contacts include both Democrats and Republicans. While in the state legislature, Bus established some long-term relationships with members from both parties as well as with many business professionals. These relationships turn into very credible endorsements when it comes time to run for office. Further, these endorsements turn into votes when constituents are unsure of Bus's qualifications, but feel strongly about one of the public figures that endorsed him.

Through working in a campaign and meeting important people, volunteers can also make important political contacts and, perhaps, even establish their own network of potential supporters. By being part of Bus's campaign staff, I have had the unique opportunity to get to know several of these politicians, some more than others have. I plan to develop these relationships so that when I am ready to run for public office, I too can reap the advantages of such long-standing relationships.

BENEFITS AND PROFESSIONAL DEVELOPMENT

I have realized several things in my tenure as an intern. First, a volunteer's job is extremely important to the success of an election. At first, when given very tedious responsibilities, I questioned my overall usefulness. But as I became more interested in politics I have come to the realization that the only way to learn is through being in the arena in some capacity. I have experienced many things, thanks to the responsibilities Bus has given me as well as the dedication I have to Worth Township politics.

Moreover, as a volunteer, I have acquired a great deal of knowledge that I otherwise would not have learned. The knowledge I have gained about politics at the local, state, and national level is something that will forever be useful to me no matter what career I enter. I have a greater appreciation of the value of constituency service, candidate credibility, name recognition, and of volunteers in winning campaigns. In particular, I have a deeper appreciation of the value of political connections, political participation, and political education.

All this became very clear to me when I was talking to a top executive at Chrysler Corporation. He said, "Caryn, although your knowledge of the Chrysler Corporation is not near to what mine is, your knowledge of politics is far beyond that of mine. We can teach each other something." In light of this executive's comment, I feel extremely grateful for having this internship experience. Working for Bus has not only made me realize my importance as a volunteer but also has broadened my appreciation for the knowledge I have gained both in the classroom and in the field. More importantly, it appears to have enhanced my potential for a career in politics.

LOG OF INTERNSHIP FIELDWORK

By

Caryn M. Cieplak
(Reprinted with permission)

October 9, 1988
2 pm–5 pm
Worth Township Democratic Headquarters (WTDH)

Today was an interesting day at the office. Harry "Bus" Yourell (Bus) was his usual witty self, asking me why I was home for the weekend and not at school studying. So, I told him that I had to come home because, without my help, he might lose the election in November for Commissioner of the Metropolitan Sanitary District of Cook County. After our usual exchange of personal stories, we (his staff consisting of Mary, Mary Ann, and Ray) decided to do some work. The first thing that needed to be done was telephone calls. One of the things I think I hate the most, but one of the things that clearly emerges as one of the most important parts of any campaign. This campaign's success almost totally relied upon calling constituents to make sure that they were aware of the fact that "Bus" was running for a position that would make him less visible but more powerful. Many of his supporters have been backing him for 30+ years now and helping him remain in the limelight. We needed to explain to people the importance of putting Bus on the county ticket in this position in order to be sure that all the candidates were elected.

The only exciting thing about today's work was the fact that, through the use of an automatic dialing system hooked up to the phone, no one could fight over not wanting to talk to those well-known citizens who will give you a three-hour dissertation.

It was interesting to see how truly uneducated the voters are, and how well known Bus really is.

October 10, 1988
5 pm–7 pm
Condesa DelMar

Last night was a great night; I almost didn't mind volunteering my time at Marty Russo's cocktail party. Marty is running for his 8th election into the House of

Representatives of the United States and I had the opportunity to serve as an intern in his Washington, D.C., office this past summer. I was given the responsibility of handing out literature on the candidates running for the local election, while watching all the bigshots walk around playing important. Little did they know that there would be a private party for all Marty's past "staffers" (never use the word employee when speaking of those who work on Capitol Hill). Anyway, after the dignitaries all got their chance to speak and everyone drank their money's worth, the cocktail party ended and we (the "staffers") got to enjoy a D.J. while mingling with the local candidates and Marty's special guests, which included twelve congressmen from around the country. It was a great opportunity for me to see what these people are like outside of their public appearance. They're great.

Anyway, the night ended around 1 am but not until I was invited back to Washington to interview with several different offices after graduation. I guess that doing the piddly work for a while really does pay off. I'm actually considering interviewing with the offices that offered me the opportunity, but only because someday I plan to run for office.

Writing a Grant

Purpose

Grant proposals are requests for funding projects that fall within the general or specific guidelines of the funding organization. Grant funding is often available from federal agencies, state agencies, and/or nonprofit organizations. Institutional (nonprofit) foundations and internal grants at colleges and universities are frequently a source for small grants available to students. Organizations may offer grant funding to individuals or may restrict the funding to organizations; they may also restrict funding geographically. Who (individual or institution) receives the grant and for what activities is a decision at the discretion of the funding institution. Organizations generally indicate whether they are accepting proposals for specific activities or general activities within the scope of the funding.

Grants proposals are generally a prepared response to the organization's *RFP* (request for proposal) whereby the organization is requesting an application. The *proposal* is the application in which students state what actions they would perform and how much money they need to perform those activities. Large sums of grant funding often require a detailed budget. If the funding organization accepts the proposal, it will issue a contract for granting the money, including deadlines for completion of the activities (often referred to as deliverables), any requirements for interim or final project reports, and accounting for how the money was spent. (This section is based on information gathered from Ward 2006; Barbato and Furlich 2000; Lock, Spirduso, and Silverman; McNamara 2005; Pfeifer and Keller 2000; Johnson 2005.)

How to Construct a Grant Proposal

Grant proposals must be constructed according to the specifications of the RFP. Some RFPs are direct and require specific information in a specific order that is supplied through a *requirements matrix* or list; other RFPs are general and depend on the requester to supply information appropriate for making a decision on whether to fund the request. Most RFPs also have a *compliance matrix* or list of eligibility requirements that must be met by the requester. It is important that requesters clearly show they are eligible for the funds. Most granting institutions have a contact person listed on the RFP to answer questions for clarification about requirements and compliance. It is good practice to contact this person prior to writing as well as during the construction of the proposal to verify compliance with the RFP as well as for clarification about number of copies needed, delivery (mail, e-mail, fax), and confirmation of delivery. All proposals (even those for internal grants of money available to students from programs at their schools) need to include the following:

- **Problem:** Summary of the problem to be solved. Be sure to link this problem directly with the granting organization's request.
- **Solution:** A recommendation for solving the problem. Be sure to link this solution to any end product or result specifically mentioned in the RFP.
- **Goals:** State the goals of the grant activities relating the solution to the problem. Be sure to link the goals to the goals specified in the RFP; use similar language wherever possible.
- **Objectives:** List the specific actionable tasks (services/actions/activities) planned to achieve the goal. Be sure to link these tasks to any tasks specified in the RFP. Do not list tasks that are restricted or listed as prohibited in the RFP.

- **Key Personnel:** Identify who is to perform each task listed in the objectives.
- **Time Line:** Provide a detailed time line from receipt of funding to delivery of service/tasks.
- **Evaluation:** Describe how progress and accomplishments will be evaluated; describe how the tasks are related to accomplishing the goal.
- **Cost:** Provide a budget, including costs for personnel, overhead (supplies, utilities, travel, etc.), and equipment (if any). For simple grants, this may include only the cost of the student's time, books, and mileage, for example. For larger grants, it may include the cost of several people's time, paper, postage, mileage, lodging, computer equipment, etc.

Structure of a Grant Proposal

The structure of a grant proposal is determined by the RFP. If the RFP is nonspecific, then the following annotated template provides the general information and structure granting institutions expect. Use headings and subheadings for each component of the proposal. Use single spacing or double spacing as permitted by the RFP. Unless specified otherwise, use a 12-point, Times New Roman font, with one-inch margins. If permitted, use a binder for complicated proposals and use professionally presented organizing tabs (not hand labeled).

Annotated Template for Formal Grant Proposals: Nonspecific RFP

The following is a list of information or items that are generally found in most grants. If there are no specific instructions in the RFP, then include all of the following material.

Cover Letter (about a page at most)

Title Page (with a proposal title that includes language implying/stating the applications' contribution; one page)

Table of Contents (especially for long proposals; no more than a page)

List of Tables and Figures (where there are more than a few; no more than a page)

Executive Summary (about a page)

Introduction (summarizing the focus of the proposal, the problem/unmet need, the scope of the proposal, and a description of objectives for resolving the problem; about a page)

Problem Identification (statement of the problem/need; anywhere from about a page to two pages— more material can be placed in an appendix as background)

Project Goals (Technical Approach) (a persuasive discussion about goals for addressing—mediating/resolving/fixing—the problem/unmet need; often about a page or two)

Project Objectives and/or Deliverables (a discussion of the methods used— tasks/activities/tools/means—for achieving goals and the expected outcomes from those methods; often about a page or more for every activity or task performed as long as the methods are clearly linked to the needs; highly technical information can be placed in an appendix)

Project Schedule (Management Approach) (project schedule by date, task, who performs the task, deliverables, and accountability activities; about a page or two, often done in landscape format)

Project Cost (budget with item justification; usually about a page or two with direct reference to a line-item budget, either in the text or in an appendix, showing how the costs were determined, why money is necessary for the task, and how the money will be spent)

Project Evaluation (Evaluation Approach) (a discussion of how to determine that the project objectives have been met; usually no more than about a page for simple proposals, although each task/objective will need about a paragraph at least)

Conclusion (summarizing how the project meets the needs as well as requirements of the grant; how the money will make a difference; about a page)

Appendices (including but not limited to additional background, references, line-item budget, tables, graphs, organizational credentials, personnel credentials, letters of support, etc.; each type of item should be in a separately labeled appendix, which are usually labeled with capital letters—A, B, etc.)

Checklist for Traditional Grant Proposals

Before submitting the grant proposal, make sure that all the requirements for the application have been addressed and clearly identified. The following checklist covers general expectations for all types of grant proposal applications.

General Guidelines and Checklists for General Grant Proposals

1. Does the grant proposal contain all required sections and materials **using the order, format, and terminology** specified by the agency/program guidelines?
   - Is there a clear **requirements matrix?**
   - If there are no requirements specified, then, make sure it includes sections identified as Executive Summary, Introduction, Problem Identification, Project Goals and Objectives, Project Schedule, Project Cost, Conclusion, and Appendices.
2. Does the proposed project meet agency/program priorities and interests?
   - Is there a **compliance matrix** required?
   - How does the proposal meet eligibility for funding under agency/program guidelines?
   - Does the compliance matrix include all amendments issued after the initial RFP or call for proposals?
3. Does the proposal clearly establish and document a need for the project?
   - Is the problem explained succinctly with each facet or component identified (the more complex the problem, the greater the reasons for breaking it into parts or facets).
   - Is each need or problem supported with facts or other evidence from credible sources such as a needs assessment, scholarly studies, government reports, etc?
   - Are causal relationships and/or processes clearly and simply described? (Use flow charts and diagrams for complex relationships.)
   - Does the project seem likely to make an important contribution to the community or advance the state of knowledge in the field?

4. Are project objectives realistic and measurable?
   - Are the stated objectives actionable and clearly distinguished from broadly stated goals?
   - Do the objectives lead logically to the achievement of project goals?
   - Is each objective clearly linked to a need as it is described in the proposal? (It is best to discuss each objective in the same order in which each problem/unmet need was identified in the problem statement.)
   - What tasks must be performed to achieve these objectives?
   - Are there limitations or risks to addressing these unmet needs/problems?
5. Is the project design adequate for achieving the project objectives?
   - Do proposed activities build sufficiently on existing literature/research?
   - Is enough information provided about the methodology to judge that it is sound and appropriate?
   - Is the data collection adequately planned?
   - Is the proposed data analysis appropriate for the aims of the project?
   - Is there primary or secondary evidence/support presented to support the assertion that the objectives will meet identified needs?
6. Is there evaluation criteria included in the proposal?
   - Who will conduct the evaluation?
   - What are the expected outcomes or deliverables?
   - Are the deliverables related to the tasks performed?
   - What indicators, data, etc., will be used to determine a successful outcome?
   - Are there direct and indirect deliverables associated with the tasks performed?
7. Is a detailed timetable provided?
   - Is there a schedule with target dates for each activity?
   - Can the planned activities or tasks reasonably be carried out as scheduled?
   - Are there possible constraints to meeting the target dates?
8. Is the function of the project director described in detail?
   - Does the director have the qualifications and experience to carry out the project?
   - What is the director's track record in the area of interest?
9. Are other key personnel well qualified?
   - Are job responsibilities and time commitments clearly delineated?
   - Is each staff person's role in each task identified specifically and directly?
   - Is each task performed by people who have the skills, knowledge, and experience to perform them?
   - Are staff resources sufficient and appropriate for carrying out the project?
   - Does it seem likely that the project will be understaffed or overstaffed?
10. Are the facilities and equipment adequate for the needs of the project?
    - Is there a clear need for any equipment requested?
    - Is each request for equipment related directly to operationalizing (performing) an objective?
    - Is the request reasonable?

11. Are other resources adequate for the needs of the project?
    - Is planned use of current resources efficient and cost-effective?
    - Is there adequate access to resources not under the applicant's control?
12. Are the costs reasonable?
    - Are the costs presented in spreadsheets or formal tables?
    - Are the costs separated into categories, including personnel (salaries, wages, and benefits), equipment, travel, operating expenses, indirect costs (overhead), and incidental?
    - Are the costs measured in the same units and in present value?
    - Are they adequate? Why?
    - Do they underestimate or overestimate likely project expenses? If so, be sure to explain why more reliable figures are not being used.
    - Does the budget justification present a clear rationale for the funding requested?
    - Does the budget justification present an item justification for each set of expenses?
    - Is the budget table presented with section totals and a full project total?
13. Is the overall proposal well written, logical, and persuasive?
    - Are arguments presented deductively?
    - Are all problems, goals, and objectives discussed in rank order consistently across the document?
    - Are arguments made in active voice?
    - Are most paragraphs controlled by assertive topic sentences?
    - Are there introduction paragraphs at the beginning and conclusion paragraphs at the end of each section?
    - Are the paragraphs concise, compact, and well written (usually no longer than half a page or no shorter than three sentences)?
    - Is the evidence from secondary sources referenced and fully credited?
    - Is the proposal supported by a balance of evidence (qualitative to quantitative)?
    - Is the writing style professional, consistent, and coherent?
14. Is the proposal presented well, with easily readable type, clearly distinguishable subheadings, sufficient margins, etc.?
    - Does the proposal meet the format criteria stated in the call for proposals (margins, fonts, type of paper, page numbering, placement of page numbering)?
    - Are there headings and subheadings that distinguish between sections in the proposal?
    - Are the grantor's headings and subheading *identical* to those listed in the call for proposals?
    - Are the tables, figures, etc., professionally labeled?
    - Are the page limitations (if any) for each section met?
    - Is the space and layout professional and used efficiently (no white or blank space, no widowed or orphaned headings)?
    - Are all appendix materials clearly referenced in the text (such as "see Appendix D")?

Example: A Simple RFP with a Requirement Matrix

CALIFORNIA BAR FOUNDATION
GRANT APPLICATION QUESTIONNAIRE

(Abridged from http://www.calbarfoundation.org/programs/grants/2008-2009Grant
ApplicationPacket.pdf.)

Applicant Information and Project Description

Provide the following information about the Applicant and the Project for which
Applicant is requesting funding:

1. Applicant's mission statement and a brief history of Applicant.
2. Detailed Project description.
3. Identify the target group, the estimated number of persons to be reached, and the geographic impact of the Project.
4. Identify the need Applicant's Project will serve and how Applicant's Project will address that need.
5. Describe how Applicant will measure the success of the Project.
6. Describe how the Project will be implemented, including listing which staff members will be involved, and the general time line for implementation of the Project.
7. Identify any other organization with which Applicant is collaborating on this Project.
8. If funding in addition to any Foundation Grant awarded is necessary, indicate where Applicant will obtain the additional funding that the Project needs for implementation and whether the Project can be implemented without such additional funding.
9. Describe how Applicant will be able to implement this program within the Project's estimated time line without Foundation funding, if at all.
10. If the Project will continue beyond the 2009 calendar year, describe how the Project will be funded in the future.

Project Budget

Provide a detailed budget for the Project for each of the following items. Identify
which of the Project costs are already accounted for in Applicant's annual budget
by marking such costs with an asterisk (*).

Project Staff	$
Materials/Supplies	$
Space	$
Travel	$
Copying/Printing	$
Meeting/Conference Costs	$
Telephone	$
Other: _____	$
Other: _____	$
Other: _____	$
Amount of Total Project Budget	**$**
Amount of funding requested from the California Bar Foundation	$
Amount of other funding for the Project	$
Anticipated source(s) of other funding: _____	$

Example: A Grant Letter and Grant Proposal Application

December 8, 2005

Ms. Karen Hughes
Grant Program Manager
Foundation of the State Bar of California
180 Howard Street
San Francisco, CA 94105-1639

Enclosure: "SHARP Knowledgebase Project" in response to the 2005 State Bar of California Foundation Annual Grants Program.

Dear Ms. Hughes,

Legal assistance is undoubtedly a significant barrier for access to the judiciary by the public. Handling cases that involve self-represented litigants is a daily process that affects the court at every level, from the filing of paperwork, to case management, to courtroom proceedings. Programs such as the Butte, Glenn, and Tehama County Court Self-Help and Referral Program (SHARP) provide a pivotal service to self-represented litigants by educating them in proper legal logistics and by assisting them with the completion of court forms and filing procedures. This proposal offers to augment the delivery of services that SHARP provides to the public.

The SHARP knowledge-base proposal focuses on improving program efficiency, effectiveness, and equity by implementing a computer knowledgebase for use by staff. Knowledgebases have been proven tools in improving staff development, increasing customer satisfaction, and creating cost savings when used in customer service environments. By organizing and retrieving program information in a convenient and centralized digital repository, staffs are able to serve program clients in a prompt, efficient, and consistent manner.

By increasing the quality of information to self-represented litigants through the knowledge-base project, SHARP will be better able to help litigants successfully navigate through the court case flow process. A 2005 Judicial Council–sponsored evaluation has shown that litigants who are properly prepared for court, and who are cognizant of legal procedures, ultimately develop confidence in the judicial system and help court calendars operate more efficiently. With these outcomes in mind, the knowledge-base project will assist SHARP staff in the effective delivery of vital information for self-represented litigants.

I would like to thank you for giving the SHARP program the opportunity to pursue this project. With your help, we can increase the effectiveness of our assistance to litigants in need. I look forward to working with you.

Please do not hesitate to contact me should you have any questions.

Sincerely,

Michael Scott Miller

CALIFORNIA BAR FOUNDATION GRANT APPLICATION: SHARP KNOWLEDGEBASE PROJECT

1. Organizational Details

- ***Mission Statement:*** SHARP's mission statement is to provide legal assistance and community-based referrals to self-represented litigants in areas of family and general civil law.
- ***Brief History:*** SHARP has been in existence for three years and has assisted some 15,000 self-represented litigants in the Butte, Glenn, and Tehama Counties since the program's inception in 2002. The program was created through the 2001 California State Budget Act, which called for the creation of five pilot programs that addressed access to the legal system and improving court efficiency. Importantly, the SHARP program recently won a KLEPS award from the AOC for program ingenuity and innovation. Finally, SHARP employs one part-time managing attorney, Ms. Suzanne Morlock, who has been with the organization since its creation, full-time paralegal Mr. Chad Sallade, who has been with the program since 2004, and full-time paralegal Ms. Starla Knight, who has been with the program for three months. Additionally, the program employs two part-time Office Assistants. The number of volunteers will vary throughout the year, but there are typically one to three part-time volunteers/student interns.

2. Detailed Project Description

This proposed project utilizes a knowledgebase to help augment service delivery of the SHARP program. The SHARP program currently assists self-represented litigants with the preparing of legal documents for filing with the court and will aid individuals with Family Law court matters by providing them with general information. SHARP staffs do not provide legal representation or counsel; staff is responsible for delivering detailed procedural information and edifying clients of the logistics of court actions and appearances. Services are currently delivered via in-person workshops, telephonic appraisals, and videoconferencing.

The knowledgebase would enhance via SHARP's existing service delivery by providing greater public access to information. The knowledgebase is a software program that acts as a digital central repository for program documents, articles, and self-help guides that can be queried through a user-friendly search portal. Users of the program can have immediate access to information in the knowledgebase. Users can access this information by visiting SHARP's Internet page or by coming into a SHARP center to use a public terminal.

There are several benefits to using a knowledgebase to enhance service delivery. First, customer service is increased due to the provision of information in a prompt and thorough manner. Due to the accessibility of the knowledgebase from a remote computer, public accessibility to the program is greatly increased. Second, staff efficiency is increased. Direct training of new employees is reduced as they are able to query the knowledgebase for answers to operational questions. Staff is also able to provide clients with consistent and reliable information based on the material listed in the knowledgebase. Finally, calls and e-mails to the program should subside as the knowledgebase is able to provide assistance to the more common questions and scenarios.

Importantly, this project can serve as a model. The project can be applied to regions that have the technical resources and infrastructure to implement the service. Forms, scripts, checklists, and handouts for self-represented litigants are available from the AOC and can be replicated, or modified for regional variations, for use on a knowledgebase. Knowledgebase software is ubiquitous, and several different vendors offer the product. Further, the project could easily be used in an urban setting to help with the volume of customer inquiries, and it could be used in a rural environment to address transportation barriers. For example, the city of Los Angeles utilized a knowledgebase in conjunction with a call center model to increase citizen access to government information. This highly successful project, known as the 3-1-1 project, allows citizens to access government information in a rapid and thorough fashion.

3. What is The Target Group to be Served/Reached?

- ***Target Group:*** The target group that is served by this project includes those individuals who do not have the ability or the desire to retain legal counsel to assist them during court proceedings. Other targets include the employees of the SHARP program.
- ***What Is the Estimated Number of Persons Served/Reached?:*** According to program statistics, SHARP serves an average of 5,000 customers per year. Approximately 60 percent of SHARP's clients are served in Butte County, 25 percent in Tehama County, and 15 percent in Glenn County. Currently, 51 percent of clients are assisted by telephone, 31 percent of clients are assisted via walk-in appointments, and 17 percent are assisted in attorney-conducted workshops. SHARP is currently limited by the office hours in each county, which vary depending on staff availability. The implementation of a knowledgebase could increase the amount of access to the program considerably.

4. What Need will The Applicant's Project Serve/How Addressed?

- ***Need Served:*** Individuals who have transportation barriers, or who have day care, work, or school commitments cannot attend SHARP during normal operating hours, which fluctuate depending on staff availability, thus making it difficult for those individuals to obtain procedural assistance with court paperwork and appearances. Clients may have time-sensitive questions or may need to complete judgments to complete their cases. Access to SHARP is currently limited by staff availability. Additionally, SHARP has had difficulty in training new employees due to the limited time of the managing attorney who must attend to both administrative issues and service delivery. The knowledgebase will assist in the training of new employees.
- ***How Needs Addressed:*** With the implementation of a knowledgebase, clients will be able to procure procedural and filing information remotely at any time during the day. Clients and potential clients are not reliant on the physical hours of the individual SHARP centers. For those individuals who do not have home Internet access, SHARP information can still be obtained via Internet connections at public libraries. In addition, staff training will also be enhanced with the knowledgebase, as new information can be researched and obtained from the database. New employees can search the database to ascertain procedural information. This will assist with the development of new employees.

5. **How Will Applicant Measure The Success of The Project?** The knowledge-base has reporting and metric capabilities that can record the client's needs and preferences. Additionally, Information Technology staff can maintain statistics as to the number of Web site visits. Finally, online customer surveys can generate useful demographic data and allow for immediate public feedback of the online resources.

6. **How Project Will be Implemented/Staff/Time Line.** First, the knowledgebase has to be built by centralizing, updating, evaluating, and codifying all programmatic data (forms, procedures, graphs, checklists, etc.) that will be available to the public. This action would be performed by the current SHARP managing attorney with the help of her paralegal assistants within the first six months.

   Second, standard operating procedures have to be drafted to determine how the knowledgebase will be maintained and updated and how material will be reviewed for currency. This action would be performed by the SHARP managing attorney within the next three months.

   Third, technical deployment would be performed by Butte County Information Technology and Tehama County Information Technology staff. This action of implementing the software would be performed by one senior-level Information Technology Analyst in Butte County, as Butte County currently has the technological infrastructure in place for such a project. The action of setting up desktop equipment for the public would be performed by one Information Technology Technician in Butte County and one Information Technology Technician in Tehama County within the next three months.

   Finally, one senior- or journeyman-level Information Technology Analyst from Butte County would be required to provide staff training for the remaining three months.

7. **Identify Any Other Organization That is Working on This Project** This project would work with the local Butte County Bar Association to solicit information with regard to online documentation and content. This project would also work with the Family Law Facilitator in Glenn and Tehama Counties for additional online content advice. Both document centralization and technological deployment will be conducted by current staff members of SHARP and the Butte and Tehama courts (Butte County provides technical service to Glenn County on a contract basis).

8. **Have You Sought Funding Elsewhere? If Additional Funding is Necessary, Where Will You Obtain the Additional Funding that your Project Needs for Implementation?** Current program operations are funded by a grant from the Administrative Office of the Courts (AOC). The AOC also provides funding for technological tools such as teleconferencing and videoconferencing. Workshops are funded through monies obtained from Assembly Bill 1058. Funding from these two grants provides the fiscal foundation for SHARP. The knowledgebase would not be implemented without additional funding because the two grants are already completely committed to other tasks.

9. **Without Foundation Funding, Will You be able to Implement This Program Within Your Estimated Time Line?** Without additional funding, this project will not be implemented. The current grants that sustain SHARP do not

provide enough funding for such a project. This project continues SHARP's tradition of using technology to increase public access to legal resources. While knowledgebases are used extensively in private-sector call center environments, there are no public self-help centers in California that utilize this technology.

10. **If the Project will Continue Beyond the 2009 Calendar Year, Describe how the Project will be Funded in the Future.** The project is designed to be completed within a calendar year. Any remaining tasks will be completed by SHARP staff.

Project Budget for Sharp Knowledgebase Project		
Project Expense	**Expense Details**	**Amount**
Project Staff°:	Currently covered in the operational budget of the program	$0
Materials/Supplies:	25 binders/dividers at $10 per binder and divider bundle	$250
Space°	Currently covered in the operational budget of the program	$0
Travel:	Transportation to three facilities covering over 150 miles for two staff members, traveling three times each at 34 cents a mile	$153
Copying/Printing:	4 cases of paper at $25 per case	$100
Meeting/Conference:	Not applicable	$0
Telephone°:	Currently covered in the operational budget of the program	$0
Other: Software:	One unit	$1,200
Other: Licensing:	One unit that allows unlimited workstation installations	$300
Other: Desktop PCs:	Three units at $1,300 per unit	$3,900
Amount of Total Project Budget		**$5,903**
Amount of funding requested from the California Bar Foundation		$5,903
Amount of other funding for the Project		$0
Anticipated source(s) of other funding		$0

Writing a Project Report

Purpose

Project report writing is a form of technical writing used in many disciplines. It is often used to report results from funded research or program development in the private, public, and nonprofit sectors. For students in political science, public administration, and public policy, these types of reports are often required for courses or course activities involving civic engagement, service learning, experiential education, or other community outreach or work projects. The goal for the project report is to provide a written record of the students' activities, either in the interim (before the tasks are completely finished) or when the project is completed. The report provides a description of the project, the resources used and produced in the project, and evidence of the project results. (For additional discussion, see Hazen 2004; Fisher n.d.; Martin 2002).

How to Construct a Project Report

- Project reports are expected to be brief and succinct. Reports for complex projects are rarely over 20 pages; small, simple project are generally well represented by a 5–10 page report. These reports are professionally presented and use a standard professional presentation style of single spacing and 12-point font.
- The audience level is intelligent nonspecialist unless the student is told otherwise. The writing style is direct, using short words, very little, if any, jargon, and short sentences. The paragraphs should be no shorter than three sentences, but no longer than five sentences. The report is not written as a diary or story; it is a *summary* of the project and is written in the past tense for all completed tasks.
- Project reports generally do not have verbatim quotes, contractions, or personal references (no "I, me, you, we," etc.).
- Project reports require references as sources for any information that has been used that was not produced by the project activities. This is particularly important for the justification, historical context, and strategy discussions.
- Project reports require topic headings and subheadings throughout the document.
- Project reports should include a table or graph of the results. The tables and graphs are usually embedded in the text.
- Project reports may include bulleted or numbered lists.
- Project reports always include an appendix or appendices with copies of any and all evidence of the project results or materials produced by the project.

Structure of a Project Report

Project reports usually reflect the structure of the project, yet there are several expected conventions in all project reports. They always include a summary of the issues addressed by the project, the context of the project, justification for the project, strategy for accomplishing goals, resources used or needed to accomplish project goals, and a conclusion. A project report generally includes the following (use headings to indicate them):

Title Page (Include the name of the organization, community, and a simple title.)

Table of Contents/List of Figures and Tables (This is particularly important for complex project reports with numerous figures, tables, and appendices.)

Executive Summary   (Including a brief introduction to the project, a statement of the problem, a description of the approach or structure of the project, the main accomplishments of the project, and conclusions.)

Summary of the Issues   (This generally functions like an introduction where the saliency of the problem is explored, the scope is explained, objectives are clarified, and an assertion or hypothesis is provided. When possible, a concept map should be used to illustrate relationships.)

Historical Context of the Project Problem   (This provides a general overview or background about the problems and issues involved in the project and a literature review of previous work related to the project goals.)

Justification for Project   (The veracity of the project is defended; discuss when, how, and under what circumstances intervention in this problem/issue is valid.)

Project Strategy   (Include a discussion of the methodology used to structure the strategy, what/which tasks were done or still need to be done, by whom, the resources necessary for completion, source of resources used in the project, what data were used, procedures used, and any process or standards used; illustrate whenever possible.)

Findings and Results of the Project   (Present the results of the project to date, provide descriptions of how well or poorly resources were used and/or tasks were completed, provide explanations for unfinished tasks, use tables, graphs, and/or illustrations to summarize results whenever possible, identify where results reach or accomplish the goals of the project.)

Conclusion   (Discuss the results as they relate to the goals of the project, draw conclusions about the value of the project, make assertions about how the results relate to previous work, suggest next steps if necessary, explore the implications of the results.)

References   (Provide a list of all secondary sources of information used to develop the report.)

Appendices   (All materials included in appendices must have a text reference and should include all supporting detail in separate appendices including, but not limited to, source documents, data, pictures, pamphlets, brochures, activity logs, news coverage about the project, and any supporting materials used in the research; original data are often included on a CD.)

because the program lacked the ability to serve them (Legal Services Corporation 2005). Additionally, the LSC noted that there is only one legal aid attorney for every 6,861 low-income persons in the United States (Legal Services Corporation 2005). Funding for legal aid centers has not increased with the increase in population, which further contributes to the rise of unmet legal needs for the poor (Smith 1991).

The Issue of Self-Representation: Impact on Court Operations

Court procedures are primarily designed for legal counsel, not for the layperson (Zeleznikow 2002). The significance of the lack of legal aid to individuals from low economic groups is that litigants are forced to navigate through the justice system without the aid of an attorney, which impacts the efficient operation of court calendars (National Center for State Courts 2005). The rise of self-represented litigants poses significant challenges to judicial officers as self-represented litigants are often unfamiliar with legal terminology, process, and substantive legal understanding (National Center for State Courts 2005). Self-represented litigants who are unfamiliar with legal lexicon, case procedures, and proper legal decorum ultimately slow case processing and court calendars (State Judicial Institute 2001).

The problem of self-represented litigation posed ethical and legal dilemmas and prompted court leaders to take action to draft solutions (Albrecht 2003). Judicial officers were concerned that to fairly adjudicate cases with self-represented litigants they would have to depart from their role as a neutral arbiter of facts by explaining legal procedures to litigants (Albrecht 2003). A survey of Virginia judicial officers indicated that 75 percent of judicial officers had concerns with admissibility of evidence issues, and nearly 50 percent of judicial officers cite concerns of litigant understanding in the courtroom (State Justice Institute 2001). Ultimately, judicial officers felt that litigants were ill-equipped to handle the judicial process without representation.

The problem of self-represented litigants was defined as an operational dilemma for courts and policy was considered when judicial officers were impacted by legal and ethical quandaries. The focus of policy makers was to then determine how court efficiency could be improved, given that the number of self-represented litigants continues to increase (Zeleznikow 2002). The court community approached the problem from the aspect of improving judicial support systems (Zeleznikow 2002). Social and economic precursors to self-represented litigants, while acknowledged, were not addressed at the judicial level of problem intervention.

HISTORICAL CONTEXT

To combat the rise of self-represented litigants in the area of family law, the California legislature created California Family Code 10002 in 1997 to create the office of the Family Law Facilitator (Hough 2004). The Family Law Facilitator is responsible for providing procedural assistance to individuals in areas such as divorce and custody (Hough 2004). In 1999, the California legislature funded three Family Law Information Centers in Los Angeles, Fresno, and Sutter counties to assist low-income individuals in understanding their rights and responsibilities in family law matters (Hough 2004). The Family Law Information Centers have proven to be successful by initiating cost savings to the courts and in providing assistance to needy clients (Judicial Council 2003).

The impetus for the creation for California's Self-Help programs started at a national judicial conference on self-represented litigants in Arizona in 1999 (Hough 2005). Bonnie Hough, Chief Counsel for the Children and Families Division at the Administrative Office of the Courts, was responsible for drafting the action plan for the State of California that would allow for Self-Help centers to be created throughout the state (Hough 2005). California Chief Justice Ronald George and William Vickery, the Director of the Administrative Office of the Courts, were the key individuals in pursuing the pilot programs (Hough 2005).

Director William Vickery soon called for a budget change proposal to be presented to the California legislature. Initially, funding was to be for all 58 California counties, but this idea was modified by the finance division at the Administrative Office of the Courts due to the costs that would have been incurred (Hough 2005). The finance division decided that five programs could be allocated a total of $166,400, for a total of $832,000 to be included in the judicial branch's annual budget (Hough 2005). This funding would then be allocated on a competitive basis, as counties would have to submit their action plans to receive funding for Self -Help Centers (Strickland 2005). Funding was originally set for three years, with the hope that the legislature would continue to fund the projects into the future (Hough 2005).

Initial objections to the program were mainly financial, but interviews with program administrators indicated that there continues to be some resistance from local bar associations with regards to Self-Help Centers (Rasnow 2005). Some attorneys feel that self-represented litigants are receiving preferential treatment from the court system (Goldschmidt 2002), and that Self-Help Centers draw business away from law practices (Rasnow 2005). Additionally, some judicial officers expressed concern that Self-Help centers create a bifurcated system where one set of rules exists for attorneys and one set of rules exists for unrepresented litigants (Goldschmidt 2002).

Without much controversy, the request for self-help funding was incorporated by the Department of Finance into the state budget of 2001 (Hough 2005). Governor Gray Davis signed the State Budget Act on July 26, 2001 (Judicial Council 2004). The impetus for the creation of the Self-Help centers was then created.

Objectives and Tools of the Pilot Programs

With the passage of the California State Budget Act in 2001, funding was soon allocated to five different programs, including a regional collaboration in Butte, Glenn, and Tehama counties. By consolidating their resources, the northern California counties were able to develop a program that could utilize technology with workshops to service their population base over a broad area (Appendix A). Attorney Suzanne Morlock was soon hired to oversee and manage the program on a contract basis (Judicial Council 2005).

The Self-Help pilot programs were created in part to satisfy the California Judicial Council's strategic goals of increasing access to justice and to improve the quality and services delivered to the public (Judicial Council 2004). The centers were implemented to see if the pilot programs would be successful enough to be applied to other courts throughout the state. The centers were to meet the following objectives from the Judicial Council (Hough 2003):

- increase litigant understanding of, and compliance with, court orders.
- increase access to justice.
- increase user satisfaction with the court process.
- increase efficiency of court operations.
- increase education for court users so that they may expect realistic case outcomes.
- increase education to allow court users to present their "best case" in court.

The Self-Help Centers are the tools to meet the objectives to increase user knowledge of the court system so that they may effectively represent themselves. The targets of the Self-Help Centers are those individuals who do not have the means to hire legal counsel (Judicial Council 2005). The Self-Help Centers do not provide resources for legal advocacy, nor do they provide licensed legal representation in court (Judicial Council 2004). Based on the objectives listed above, the Self-Help Centers do aim to satisfy the Judicial Council's goal of accessible justice. The Self-Help Centers do not address the problem of the cost of hiring counsel. The fees for legal representation were not addressed by the Judicial Council and were not identified as an objective.

JUSTIFICATION OF THE COLLABORATION

Based on interviews with SHARP staff and a 2003 Judicial Council–sponsored program evaluation, SHARP suffers from program deficiencies in that it is unable to retain institutional memory due to high staff attrition that is a result of inadequate funding levels for the program. Although the professional evaluation performed by the Judicial Council indicated that client satisfaction with the program remains high, the evaluation did note recurring problems of staff attrition (Judicial Council 2005).

Collaborative Focus: SHARP Staff Attrition and Courtroom Efficiency

The effects of staff attrition impact the effectiveness, efficiency, and equity in the implementation of the program and impact court operations in the three courts served by SHARP. Clients of the program are impacted as the program has to alter service hours due to staff attrition (Morlock 2005). The managing attorney devotes a substantial portion of her time to staff training due to frequent staff turnover and has little time to devote to administrative tasks such as outreach, pursuing new funding sources, or developing program enhancements (Morlock 2005). Court operations are also impacted, as clients do not always receive optimal service from SHARP due to lack of program knowledge of new staff (Hovsepian 2005). Court staff then has to shift resources to assist court users with incorrect paperwork, reducing the efficiency of courtroom operations.

Collaborative Project: A Knowledgebase Solution

To address the issue of the lack of institutional memory of SHARP staff, a collaborative venture between the SHARP program and the Butte County Superior Court was developed to allow SHARP staff to house and access digital training data on the Butte County Superior Court's electronic knowledgebase (Appendix B). This allows SHARP staff to improve their knowledge capacity while the Butte County Superior Court staff enhances their collaborative capacity. Therefore, the SHARP program and the Butte County Superior Court can achieve more in collaboration than they are able to achieve separately. SHARP currently does not have the financial ability to procure a knowledgebase for its staff, and the Butte County Superior Court does not have the ability to provide the services of SHARP with court staff (Strickland 2005). The condition of mutual and reciprocal success creates an incentive for both parties to pursue collaboration (Straus 2002).

Donor-Recipient Model of Collaboration

The Butte County Superior Court and SHARP program collaboration may be classified as a donor-recipient model of collaboration. The donor-recipient model of collaboration is a vertical collaboration in which the donor does not have the ability to deliver the services within the organization (Agranoff and McGuire 2003). The parties in a donor-recipient model rely on one another to provide assistance in order to satisfy the goal of both parties through shared administration of the collaboration (Agranoff and McGuire 2003).

For the Butte-SHARP collaboration, SHARP does not have the financial or technical capacity to host a knowledgebase for its program (Morlock 2005). The Butte County Superior Court does not have the ability to deliver services that SHARP provides (Strickland 2005). Thus, the Butte County Superior Court can provide a resource (an electronic knowledgebase) to SHARP to expand SHARP's collaborative capacity, which allows SHARP to address its goal of retaining institutional memory, while the Butte County Superior Court's goal of enhancing courtroom efficiency is addressed.

Knowledgebase Benefits

A knowledgebase is an electronic repository of information that is quickly accessible by either internal or external users of an organization. The central premise of a knowledgebase is identifying, capturing, and disseminating knowledge within an organization (Repath and Foxlow 1994). By creating, codifying, and transferring information in an immediately accessible digital format, the preservation and creation of knowledge can be ensured within an organization (Bhatt 2000). Therefore, a knowledgebase becomes a desirable tool to prevent the leakage of knowledge in an organization.

First, a knowledgebase is a useful tool for organizations that operate in a dynamic setting. Organizations that experience internal or external change need the capability to increase their storage and dissemination of knowledge (Chaharbargi and Nugent 1994). The significance of this is that an organization with effective knowledge management is not reliant on a select few individuals for expertise; a knowledgebase captures information from several sources and allows information to be accessed by anyone in the organization rapidly (Repath and Foxlow 1994). Furthermore, a knowledgebase retains information even after the human expert has left the organization (Martinsons 1995). Therefore, a knowledgebase may improve the efficiency of an organization.

Second, a knowledgebase can improve the consistency and equity of the services being delivered by an organization. Knowledgebases promote decision consistency because the knowledgebase acts as a common foundation for service delivery in the organization (Martinsons 1995). This also allows for best practices to be identified and then delivered on a consistent basis by service providers (Repath and Foxlow 1994). Thus, a knowledgebase is able to provide improvements in organizational equity.

The integration of SHARP into the Butte County Superior Court's knowledgebase is an appropriate objective to increase the institutional memory of SHARP staff. SHARP has had difficulty with knowledge retention and equitable service delivery (Hovsepian 2005). SHARP has also had difficulty in that additional resources have to be frequently diverted to training (Morlock 2005). The implementation of a knowledgebase helps address these programmatic challenges.

COLLABORATIVE STRATEGY

The implementation of a knowledgebase for the SHARP program required the assistance of SHARP administration staff and Butte County Superior Court's operations and information systems division to ensure that SHARP staff is cognizant of how to utilize the knowledgebase, that SHARP administrators are familiar with article creation, and that ongoing support is established between both organizations to enable continuous quality improvement on the knowledgebase project. The central objective of this project is making certain that all relevant stakeholders would be included and that sufficient bonds of trust would be established and maintained throughout the collaborative process.

Principle of Inclusion

Inclusion of all stakeholders is a pivotal part of a successful collaborative effort (Straus 2002). The inclusion of all stakeholders in a collaborative process helps to minimize the rejection of the collaborative efforts (Kaner 1996). The significance here is that the process of collaboration should remain an open and transparent venture where feedback loops can be established between stakeholders so that a variety of viewpoints can be established in the final product. This is important, as even ancillary groups can offer input back to the core group of a collaborative effort (Boris and Steuerle 2006).

The Butte County Superior Court and the SHARP program have benefited from having a nearly seven-year collaborative relationship. Both organizations have achieved trust through action and through progressive accomplishments (Strickland 2005). Incremental accomplishments can help to strengthen the bonds of a collaborative effort (Boris and Steuerle 2006). Thus, the foundation for a successful collaboration is in place for the SHARP and Butte County Superior Court collaborative to achieve success.

Structure of Work

The work for the Butte-SHARP collaboration consists of three general phases: an orientation phase, an implementation phase, and an evaluation phase (Figure 1).

Figure 1: Gantt Chart for Knowledgebase Project 2008

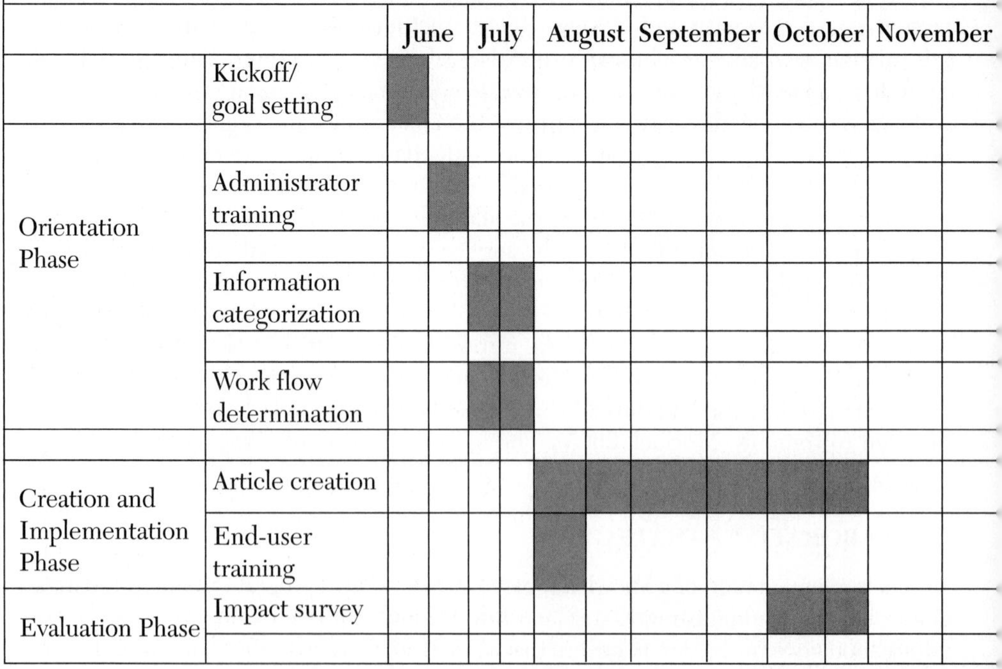

		June		July		August		September		October		November	
	Kickoff/ goal setting	▓											
Orientation Phase	Administrator training			▓									
	Information categorization					▓							
	Work flow determination					▓							
Creation and Implementation Phase	Article creation						▓	▓	▓	▓	▓		
	End-user training						▓						
Evaluation Phase	Impact survey										▓	▓	

Each phase represents a distinct set of activities that must be enacted before the next phase can begin. These phases are predicated on the Butte County Superior Court's previous experience with implementing a knowledgebase in the summer of 2007. The key individuals are identified in Table 1.

Table 1: Key Individuals

Person	Organization	Responsibility
Andrea Nelson	Butte County Superior Court	Butte County Superior Court administrative liaison; evaluation
Michael Miller	Butte County Superior Court	Staff and administrator training
Phillip Simpson	Butte County Superior Court	Technical support
Tammy Grimm	SHARP	Procedure writing
Nancy McGie	SHARP	SHARP administrative liaison; evaluation

The orientation phase. The orientation phase primarily consists of administrator training on the use of the knowledgebase. Figure 1 shows that a kickoff meeting was held to summarize the knowledgebase and identify key areas that SHARP administrators would like to identify first in the collaborative effort. Second, training was provided by Michael Miller of Butte County Superior Court to Tammy Grimm and Nancy McGie of SHARP. This training is primarily designed to instruct SHARP staff how to create articles in a knowledgebase and how to navigate though the screens of the knowledgebase software. The orientation phase identifies how SHARP procedures should be categorized for logical retrieval by staff and exactly which SHARP staff has the ability to create and approve articles. Tammy Grimm, administrative coordinator for SHARP, assumed oversight for article creation for SHARP.

The creation phase. The creation phase consisted of SHARP personnel creating articles that will be placed into the knowledgebase. It is important to create articles that are accurate and useful for staff to increase the effectiveness of the knowledge in improving service delivery. At least 50 articles will have been completed by the end of October, allowing SHARP administrators to create and approve approximately 3 articles per week. End-user training was also provided to staff in all three SHARP locations by Michael Miller. The knowledgebase was accessible to end users during the creation stage in an attempt to provide immediate assistance to the SHARP program.

The evaluation phase. The evaluation phase features a joint evaluation of the knowledgebase collaborative project by SHARP administrative liaison Nancy McGie and the Butte County Superior Court administrative liaison Andrea Nelson. An impact survey of SHARP staff and Butte County Superior Court staff will be administered to ascertain if the knowledgebase has increased staff knowledge and if it has improved the efficiency of case flow processes. The work product of SHARP staff will be audited through a random sampling of case files and by shadowing SHARP client interviews to determine if staff is providing consistent information to the public.

FINDINGS AND RESULTS

The Butte-SHARP collaboration will need continued technical, physical, and human resources to fully implement the project. SHARP staff will need continued access to the knowledgebase, conference facilities will have to be available to provide training, and personnel must continue to be available to deliver training and offer support to end users and program administrators. These resources are important to adequately implement the strategic collaborative plan.

Technical Resources

The Butte-SHARP collaborative will utilize the existing knowledgebase currently in use by the Butte County Superior Court. Butte County Superior Court Information Systems staff will be responsible for creating the necessary accounts for SHARP users and ensuring adequate access by SHARP employees from all three counties. The Butte County Superior Court currently provides information systems support for general operations on a contract basis; therefore, the framework for data integration is already in place.

Physical Resources

Physical resources will be needed to conduct training for administrators and end users. The Butte County Superior Court currently has training space for eight SHARP employees in a single session. Conference rooms and training laptops will be reserved to facilitate the training process on the knowledgebase. Videoconferencing capabilities exist in all SHARP offices (Judicial Council 2005) and at all Butte County Superior Court facilities for remote meetings.

Human Resources

Administrative staff from the SHARP program and the Butte County Superior Court will need to schedule adequate time for the implementation of the project. Butte County Superior Court administrative staff and SHARP administrative staff need to be accessible throughout all three phases of project implementation. Time must also be scheduled for SHARP line staff to attend training sessions. Finally, time for evaluative staff must be made available to measure the project's outcome in the evaluation phase.

CONCLUSION

The Butte-SHARP collaborative project addresses the challenge of attrition in the SHARP program. The challenge of SHARP's attrition is that services to the public are reduced as the quality of service declines and courtroom operations are encumbered. By developing a system to capture and retain institutional memory, the Butte-SHARP collaborative

- improves the effectiveness of SHARP by providing a system that delivers accurate and thorough information,
- improves the efficiency of SHARP, as fewer resources have to be devoted to the training of SHARP staff, and
- improves equity of access to SHARP, as the information provided to clients is consistent and reliable, allowing different clients to receive the same information.

The Butte County Superior Court benefits from the collaboration. As the SHARP program staff improves their service delivery to the public, courtroom operations are improved because the court devotes fewer resources to assisting unrepresented litigants in court cases. This allows court calendars to operate more efficiently and effectively.

Ultimately, the Butte-SHARP collaborative is a model in which one organization possesses the technical ability to assist another organization in a vertical arrangement. The central focus of this collaboration is that neither the Butte County Superior Court nor the SHARP program could implement this program without the other agency being involved. Therefore, collaboration is the most effective arrangement for improving service to the public, as both organizations can achieve more working towards a common goal.

REFERENCES

Agranoff, Robert, and Michael McGuire. 2003. *Collaborative public management.* Washington, DC: Georgetown University Press.

Bhatt, Ganesh. 2000. Information dynamics: Learning and knowledge creation in organizations. *The Learning Organization* 7 (2): 89–98.

Chaharbaghi, Kazem, and Edward Nugent. 1994. Towards the dynamic organization. Management Decision 32 (6): 45–48.

Frederickson, Teresa. 2001. *Service to the self-represented litigant and court staff training: The disconnect.* http://www.nsconline.org/D_ICM/Research_Papers_2001/Service_to_the_Self_Represented/pdf.

Goldschmidt, Jona. 2002. *Meeting the challenge of pro se litigation: A report and guidebook for judges and court managers.* Chicago, IL: American Judicature Society.

Greacean, John. 2001. *Self-represented litigants and court and legal services responses to their needs: What we know.* http://www.courtinfo.ca.gov/programs/cfcc/pdffiles/SRLwhatweknow.pdf.

Hannaford-Agor, Paula L. 2003. Helping the pro se litigant: A changing landscape. *Court Review* 39 (4): 8–16.

Hough, Bonnie. 2003. Description of California courts' programs for self-represented litigants. *International Journal of the Legal Profession* 11 (3): 305–334.

Hough, Bonnie. 2004. Self-represented litigants in California: Court programs helping litigants help themselves. http:www/nsconline.org/D_KIS/Trends/Trends04MainPage.html.

Hough, Bonnie. 2005. Supervising attorney for the Center of Children, Families, and the Courts. Personal interview. October 14, 2005.

Hovsepian, Vahan. 2005. Family and Children Services Director, Butte County Superior Court. Personal interview. October 21, 2005.

Judicial Council of California. 2003. *A report to the legislature—family law information centers: An evaluation of three pilot programs.* San Francisco, CA. Government Printing Office.

Judicial Council of California. 2004. *Statewide action plan for serving self-represented litigants.* San Francisco, CA: Government Printing Office.

Judicial Council of California. 2005. *Model self-help pilot programs: A report to the legislature.* San Francisco, CA: Government Printing Office.

Kaner, Sam, et al. 1996. *Facilitator's guide to participatory decision-making*. Gabriola Island, BC: New Society Publishing.

Legal Services Corporation. 2005. *Documenting the justice gap in American*. Washington DC: Legal Services Corporation Press.

Martinsons, Maris. 1995. Knowledge-based systems leverage human resource management expertise. *International Journal of Manpower* 16 (2): 17–34.

Mather, Lynn. 2003. Changing patterns of legal representation in divorce from lawyers to pro se. *Journal of Law and Society* 30 (1): 137–155.

Morlock, Suzanne. 2005. Managing Attorney of SHARP (2001–2006). Personal interview. October 19, 2005.

National Center for State Courts. 2005. *The future of self-represented litigation: Report from the March 2005 summit*. Denver, CO: Government Printing Office.

Rasnow, Tina. Managing Attorney of the Ventura County Superior Court Self-Help Center. 2005. Personal interview. October 19, 2005.

Repath, Kathleen, and Tim Foxlow. 1994. Knowledgebase manufacturing. *Assembly Automation* 14 (4): 21–25.

Smith, Christopher E. 1991. *Courts and the poor*. Chicago, IL: Nelson-Hall Publishers.

State Justice Institute of Virginia. 2001. *Enhancing access to justice*. Richmond, VA: Government Printing Office.

Straus, David. 2002. *How to make collaboration work*. San Francisco, CA: Berrett-Koehler Press.

Strickland, Sharol. 2005. Court Executive Officer, Butte County Superior Court. Personal interview. October 17, 2005.

Zeleznikow, John. 2002. Using web-based legal decision support systems to improve access to justice. *Journal of Information and Communications Technology* 11 (1): 15–33.

Appendix A: Screenshot of SHARP's Public Web Site

Butte County Superior Court - Microsoft Internet Explorer provided by Butte County Courts GP

http://www.buttecourt.ca.gov/departments/self_help/sharp.htm

Live Search

Butte County Superior Court

Page ▾ Tools ▾

Superior Court of California
County of Butte

Career Opportunities	Family Law	Jury & Appeals	Self Help	Traffic	

Home
Alt Dispute Resolution
Case Information
Court Calendars
Courthouses
Fee Schedule
General Information
Local Rules & Forms
Notices & Press Info
Tentative Rulings

SHARP

Self-Help Assistance and Referral Program (SHARP)

The SHARP Program provides several services in the family law area that are not offered by the Family Law Facilitator's Office. These services include the following:

- Providing assistance to the parties in finalizing their divorce (obtaining a final judgment);
- Providing assistance to parties in initiating and responding to Orders to Show Cause and Notice of Motion for issues other than child and spousal support (How to get interim orders for control of property, use of vehicles, assignment of responsibility for the payment of debts, etc.);
- Providing assistance to parties in initiating and responding to Change of Venue Motions;
- Providing information to parties on how to proceed with summary dissolution (How to obtain an uncontested divorce);
- Providing assistance to parties in initiating and responding to domestic violence restraining orders;
- Providing assistance to all parties in the preparation of all documents involved in guardianships; and
- Providing assistance to parties in initiating and responding to injunctions prohibiting harassment (civil harassment).

Oroville SHARP Facility
1675 Montgomery St.
Lower Level
(USE OAK STREET ENTRANCE)
Oroville, CA 95965
View Map

Tel: (530) 532-7015

Chico SHARP Facility
655 Oleander Avenue
Chico, CA 95926
View Map

Tel: (530) 532-7024

Hours:
Tue - Wed: 9am - 4pm
Thursday: 10am - 4pm

Privacy Statement | Contact the Court

[Home] [Case Information] [Court Calendars] [Courthouses] [Family Law] [Fee Schedule] [General Information] [Human Resources] [Jury] [Local Rules & Forms] [Notices & Press Releases] [Self Help] [Traffic] [Tentative Rulings]

1 Court Street, Oroville CA 95965
webmaster@buttecourt.ca.gov
Copyright © 2005 Superior Court of California, County of Butte

Done

Internet

100%

Appendix B: Screenshot of Butte County Superior Court's Knowledgebase

REFERENCES

Association of College and Research Libraries. 2000. *Information literacy competency standards for higher education*. Chicago, IL: Association of College and Research Libraries.

Association of Research Libraries. 2002. *Timeline: A history of copyright in the United States*. http://www.arl.org/info/frn/copy/timeline.html (accessed April 14, 2004).

Babbie, Earl. 1998. *Plagiarism*. Social Science Research and Instructional Council Teaching Resources Depository: Other Teaching Tools. http://www.csubak.edu/ssric/Modules/Other/plagiarism.html (accessed March 28, 2004).

Bailey, Kenneth D. 1994. *Typologies and taxonomies: An introduction to classification techniques*. Thousand Oaks: Sage Publications.

Barbato, Joseph, and Danielle Furlich. 2000. *Writing for a good cause*. New York: Simon and Schuster.

Benzinger, Brian. 2006. 50 ways to take notes. *Solution Watch* (April 17). Boca Raton, FL: CRC Press. http://solutionwatch.com/368/fifty-ways-to-take-notes/.

Chicago manual of style. 2003. Revised and expanded. 15th ed. Chicago: University of Chicago Press.

Coplin, William D., and Michael K. O'Leary. 1988. *Policy skills workbook*. Croton-on-Hudson, NY: Policy Studies Associates.

Corder, Jim, and John Ruszkiewicz. 1989. *Handbook of current English*. 8th ed. Chicago, IL: Scott Foresman.

Downes, Stephen. n.d. *The logical fallacies*. http://onegoodmove.org/fallacy.toc.htm.

Dunn, William N. *Public policy analysis: An introduction*. 4th ed. Upper Saddle River, NJ: Pearson Education.

Fisher, A. J. n.d. *How to write a project report*. http://www.cs.york.ac.uk/projects/howtowrt.html.

Fowler, H. Ramsey, and Jane Aaron. 1989. *The little, brown handbook*. 4th ed. Chicago, IL: Scott Foresman.

Galvan, Jose L. 2006. *Writing literature reviews: A guide for students of the social and behavioral sciences*. 3rd ed. Glendale, CA: Pyrczak Publishing.

Gibaldi, Joseph. 2003. *MLA handbook for writers of research papers*. 6th ed. New York: Modern Language Association of America.

Goehlert, Robert U., and Fenton S. Martin. 1989. *Congress and law-making: Researching the legislative process*. 2nd ed. Santa Barbara, CA: ABC-CLIO.

Harnack, Andrew, and Eugene Kleppinger. 1998. *Online!: A reference guide to using Internet sources*. New York: St. Martin's Press.

Hazen, Gordon B. 2004. *Writing effective project reports*. Northwestern University. http://users.iems.northwestern.edu/~hazen/Writing%20Project%20Reports%202004a.pdf.

Indiana University, Bloomington. 2004. *How to recognize plagiarism*. School of Education. http://www.indiana.edu/~istd/examples.htm (accessed March 28, 2004).

Johnson, Diane. *Grant writing for smarties*. Chico, CA: CSUC Office of Sponsored Programs.

Johnson, Kristin, and Sarah Blakselee. 2004. *The information timeline*. Chico, CA: Meriam Library's Information Literacy/Instruction Program.

Jones, Laurence F., and Edwards C. Olson. 2005. *Researching the polity: A handbook of scope and methods*, 2nd ed. Mason, Ohio: Atomic Dog Publishers.

Kalvelage, Carl, Albert Melone, and Morely Segal. 1984. *Bridges to knowledge in political science: A handbook for research*. Pacific Palisades, CA: Palisades Publishers.

Kurian, George. 1994. *Datapedia of the United States, 1790–2000*. Lanham, MD: Bernian Press.

Leahy, Richard. Spring 1990. What the college writing center is—and isn't. *College Teaching* 38: 43–48.

Lester, James D. 1990. *Writing research papers: A complete guide*. Chicago, IL: Scott, Foresman.

Locke, Lawrence, Waneen Wyrick Spirduso, and Stephen Silverman. 2007. *Proposals that work*. 5th ed. Thousand Oaks, CA: Sage Publications.

Mackenzie, G. C. 1996. The presidential appointment process: Historical development, contemporary operations, current issues. In *Obstacle course: The report of the twentieth century fund task force on the presidential appointment process*. ed. G. C. Mackenzie and Robert Shogan. New York: The Twentieth Century Fund Press.

Martin, Vivien. 2002. *Managing projects in health and social care*. New York: Routledge.

McNamara, Carter. 2005. *Field guide to nonprofit program design, marketing, and evaluation*. Minneapolis MN: Authenticity Consulting, LLC.

Melone, Albert P. 1990. *Researching constitutional law*. Chicago, IL: Scott, Foresman.

Novak, J. D., and A. J. Cañas. 2006. The theory underlying concept maps and how to construct them. *Technical Report IHMC CmapTools 2006-01*. Florida Institute for Human and Machine Cognition. http://cmap.ihmc.us/Publications/ResearchPapers/TheoryUnderlying ConceptMaps.pdf.

OWL. 1995–2004. Avoiding plagiarism. *Purdue University Online Writing Lab*. Purdue University. http://owl.english.purdue.edu./handouts/print/research/r_plagiar.html (accessed March 28, 2004).

Pan, Ling M. 2008. *Preparing literature reviews: Qualitative and quantitative approaches*. 3rd ed. Glendale, CA: Pyrczak Publishing.

Paul, Richard, and Linda Elder. 2005. *The thinker's guide to the art of Socratic questioning*. Dillon Beach, CA: Foundation for Critical Thinking.

Pfeiffer, William, and Charles Keller. 2000. *Proposal writing*. Upper Saddle River, NJ: Prentice Hall.

Plotnick, Eric. 1997. Concept mapping: A graphical system for understanding the relationship between concepts. *ERIC Digest*. ED407938. http://www.ericdigests.org/1998-1/concept.htm.

Policy memos. n.d. http://www.duke.edu/~nrt/memoguide.pdf.

Publication manual of the American Psychological Association. 5th ed. 2001. Washington, DC: American Psychological Association.

Rabin, Jack. Ed. 2003. *Encyclopedia of public administration and public policy*. New York, NY: Taylor and Francis Group.

Ruggiero, Vincent Ryan. 1991. *The art of thinking: A guide to critical and creative thought*. 3rd ed. New York: Harper-Collins.

Salisbury, Robert H. 1968. The analysis of public policy: A search for theories and roles. In *Political science and public policy*. ed. Austin Ranney. Chicago, IL: Markham Publishing.

Schmidt, Steffen, Mack Shelley II, and Barbara Bardes. 1989. *An introduction to critical thinking in American politics*. New York: West Publishing Co.

Schrems, John. 2006. *Understanding principles of politics and the state*. Otsego, MI: PageFree Publishing.

Shappell, Scott A., and Douglas Wiegmann. 2000. *The human factor analysis and classification system-HFACS*. Springfield, VA: National Technical Information Service. http://www.nifc .gov/safety/reports/humanfactors_class&analy.pdf.

Silverberg, Robert. 1986. *Star of the gypsies*. New York: Warner Bros.

Standler, Ronald. 2000. *Plagiarism in colleges in USA*. http://rbs2.com/plag.htm. (accessed March 28, 2004).

Stanley, Harold W. and Richard G. Niemi. 1998. *Vital statistics on American politics*. Washington, D.C.: Congressional Quarterly Press.

Strunk, William Jr. and E. B. White. 2000. *The elements of style*. 4th ed. New York: Pearson-Longman Publishing.

Twain, Mark. 1961. *Wit and wisecracks*. Selected by Doris Bernardete. White Plains, NY: Peter Pauper Press, Inc.

U.S. Congress. House. Office of the Clerk. n.d. *History of congressional elections*. http://clerweb .house.gov/histrecs.../elections/political/divisions.html (accessed March 10, 1999).

University of California, Davis. 2001. *Avoiding plagiarism*. Student Judicial Affairs. http://sja .ucdavis.edu/avoid.html (accessed March 28, 2004).

Ward, Deborah. 2006. *Writing grant proposals that win*. 3rd ed. Sudbury, MA: Jones and Bartlett Publishing.

Ward, Kathryn. 1990. *Curriculum integration workbook*. Southern Illinois University, Carbondale. Unpublished manuscript.

Written word II. 1983. Boston: Houghton Mifflin.

TEXT ACKNOWLEDGMENTS

Reprinted by Permission from the Following Books

Coplin, William D., and Michael K. O'Leary. 1988. *Policy skills workbook*. Croton-on-Hudson, NY: Policy Studies Associates. Copyright 1988, William D. Coplin and Michael K. O'Leary. Adaptation of policy analysis.

Corder, Jim, and John Ruszkiewicz. 1989. *Handbook of current English*. 8th ed. Chicago, IL: Scott Foresman. Copyright 1989, Scott Foresman Publishers. Adaptation from pages 631, 731.

Fowler, H. Ramsey, and Jane Aaron. 1989. *The Little, Brown Handbook*. 4th ed. Chicato, IL: Scott Foresman. Copyright 1989, Scott Foresman Publishers. Adaptation of pages 95–96, 115, 117, 118, 119.

Kalvelage, Carl, Albert Melone, and Morely Segal. 1984. *Bridges to knowledge in political science: A handbook for research*. Pacific Palisades, CA: Palisades Publishers. Copyright 1984, Palisades Publishers. Adaptation of pages 118–119.

Reprinted by Permission from the Following Student Manuscripts

Adams, Noel. *Annotated bibliography*. Unpublished manuscript.

Allison, Annette. *Building inspection expense analysis: Building inspection department*. Unpublished manuscript.

Brown, Patrick. *Youth influence in political outcomes*. Unpublished manuscript.

Carter, Kari. *Endangered Species Act: Preserving species and industrialism*. Unpublished manuscript.

Cieplak, Caryn. *Campaign volunteers: VIPs or peons?* Unpublished manuscript.

Dueñas, Gilbert Peña. 2003. Policy implementation and the collaborative management process. Chico, CA: California State University, Chico.

Ford, Josh. *The No Child Left Behind Act of 2001: Accountability, standardization, and federal sanctions*. Unpublished manuscript.

Funes, Rebekah. *Reciprocity in collaboratives*. Unpublished manuscript.

Gifford, Alicia. *Distributive justice and community: A literature review*. Unpublished manuscript.

Gifford, Alicia. *The Terminal: Analysis of popular portrayals of ethical, group dynamic, and leadership behaviors*. Unpublished manuscript.

Goard, Steve. *Dysfunctional behavior in the FBI*. Unpublished manuscript.

Harmon, Marion. *Research proposal: Copyright protection and fair use in the digital age*. Unpublished manuscript.

Kozenski, Chris. *Chief Justice Rehnquist: Does he lead the court?* Unpublished manuscript.

Miller, Michael Scott. *California Bar Foundation grant application: SHARP Knowledge Base Project*. Unpublished manuscript.

Miller, Michael Scott. *Knowledgebase Project collaboration between the Butte County Superior Court and The Self Help Assistance and Referral Program (SHARP): Interim report*. Unpublished manuscript.

Miller, Michael Scott. *PowerPoint presentation*. Unpublished manuscript.

Mitchell, Thomas. *Outlines*. Unpublished manuscript.

Pettit, Edward. *Midterm Exam: Question 5*. Unpublished manuscript.

Pettit, Edward. *The Reagan administration policies on social welfare spending*. Unpublished manuscript.

Root, Alyssum. *Foster Care Independence Act Of 1999: A coordinated effort*. Unpublished manuscript.

Rueda-Lynn, Christine N. 1997. Just a housewife? Think about it a bit longer! *Springfield News Leader* (Dec. 1): 8a.

Schmidt, Alan. *Federal funding for NEA*. Unpublished manuscript.

Schuberth, Jean M. *Why should we worry about a judge's ideology if judicial decisions are based on precedent?* Unpublished manuscript.

Sullivan, John T. *The Kennedys and the Rockefellers: Political dynasties' effect on the American electorate*. Unpublished manuscript.

Walka, Christopher. A review of the *Politics of Congressional Elections*. Unpublished manuscript.

INDEX